D1271056

Springer Series in Cognitive Development

Series Editor
Charles J. Brainerd

Springer Series in Cognitive Development

Series Editor: Charles J. Brainerd

Children's Logical and Mathematical Cognition:
Progress in Cognitive Development Research
Charles J. Brainerd (Ed.)

Verbal Processes in Children:
Progress in Cognitive Development Research
Charles J. Brainerd/Michael Pressley (Eds.)

Adult Cognition:
An Experimental Psychology of Human Aging
Timothy A. Salthouse

Recent Advances in Cognitive-Developmental Theory:
Progress in Cognitive Development Research
Charles J. Brainerd (Ed.)

Learning in Children:
Progress in Cognitive Development Research
Jeffrey Bisanz/Gay L. Bisanz/Robert Kail (Eds.)

Cognitive Strategy Research:
Psychological Foundations
Michael Pressley/Joel R. Levin (Eds.)

Cognitive Strategy Research:
Educational Applications
Michael Pressley/Joel R. Levin (Eds.)

Equilibrium in the Balance:
A Study of Psychological Explanation
Sophie Haroutunian

Crib Speech and Language Play
Stanley A. Kuczaj, II

Cognitive Strategy Research
Psychological Foundations

Edited by
Michael Pressley and Joel R. Levin

Springer-Verlag
New York Berlin Heidelberg Tokyo

Carlyle Campbell Library
Meredith College

Michael Pressley
Department of Psychology
University of Western Ontario
London, Ontario
Canada N6A 5C2

Joel R. Levin
Department of Educational
Psychology and Wisconsin Center
for Education Research
University of Wisconsin
Madison, Wisconsin 53706, U.S.A.

Series Editor
Charles J. Brainerd
Department of Psychology
University of Western Ontario
London, Ontario
Canada N6A 5C2

With 4 Figures

Library of Congress Cataloging in Publication Data
Main entry under title:
Cognitive strategy research: psychological foundations.
   (Springer series in cognitive development)
   Bibliography: p.
   Includes index.
   1. Cognition—Research. I. Pressley, Michael.
II. Levin, Joel R. III. Title. IV. Series.
[DNLM: 1. Cognition. 2. Psychology. BF 311 P935c]
BF311.C5533   1983   153   82-19635
ISBN 0-387-90818-8

© 1983 by Springer-Verlag New York Inc.
All rights reserved. No part of this book may be translated or reproduced in any form
without written permission from Springer-Verlag, 175 Fifth Avenue, New York,
New York 10010, U.S.A.
The use of general descriptive names, trade names, trademarks, etc., in this publication,
even if the former are not especially identified, is not to be taken as a sign that such
names, as understood by the Trade Marks and Merchandise Marks Act, may accordingly
be used freely by anyone.

Typeset by Ms Associates, Champaign, Illinois.
Printed and bound by R. R. Donnelley & Sons Company, Harrisonburg, Virginia.
Printed in the United States of America.

9 8 7 6 5 4 3 2 1

ISBN 0-387-90818-8   Springer-Verlag   New York   Berlin   Heidelberg   Tokyo
ISBN 3-540-90818-8   Springer-Verlag   Berlin   Heidelberg   New York   Tokyo

Series Preface

For some time now, the study of cognitive development has been far and away the most active discipline within developmental psychology. Although there would be much disagreement as to the exact proportion of papers published in developmental journals that could be considered cognitive, 50% seems like a conservative estimate. Hence, a series of scholarly books devoted to work in cognitive development is especially appropriate at this time.

The *Springer Series in Cognitive Development* contains two basic types of books, namely, edited collections of original chapters by several authors, and original volumes written by one author or a small group of authors. The flagship for the Springer Series is a serial publication of the "advances" type, carrying the subtitle *Progress in Cognitive Development Research*. Each volume in the *Progress* sequence is strongly thematic, in that it is limited to some well-defined domain of cognitive-developmental research (e.g., logical and mathematical development, development of learning). All *Progress* volumes will be edited collections. Editors of such collections, upon consultation with the Series Editor, may elect to have their books published either as contributions to the *Progress* sequence or as separate volumes. All books written by one author or a small group of authors are being published as separate volumes within the series.

A fairly broad definition of cognitive development is being used in the selection of books for this series. The classic topics of concept development, children's thinking and reasoning, the development of learning, language development, and memory development will, of course, be included. So, however, will newer areas such as social-cognitive development, educational applications, formal modeling, and philosophical implications of cognitive-developmental theory. Although it is

136939

anticipated that most books in the series will be empirical in orientation, theoretical and philosophical works are also welcome. With books of the latter sort, heterogeneity of theoretical perspective is encouraged, and no attempt will be made to foster some specific theoretical perspective at the expense of others (e.g., Piagetian versus behavioral or behavioral versus information processing).

                                                                    C. J. Brainerd

Preface

This is one of two companion volumes on cognitive strategy research within the *Springer Series in Cognitive Development*. These volumes were motivated by the large number of studies in recent years on cognitive strategy training, studies that have appeared in the developmental, educational, and clinical literatures. The present volumes summarize much of the most important work on the topic, juxtaposing diverse applications and theoretical perspectives. We hope that by bringing together so many different approaches, the volumes will promote general knowledge about strategies that will integrate future research and practice.

This volume is concerned with the development of cognitive strategies, and the training of both cognitive and social-behavioral strategies in various contexts. As editors, we have provided introductory comments for each of the three major sections of the book. Readers interested in quickly identifying the major themes developed in the volume should begin with these introductions.

The authors were not asked to provide exhaustive reviews of research. Instead, we wanted them to summarize exemplary research studies and programs of research. In doing so, authors were requested to provide a discussion of what the term "strategy" meant in their particular domain. Authors were also asked to present a brief historical account of strategy research in their area, and to suggest future research directions. We feel that the authors succeeded in separating the wheat from the chaff, providing references to much of the best research available in the cognitive strategy field.

In order to promote continuity from chapter to chapter, and to assist readers in identifying themes that cut across chapters, we inserted cross-references in each contribution to other chapters in the volumes. In many ways this was a difficult task for us because of the many potential interconnections that could have been built, and because we did not want to clutter the chapters with cross-references. Thus, we inserted only what we regarded to be the most relevant citations across the two volumes, which appear in the authors' running text.

Editorial work on this book was supported partially by a grant to Michael Pressley from the Natural Sciences and Engineering Research Council of Canada. Joel Levin's participation was supported in part by a grant from the National Institute of Education to the Wisconsin Center for Education Research. We also wish to acknowledge the encouragement and assistance of the Series Editor, Charles Brainerd, and the staff of Springer-Verlag.

Michael Pressley
Joel R. Levin

Contents

Part I   Memory Strategies Across the Life Span **1**

Chapter 1   Children's Use of Memory Strategies Under Instruction ... **3**
Harriet Salatas Waters and Carol Andreassen

A Developmental Framework for Strategy Use 3
Training Procedures for Acquisition and Generalization of
Strategy Use 12
Changes in Strategy Effectiveness with Age 19
Concluding Comments 20
Reference Notes 21
References 21

**Chapter 2   Memory Strategy Instruction During Adolescence: When
Is Explicit Instruction Needed?** **25**
Michael Pressley, Joel R. Levin, and Susan L. Bryant

Does Memory Develop During Adolescence? 25
Five Frequently Asked Questions About Memory Strategy
Instruction 36
Concluding Remarks 42
Reference Notes 43
References 44

Chapter 3   **Mnemonic-Device Instruction with Adults**.................. **51**
                Francis S. Bellezza

                The Scope of the Chapter..................................... 52
                List-Learning Techniques 54
                Mnemonic Techniques for Prose Materials..................... 61
                Summary 67
                Reference Notes 68
                References 68

Chapter 4   **Memory Strategy Instruction with the Elderly: What
                Should Memory Training Be the Training Of?** **75**
                Pamela Roberts

                Memory Decline in Old Age................................... 76
                Memory Strategy Instruction Research........................ 78
                Memory-Training Programs.................................... 86
                Important New Developments 87
                Motivation 88
                Summary and Conclusions.................................... 94
                Reference Notes 95
                References 96

Part II   Cognitive Strategies and Special Populations.................... **101**

Chapter 5   **Learning and Memory Strategies in the Mentally
                Retarded** **103**
                John G. Borkowski and Fredi P. Büchel

                Toward a Paradigm for Strategy-Training Research............ 104
                Research on Strategy Acquisition and Transfer 106
                Theory and Strategy-Training Research 119
                New Directions for Strategy-Training Research............... 123
                Reference Notes 124
                References 125

Chapter 6   **Memory Strategy Instruction with the Learning Disabled**.. **129**
                Patricia E. Worden

                Definition of Learning Disabilities 130
                Studies of Cognitive Disabilities 132

Research on Memory Strategy Instruction 140
Future Directions for Memory Strategy Instruction 147
Reference Notes 148
References 149

Chapter 7   The Zone of Proximal Development **155**
Jeanne D. Day

Philosophical Background..................................... 156
Zone of Proximal Development............................... 158
Dynamic Assessments of Intelligence......................... 161
Empirical Studies of the Zone of Proximal Development 165
Implications for Future Research............................. 169
Reference Notes 170
References 171

Part III   Strategies for Attitudinal and Social-Behavioral Change **177**

**Chapter 8   Cognitive Processes in Television Viewing: Description and
Strategic Implications** **179**
W. Andrew Collins and Mary Wiens

Aspects of the Viewing Process.............................. 180
Research on Interventions in Viewing 190
Implications and Possibilities 196
Reference Notes 197
References 198

Chapter 9   Cognitive Strategies in Advertising Design **203**
Kathryn Lutz Alesandrini

Issues in Strategy Effectiveness.............................. 203
Visual Strategies 206
Organizational Strategies.................................... 214
Conclusion... 216
Reference Notes 218
References 219

**Chapter 10   Cognitive Behavior Modification: The Clinical Application
of Cognitive Strategies**.................................... **221**
William M. Reynolds and Kevin D. Stark

A Cognitive-Behavioral Perspective........................... 222
Clinical Applications... 228
Methodological Issues 253
Summary 255
Reference Notes 256
References 257

Chapter 11   Cognitive Strategy Training and Children's Self-Control... **267**
*Michael Pressley, William M. Reynolds, Kevin D. Stark, and
Maribeth Gettinger*

Development and Verbal Control of Motor Behavior 268
Cognitive Intervention Effects on Children's Delay of
Gratification and Resistance to Temptations 273
Effects of Cognitive Strategies in Modifying Impulsive
Behaviors 278
General Discussion 292
References 293

Author Index **301**
Subject Index **315**

Contributors

Kathryn Lutz Alesandrini College of Education, Lindquist Center, University of Iowa, Iowa City, Iowa 52242, U.S.A.

Carol Andreassen Department of Psychology, State University of New York, Stony Brook, New York 11794, U.S.A.

Francis S. Bellezza Department of Psychology, Ohio University, Athens, Ohio 45701, U.S.A.

John G. Borkowski Department of Psychology, University of Notre Dame, Notre Dame, Indiana 46556, U.S.A.

Susan L. Bryant Department of Psychology, University of Western Ontario, London, Ontario N6A 5C2, Canada.

Fredi P. Büchel University of Basel, Basel, Switzerland.

W. Andrew Collins Institute of Child Development, University of Minnesota, Minneapolis, Minnesota 55455, U.S.A.

Jeanne D. Day Department of Psychology, University of Notre Dame, Notre Dame, Indiana 46556, U.S.A.

Maribeth Gettinger Department of Educational Psychology, University of Wisconsin, Madison, Wisconsin 53706, U.S.A.

Joel R. Levin   Department of Educational Psychology and Wisconsin Center for Education Research, University of Wisconsin, Madison, Wisconsin 53706, U.S.A.

Michael Pressley   Department of Psychology, University of Western Ontario, London, Ontario N6A 5C2 Canada.

William M. Reynolds   Department of Educational Psychology, University of Wisconsin, Madison, Wisconsin 53706, U.S.A.

Pamela Roberts   Department of Psychology, University of California, Riverside, California 92521, U.S.A.

Kevin D. Stark   Department of Educational Psychology, University of Wisconsin, Madison, Wisconsin 53706, U.S.A.

Harriet Salatas Waters   Department of Psychology, State University of New York, Stony Brook, New York 11794, U.S.A.

Mary Wiens   Institute of Child Development, University of Minnesota, Minneapolis, Minnesota 55455, U.S.A.

Patricia E. Worden   Department of Psychology, California State University, Fullerton, California 92634, U.S.A.

Part I
Memory Strategies Across the Life Span

The first four chapters in this volume are concerned with memory-strategy development. They represent a good sampling of the paradigms, theories, and research approaches of investigators interested in memory development. The four chapters provide information on strategy usage and training during childhood, adolescence, early adulthood, and late adulthood, with the chapters ordered in a life-span chronological fashion. The authors of these chapters convey both traditional positions and novel perspectives on memory development.

Waters and Andreassen's chapter on children's memory-strategy usage deals with the acquisition and generalization of memory strategies. These authors make the point that strategies are at first usually confined to a very few situations and are often applied ineffectively. With increasing age, broader and more effective usage of strategies occurs. Waters and Andreassen make a number of suggestions about how to increase the likelihood of generalized strategy usage and how to study its development. They also offer interpretations of strategy development with reference to theories (e.g., perceptual learning theory) and aspects of data (e.g., sex differences) that workers in children's memory have traditionally ignored.

Pressley, Levin, and Bryant provide an overview of memory-strategy development during adolescence, a period of the life span often neglected by memory-development researchers. The authors discuss developments in strategy usage that occur between 10 and 20 years of age. Pressley and his colleagues consider a number of rather complex strategies that first appear only after middle childhood. Individual differences in spontaneous strategy usage and the susceptibility of adolescents to strategy instruction are also considered. The authors conclude the chapter by providing answers to questions about memory development which have been posed to them frequently. In doing so, they touch on both theoretical implications of strategy research (incorporated into what they refer to as the *developmental strategy hypothesis*) and practical issues (e.g., the feasibility of cognitive strategy instruction in the classrooms).

Bellezza provides a summary of mnemonic-device instruction with adults. In doing so, he discusses both list learning and prose learning, emphasizing the linkages between studies of purely laboratory tasks and the more ecologically valid prose-learning research. The author considers in-depth the nature of the representations constructed during mnemonic mediation, touching on such diverse positions as dual coding and schema theory. Bellezza reviews many imagery-based mnemonics, including the method of loci, the pegword method, the use of graphic locations, and the keyword mnemonic. In considering the various techniques, the author reviews situational and personological (e.g., information-processing capacity) variables that may constrain the effects of mnemonic aids on learning.

For many years little attention was paid to the cognitive-skill differences between college-age learners and older adults. Recently, however, there has been a substantial increase in interest in the cognitive competencies of the elderly. To complete the overview of life-span memory development presented in this volume, Roberts summarizes some of the more visible work on memory-strategy usage by the elderly. She provides extensive commentary on the use of imagery strategies by the elderly and on prose learning by the elderly. Thus, the author adds to the discussion of several topics considered by Bellezza and by Pressley, Levin, and Bryant in their chapters. In general, Roberts offers a justifiably optimistic summary of evidence that older people are quite capable of executing memory strategies, and that they benefit from using those strategies. Importantly, the case is cogently developed that the elderly perceive that their memories are not what they used to be, thereby focusing attention on an important human need that strategy instruction can help to fill. Roberts then discusses motivational aspects of memory-strategy instruction with the elderly, and she provides concrete suggestions for addressing this issue. The chapter offers good reason for skepticism about generalizing procedures and paradigms used with younger populations to the elderly.

1. Children's Use of Memory Strategies Under Instruction

Harriet Salatas Waters and Carol Andreassen

This chapter is concerned with training procedures for the acquisition and generalization of learning and memory strategies during the early and middle childhood years. The first section of the chapter presents a general developmental framework in which all strategy development can be viewed. Its emphasis is on the change from limited, context-specific, and often inconsistent strategy use to broader, more consistent, context-free strategy use. It is proposed that strategy generalization proceeds from specific contexts that encourage strategy use to a broader range of contexts in which the individual is more active in initiating appropriate strategy use. Several common memory strategies that develop during childhood are examined within this general developmental framework. Its application to and usefulness in new domains are also examined. After the general developmental framework is presented, the question how best to promote the acquisition and generalization of appropriate learning and memory strategies is addressed. The roles of task procedure and materials, practice and familiarity with learning and memory tasks, and verbalizable knowledge of strategies and task demands in strategy development and training are examined. It is suggested that all could be effective in promoting strategy use, with the possibility that some approaches would work better at certain ages (i.e., an age-instruction interaction). Changes in strategy effectiveness with age are also discussed with respect to the evaluation of training procedures.

A Developmental Framework for Strategy Use

Present-day research on memory has focused on the general processing of information—both its initial comprehension and storage and its later retrieval upon demand. Within this general framework, research efforts have focused on the development and use of effective learning and memory strategies, those procedures that individuals elect to use to enhance learning and memory (for reviews see Kail & Hagen, 1977; Ornstein, 1978). Some common strategies include rehearsal, organization during study, and elaboration of the meaning of the material to be learned. They are strategies because they are not a necessary consequence of doing the task, and because individuals who spontaneously engage in the use of these strategies appear to have some intent behind their activities. Thus, it is difficult to imagine a child rehearsing aloud without imagining that he or she can start or stop the activity at will. Of course, within this definition there are degrees of intent, with the individual more or less aware of his or her activities and their consequences on performance.

Obviously, there are other developments in the area of memory besides those that involve the use of appropriate learning and memory strategies. There are increases in memory span that cannot be attributed to strategy development (Huttenlocher & Burke, 1976); semantic representations of concepts become more elaborate as general levels of knowledge increase (Chi, 1978); and changes occur in encoding and retrieval processes that are not readily attributed to changes in strategy use (e.g., the effects of encoding variability, Waters & Waters, 1976, 1979). Nonetheless, it is to our advantage in a discussion of strategy instruction that so much of what develops is indeed the use of appropriate memory strategies. It is important to note that developmental studies of strategies have generally found that when young children fail to use a particular strategy, they can often be trained to do so, and show immediate benefits. Strategy instruction thus seems both a plausible and potentially a highly beneficial undertaking.

In examining the literature on memory development and the early use of strategies, we can abstract a number of general principles that can serve as a developmental framework within which to describe the acquisition and generalization of strategy use with age. The first of these is that a particular memory strategy or skill will first appear under task conditions that encourage optimal processing of the material to be learned (a theme continued in Chapters 2 and 7 of this volume). Any number of procedures can serve to improve the processing conditions of a task: more time to study the materials, instructions that focus the individual's attention on relevant aspects of the task, and the like. What these procedures have in common is that they increase the likelihood that appropriate processing strategies will be adopted, and that memory performance will be enhanced. The memory literature is full of examples of particular strategies that develop first under more favorable processing conditions, and several such strategies will be discussed below. The second general principle of strategy use is that a particular strategy will first appear with materials that encourage the use of that strategy (e.g., Pressley, this volume). This could be due to the structural characteristics of the material, the familiarity or meaningfulness of the material, the imagery value of the material, and so on. Once again, what these characteristics have in common is that they serve to encourage the use of appropriate learning and memory strategies. Examples are provided in the discussion below of specific strategies and their development. The third and final principle is that individuals become more active in initiating strategy use in

Table 1-1 Developmental Principles of Strategy Use
and Strategy Generalization

Principle 1: Characteristics of the Task
　　Memory strategies will first appear under enhanced
　　processing conditions.
Principle 2: Characteristics of the Materials
　　Memory strategies will first appear with materials
　　that encourage the use of that strategy.
Principle 3: Characteristics of the Learner
　　Individuals become more active in initiating
　　strategy use in a variety of situations as they
　　become older and more experienced.

---

a variety of situations as they become older and more experienced (again, also considered by Pressley et al. in Chapter 2). Thus strategy use generalizes to less favorable processing conditions and more varied types of materials. Strategy generalization, as well as strategy acquisition, is an important aspect of strategy development. Table 1-1 presents the three developmental principles of strategy use and strategy generalization. Although the present discussion will focus on memory strategies that develop during early and middle childhood, the present developmental principles apply to all strategy development. A similar analysis of the development of elaborative strategies in late childhood and adolescence is presented in Rohwer's (1973) discussion of effective prompt conditions for elaboration and developmental level.

The Development of Specific Strategies

Several common memory strategies develop during the middle childhood years. For purposes of discussion, these strategies can be grouped into those that encourage attention to relevant aspects of the material and task, and lead to more elaborate and meaningful representations in memory (i.e., encoding strategies); and those that emphasize organization during study and recall. Whereas the individual encodes structural characteristics at the time of presentation, organization of material is particularly useful at the time of retrieval, when the individual must access the information stored in memory. In line with the developmental principles described earlier, it is instructive to examine the conditions under which these strategies first appear and the course of development as use becomes more frequent. The two encoding strategies that will be discussed are rehearsal and semantic processing of materials. Organization strategies during study and recall—including those with text materials—are examined in a subsequent section.

Encoding Strategies. One of the classic studies in the literature on strategy use concerns the spontaneous use of rehearsal by first-grade children in a simple serial learning task (Keeney, Cannizzo, & Flavell, 1967). A row of pictures is placed in front of the child one at a time, and he or she is asked to study the pictures so that he or she can later identify the pictures in their appropriate order (after the pictures have been covered). Children were observed during the study period in order to check for spontaneous rehearsal, which at this age is often evident as spontaneous lip movements or speaking aloud. Observations were later confirmed by asking the children if they had rehearsed. The first-grade group was then divided into those who had rehearsed and those who had not. Recall was compared. Rehearsers did much better on the memory task than the nonrehearsers. The nonrehearsers were then instructed to rehearse, and then did as well as the spontaneous rehearsers. It is an impressive demonstration, not only of rehearsal as an effective strategy for this age with this task, but also of the powerful effects of training. Children who had not used the appropriate strategy could benefit from its use if instructed. In a classic example of production deficiency, they had simply failed to produce the relevant strategy (Flavell, 1970). We will see that there are many cases in which children simply fail to use strategies that would otherwise help their performance.

Rehearsal can be a useful strategy, particularly if it is used as an opportunity to engage in more elaborate processing of the material (Craik & Watkins, 1973). Several studies indicate that as children become older, they are more likely to use rehearsal in relevant situations (for reviews see Hagen & Stanovich, 1977; Ornstein & Naus, 1978). In addition, they are less likely to use rote-type rehearsal strategies, rehearsing only one or two recent items, and more likely to use cumulative rehearsal, with many different items rehearsed together (Cuvo, 1975; Kellas, McCauley, & McFarland, 1975; Ornstein, Naus, & Liberty, 1975). With respect to the developmental principles described earlier, the question of interest is whether the use of rehearsal in younger children is encouraged by constructing favorable processing conditions for strategy utilization. A number of studies relate to this point. Naus, Ornstein, and Aivano (1977) presented third- and sixth-grade children with a list of unrelated words with either a 5-sec or 10-sec presentation time (for each item). The results indicated that the 10-sec presentation rate (a more favorable processing condition) resulted in more effective multi-item rehearsal by third graders, and recall performance improved accordingly. Sixth graders did not improve with additional time, primarily because they were already engaging in effective multi-item rehearsal even with the 5-sec rate. Naus et al. (1977) and Ornstein, Naus, and Stone (1977) demonstrated that instructions to engage in multi-item rehearsal (which can also be viewed as a more favorable processing condition for strategy use) benefited younger children (second and third graders) compared to a noninstruction group, but did not improve performance in older children (sixth graders). Once again, the older children were already engaging in effective strategy use in the less favorable processing condition (no specific rehearsal instructions).

One of the interesting aspects of rehearsal as a strategy is the qualification that in order to benefit performance it must set the stage for more in-depth semantic processing of the material. Repetition of the material per se does not guarantee semantic processing (Craik & Watkins, 1973). This finding fits nicely with recent perspectives on memory in which depth of processing is emphasized (Craik & Lockhart, 1972). Within the more contemporary depth of processing approach, one must encode the semantic features of a word, picture, or more complex material in order to ensure successful long-term retention. The key is to process the meaning of the material. The processing of acoustic, syntactic, or other nonsemantic characteristics does not typically benefit learning and memory as much as semantic processing (Craik & Tulving, 1975; Hyde & Jenkins, 1969, 1973). One possible developmental hypothesis from this depth-of-processing analysis is that children do not necessarily engage in effective in-depth semantic processing when told to remember a set of materials, whereas adults do. If this were the case, we would expect children to benefit from a semantic orienting task in which the child is asked to consider the meaning of the material. Adults, who would be expected to engage in effective semantic processing when told to study and remember material, should do as well with instructions to remember as with semantic orienting task instructions. The experimental evidence confirms these two hypotheses. Adults asked to make "pleasantness" ratings, to judge the frequency of occurrence in the language of words on a word list, and the like (semantic orienting tasks) will recall as many words as when asked to study and remember the material (Hyde & Jenkins, 1969, 1973). Children of elementary school age asked to engage in semantic processing through the use of semantic orienting tasks (e.g., "Is it nice, would you like to have one?") do better than when they are asked to study and remember the materials (Waters & Waters, 1976, 1979). These findings correspond nicely to the developmental principle that a learning and memory strategy (in this case, in-depth semantic processing) will first appear under enhanced processing conditions (semantic orienting task instructions) and then generalize to less favorable conditions (instructions to study and recall the material).

Variations in materials can also be identified that influence the likelihood of in-depth semantic processing during the early elementary school years. More effective in-depth semantic processing can be encouraged with more meaningful material (Waters & Waters, 1979). One can probably assume that because words become more meaningful with age, an individual can take advantage of semantic processing instructions across a wider range of materials. This trend, however, has not been directly demonstrated. If the use of elaboration (e.g., imagery) is included within the broader range of semantic processing, then there are a number of developmental studies with elementary school children (7 and older) that show that younger children are better able to use elaborative strategies when instructed with pictures than with words, and that this difference decreases with age (Hughes & Walsh, 1971; Pressley & Levin, 1978). These results conform to the second developmental principle concerning strategy use and materials.

Organization Strategies. The experimental literature is replete with demonstrations of the importance of organization for learning and memory (see Tulving & Donaldson, 1972, for reviews). Organization is particularly effective when the material is grouped during study (Cofer, Bruce, & Reicher, 1966). Because of this fact, spontaneous organization of materials during study becomes an important strategy for study and investigation during the elementary school years. The classic developmental study on this topic was conducted by Moely, Olsen, Hawles, and Flavell

(1969). They presented children in kindergarten and in the first, third, and fifth grades with a set of pictures to be recalled. The picture set comprised several familiar categories (e.g., animals, clothing, furniture). The pictures were randomly arranged on a tabletop and children were asked to study the material for later recall. They were told they could rearrange the materials in any way they chose. Only children in the oldest age group (fifth graders) spontaneously grouped the pictures by category. If the categories were labeled before the study session began, then when the children were given the opportunity to rearrange the pictures for study, even third graders spontaneously grouped the pictures for study. Salatas and Flavell (1976) were able to obtain spontaneous grouping in children as young as first graders (without explicit instructions to group) by asking the children to place pictures on a lecternlike apparatus that had four rows that "paralleled" the four semantic categories in the picture set, labeled at the beginning of the study session. Table 1-2 presents these results. They are quite clear and quite dramatic. Under limited, highly structured conditions, young elementary school children are able to take advantage of a learning and memory strategy that does not spontaneously appear under more typical learning conditions until late elementary school. These results not only demonstrate the generalization of a memory strategy to less favorable conditions with age, but highlight the vast potential of appropriate training procedures for increasing the use of memory strategies in young children.

In addition to the use of category organization during study, the use of category organization during recall has also been examined. Typically, in these learning situations, the subject has no opportunity to reorder the materials during study. Nonetheless, structure is present in the materials and the individual can benefit from identifying the conceptual categories in the material. Organization of items for recall shows a steady increase across a wide range of ages (e.g., Cole, Frankel, & Sharp, 1971; Moely & Shapiro, 1971; Neimark, Slotnick, & Ulrich, 1971). Grouping of semantically related items has been found with children as young as 2 and 3 years of age (Goldberg, Perlmutter, & Myers, 1974; Rossi & Rossi, 1965), whereas grouping of unrelated items (subjective organization) does not appear consistently

Table 1-2 Significant Category Grouping During Study Under Varying Experimental Conditions

Grade Level	Randomly Arranged	Category Labels	Category Labels and Structured Display
First	–	–	+
Third	–	+	(+)
Fifth	+	+	(+)

Note. A "+" indicates significant organization; parentheses mean that specific experimental conditions were not used with that age group, but that results can be inferred from other data in the table.

until early adolescence (Laurence, 1966; Rosner, 1971; Shapiro & Moely, 1971). Moely (1977) provides a comprehensive review of the developmental literature.

We know that the use of organization as a memory strategy develops during the elementary school years. To what extent is the development of this important strategy tied to processing conditions and the structure of materials? Waters and Waters (1976) presented kindergarten and second-grade children with a list of categorizable words randomly arranged. The processing conditions of the task were varied by asking some children to respond to a semantic orienting task while listening to the list of words presented one at a time on a tape recorder. This assured semantic processing of all the items (enhanced processing condition). Others were just asked to listen to the words carefully for later recall. In the kindergarten group there was significant organization during recall (remembering the furniture items together, the clothing items together, etc.) only under semantic orienting task instructions. In second grade there was significant organization under standard instructions as well, which represents a generalization of strategy use to less favorable processing conditions.

Kobasigawa and Middleton (1972) and Furth and Milgram (1973) manipulated structural characteristics of material across a wide age range. Sets of categorizable pictures could either be blocked by category for presentation (more structured condition) or randomly presented. Alternatively, categories could either be labeled before the task began (more structured condition) or not. Children of preschool age did not benefit from either blocked presentation or labeling of categories. No significant organization of materials during recall was observed. Children from kindergarten to the third grade benefited from blocked presentation, but not from labeling of categories. Fifth graders benefited from blocked presentation and from labeling of categories under random presentation. Table 1-3 presents the results from these two studies. The generalization of strategy use to less structured conditions with age is apparent. Older students are better able to capitalize on a range of provided structure in the materials.

Waters (1981) has examined the use of organizational strategies in memory for prose. Third-grade, sixth-grade, and college students either generated (enhanced comprehension condition) or listened to (less favorable comprehension condition)

Table 1-3 Significant Organization During Recall Under Varying Experimental Conditions

Grade Level	Random Presentation	Category Labels	Blocked Presentation
Preschool	−	−	−
Kindergarten to third grade	−	−	+
Fifth grade	−	+	+

Note. A "+" indicates significant organization.

narrative (more structured materials) or descriptive (less structured) passages for later recall. Younger children initiated organizational activity only with more structured (narrative) materials and only under enhanced comprehension (generate passage) conditions. Older children initiated organizational activity with either more structured passages or under enhanced comprehension conditions. Adults initiated organizational activity under a wide range of situations, and only the combination of relatively unstructured (descriptive) passages and average comprehension (listened-to passages) conditions significantly impeded recall. Thus, the use of organizational strategies with more complex verbal materials shows the same pattern of development as the strategies discussed earlier. Organizational activity first appears in limited circumstances (enhanced processing and more structured materials) and then generalizes to less favorable conditions.

Application of Developmental Framework to New Domains

The developmental framework discussed above should serve both to organize existing literature on strategy development and to promote new investigations of strategy use that focus on the effects of processing and materials variables, as well as on the pattern of strategy use across experimental conditions. As a demonstration of the power of this perspective, we will report some recent work on sex differences in the use of organizational strategies (with word list materials). Reports of sex differences appear and disappear in the literature on strategy use in what appears to be an inconsistent patterning of results. At the same time, we are well aware of the differences in verbal skills between males and females, and would expect females to show superiority in the use of relevant memory strategies with verbal materials. Cox and Waters (Note 1) undertook an investigation of sex differences in the use of organization, hypothesizing that females should show earlier use of organizational strategies and should generalize sooner to less favorable processing conditions. First-grade, third-grade, and fifth-grade students were asked to listen to and recall lists of categorizable items (e.g., animals, furniture) randomly presented. Their recall protocols were scored for degree of organization (category clustering). Some children processed the materials under enhanced processing conditions (semantic orienting task instructions), others under less favorable processing conditions (standard instructions in which children are asked to listen to and recall the words). The results are presented in Table 1-4. They show that females first use organization under enhanced processing conditions in first grade, whereas males first use organization under enhanced processing conditions in third grade. They also show that females generalize their use of organization to less favorable conditions in fifth grade, whereas males have not yet done so. Thus, it appears that there are reliable sex differences in the use of organization with verbal materials, and that the differences can be explained as a developmental lag (for males) in the initial use and subsequent generalization of organization across experimental conditions. What is interesting is that if we examine the sex differences presented in the Cox and Waters data at each age—instead of examining the changing patterns across age—we would note a sex difference in first grade, no difference in third grade, and

Table 1-4 Significant Organization Across
Instructions and Age for Males and Females
(Data from Cox & Waters, Note 1)

Grade Level	Semantic Processing	Standard Conditions
First		
Males	—	—
Females	+	—
Third		
Males	+	—
Females	+	—
Fifth		
Males	+	—
Females	+	+

Note. A "+" indicates significant organization.

a reemergence of a sex difference in fifth grade. Taken separately, the results might suggest an inconsistent pattern of sex differences across age. Clearly, the use of a general developmental framework of strategy use is necessary in order to interpret these results correctly.

In addition to the Cox and Waters sex differences results, Waters (1981) found similar patterns of results for sex differences in the use of organization with complex verbal materials (prose passages). Once again, these differences are only interpretable in the context of the general developmental framework of strategy use outlined above.

Summary

A general developmental framework was proposed in which strategy use first appears in limited, context-specific conditions, and then generalizes with development to a range of possible processing conditions and materials. We demonstrated not only that this framework organizes the existing literature on the development of familiar learning and memory strategies, but that it can be used to investigate new domains and issues in strategy development. The developmental framework is important not only as an organizational scheme, but because it highlights a point often overlooked in the developmental literature on strategy development. There is strategy development beyond the initial acquisition of a strategy, as concretized by research we have cited and by data considered in Chapter 2. Much of the strategy development literature has focused on the circumstances in which we first observe strategy use. Although initial acquisition is important, the question of how and why strategy use generalizes is equally important. The present developmental framework highlights both questions. Research on the generalization of strategy use is particularly important in the context of strategy training, in which generalization to new situations would be an expected outcome of training procedures.

Training Procedures for Acquisition
and Generalization of Strategy Use

In a general sense, the memory development literature has much to offer anyone interested in the training of appropriate learning and memory strategies. There is a wealth of information, particularly for elementary school children, concerning the conditions that encourage strategy use. Some of this literature has been discussed above. However, there is less information from actual training studies, and many of these studies do not assess transfer to other similar tasks that might require the strategy, or do not assess long-term retention and use of the strategy in question. In the following section, we will take advantage of the extensive literature on memory development to identify several mechanisms by which strategy use can be encouraged and generalization promoted. In discussing both the acquisition and generalization of strategy use, we will be defining the type or types of training studies that would be of greatest value in our efforts to understand strategy development, and the role the psychologist might play in promoting this developmental progression in children. The following discussion is not only a summary of the memory development literature, but a prescription for future research on the training of memory strategies. Our discussion will continue to be guided by the general developmental framework outlined in earlier sections of the chapter.

Manipulations of Task Procedure and Materials

It is clear from the literature that task procedures and materials can be set up in such a way that they encourage strategy use in individuals who are unlikely to demonstrate strategy use in what we might consider typical or standard conditions. Strategy use in young children can be observed, although in limited, context-specific situations. The progression follows from limited strategy use to strategy use across a wider range of situations with age. The progression is plausible, in that those limited, context-specific situations entail highly structured and concrete materials and processing conditions that can direct a child's attention, limit memory requirements, and take advantage of already acquired cognitive skills and predispositions. We would certainly not expect early strategy use to appear with unfamiliar materials and with task procedures that are relatively unstructured, and then generalize to more concrete, structured situations with age.

The relevant research findings on developing strategy use, discussed in some detail in earlier sections, provide a set of procedures for encouraging early strategy use, and can be viewed as training procedures for the acquisition of strategy use. For example, labeling of categories in advance, blocked presentation of category items, and providing an array in which to place the pictures (rows corresponding to number of categories) all encourage the use of organization at earlier ages. In using these procedures, we can promote organization during study at an age at which it is not "typically" used. Obviously, both in our example and in other tasks designed to assess different strategies, what is typical is somewhat arbitrary. Nonetheless, there is often a standardized procedure for the presentation of a particular task, whether in a laboratory setting or in a classroom; and this procedure, *ipso facto,* becomes the typical or standard circumstance against which strategy use is evaluated. The point to remember is that whatever the standard procedure might be, variants can be found to encourage strategy use at an earlier age. It is a matter for researchers to determine exactly what these circumstances are for a particular strategy.

From the point of view of strategy acquisition and generalization, we would like to know what is gained by initiating strategy use in individuals who would not otherwise use the strategy. At the very least, we would hope that these individuals would be likely to continue strategy use under the same conditions at a later point in time. We would perhaps hope that strategy use in the training procedure would lead to generalization to other similar circumstances in which the particular strategy would be appropriate, but that were less favorable in terms of processing conditions and structure of task and materials. This generalization process would then continue to even less favorable conditions. The proposed consequences of initiation of early strategy use are presented in Table 1-5. Strategy use would be initiated under more favorable conditions, maintained through repeated task presentations, and (it is hoped) would in time generalize to less favorable conditions. Thus, we are concerned with both continued strategy use under training conditions (strategy maintenance) and strategy use in new circumstances (strategy generalization).

In addition to the specific consequences of strategy training presented in Table 1-5, there is the possibility of more general consequences in which initiation of one strategy would lead to the use of other strategies in appropriate learning and memory situations. That is, we would not only be teaching the child that strategy A is effective in a particular set of circumstances, but that strategic behavior often improves performance in learning and memory situations generally.

Studies in the literature that are presented as training studies often involve verbal instructions to engage in strategy use, and thus do not fall under the present heading of initiating strategy use through manipulation of task variables. Nonetheless,

Table 1-5 Strategy Acquisition and Generalization Through the Use of Enhanced Processing Conditions and Structured Materials

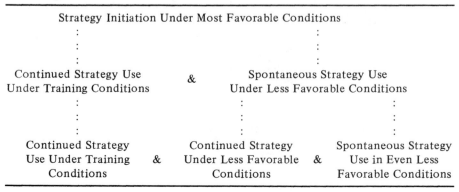

we can identify studies—and have done so in previous sections—that successfully initiate strategy use through task manipulations in individuals who would otherwise not use the strategy. It is difficult, however, to identify studies of this type that take the research one step further and investigate either long-term strategy maintenance or generalization of strategy use to new situations through the use of transfer paradigms. One study that did include a second session in which the same task was presented 6 weeks later and assessed continued strategy use (long-term strategy maintenance) was that of Salatas and Flavell (1976), who encouraged spontaneous organization of materials during study in first graders by labeling the semantic categories contained in the picture sets and by providing a display board whose rows matched the number of categories in the picture set (as described previously). Thirty-three percent of the subjects significantly categorized pictures on the display board during study on the initial trial of the first session. Seventy-one percent of these subjects continued to organize during study on the second session, demonstrating a high degree of strategy maintenance. In addition, the number of children organizing during the second session increased from 33% to 63%. This represents a significant increase in strategy use across the two sessions, and suggests that repeated exposure to favorable task conditions can encourage the initiation of strategy use across time. Obviously, many more studies of this type are needed in order to test the power of training procedures that manipulate task procedures and materials and encourage early strategy use. These procedures should be assessed for both effectiveness in long-term strategy maintenance and generalization of strategy use to new circumstances.

Familiarity with Task Through Practice

The idea that acquiring familiarity with the task and materials will increase the likelihood of a person's exhibiting strategic behavior is not new. It has its roots in the developmental work on discrimination learning and in the Gibsons' theory of perceptual learning (Gibson, 1969; Tighe & Tighe, 1968a). Perceptual learning theory proposes that with repeated exposure to material, the individual will increasingly be able to discriminate the distinctive features of the material—something that is particularly important in discrimination learning. The Gibsons' famous scribble task illustrates this point (Gibson & Gibson, 1955). The stimulus population of scribbles differs on three dimensions: number of coils, density of coils, and orientation of scribble. A prototype scribble is presented, and individuals of different ages (7- and 10-year-olds and adults) are asked to go through a deck of scribbles, selecting those scribbles that match the prototype. The subjects are asked to repeat the process (without feedback) until they complete a perfect run through the deck. All subjects improve with repeated exposure to the deck of scribbles, although the older the subject, the faster he or she reaches one perfect trial. The point to remember is that improvement occurs with repeated exposure to task, even without feedback.

One of the key steps to sophisticated problem solving in discrimination learning is identification of the dimensions of the stimulus population (and their individual values). A stimulus population could be composed of geometric stimuli that vary in form (e.g., square, circle), color, size, and so forth. Gaining familiarity with the dimensions in an initial training session can have dramatic effects on children's performance (Johnson & White, 1967; Tighe & Tighe, 1968b). Shift problems in discrimination learning involve changing the rule (e.g., changing from "black" ones being positive to "squares" being positive) on the subject after he or she has reached criterion on the first problem. Typically, adult learners find intradimensional shift problems easier (e.g., "black" to "white") than extradimensional shift problems ("black" to "square"). Young children and rats find the reverse easier (Kendler & Kendler, 1962). Training studies have been conducted to determine if young children can be made to perform like adults and find intradimensional shifts easier. This pattern of performance is indicative of attention to relevant dimensions and of the abstraction of a rule identifying the relevant values on the dimension. Training sessions in which the child can manipulate objects that vary systematically on those dimensions that will be included in the discrimination learning task change a young (4- to 6-year-old) child's performance from "ratlike" to "adultlike."

These examples from the children's learning literature strongly suggest that familiarization with task and materials can improve children's performance in problem-solving tasks and make the children more strategic in their approach. The results also suggest that familiarization with task is more useful for younger subjects. The older subject has already acquired some familiarization with task and materials through his or her greater experience with learning, memory, and problem-solving tasks.

With regard to developing memory strategies, we would expect the effects of familiarization and practice to be similar. That is, as the individual learner becomes accustomed to the task, he or she would be more likely to use an appropriate learning or memory strategy. Although it is rare for developmental psychologists to use repeated sessions on the same task in order to determine the effects of practice on performance, administering several trials within one session is often done. With respect to rehearsal, studies investigating the use of rehearsal have not found changes in serial position effects across trials, or spontaneous changes in the quality of rehearsal that would suggest strong practice effects in the use of the strategy (e.g., Ornstein et al., 1975). However, some of these studies have not examined strategy use across trials, and the vast majority have not examined practice effects across different lists or sets of materials, or across sessions.

With respect to semantic processing, improvement across trials would be signaled by increases in recall relative to a semantic processing condition. We know that semantic processing and subsequent recall are improved when semantic orienting tasks are used with children of elementary school age (Waters & Waters, 1976, 1979). If recall improves across trials under standard conditions (no semantic orienting task) and recall differences between semantic processing and standard conditions decrease, then we would have evidence of more effective semantic processing with practice. Waters and Waters did not find this interaction across the elementary school groups tested with three trials on a single list. However, Cox and Waters (Note 2) have found processing-condition-by-trials interactions (three trials) with adult subjects, with the beneficial effects of semantic orienting task instructions decreasing across trials. Perhaps a similar interaction would appear with elementary school children with more trials, more lists, or repeated sessions. The studies have not yet been done.

To date, there is not much evidence that the use of encoding strategies (e.g., rehearsal, semantic processing) is encouraged in young elementary school children with practice and familiarity with task. However, there has been little systematic effort to collect such evidence. The results of practice and the use of organizational strategies are more positive. Significant levels of organization during recall increase for both category clustering and subjective organization across trials (Nelson, 1969; Laurence, 1966, 1967; Rosner, 1971). Increased use of organization during study has also been found across sessions (Salatas & Flavell, 1976). The use of organizational strategies with prose materials has not been investigated across repeated presentations and recall of passage material.

In sum, we would expect that repeated exposure to a particular task and one's becoming familiar with the task procedure would lead to increased use of appropriate memory strategies. There is some evidence to support this statement (discussed above), although the question has not been investigated systematically, in spite of its importance for training and generalization of appropriate learning and memory strategies. Assuming that becoming familiar with and practicing a particular task will increase the likelihood of strategy use, the question is whether the effects of practice on one task will lead to generalization of strategy use to new tasks. Table 1-6 presents a model of the effects of practice on both strategy acquisition and generalization. Once task familiarization results in strategy initiation, we would expect some generalization of strategy use across other similar tasks. The pattern of generalization may follow that described in Table 1-5 from more favorable to less favorable task circumstances. We might also discover that familiarization leads to strategy initiation more readily if we select enhanced processing condi-

Table 1-6 Strategy Acquisition and Generalization Through Practice

Initial Task Performance:
No Strategy Use
:
:
:

Task Familiarization
(through repeated practice or specific training)
Appearance of Strategy Use

Continued Strategy Use: Subsequent Generalization
Increased Effectiveness;   &   of Strategy to New Contexts
Subject Awareness of Strategy Use

tions for the initial training session, as would also be suggested from the model of strategy acquisition and generalization presented in Table 1-5. Obviously, one can combine the use of optimal task conditions and the effects of practice to design an optimal training procedure. The use of one technique does not preclude the use of the other. There may also be some additional benefits from continued practice on the initial task after strategy initiation has occurred, which would make strategy generalization more likely and which would be solely attributed to practice effects. Continued use of the strategy in question might very well lead to increased strategy effectiveness, more consistent strategy use, and a growing awareness of the strategy that has been adopted and its effect on performance. Insofar as the "availability" of the strategy for use changes with practice, then perhaps it would be more likely to generalize to new situations after repeated use. More consistent and effective strategy use would all seem to be indicators of increased strategy availability. Research is needed to determine if these consequences of repeated strategy use are tied to strategy generalization.

Verbal Instruction

Verbal instruction followed by an opportunity to engage in the strategy described is the more typical training situation, and studies that use this technique are more often identified as training studies, although they are not necessarily as extensive as we might like. The question whether children who do not use a particular strategy could do so if asked has been a major question in the study of memory development (Flavell, 1970). When this question has been tested, the answer has often been positive. Failure to use a particular strategy may not be due to limitations in the memory system itself. Instead, it may be a failure on the part of the individual to produce the appropriate strategy. Consequently, efforts to instruct elementary school children in the use of a particular strategy who do not spontaneously use the strategy have been successful. For example, children can be instructed to use rehearsal strategies, and when they do, their performance improves accordingly (Keeney et al., 1967; Naus et al., 1977); and although Keeney et al. (1967) failed to elicit continued strategy use when instruction was terminated, Kennedy and Miller (1976) found that feedback concerning the effects of strategy use was sufficient to maintain rehearsal activity. Children can also be encouraged to use semantic processing and organizational strategies during study by appropriate instructions to study the material for later recall (Appel, Cooper, McCarrell, Sims-Knight, Yussen, & Flavell, 1972; Yussen, Gagne, Garguilo, & Kunen, 1974; Salatas & Flavell, 1976). Interestingly, preschool children and young elementary school children are less sensitive to the implications of verbal instructions to remember. More specific orienting tasks requiring semantic processing of the material also encourage semantic processing (Murphy & Brown, 1975; Waters & Waters, 1976). Organizational strategies during study and/or recall can be induced through verbal instruction (Lange, 1973; Moely et al., 1969; Rosner, 1971; Scribner & Cole, 1972). Finally, organization of text materials can be encouraged by reminding children of schemata that can be used to organize materials (see Levin & Pressley, 1981, for a relevant discussion).

It is certainly the case that verbal instruction can be effective in inducing strategy use. We must go on to ask in what circumstances, or in what form, verbal instruction is most effective. There is evidence, for example, that more detailed instruction is needed with younger children (e.g., Bray, Justice, Ferguson, & Simon, 1977; Pellegrino, Posnansky, & Vesonder, 1977). We might also expect, given previous discussions, that verbal instruction would be more effective the more structured the task and the more favorable the processing conditions, and the more experience the individual has had with the type of task in question. In addition, these relationships are likely to undergo change with development, as the child becomes better able to use language to represent task requirements and demands and to represent his or her own knowledge about memory strategies and their effect on performance. All of these possibilities need further investigation.

The effects of verbal instruction on strategy acquisition and generalization are represented in Table 1-7. Once strategy use has been initiated with verbal instruction, it is likely to be maintained in the same situation, although this is not always the case. Explicit information on why the child was asked to engage in a particular procedure, and feedback on performance, are probably necessary in order to maintain strategy use in the same context. Subsequent generalization to new contexts may follow patterns similar to that described in previous sections on mechanisms of strategy acquisition and generalization. It is, however, possible that the likelihood of strategy generalization is increased because of the availability of verbalizable knowledge about strategy use, a consequence of verbal instruction. Although several researchers have discussed "metamemory" (knowledge about how the memory system operates) and its possible role in strategy generalization (Borkowski, in press; Campione & Brown, 1978), Waters and Foley (Note 3) have explicitly defined it as *verbalizable* knowledge of the memory system. This definition of metamemory not only avoids difficult problems of assessment that can occur with more open-ended definitions of metamemory, but also suggests that verbal instruction is one mechanism to enhance metamemory about strategy use, as well as to

Table 1-7 Strategy Acquisition and Generalization Through Verbal Instruction

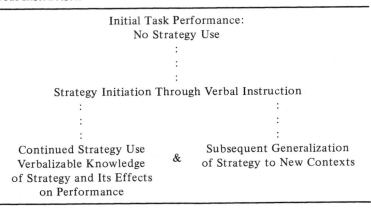

Initial Task Performance:
No Strategy Use

⋮

Strategy Initiation Through Verbal Instruction

⋮

Continued Strategy Use   Subsequent Generalization
Verbalizable Knowledge & of Strategy to New Contexts
of Strategy and Its Effects
on Performance

initiate actual strategy use (Borkowksi & Büchel, in Chapter 5, and Worden, in Chapter 6, also consider metamemory). There are many examples in the literature of children of elementary school age who use a particular strategy, but who are unable to identify the strategy as useful for memory performance when asked (e.g., Moynahan, 1973; Salatas & Flavell, 1976). Verbal instruction may very well improve the correspondence between verbalizable knowledge and performance in elementary school children, and set the stage for strategy generalization. Positive knowledge-behavior relationships have been demonstrated for adolescent subjects with elaborative memory strategies (Waters, 1982), and suggest a developmental change in the correspondence between verbalizable knowledge and behavior in a memory task. Verbal instruction may minimize this developmental difference and encourage strategy generalization in young children who would not otherwise generalize strategy use from one context to another. Studies that assess metamemory, strategy use, and performance, and that use a transfer paradigm to assess strategy generalization, are needed in order to evaluate these possibilities.

Summary

Three possible procedures for encouraging strategy use and generalization have been identified: manipulation of task structure and procedure, task familiarization and practice, and explicit verbal instruction. Evidence and logical argument supporting each of these as possible training procedures has been discussed. Further investigations into the effects of strategy training and generalization with these procedures is obviously necessary. The three procedures are not mutually exclusive, and could interact in ways as yet undetermined. One might expect the procedures, when used in combination, to enhance strategy training and lead to strategy generalization more readily. In addition, there is the possibility that different procedures could be more effective at different ages. One might imagine, for example, that task manipulation and practice would be more effective at younger ages, with verbal instruction taking on added significance with age (when the individual is better able to use language to represent task demands and his or her own knowledge about how the memory system operates). Mechanisms for strategy generalization may also become more verbal with age. Further research is needed. (Peterson & Swing, 1983, as well as Chapters 2, 4, and 5 of this volume also discuss generalization.)

Changes in Strategy Effectiveness with Age

In addition to strategy acquisition and generalization, researchers must concern themselves with strategy effectiveness in evaluating the success of their training procedures. Although developmental psychologists in the field of memory have emphasized the acquisition of strategies as a major developmental achievement (Flavell, 1971) in memory development, there is no doubt that development continues after acquisition, not only in terms of generalization but also in terms of effectiveness. Training procedures may need to be modified in order to improve strategy effectiveness. Developmental findings that suggest improvement in strategy effectiveness with age should be taken into account when initiating strategy use. Naus et al. (1977) have shown that when young elementary school children do rehearse, they do not use the more effective multiple-item technique that older elementary school children adopt. Sorting studies that ask children to group together material that is to be recalled later suggest that older children generate more cohesive and effective groupings, and do so more quickly, than younger children (Lange & Jackson, 1974; Liberty & Ornstein, 1973; Worden, 1975). Although studies examining category organization and performance across age have not reported changes in the relationship between organization and recall, such developmental changes have been reported with organization of unrelated word lists, with increasingly positive relationships with age (Laurence, 1966). Waters and Lomenick (in press) report increasingly positive correlations (with age) between structure in descriptive passages and recall performance. Finally, Waters (1982) has shown that when eighth graders report the use of elaborative strategies in paired-associate learning, the probability of recall is less than that of tenth graders reporting the use of elaborative strategies.

From the point of view of training strategy use, researchers must ask whether these developmental steps in strategy effectiveness must be replayed in the training situation. Is it necessarily the case that initial strategy use will be less effective? Or is the improvement in the spontaneous use of strategies a consequence of the discovery process in the natural setting, and can it thus be bypassed with explicit training in strategy use? The answer may be yes for some strategies and no for others. For example, Naus et al. (1977) have shown that more sophisticated rehearsal strategies (multi-item rehearsal) can be taught to younger children. At the same time, some of the improvements in organizational strategies may depend on the developing knowledge base in semantic memory (e.g., category structure in semantic memory), and thus limitations on training strategy effectiveness would occur at the younger elementary school ages. Before we can answer these questions we need to know the reasons for changes in strategy effectiveness with age. To date, these questions have not been investigated systematically. Finally, it is worth noting that some of the training procedures discussed for strategy acquisition and generalization may be more readily adapted for improving strategy effectiveness than others. Verbal instruction would be a particularly good bet, whereas task manipulations and practice are more likely to recreate the developmental progression in strategy effectiveness seen in naturalistic settings.

Concluding Comments

Memory development is largely based on the acquisition and generalization of memory strategies. It is not an all-or-none process and initially involves limited, often inconsistent, strategy use followed by more consistent and broader use of appropriate learning and memory strategies. Training in the use of memory strategies must therefore be concerned with several aspects of strategy development. In what circumstances will strategy use be initiated with young children? How can we assure consistent and effective strategy use? Finally, in what circumstances will strategy use generalize to new contexts? This series of questions requires that we assess not only the presence of strategy use, but also the quality of strategy use and its relationship to performance. In addition, transfer of the strategy to new contexts must be assessed, not in a haphazard manner, but by systematically varying the transfer tasks in terms of similarity to the original task. Emphasis should be placed on changing structural and processing characteristics to determine whether generalization in a training setting follows a course similar to strategy generalization in a natural setting.

Although there is additional work to be done in the area of strategy instruction, the memory development literature does offer a possible set of procedures to be used: manipulation of task procedure and materials, task familiarization and practice, and verbal instruction and the induction of metamemory. These mechanisms of strategy initiation and generalization need to be evaluated within a developmental context. Do certain procedures work better at different ages, or for different purposes (e.g., acquisition vs. generalization)? There are also changes in the structure and elaborateness of children's knowledge, and in their use of language as a representational system with age. How do these changes affect strategy instruction? The answers to these questions can play a valuable role in the design of effective strategy instruction.

Reference Notes

1. Cox, D., & Waters, H. S. *Sex differences in the use of organizational strategies: A developmental analysis.* Unpublished manuscript, 1983. (a)
2. Cox, D., & Waters, H. S. *Memory and organization in late adulthood: Qualitative or quantitative decline?* Unpublished manuscript, 1983. (b)
3. Waters, H. S., & Foley, M. *The origins and influence of verbalizable knowledge of strategy use in memory development.* Unpublished manuscript, 1983.

References

Appel, L. F., Cooper, R. G., McCarrell, N., Sims-Knight, J., Yussen, S. R., & Flavell, J. H. The development of the distinction between perceiving and memorizing. *Child Development,* 1972, *43,* 1365–1381.

Borkowski, J. C. Signs of intelligence: Strategy generalization and metacognition. In S. R. Yussen (Ed.), *The development of reflection.* New York: Academic Press, in press.

Bray, N. W., Justice, E. M., Ferguson, R. P., & Simon, D. L. Developmental changes in the effects of instructions in production-deficient children. *Child Development,* 1977, *48,* 1019–1026.

Campione, J. C., & Brown, A. L. Toward a theory of intelligence: Contributions from research with retarded children. *Intelligence,* 1978, *2,* 279–304.

Chi, M. T. H. Knowledge structures and memory development. In R. S. Siegler (Ed.), *Children's thinking: What develops?* Hillsdale, NJ: Erlbaum, 1978.

Cofer, C. N., Bruce, D. R., & Reicher, G. M. Clustering in free recall as a function of certain methodological variations. *Journal of Experimental Psychology*, 1966, *71*, 858–866.

Cole, M., Frankel, F., & Sharp, D. Development of free recall in children. *Developmental Psychology*, 1971, *4*, 109–123.

Craik, F. I. M., & Lockhart, R. S. Levels of processing: A framework for memory research. *Journal of Verbal Learning and Verbal Behavior*, 1972, *11*, 671–684.

Craik, F. I. M., & Tulving, E. Depth of processing and the retention of words in episodic memory. *Journal of Experimental Psychology: General*, 1974, *104*, 268–294.

Craik, F. I. M., & Watkins, M. J. The role of rehearsal in short-term memory. *Journal of Verbal Learning and Verbal Behavior*, 1973, *12*, 599–607.

Cuvo, A. J. Developmental differences in rehearsal and free recall. *Journal of Experimental Child Psychology*, 1975, *19*, 265–278.

Flavell, J. H. Developmental studies of mediated memory. In H. W. Reese & L. P. Lipsett (Eds.), *Advances in child development and behavior* (Vol. 5). New York: Academic Press, 1970.

Flavell, J. H. First discussant's comments: What is memory development the development of? *Human Development*, 1971, *14*, 272–278.

Furth, H. G., & Milgram, N. A. Labeling and grouping effects in the recall of pictures by children. *Child Development*, 1973, *44*, 511–518.

Gibson, E. J. *Principles of perceptual learning and development.* New York: Appleton-Century-Crofts, 1969.

Gibson, J. J., & Gibson, E. J. Perceptual learning: Differentiation or enrichment? *Psychological Review*, 1955, *62*, 32–41.

Goldberg, S., Perlmutter, M., & Myers, N. Recall of related and unrelated lists by 2-year-olds. *Journal of Experimental Child Psychology*, 1974, *18*, 1–8.

Hagen, J. W., & Stanovich, K. G. Memory: Strategies of acquisition. In R. V. Kail, Jr., & J. W. Hagen (Eds.), *Perspectives on the development of memory and cognition.* Hillsdale, NJ: Erlbaum, 1977.

Hughes, S. E. D., & Walsh, J. F. Effects of syntactic mediation, age, and modes of representation on paired-associate learning. *Child Development*, 1971, *8*, 1–31.

Huttenlocher, J., & Burke, D. Why does memory span increase with age? *Cognitive Psychology*, 1976, *8*, 1–31.

Hyde, T. S., & Jenkins, J. J. Differential effects of incidental tasks on the organization of a list of highly associated words. *Journal of Experimental Psychology*, 1969, *82*, 472–481.

Hyde, T. S., & Jenkins, J. J. Recall of words as a function of semantic, graphic, and syntactic orienting tasks. *Journal of Verbal Learning and Verbal Behavior*, 1973, *12*, 471–480.

Johnson, P. J., & White, R. M., Jr. Concept of dimensionality and reversal shift performance in children. *Journal of Experimental Child Psychology*, 1967, *5*, 223–227.

Kail, R. V., Jr., & Hagen, J. W. (Eds.), *Perspectives on the development of memory and cognition.* Hillsdale, NJ: Erlbaum, 1977.

Keeney, T. J., Cannizzo, S. R., & Flavell, J. H. Spontaneous and induced verbal rehearsal in a recall task. *Child Development*, 1967, *38*, 953–966.

Kellas, G., McCauley, C., & McFarland, C. E. Developmental aspects of storage and retrieval. *Journal of Experimental Child Psychology*, 1975, *19*, 51–62.

Kendler, H. D., & Kendler, T. S. Vertical and horizontal processes in problem-solving. *Psychological Review*, 1962, *69*, 1–16.

Kennedy, B. A., & Miller, D. J. Persistent use of verbal rehearsal as a function of information about its value. *Child Development,* 1976, *47,* 566–569.

Kobasigawa, A., & Middleton, D. B. Free recall of categorized items by children at three grade levels. *Child Development,* 1972, *43,* 1067–1072.

Lange, G. The development of conceptual and rote recall skills among school age children. *Journal of Experimental Child Psychology,* 1973, *15,* 394–407.

Lange, G., & Jackson, P. Personal organization in children's free recall. *Child Development,* 1974, *45,* 1060–1067.

Laurence, M. W. Age differences in performance and subjective organization in the free-recall learning of pictorial material. *Canadian Journal of Psychology,* 1966, *30,* 388–399.

Laurence, M. W. A developmental look at the usefulness of list categorization as an aid to free recall. *Canadian Journal of Psychology,* 1967, *21,* 153–165.

Levin, J. R., & Pressley, M. Improving children's prose comprehension: Selected strategies that seem to succeed. In C. Santa & B. Hayes (Eds.), *Children's prose comprehension: Research and practice.* Newark, DE: International Reading Association, 1981.

Liberty, C., & Ornstein, P. A. Age differences in organization and recall: The effects of training in categorization. *Journal of Experimental Child Psychology,* 1973, *15,* 169–186.

Moely, B. E. Organizational factors in the development of memory. In R. V. Kail, Jr., & J. W. Hagen (Eds.), *Perspectives on the development of memory and cognition.* Hillsdale, NJ: Erlbaum, 1977.

Moely, B. E., Olson, F., Hawles, T. G., & Flavell, J. H. Production deficiency in young children's clustered recall. *Developmental Psychology,* 1969, *1,* 26–34.

Moely, B. E., & Shapiro, S. I. Free recall and clustering at four age levels: Effects of learning to learn and presentation method. *Developmental Psychology,* 1971, *4,* 490.

Moynahan, E. D. The development of knowledge concerning the effect of categorization upon free recall. *Child Development,* 1973, *44,* 238–246.

Murphy, M. D., & Brown, A. L. Incidental learning in preschool children as a function of level of cognitive analysis. *Journal of Experimental Child Psychology,* 1975, *19,* 509–523.

Naus, M. J., Ornstein, P. A., & Aivano, S. Developmental changes in memory: The effects of processing time and rehearsal instructions. *Journal of Experimental Child Psychology,* 1977, *23,* 237–251.

Neimark, E., Slotnick, N. S., & Ulrich, T. Development of memorization strategies. *Developmental Psychology,* 1971, *5,* 427–432.

Nelson, K. J. The organization of free recall by young children. *Journal of Experimental Child Psychology,* 1969, *8,* 284–295.

Ornstein, P. A. (Ed.). *Memory development in children.* New York: Wiley, 1978.

Ornstein, P. A., & Naus, M. J. Rehearsal processes in children's memory. In P. A. Ornstein (Ed.), *Memory development in children.* New York: Wiley, 1978.

Ornstein, P. A., Naus, M. J., & Liberty, C. Rehearsal and organizational processes in children's memory. *Child Development,* 1975, *46,* 818–830.

Ornstein, P. A., Naus, M. J., & Stone, B. P. Rehearsal training and developmental differences in memory. *Developmental Psychology,* 1977, *13,* 15–24.

Pellegrino, J. W., Posnansky, C., & Vesonder, G. T. Developmental changes in free recall: The interaction of task structure and age. *Journal of Experimental Child Psychology,* 1977, *24,* 86–96.

Peterson, P. L., & Swing, S. R. Problems in classroom implementation of cognitive strategy instruction. In J. R. Levin & M. Pressley (Eds.), *Cognitive strategy research: Educational applications.* New York: Springer-Verlag, 1983.

Pressley, M., & Levin, J. R. Developmental constraints associated with children's use of the keyword method of foreign language vocabulary learning. *Journal of Experimental Child Psychology,* 1978, *26,* 359–372.

Rohwer, W. D., Jr. Elaboration and learning in childhood and adolescence. In H. W. Reese (Ed.), *Advances in child development and behavior* (Vol. 8). New York: Academic Press, 1973.

Rosner, S. R. The effects of rehearsal and chunking instructions on children's multi-trial free recall. *Journal of Experimental Child Psychology,* 1971, *11,* 93–105.

Rossi, E. L., & Rossi, S. I. Concept utilization, serial order and recall in nursery-school children. *Child Development,* 1965, *36,* 771–778.

Salatas, H., & Flavell, J. H. Behavioral and metamnemonic indicators of strategic behavior under remember instructions in first grade. *Child Development,* 1976, *47,* 81–89.

Scribner, S., & Cole, M. Effects of constrained recall training on children's performance in a verbal memory task. *Child Development,* 1972, *43,* 845–857.

Shapiro, S. I., & Moely, B. E. Free recall, subjective organization and learning to learn at three age levels. *Psychonomic Science,* 1971, *23,* 189–191.

Tighe, T. J., & Tighe, L. S. Differentiation theory and concept-shift behavior. *Psychological Bulletin,* 1968, *70,* 756–761. (a)

Tighe, T. J., & Tighe, L. S. Perceptual learning in the discrimination processes of children: An analysis of five variables in perceptual pretraining. *Journal of Experimental Psychology,* 1968, *77,* 125–134. (b)

Tulving, E., & Donaldson, W. (Eds.). *Organization of memory.* New York: Academic Press, 1972.

Waters, H. S. Organizational strategies in memory for prose: A developmental analysis. *Journal of Experimental Child Psychology,* 1981, *32,* 223–246.

Waters, H. S. Memory development during adolescence: Relationship between metamemory, strategy use, and performance. *Journal of Experimental Child Psychology,* 1982, *33,* 183–195.

Waters, H. S., & Lomenick, T. L. Levels of organization in descriptive passages: Production, comprehension, and recall. *Journal of Experimental Child Psychology,* in press.

Waters, H. S., & Waters, E. Semantic processing in children's free recall: Evidence for the importance of attentional factors and encoding variability. *Journal of Experimental Psychology: Human Learning and Memory,* 1976, *2,* 370–380.

Waters, H. S., & Waters, E. Semantic processing in children's free recall: The effects of context and meaningfulness on encoding variability. *Child Development,* 1979, *50,* 735–746.

Worden, P. E. Effects of sorting on subsequent recall of unrelated items: A developmental study. *Child Development,* 1975, *46,* 687–695.

Yussen, S. R., Gagne, E., Garguilo, R., & Kunen, S. The distinction between perceiving and memorizing in elementary-school children. *Child Development,* 1974, *45,* 547–551.

2. Memory Strategy Instruction During Adolescence: When Is Explicit Instruction Needed?

Michael Pressley, Joel R. Levin, and Susan L. Bryant

This chapter is about memory development and memory strategy instruction during adolescence. Although there is some debate about the age boundaries associated with this developmental interval (e.g., Conger, 1977), for purposes of this chapter we will consider people from roughly 10 to 22 years of age as adolescents. In doing so, it is recognized that we may be invading the territories that Waters and Andreassen (Chapter 1), Cook and Mayer (1983), and Bellezza (Chapter 3) cover in their discussions of children's and adults' strategy use. However, the real developmental significance of the discussion would be missed if it were not possible to compare the performance of teenagers with preteens and people slightly older. Thus, we apologize to the authors of the other chapters, but will poach anyway!

The chapter will be divided into two parts. The first section will be concerned with description and discussion of three research domains concerning memory during middle childhood and adolescence. This survey of research illustrates the types of paradigms and strategies that have been included in studies of adolescent memory. Both spontaneous use of strategies and use of strategies under instruction will be considered. The review of the three research domains will be followed by a section in which we address questions that are commonly asked about memory strategy instruction.

Does Memory Develop During Adolescence?

After reading certain summaries of memory development—mainly those that focus on list learning and simple cumulative rehearsal strategies (i.e., Lange, 1978; Ornstein & Naus, 1978)—one might come away with the sense that memory strategy development is a *fait accompli* by age 10. One purpose of this chapter is to convince the reader that this is not in fact the case. What will become apparent, however, as we review the relevant literature is that the evidence bearing on strategy development during adolescence is relatively sparse compared to that bearing on memory development in preadolescents. Nonetheless, the findings that have emerged suggest some interesting progressions in memory strategy usage during adolescence, developments that are of concern to more people than just those who make a living by studying cognitive development.

These points can be illustrated by some bits of conversation that occurred in a course on adolescent psychology taught by the first author. Many of the students in the course were junior and senior high school teachers returning to the university for additional certification credits. At one point during the discussion section on learning during adolescence, several students commented that adolescents were in many ways more fun to teach than younger children. As one student expressed it, "You can teach them so much, yet they still have a lot to learn." Another student added, "There are such big differences between kids in how clever they'll be at going at a problem, and the differences between the seventh and twelfth graders are just amazing." In general, memory development researchers have made exactly these points, and most of what will be presented here will substantiate the observations of these teachers of adolescents.

Before beginning our discussion, we offer a few cautionary remarks. First, our consideration of adolescent memory strategies will not be comprehensive. Rather, specific studies were selected largely because they presented especially exciting findings, and at the same time were conducted in situations that are fairly typical of memory strategy investigation. The studies were selected in this fashion so that the chapter will increase in the readership an awareness of the problems and methodologies common in the study of adolescent memory strategies. Because of this bias toward representativeness, most of the work presented here involves laboratory tasks and studies. However, some of the studies chosen do have an applied focus. This was done to illustrate that bridges can be built from purely basic research (e.g., paired-associate learning) to applied problems (e.g., vocabulary learning). It is the authors' hope that on the basis of the discussion presented here, some readers will gain insights into the potential linkages that exist between the laboratory and the classroom (for additional discussion see Brown, Campione, & Day, 1981; Peterson & Swing, 1983).

As noted earlier, the studies discussed in this section will substantiate the main points made by the teachers of adolescents:

1. There are clear developments in the deployment of memory strategies during adolescence. For example, some adolescents *spontaneously* employ strategies that younger children do not.
2. The word *some* in the last sentence is important, in that there are pronounced individual differences among adolescents in their spontaneous use of strategies.
3. Nonetheless, those adolescents who do not use sophisticated strategies spontaneously will often benefit from explicit instruction in their use.

Given the "application" goals of this book, the last point may be the most important of all, and it is one completely consistent with the framework developed by Waters and Andreassen and by Day in Chapters 1 and 7, respectively.

Research from three different paradigms will be used to illustrate these points: constrained recall of list items, memory for associated terms, and memory for connected discourse.

Constrained Recall

Barclay (1979) conducted a study that clearly illustrates all of the above-cited principles. This study also highlights the neglect of strategy development during adolescence by memory development researchers. Despite a large number of studies of recall and rehearsal with elementary school children as subjects (e.g., Orstein & Naus, 1978), very little research on the topic has been conducted with secondary school students. [Note, however, that in addition to Barclay's (1979) study, there are scattered references documenting increases in strategy sophistication during the transition from childhood to adulthood (e.g., Bisanz, Vesonder, & Voss, 1978; Brown, Campione, Bray, & Wilcox, 1973; Cuvo, 1974, 1975; Kellas, McCauley, & McFarland, 1975).]

Barclay's (1979) study included subjects from Grades 6, 10, and 12, as well as a group of university students. The study was conducted in four phases: assessment, training, maintenance, and generalization. In the *assessment* phase, subjects were given a series of constrained recall trials in which their spontaneous strategy usage was monitored. The subjects were seated in front of a display panel with 13 small windows. They were told by the experimenter that they would see six pictures (one at each of the first six windows) and that they would be required to recall these pictures, beginning with Items 5 and 6 and then Items 1–4. The subjects were also informed that they could take as long as they wanted during each trial, and that they could do anything they wanted to help them remember the pictures. During each trial, the subjects themselves exposed the six pictures one at a time by pressing the windows on the display panel from left to right. The subjects were able to control the exposure time for each item, but had to expose the items in the fixed serial order of Items 1, 2, 3, 4, 5, and 6. Each picture could be viewed only once, and the subjects were required to press the 13th window when they were ready to recall the six pictures. The pause times between presses signaling picture presentations were recorded. During the assessment phase, all of the university student participants used what is known to be an optimal strategy for this type of task, namely a "cumulative rehearsal, fast-finish" strategy (Butterfield & Belmont, 1977). That is, they cumulatively rehearsed the first four items and then studied the last two items very quickly. This was evidenced by increased pause times from Items 1 to 4 with a dramatic decrease in pause times for Items 5 and 6. In contrast to the data generated by the university students, this pattern never occurred among Grade 6 subjects. Among Grade 10 participants, two of them (10%) used the strategy, and three (14%) of the Grade 12 subjects did so. In general, the Grade 6, 10, and 12 subjects evidenced increasing pause times in going from Items 1 to 6, indicating a simple cumulative rehearsal strategy (i.e., after each item presentation, that item and each of the previous ones were rehearsed). In general, study pause times in these grades increased dramatically on the last item for most subjects, a pattern completely opposite to the cumulative rehearsal, fast-finish pattern. Barclay (1979) concluded that these "subjects viewed all six items and then rehearsed them as a group" (p. 268). In summary, the results were consistent with the position that there are developmental increases during adolescence with respect to adopting a cumulative rehearsal, fast-finish technique, and that there are individual differences among teenagers in the deployment of the strategy.

In the *training* phase of the experiment, all of the subjects who had not employed the cumulative rehearsal, fast-finish technique in the assessment phase were included in a two-group experiment. Half of the subjects were given training in the use of the technique in the following fashion (Barclay, 1979):

> The experimenter demonstrated a cumulative rehearsal, fast-finish routine by exposing the first four pictures, labeling and including each new picture in a cumulative rehearsal set. For example, if the first picture was that of a cat, the experimenter said "cat," then, if the second picture was a dog, the experimenter said "dog, cat-dog, cat-dog, cat-dog." Picture items were added to the set up through item No. 4 and rehearsed cumulatively three times. The experimenter then exposed the fifth and sixth pictures, labeling, but not rehearsing them, pressed [the window that was to be pressed to signify the test], and then said quickly (pointing to the appropriate window) the names of the last two items followed by the first four. Ten training trials followed which were identical to this demonstration, and the subjects were directed to use the "cumulative rehearsal, fast-finish" strategy. (pp. 266–267)

The no-training control subjects were exposed to the same lists as training subjects, but their task was to learn the items according to their own devices.

During the third phase, the *maintenance* phase, the subjects received a series of 10 six-item recall tests. No prompting to use a strategy was provided to the subjects during this phase. The results were clear-cut. The trained subjects in all grade levels evidenced the cumulative rehearsal, fast-finish strategy (as reflected by their pause times), and the untrained subjects continued to use the simple cumulative rehearsal strategy. Also, the recall of trained subjects was higher during this phase than was the recall of untrained subjects. Thus, it was possible to teach these adolescents to use a more complex strategy than they would employ normally.

In the final phase of the experiment (the *generalization* phase), both trained and untrained subjects were administered a task somewhat different from the previous recall task, but one in which a cumulative rehearsal, fast-finish technique could be employed profitably. In this task the subjects were presented with 12 items, six from each of two different categories. The subjects were told before the presentation of the items that they were to learn the items from only *one* of the categories, and that there was no need to remember the other six pieces of information. Subjects were not prompted to use any particular strategy during the generalization trials.

A very interesting developmental pattern occurred among the trained subjects. They spontaneously transferred the cumulative rehearsal, fast-finish strategy of the previous task to this one, with strategy usage again inferred from the patterns of study pause times. A subject was classified as "clearly using" a cumulative rehearsal, fast-finish strategy "if (s)he paused cumulatively longer before items 1-4, with shorter pause times after items 5 and 6 than after item 4." If the pause time increased between Items 1 and 4, but continued to increase on either Item 5 or 6, the subject was classified in the "partially using" category, and a subject with low or variable pause times after each item was classified as "not using" the strategy.

All of the (untrained) adult subjects, who had used the cumulative rehearsal, fast-finish strategy on the assessment task, also evidenced use of the strategy on the generalization task. Among Grade 6 trained subjects, one (11%) clearly used the strategy, one partially used it, and seven (78%) definitely did not use it. At the Grade 10 level, the subjects were equally divided between those who partially used it and those who did not use it. At the Grade 12 level, three (33%) subjects clearly used the strategy, five (56%) partially used it, and one (11%) did not use it. In general, the untrained subjects showed no use of the strategy on the generalization task. In summary, there was greater evidence of generalization among older trained subjects than among younger ones.

Thus, Barclay (1979) presented evidence consistent with all three of the assertions made earlier in the article. His older subjects were more likely to use the more sophisticated strategy spontaneously than were the younger subjects, although there were individual differences in spontaneous strategy deployment among the Grade 10 and 12 subjects. Subjects who did not evidence spontaneous strategy usage could be trained to use the strategy, although again there were individual differences in transfer of the strategy. Research in other paradigms has also substantiated these points, and it is to some other learning paradigms that the discussion now turns.

Associative Learning

The most frequently studied associative learning task is noun pair learning, which involves the presentation of pairs of items (e.g., *turkey–rock*, *cat–apple*) with the requirement that subjects learn the pairs so that one item can be recalled when its pairmate is given (i.e., *rock* can be remembered given *turkey*, and *apple* can be recalled on presentation of *cat*). Variants of noun pair learning that have been included in recent studies are vocabulary and definitions (e.g., Pressley & Levin, 1978), states and their capitals (Levin, Shriberg, Miller, McCormick, & Levin, 1980), presidents and their numbers (Levin, McCormick, & Dretzke, 1981), occupations (Jones & Hall, 1982; Shriberg, Levin, McCormick, & Pressley, 1982), and cities and their products (Pressley & Dennis-Rounds, 1980), among others (see Pressley, Levin, & Delaney, 1982). The most efficient associative learning strategy has been termed an *elaboration* strategy (Rohwer, 1973), and a variant of the elaboration strategy is the "keyword method" (Atkinson, 1975); see also Paivio (1983) and Chapter 3 in this volume. Elaboration of a paired associate involves constructing either an interactive visual image or a meaningful verbal context (e.g., a phrase, sentence, or story) involving the to-be-associated items. For example, to remember that the English word *carlin* means *old woman* via the keyword method, one first notes that part of *carlin* sounds like the familiar word *car*. Then, the learner constructs an interactive image or sentence that relates a car and an old woman. An image of an old woman driving a car would likely be an effective keyword elaboration for *carlin*.

Several studies have been conducted in which subjects were interviewed about their strategy usage during associative learning (e.g., Kemler & Jusczyk, 1975; Pressley & Levin, 1977a; Beuhring, Note 1; Greer & Suzuki, Note 2). In these studies (1) individual differences in strategy usage have been discovered, with some adolescents reporting elaborative activity and others not doing so; (2) the proportion of subjects reporting elaboration has been found to increase with increasing age during adolescence; and (3) elaborative usage has consistently been associated with higher learning performance than that observed among nonelaborators.

The interview data collected by Pressley and Levin (1977a) will be used to illustrate each of these points. The study included children from Grades 5, 7, and 9 who were presented with a list of noun pairs to learn. After studying the pairs, subjects were given a structured interview regarding their strategy usage. At the Grade 5 level, the majority of subjects (53%) reported exclusively using an inefficient repetition strategy, that is, saying each pair over and over until the next pair was presented. Only 6% of the Grade 5 children used elaboration exclusively to learn the associations. The percentage of pure repeaters declined with increasing age, with 26% of Grade 7 subjects relying on repetition only and 6% of Grade 9 subjects doing so. Exclusive usage of elaboration increased with age, with 15% of Grade 7 subjects classified as pure elaborators and 22% of ninth graders falling into this category. Note, however, that despite the developmental increases in elaborative usage, the efficient elaboration strategy was exhibited by a minority of students, including ninth graders (the highest grade level represented in the study).

The Pressley and Levin (1977a) results are consistent with the positions that increased sophistication in the use of elaborative strategies begins during the adolescent years, and that use of such strategies is predictive of recall performance. The results of three recent studies, however, indicate that in more complex associative tasks, such as vocabulary learning (O'Sullivan & Pressley, Note 3; Scruggs, Note 4) and learning the numbers of the presidents (Levin, Dretzke, McCormick, & McGivern, Note 5), even though young adolescents may spontaneously attempt to produce elaborative mediators, their elaborations will be incomplete and ineffective. Thus, as regards spontaneous elaboration competence, these initial results suggest that the complexity of the task likely affects whether young adolescents will generate effective elaborations.

However, even though not all adolescents evidence spontaneous usage of elaborative strategies, and even though those who do probably experience difficulty with complex associative tasks, it is encouraging to note that by the age of 11 or 12 children can capably execute both imaginal and verbal elaborations on request (see Pressley, 1982, for a review). Also, there is a substantial body of evidence documenting that after elaboration training for paired-associate learning, even young grade school children will maintain the elaboration strategy on another paired-associate task (e.g., Borkowski, Levers, & Gruenenfelder, 1976; Kestner & Borkowski, 1979; Moynahan, 1978; Rohwer, 1980). However, the picture is not as uniformly positive with respect to generalization to slightly different tasks or situations.

Pressley and Dennis-Rounds (1980) provided evidence that transfer of an elaborative strategy from a training domain to another associative problem increases from the upper elementary grades to the high school years. In that experiment, 10- to 11-year-old and 16- to 17-year-old subjects were presented with two associative tasks. In the first task, subjects were asked to remember the products associated with various cities, and in the second task they had to remember the meanings of unfamiliar Latin words. Subjects in three of the four conditions were given explicit instruction in keyword method usage to learn the city-product pairs. Thus, to learn that *flour* is produced in *Appleton*, subjects were taught to derive a keyword from the town name (e.g., *apple* from *Appleton*) and then to generate an interactive image between the keyword and the product referents (e.g., an apple covered with flour). Subjects in the fourth condition were given no-strategy control instructions (i.e., they had to use their own strategies for remembering the city-product pairs). As expected, at both age levels subjects in the three keyword training conditions correctly associated far more cities and their products than did subjects in the control condition.

Immediately following the "cities" training task, subjects in all four conditions were presented with the Latin vocabulary transfer task. Previous control subjects were given no-strategy control instructions, as was one third of the subjects at each age level who had previously been taught the keyword method for the cities task. A second third of the previously trained subjects was given a hint to use a keyword strategy on the Latin task. These subjects were told "to do something like what you did to learn what the cities were famous for" in order to remember the Latin words. The final third of the previously trained subjects was given actual instruction in keyword method usage as specifically applied to Latin vocabulary items.

At the younger (10- and 11-year) age level, prior keyword instruction on the cities task was not spontaneously transferred to the Latin task. That is, performance did not differ significantly in the two conditions given control instructions immediately prior to the Latin task. Transfer did occur at the older (16- and 17-year) age level, however, for even with no hint or instruction regarding the keyword method, subjects who had used the method on the cities task remembered more Latin words than did control subjects who had not been taught the method initially. At both age levels, "hint" subjects and subjects explicitly instructed to use the keyword method for the Latin task recalled more definitions than did control subjects who were never provided with keyword instructions on either task. These data are consistent with the position that older adolescents are more likely to generalize an elaborative strategy than are younger subjects. Thus, the Pressley and Dennis-Rounds findings add to the weight of evidence that there is greater spontaneous usage of sophisticated strategies by older than by younger adolescents.

Prose Learning

A series of prose-learning experiments by Ann Brown and her associates illustrates some of the developmental increases in strategy usage that can be expected during adolescence. As in other learning and/or memory domains, Brown has unearthed individual differences in students' spontaneous deployment of effective prose-recall strategies.

Encoding. Brown and Smiley (1977) showed that adolescents and college students were more sensitive than elementary school students to important versus unimportant aspects of text (see also Cook & Mayer, 1983, and Chapter 6 in this volume). Grade 3, Grade 5, Grade 7, and college students were presented with four consecutive prose passages to read. For two of the passages, subjects were asked to study and recall the passage content. For the other two passages, subjects were asked to rate the importance of each idea unit in the text, ranging from 1 (least important) to 4 (most important). Importance-rating norms had previously been obtained from a sample of adult subjects. The findings can be summarized as follows: At each grade level the probability of recall of any given idea unit was a positive monotonic function of its normed importance rating. That is, the probability of a subject's recalling a Level 4 unit was higher than the probability of his or her recalling a Level 3 unit, as was the probability of Level 3 over Level 2 recall, and Level 2 over Level 1. However, the pattern of data was quite different with respect to subjects' own ratings of idea unit importance. Grade 3 subjects rated units at all four normed levels to be equally important. Grade 5 subjects realized that Level 4 units were more important than the other ones, but did not differentiate among Level 1, Level 2, and Level 3 units. Grade 7 subjects were able to indicate that the Level 1 units were the least important and the Level 4 units the most important. The clearest differentiation among the four importance levels was evident at the college level, where subjects' rated importance of the idea units reflected the same monotonic statistical pattern that appeared in their recall data. Thus, the Brown and Smiley (1977) data offer support for the notion that the ability to discriminate between more and less important text content is developmentally sensitive, with clear improvement occurring during the transition from childhood to adulthood.

The question that followed these observations was whether students' appraisal of the importance of various idea units in a text would affect the kind of strategy they adopted while studying that text. Brown and Smiley (1978, Experiment 3) offered data consistent with the position that strategic study of text is guided by students' understanding of the important versus unimportant information contained therein. That experiment included Grade 5, junior high school (Grades 7 and 8), and senior high school (Grades 11 and 12) students. Subjects were presented with two of the stories from the Brown and Smiley (1977) study, with instructions to study the stories so that they could be recalled. The first story was presented orally, with the subjects simultaneously reading a printed copy of it. After two such presentations of the story, subjects wrote down what they remembered of the content of the story. Then, subjects were again given the printed version of the story and told to do whatever they wanted in order to increase their recall. During this phase, notepads and pens were available, but the subjects were not given explicit instructions to use them. After 5 minutes had passed, subjects were once again tested for their free recall of story content. The same procedure was repeated for the second story, except that before the 5-minute study period, subjects were given a mild hint to use the pens and paper. They were told that "it helps some people to underline or take notes," and that they had the option to do so if they wished.

As in the Brown and Smiley (1977) study, the probability of recall of any particular idea unit was a positive monotonic function of the normed importance level of that item. Of concern here, however, was how the subjects spent their 5 minutes after the first recall test. Brown and Smiley (1978) argued that study of a particular idea unit could be inferred by increased recall of that unit from the first to the second test. They concluded that the secondary school students studied effectively during the 5 minutes and that the Grade 5 children did not, in that the junior and senior high students' recall increased where the recall of the Grade 5 children did not. The most interesting aspect of the data was that at both the junior and senior high levels, increased recall occurred only for the Level 3 and Level 4 units (and not for the Level 1 and Level 2 units), suggesting that the extra study time was devoted primarily to the most important passage content.

Analysis of the notes and underlining produced by subjects during the 5-minute period provided some insights into the specific study-strategy differences between younger and older subjects. First, strategy usage increased with increasing age, with 28% of Grade 5 subjects either taking notes or underlining, in contrast to 41% of junior high school and 76% of senior high school students doing so.

At all grade levels, subjects who "spontaneously" *underlined* (i.e., those who underlined on the first passage when no underlining prompt was provided) were more likely to underline Level 4 idea units than units at other levels during the 5-minute study period. Moreover, at the junior high and senior high levels, spontaneous *note takers* were much more likely to take notes on the more important aspects of the texts than on the less important ones. At both of these grade levels, recall of the higher order text idea units (especially Level 4 units) increased from the first to the second recall test for these spontaneous note takers. There was very little increase in the recall of Level 1 and Level 2 units for these subjects. (Because there were so few Grade 5 spontaneous note takers, no corresponding analysis was carried out at that grade level.)

What happened on the second text passage when it was suggested to subjects that they could take notes and underline? Previously "nonspontaneous" subjects who did take the suggestion to use the strategies did *not* exhibit the proficiency at strategy usage that the spontaneous subjects had displayed. They produced notes and underlinings more equitably across the four levels of importance. Thus, Brown and Smiley (1978) have identified a memory strategy that cannot be induced by a simple suggestion to use it. As Levin and Pressley (1981) have suggested, perhaps more elaborate instruction would induce efficient usage, but that is a question that will require additional research.

Retrieval. Until this point we have restricted our attention to encoding or *storage* strategies. Nonetheless, Brown et al. (1978) were able to show that strategic development during adolescence also occurs with respect to *retrieval*, and highlights of that study that are relevant to the present discussion are presented here. Grade 5, junior high school, senior high school, and college students heard and read one of the stories used in the previous Brown studies. Subjects were given the task of selecting 12 idea units (of the total of 50 units in the story) that they would prefer to have with them if they were trying to remember the story. That is, the subjects were instructed to select retrieval cues, with some of the subjects performing this task before they attempted recall and some doing so after one recall attempt.

When subjects selected retrieval cues *before* they had attempted recall, the pattern of results was the same at all four age levels. Subjects selected Level 4 idea units more frequently than Level 3 units, Level 3 units more frequently than Level 2 units, and Level 2 units more frequently than Level 1 units. When subjects selected retrieval cues *after* they had attempted recall, the same pattern that had been obtained for the cue selection before recall was obtained at the Grade 5, junior high, and senior high levels. At the college level, however, there was a clear difference. The after-recall college students preferred Level *3* units most of all, and to a lesser extent, Level *2* units. Level 1 and Level 4 ideas trailed far behind the Level 2 and Level 3 units as preferred retrieval cues. Why the change? In a postexperiment interview, the college students indicated that they knew that they could recall the Level 4 idea units. Consequently, there would be no need to enlist them as retrieval cues. Being less certain of recalling the next most important text information (Level 3 and Level 2 units), the college students selected cues from those levels instead. Thus, the college students displayed a sophistication in their choice of retrieval cues that younger children did not. At the same time, it should be noted that 7 of the 20 college students did not show the preference for the Level 3 over the Level 4 cues, so that it is not the case that *every* college student evidences this type of strategy in retrieval cue selection.

Discussion

Older adolescents are clearly more strategic than younger adolescents. As discussed here, they are more likely to use a cumulative rehearsal, fast-finish strategy in constrained recall, more likely to use elaboration in associative learning, and more likely to be aware of effective encoding and retrieval strategies in a prose-learning situation. A more optimistic aspect of the associated research to date is that it appears that younger adolescents can, in many cases, be trained to use the strategies that they do not spontaneously employ.

In addition to across-age differences, there are also pronounced individual differences within age levels in the use of all of the strategies discussed here. Only a few high school students in Barclay's (1979) study spontaneously adopted a cumulative rehearsal, fast-finish strategy. Individual differences in elaboration propensity within age levels are found from at least 10 years of age on up (e.g., Pressley & Levin, 1977a); and not all of even the oldest subjects in Brown's prose-learning studies used the most sophisticated strategies that were available to them. These profound individual differences present several challenges to researchers in adolescent cognition.

One challenge is simply to explain the individual differences. Why is it that some adolescents become highly strategic and others do not? Is it because of differences in schooling or instruction, or is it because of organismic differences (e.g., intellectual maturity)? Very little progress has been made toward resolving these issues, although there have been attempts to relate use of specific strategies to psychometric intelligence (e.g., Kennedy & Suzuki, 1977; Rohwer, Raines, Eoff, & Wagner, 1977), formal operational structures (Greer, 1979), and general metacognitive abilities (e.g., Flavell & Wellman, 1977). Given the striking advantages in learning that sophisticated users have, it is easy to justify the expenditures of great resources on the problem of the origins of sophisticated study skills.

The existence of individual differences in strategy usage also presents formidable challenges to the educator. It is axiomatic that if a child is already executing a learning strategy successfully, (s)he will probably not benefit from further instruction to use the given strategy (e.g., Flavell, Beach, & Chinsky, 1966; Hagen & Kingsley, 1968; Pressley, Heisel, McCormick, & Nakamura, 1982; Rohwer et al., 1977). The obvious conclusion is that only those who do not spontaneously evidence a strategy should be taught the learning technique in question, but that is more easily said than done! As should be evident from the studies discussed so far, it often requires more effort to diagnose efficient strategy deployment than it does to instruct in strategy usage (Pressley et al., 1982). Worse yet, there are some cognitive strategies, such as spontaneous inferencing (Paris & Lindauer, 1977; Trabasso & Nicholas, 1980) and schema activation and utilization (Levin & Pressley, 1981), that may not be as easy to detect as the ones discussed here. Those who hope to develop a strategy-training program that can be implemented in classroom settings must make some progress toward developing convenient, yet reliable, assessments of students' spontaneous strategy deployment (see Pressley et al.'s, 1982, discussion of this point, as well as the discussion by Schmeck, Ribich, & Ramanaiah, 1977). Otherwise, well-intentioned strategy interventionists may end up teaching a strategy that is not in the best interest of a particular learner. This is clearly an instructional domain that calls for different treatments for different students. Rohwer (1980) reviews in great detail the implications of differential strategy instruction. Also, Peterson and Swing (1983) review the implications of individual differences in students for classroom implementation of cognitive strategies.

We certainly would not posit that adolescence is the endpoint with respect to the development of sophisticated memory strategies. There simply have not been enough investigations of spontaneous strategy usage during early and middle adulthood for one to conclude whether or not changes occur beyond late adolescence and early adulthood. (The picture is more complete for later portions of the lifespan, however; see Poon, Fozad, Cermak, Arenberg, & Thompson, 1980.) We can be sure that there is plenty of room for improvement during the adult years, for there are many memory tasks in which college students do not display strategies as sophisticated as the ones they could be taught to use—see, for example, Levin's (in press) discussion of mnemonic, prose-learning strategies, as well as Paivio and Desrocher's (1979) and Pressley, Levin, Nakamura, Hope, Bispo, & Toye's (1980, Experiment 2) research using mnemonic strategies for foreign-language learning. It is to be hoped that investigations will be expanded upward developmentally, for it would not be surprising to find additional strategy usage by adults as they get older. In particular, it seems especially likely that many adults will have developed memorization schemes for tasks that they face in their work and everyday lives. It is also likely that the specific memory strategies employed by any particular adult will largely depend on that person's experience, a proposition consistent with general theoretical notions about cognitive development during adulthood (Flavell, 1970; Piaget, 1972).

This closes the first major section of the chapter, which was aimed at providing the reader with some knowledge about the research on memory strategy instruction between the late grade school and college years. In addition to offering the reader some "cognitive structure" about memory, it is hoped that this survey of results has prompted some thinking about promising new directions for research on adolescent memory strategies and strategy instruction. The second major section will focus on specific questions that are frequently presented to memory strategy researchers. As much as possible, the answers will be made with reference to middle childhood and adolescence, and especially with reference to the studies presented thus far.

Five Frequently Asked Questions
About Memory Strategy Instruction

The questions in this section were included because they are five of the more common questions that have been asked of strategy researchers. The issues raised have ranged from theoretical concerns of researchers searching for order in developmental memory data to the questions of educators wanting to know the relevance of strategy instruction research for teachers and students.

1. *Do the results of memory investigations conducted with middle childhood and adolescent subjects conform to a general model of memory development?* Rohwer (1973) argued that "the older the learner, the less explicit the prompt necessary to activate elaboration" (p. 8). In other words, older children are more likely to use elaboration techniques spontaneously, and when instruction is necessary to induce usage, less detailed instructions are required with older than with younger children. A wealth of empirical data has substantiated Rohwer's position (Levin, 1976; Pressley, 1982). That position and slight variations of it (Rohwer, 1976, 1980) about memory instruction can be easily adapted so that it is more general. Based on the research summarized in this chapter and elsewhere, it appears that *the older the learner, the less explicit the prompt necessary to activate any particular memory strategy that is appropriate for the task*. This position is hereafter referred to as the *developmental strategy hypothesis*. Thus, in item learning, spontaneous use of a cumulative rehearsal, fast-finish strategy was more prevalent among late adolescent than among early adolescent learners, although use of the strategy by the younger learners could be induced via explicit instructions to use the strategy. Under a simple instruction to learn the text content, Brown and Smiley's (1978) younger subjects were not as likely to focus on the more important aspects of text as were the older subjects; and in comparison to older adolescents,

Pressley and Dennis-Rounds's (1980) younger subjects required more explicit instructions to transfer the mnemonic keyword strategy to a different content domain. See Rohwer (1976, 1980) and Chapter 1 of this volume for more examples illustrating this theme.

Thus, in each of the three research areas highlighted in the first part of this chapter, studies included instructions that were explicit enough to prompt strategy usage at an older age level but not explicit enough to do so at a younger age level. Also, there was evidence that with more explicit instructions, younger subjects could capably execute strategies that were not manifested spontaneously. The Brown and Smiley (1978, Experiment 3) unsuccessful attempt to induce effective notetaking and/or underlining behavior cannot be taken as serious counterevidence to the generalization offered here, however, for the "more explicit" instructions given to subjects in that study amounted to little more than a hint that notetaking and/or underlining might be helpful (see Levin & Pressley, 1981).

The developmental strategy hypothesis rests on the assumption that the exhibition of less effective memory strategies by pre- and early adolescents (in comparison to later adolescents and adults) is not due to a structural "deficiency." In other words, effective strategies are *capable* of being elicited, given the proper eliciting conditions. At least for a visual imagery associative strategy—the one strategy that has been extensively investigated to determine whether its use is linked to the subject's developmental level (see Pressley, 1982)—it has been found that it is possible to induce effective visual imagery generation in young children with more explicit instruction or prompts (e.g., Bender & Levin, 1976; Pressley & Levin, 1978; Wolff & Levin, 1972). However, much more research is needed on a variety of strategies in order to determine whether there are some that children cannot execute at certain ages no matter how explicit the instructions. If it proves to be the case that such strategies can be found, then the developmental strategy hypothesis would have to be modified accordingly. For the time being, however, the hypothesis appears to summarize concisely and accurately the available data on memory strategy development during middle childhood and adolescence.

2. *What do memory strategy theory and research based on artificial laboratory tasks have to do with the memory tasks people are faced with in their daily lives?* Although the preponderance of work on memory strategies has been done in the context of basic paired-associate, free, serial, and discrimination learning tasks, we contend that this work is not irrelevant to the study of learning in more "ecologically valid" situations (Bracht & Glass, 1968). In our own case, much of our work on the effects of imagery strategies on children's learning in real-world tasks was more than inspired by the earlier work in basic learning situations. The studies would never have been conceived had the more basic work not supplied many hints as to how to design materials that would produce greater learning.

Consider, for example, the task of learning to associate a foreign word with its definition—a task with obvious real-world validity. Based on imagery elaboration research conducted with arbitrarily paired nouns (e.g., Danner & Taylor, 1973; Levin & Pressley, 1978; Pressley & Levin 1977b; Yuille & Catchpole, 1973), it was anticipated that children in the early grade school years would experience more difficulty applying the mnemonic keyword method when unfamiliar vocabulary items were presented in a purely verbal mode (i.e., as words) than when the items were concretized as pictures. In contrast, the results of the same noun pair learning studies suggested that by the end of the grade school years children would experience little difficulty using the imagery-based keyword method. Both of these expectations were confirmed in a vocabulary-learning context (Pressley & Levin, 1978). Other predictions about keyword effects also followed from the basic research findings. For instance, Pressley and Dennis-Rounds's (1980) hypothesis that generalized use of the keyword method would occur more readily in late rather than early adolescence was based on earlier associative learning research by Rohwer and his colleagues (Rohwer & Bean, 1973; Rohwer et al., 1977).

Now consider the real-world task of learning from text. Related to the finding just discussed, basic learning research has supported the conclusion that pictured objects are recalled better than verbally described objects (e.g., Levin, 1976; Paivio, 1971; Pressley, 1977). Consistent with the results from basic learning tasks, the case can certainly now be made that prose passages are recalled better when they are accompanied by text-relevant pictures than when they are not (Levin, 1981a, in press; Levin & Lesgold, 1978; Pressley, Pigott, & Bryant, in press; Schallert, 1980). As another example from the prose-learning domain, parallels can also be drawn between improved memory due to organization and clustering of arbitrarily formed word lists (e.g., Tulving & Donaldson, 1972) and similarly derived memory increases in meaningful prose passages (e.g., Meyer, in press).

As a final example, consider Pressley, Levin, and Delaney's (1982) discussion of the variety of specific real-world applications of mnemonic devices that have occurred in recent years. In particular, the basic components of mnemonic systems—which had earlier been studied in the context of basic learning texts—have now been applied in such diverse domains as foreign languages, language arts (both mechanics and literature), mathematics, science, social studies, medicine, social situations (e.g., to associate a name with a face), and grocery shopping! Many of the components and refinements included in the systems developed came directly from laboratory research using basic learning tasks (see also Levin, 1981b). It is obvious from even a cursory overview of the professional journals concerned with the psychology of learning that the number of memory strategy studies in real-world situations has shown a dramatic increase in the last decade. Much of this shift to real-world problems follows on the heels of expansion of theoretical conceptions of memory from more basic to more complex tasks. In the late 1960s and early 1970s, there was a plethora of theoretical statements about recall and recognition of word lists (e.g., Dixon & Horton, 1968; Tulving & Donaldson, 1972), and these motivated a great deal of research. Contemporary theoretical work on educationally relevant problems such as reading (e.g., Rumelhart, 1980; Spiro, 1980), the nature of bilingual representations (e.g., Paivio & Begg, 1981, chap. 13), children's mathematical skills (e.g., Gelman & Gallistel, 1978) and problem solving (e.g., Cook & Mayer, 1983) are expected to continue as sources of hypotheses for the current generation of memory researchers. Also, processes that have been extensively studied for many years are now being reworked by theorists, and this reworking is resulting in more sophisticated and better articulated proposals about how these processes operate in naturalistic learning situations. Mervis's (1980) discussion of categorization and memory is a good example of this type of theoretical advance (see also Levin's, 1981a, conceptualization of picture "functions" in prose-learning situations).

3. *Can memory strategies be trained in the classroom?* Controlled research related to this question is sparse indeed. There have been some efforts to carry out such research with adults (e.g., Dansereau, McDonald, Collins, Garland, Holley, Diekhoff, & Evans, 1979; Weinstein, Underwood, Wicker, & Cubberly, 1979), but the associated results cannot be unambiguously interpreted (Pressley, 1980). In particular, in many of the "classroom-training" studies, interpretive problems are created by factors such as nonrandom assignment of subjects to conditions, nonindependent treatment administrations, failure to include necessary control conditions, and inappropriate statistical treatment of the data. With these limitations in mind, we still offer the conclusion that despite typically lengthy periods of strategy training, the resulting beneficial effects are surprisingly small.

The present authors have been involved in classroom evaluations of the mnemonic keyword method in recent years. In general, our classroom vocabulary-learning studies conducted with older adolescent high school students have failed to obtain the positive keyword effects that have been observed in the laboratory research (Levin, Pressley, McCormick, Miller, & Shriberg, 1979). Why this is so is unclear, and research by these investigators is continuing. One from among seemingly countless potential explanations is that the older adolescents in the classroom are not as persevering or compliant as they are when they are instructed and tested individually in a laboratory setting.

On the brighter side, however, Levin et al. (1979) have been able to show that the keyword method can produce positive group-instruction results with younger children as subjects. In one of their experiments, 11 groups of Grade 5 children (3-6 children per group) were taught the keyword method of vocabulary learning. Subjects in the 11 groups of control subjects were never instructed in the keyword method. Using "groups" as the units of statistical analysis, Levin et al. found a substantial positive effect of the keyword method. In fact, there was almost no overlap in the distribution of the means of the two groups, with only one keyword mean as low as the highest control mean. The keyword-control manipulation accounted for 62% of the variance in recall scores.

Moreover, in a final experiment Levin et al. (1979) provided keyword method instruction to five intact *classrooms*, with another five classrooms assigned to a control condition—with "classrooms" constituting the units of analysis—and again keyword subjects by far outperformed controls. In fact, this time there was *no* overlap in the two groups' means. Eighty percent of the variance in recall was accounted for by the keyword-control manipulation.

As a final note, in three recent prose-learning experiments (Levin, Shriberg, & Berry, in press, Experiments 1 & 2; McCormick, Note 6), mnemonic strategy instruction has been provided en masse to groups of younger adolescents (junior high school students), with very encouraging positive results. Yet, given the previously mentioned problems and discrepancies in other studies, it is clear that much more research in classroom-based strategy research is needed. Just as one message of this chapter is that across-age generalizations regarding the effectiveness of memory strategies are not warranted, neither can one conclude that strategy findings based on individually tested students in the laboratory will automatically generalize to a classroom-instructional situation (see also Fuentes, 1976; Peterson & Swing, 1983).

4. *Are the strategies that are being developed by cognitive psychologists as good as the ones that teachers have been recommending for years?* Walk into any education library at a major university and you will be struck by the number of textbooks that deal with various aspects of the curriculum. Many of these books are filled with recommendations about effective learning strategies, some of which are discussed by Cook and Mayer (1983). All too often, however, the recommendations are based on either conventional wisdom or vague theoretical speculation rather than actual research evidence. Admittedly, much of the blame for this state of affairs must fall on the educational research community. As implied in the answer to the immediately preceding question, researchers have rarely provided usable classroom solutions. Even in the laboratory research, investigators have failed to include as contrast conditions the kind of educational treatments that typically occur in the classroom.

Again, however, there is a brighter side to the picture. At least as far as the mnemonic keyword method is concerned, the present authors have included contrast conditions that contain the ingredients of more "naturalistic" educational treatments. For example, in a recent series of vocabulary-learning experiments with college students, Pressley, Levin, Kuiper, Bryant, and Michener (in press) compared the keyword method with procedures designed to increase semantic and/or contextual processing of vocabulary words and their meanings. The keyword method proved to be more effective than any of the semantic alternatives that were considered. The present discussion will focus on these semantic procedures. In Pressley et al.'s (in press) third experiment, subjects were presented with English vocabulary words to learn. Half of the subjects were instructed to use the keyword method and half were presented with a variety of semantic strategies, all of which are recommended as effective vocabulary-learning supplements by reading theorists (see Johnson & Pearson, 1978). In particular, subjects in the semantic condition were provided with (a) words that were semantically related to the vocabulary items; (b) more specific definitions of the items; (c) sentences containing the vocabulary words; and (d) pictures representing the meanings of the vocabulary words. The experiment was considered an especially challenging test for the keyword method in that the semantic strategy subjects were provided with four different kinds of naturalistic support, each of which has been assumed to increase vocabulary learning in a classroom instructional context. The keyword method proved more than equal to the challenge, with over twice as many definitions recalled in the keyword than in the semantic condition.

The positive results obtained by Pressley et al. (in press) nicely complemented two other studies in which the keyword method was compared to semantically-based alternative techniques. Both Pressley, Levin, and Miller (1982) with adults and Levin, McCormick, Miller, Berry, and Pressley (1982) with children presented data showing the keyword method to be superior to various semantic alternatives (see also Paivio, 1983). The conclusion therefore follows that the mnemonic keyword method appears to be a more potent vocabulary-learning strategy than those that are held in high regard by reading theorists. A surprising finding in these experiments is that naturalistic, semantically-based alternatives have not even proven to be better than no-strategy control instructions. Thus, the research discussed here has not only advanced the development of the keyword method of vocabulary learning, but has also demonstrated that educator wisdom about what constitutes an effective learning strategy is at best premature and at worst unfounded empirically.

5. *Even if children can be taught effective strategies, will they continue to use them in the absence of explicit prompts?* This should be posed as a two-part question: Will subjects continue to use a strategy in the same situation in which it was taught (maintenance)? Will children use the strategy in new situations for which the strategy would be appropriate (generalization)?

There is a good deal of evidence that with adequate instruction and practice, children do maintain memory strategies. For instance, both retarded and normal children maintain simple elaboration strategies (e.g., Borkowski et al., 1976; Kestner & Borkowski, 1979; Moynahan, 1978; Rohwer, 1980; Wanshura & Borkowski, 1974, 1975; Yuille & Catchpole, 1974). Also, children maintain certain rehearsal and clustering strategies (Brown, Campione, & Murphy, 1974; Bilsky & Evans, 1970; Kellas, Ashcraft, & Johnson, 1973; Nye, McMannis, & Haugen, 1972; Turnbull, 1974).

Unfortunately, as can be inferred from our earlier discussion of the Pressley and Dennis-Rounds (1980) study, the picture is more pessimistic with respect to children's spontaneous generalization of an elaborative strategy (see also Borkowski, in press; Borkowski & Cavanaugh, 1979; Brown, 1975; Butterfield & Belmont, 1977; Belmont & Butterfield, Note 7; and Chapter 5 in this volume). However, the same researchers who have reported generalization failures have also offered viable suggestions as to what components may be necessary in order to induce transfer. Their arguments boil down to this: To enhance transfer, enhance the subjects' knowledge about the strategy. To accomplish this goal, strategy training should minimally include (a) information about the classes of tasks for which the strategy would be appropriate and how to recognize those situations; (b) information about the learning gains that can be expected as a result of using the strategy; and (c) practice at applying the strategy, with concomitant feedback about performance under both strategy-present and strategy-absent conditions. At present, evidence to support the contention that strategy generalization is tied to strategy knowledge is mostly correlational (Borkowski, in press; Cavanaugh & Borkowski, 1980; Belmont & Butterfield, Note 7). However, researchers interested in the relationship between strategy knowledge and strategy generalization are beginning to explore causal connections (e.g., Lodico, Ghatala, Levin, Pressley, & Bell, in press; Beuhring, Note 1). An example of an experimental investigation of the effect of strategy knowledge on strategy generalization is a recent study by O'Sullivan and Pressley

(Note 3). They varied the amount of general information that was provided during a strategy-training session. All of the Grade 5 and Grade 6 subjects were taught the keyword method in the specific context of a city-product learning task. In some conditions, however, the training was supplemented with information about the general structure of keyword mnemonics, along with information about situations that are amenable to keyword usage. As expected, greater generalization of the strategy to a Latin vocabulary-learning task was obtained with the knowledge-rich instruction than with strategy instruction per se.

Given the tremendous educational importance of research on strategy generalization (Royer, 1979), as well as the criticality of strategy generalization for those concerned with children's metacognitive development (Borkowski, in press), it is expected that much more research on transfer will be generated in the near future. See also the many comments about generalization in other chapters of this volume (e.g., Chapters 1, 4, 5, and 6).

Concluding Remarks

The most appropriate way to close this chapter seems to be to reiterate a point that was made at the outset: There has been far too little research on memory strategy instruction within the period from late childhood into adulthood. What we have attempted here has been to provide some general commentary about the research that *has* been conducted. Also, the questions presented in the latter part of the chapter suggest directions that researchers might profitably follow in order to generate a more complete picture of adolescent memory strategy development.

Five conclusions follow from the answers given to the questions:

1. The only way to discover whether the developmental strategy hypothesis is correct is to conduct more research aimed at determining whether children can always be taught to use strategies that they do not employ when minimal instruction is given. If all that is required to induce use of a particular strategy is more extensive and explicit instruction, then the extension of Rohwer's (1973) hypothesis that was presented here would be supported.

2. In addition, more research is needed in which theoretical notions about memory strategies are validated in real-world contexts. The trend away from list-learning studies relevant only to abstract, theoretical issues is to be both applauded and encouraged. By expanding investigations to include more ecologically valid domains, it is a good bet that more will be learned about the diversity and adaptability of human cognition.

3. Developing classroom interventions for memory strategy instruction should be a high priority. Given the challenges associated with diagnosing strategy deficiencies and providing instruction appropriate to children at different levels of cognitive sophistication, it is expected that the fostering of memory strategy deployment in school will be no easy task. On the other hand, the potential gains are great, which should provide motivation for classroom-relevant research.

4. Reevaluation of "ingrained" instructional recommendations is desperately needed. Many curriculum-instructional recommendations are without empirical support. In reexamining these techniques, researchers should also compare the "good old ways" with the new ideas of cognitive psychology. Few explicit comparisons have been made between techniques developed in the laboratory and those that are presumed to work by educational practitioners. However, the preliminary box score to date is heavily weighted in favor of those empirically tested strategies that have arisen from psychological principles of learning and memory, in contrast to untested traditional curriculum recommendations. Despite these suggestions, the only way to create a new tradition is for researchers who develop new strategies to substantiate their value by using real-world tasks in real-world settings.

5. Continued use of effective memory strategies once instruction is discontinued is a problem of both applied and theoretical concern. How to create a mature thinker who possesses a repertoire of strategies (i.e., strategies "for all seasons"), as well as the knowledge of when to apply them, is perhaps the ultimate goal and presents the greatest challenge to memory strategy researchers. It is hoped that more and more educational researchers can be encouraged to face that challenge in the next few years.

Acknowledgments. This chapter was prepared in part while the first and second authors were on leave to the University of Notre Dame and Arizona State University, respectively. We gratefully acknowledge the support of those institutions in the preparation of the manuscript. The manuscript preparation was principally supported by grants from the Natural Sciences and Engineering Research Council of Canada and the National Institute of Education through the Wisconsin Research and Development Center for Education Research. We are grateful to Gail Kopp and Lynn Sowle for typing the manuscript.

Reference Notes

1. Beuhring, T. *Elaboration and associative memory development: The metamemory link.* Unpublished manuscript, 1981. (Available from author, Human Sciences Research Council, Pretoria, Republic of South Africa.)
2. Greer, R. N., & Suzuki, N. S. *Development of spontaneous elaboration in concrete and abstract noun pair learning.* Paper presented at the annual meeting of the American Educational Research Association, San Francisco, April 1976.
3. O'Sullivan, J., & Pressley, M. Manuscript in preparation, University of Western Ontario, 1982.
4. Scruggs, T. E. *Verbal learning strategies in academically precocious youth.* Unpublished doctoral dissertation, Department of Special Education, Arizona State University, 1982.
5. Levin, J. R., Dretzke, B. J., McCormick, C. B., & McGivern, J. *Learning mnemonically: Analysis of the presidential process.* Working Paper No. 327,

Wisconsin Center for Education Research, University of Wisconsin-Madison, 1982.
6. McCormick, C. B. *The effect of mnemonic strategy variations on students' recall of potentially confusable prose passages.* Unpublished doctoral dissertation, University of Wisconsin-Madison, 1981.
7. Belmont, J., & Butterfield, E. *To secure transfer, train superordinates.* Paper presented at the annual meeting of the American Educational Research Association, April 1980.

References

Atkinson, R. C. Mnemotechnics in second-language learning. *American Psychologist,* 1975, *30*, 821–828.

Barclay, C. R. The executive control of mnemonic activity. *Journal of Experimental Child Psychology*, 1979, *27*, 262–276.

Bender, B. G., & Levin, J. R. Motor activity, anticipated motor activity, and young children's associative learning. *Child Development*, 1976, *47*, 560–562.

Bilsky, L., & Evans, R. A. Use of associative clustering techniques in the study of reading disability: Effects of list organization. *American Journal of Mental Deficiency*, 1970, *74*, 771–776.

Bisanz, G. L., Vesonder, G. T., & Voss, J. F. Knowledge of one's own responding and the relation of such knowledge to learning. *Journal of Experimental Child Psychology*, 1978, *25*, 116–128.

Borkowski, J. G. Signs of intelligence: Strategy generalization and metacognition. In S. Yussen (Ed.), *The development of reflection in children.* New York: Academic Press, in press.

Borkowski, J. G., & Cavanaugh, J. C. Maintenance and generalization of skills and strategies by the retarded. In N. R. Ellis (Ed.), *Handbook of mental deficiency, psychological theory and research.* Hillsdale, NJ: 1979.

Borkowski, J. R., Levers, S., & Gruenenfelder, T. M. Transfer of mediational strategies in children: The role of activity and awareness during strategy acquisition. *Child Development*, 1976, *47*, 779–786.

Bracht, G. H., & Glass, G. V. The external validity of experiments. *American Educational Research Journal*, 1968, *5*, 437–474.

Brown, A. L. The development of memory: Knowing, knowing about knowing, and knowing how to know. In H. W. Reese (Ed.), *Advances in child development and behavior* (Vol. 10). New York: Academic Press, 1975.

Brown, A. L., Campione, J. C., Bray, N. W., & Wilcox, B. L. Keeping track of changing variables: Effects of rehearsal training and rehearsal prevention in normal and retarded adolescents. *Journal of Experimental Child Psychology*, 1973, *101*, 123–131.

Brown, A. L., Campione, J. C., & Day, J. D. Learning to learn: On training students to learn from texts. *Educational Researcher*, 1981, *10*(2), 14–21.

Brown, A. L., Campione, J. C., & Murphy, M. D. Keeping track of changing variables: Long-term retention of a trained rehearsal strategy by retarded adolescents. *American Journal of Mental Deficiency*, 1974, *78*, 446–453.

Brown, A. L., & Smiley, S. S. Rating the importance of structural units of prose passages: A problem of metacognitive development. *Child Development*, 1977, *48*, 1–8.

Brown, A. L., & Smiley, S. S. The development of strategies for studying text. *Child Development*, 1978, *49*, 1076–1088.

Brown, A. L., Smiley, S. S., & Lawton, S. C. The effects of experience on the selection of suitable retrieval cues for studying text. *Child Development*, 1978, *49*, 829–835.

Butterfield, E. C., & Belmont, J. M. Assessing and improving the cognitive functions of mentally retarded people. In I. Bailer & M Steinlicht (Eds.), *Psychological issues in mental retardation*. Chicago: Aldine Press, 1977.

Cavanaugh, J. C., & Borkowski, J. G. Searching for metamemory-memory connections: A developmental study. *Developmental Psychology*, 1980, *16*, 441–453.

Conger, J. J. *Adolescence and youth*. New York: Harper & Row, 1977.

Cook, L. K., & Mayer, R. E. Reading strategies training for meaningful learning from prose. In M. Pressley & J. R. Levin (Eds.), *Cognitive strategy research: Educational applications*. New York: Springer-Verlag, 1983.

Cuvo, A. J. Incentive level influence on overt rehearsal and free recall as a function of age. *Journal of Experimental Child Psychology*, 1974, *18*, 167–181.

Cuvo, A. J. Developmental differences in rehearsal and free recall. *Journal of Experimental Child Psychology*, 1975, *19*, 265–278.

Danner, F. W., & Taylor, A. M. Integrated pictures and relational imagery training in children's learning. *Journal of Experimental Child Psychology*, 1973, *16*, 47–54.

Dansereau, D. F., McDonald, B. A., Collins, K. W., Garland, J., Holley, C. D., Diekhoff, G. M., & Evans, S. H. Evaluation of a learning strategy system. In H. F. O'Neil & C. D. Spielberger (Eds.), *Cognitive and affective learning strategies*. New York: Academic Press, 1979.

Dixon, T. R., & Horton, D. L. (Eds.), *Verbal behavior and general behavior theory*. Englewood Cliffs, NJ: Prentice-Hall, 1968.

Flavell, J. Cognitive changes in adulthood. In P. B. Baltes & L. R. Goulet (Eds.), *Life-span developmental psychology*. New York: Academic Press, 1970.

Flavell, J. H., Beach, D. R., & Chinsky, J. M. Spontaneous verbal rehearsal in a memory task as a function of age. *Child Development*, 1966, *37*, 283–299.

Flavell, J. H., & Wellman, H. M. Metamemory. In R. V. Kail & J. W. Hagen (Eds.), *Perspectives on the development of memory and cognition*. Hillsdale, NJ: Erlbaum, 1977.

Fuentes, E. J. An investigation into the use of imagery and generativity in learning a foreign language vocabulary (Doctoral dissertation, Stanford University, 1976). *Dissertation Abstracts International*, 1976, *37*, 2694A. (University Microfilms No. 76-25, 997)

Gelman, R., & Gallistel, C. R. *The child's understanding of number*. Cambridge, MA: Harvard University Press, 1978.

Greer, R. N. E. Spontaneous elaboration of paired associates and formal operational thinking: A developmental analysis (Doctoral dissertation, University of British Columbia, 1978). *Dissertation Abstracts International*, 1979, *39*, 5410A–5411A.

Hagen, J. W., & Kingsley, P. R. Labeling effects in short-term memory. *Child Development*, 1968, *39*, 113–121.

Johnson, D. D., & Pearson, P. D. *Teaching reading vocabulary*. New York: Holt, Rinehart & Winston, 1978.

Jones, B. F., & Hall, J. W. School applications of the mnemonic keyword method as a study strategy by eighth graders. *Journal of Educational Psychology*, 1982, *74*, 230–237.

Kellas, G., Ashcraft, M. H., & Johnson, N. S. Rehearsal processes in the short-term memory performance of mildly retarded adolescents. *American Journal of Mental Deficiency*, 1973, *77*, 670–679.

Kellas, G., McCauley, C., & McFarland, C. E. Developmental aspects of storage and retrieval. *Journal of Experimental Child Psychology*, 1975, *19*, 51–62.

Kemler, D. G., & Jusczyk, P. W. A developmental study of facilitation by mnemonic instructions. *Journal of Experimental Child Psychology*, 1975, *20*, 400–410.

Kennedy, S. P., & Suzuki, N. S. Spontaneous elaboration in Mexican-American high school seniors. *American Educational Research Journal*, 1977, *14*, 383–388.

Kestner, J., & Borkowski, J. G. Children's maintenance and generalization of an interrogative learning strategy. *Child Development*, 1979, *50*, 485–494.

Lange, G. Organization-related processes in children's recall. In P. A. Ornstein (Ed.), *Memory development in children*. New York: Wiley, 1978.

Levin, J. R. What have we learned about maximizing what children learn? In J. R. Levin & V. L. Allen (Eds.), *Cognitive learning in children*. New York: Academic Press, 1976.

Levin, J. R. On functions of pictures in prose. In F. J. Pirozzolo & M. C. Wittrock (Eds.), *Neuropsychological and cognitive processes in reading*. New York: Academic Press, 1981. (a)

Levin, J. R. The mnemonic '80s: Keyword in the classroom. *Educational Psychologist*, 1981, *16*, 65–82. (b)

Levin, J. R. Pictures as prose-learning devices. In A. Flammer & W. Kintsch (Eds.), *Discourse processing*. Amsterdam: North-Holland, in press.

Levin, J. R., & Lesgold, A. M. On pictures in prose. *Educational Communication and Technology Journal*, 1978, *26*, 233–243.

Levin, J. R., McCormick, C. B., & Dretzke, B. J. A combined pictorial mnemonic strategy for ordered information. *Educational Communication and Technology Journal*, 1981, *29*, 219–225.

Levin, J. R., McCormick, C. B., Miller, G. E., Berry, J. K., & Pressley, M. Mnemonic versus nonmnemonic vocabulary learning strategies for children. *American Educational Research Journal*, 1982, *19*, 121–136.

Levin, J. R., & Pressley, M. A test of the developmental imagery hypothesis in children's associative learning. *Journal of Educational Psychology*, 1978, *70*, 691–694.

Levin, J. R., & Pressley, M. Improving children's prose comprehension: Selected strategies that seem to succeed. In C. Santa & B. Hayes (Eds.), *Children's prose comprehension: Research and practice*. Newark, DE: International Reading Association, 1981.

Levin, J. R., Pressley, M., McCormick, C. B., Miller, G. E., & Shriberg, L. K. Assessing the classroom potential of the keyword method. *Journal of Educational Psychology*, 1979, *71*, 583–594.

Levin, J. R., Shriberg, L. K., & Berry, J. K. A concrete strategy for remembering abstract prose. *American Educational Research Journal*, in press.

Levin, J. R., Shriberg, L. K., Miller, G. E., McCormick, C. B., & Levin, B. B. The keyword method in the classroom: How to remember the states and their capitals. *Elementary School Journal*, 1980, *80*, 185–191.

Lodico, M. G., Ghatala, E. S., Levin, J. R., Pressley, M., & Bell, J. A. The effects of strategy-monitoring training on children's selection of effective memory strategies. *Journal of Experimental Child Psychology*, in press.

Mervis, C. B. Category structure and the development of categorization. In R. J. Spiro, B. C. Bruce, & W. F. Brewer (Eds.), *Theoretical issues in reading comprehension*. Hillsdale, NJ: Erlbaum, 1980.

Meyer, B. J. F. Organizational aspects of text: Effects on reading comprehension and applications for the classroom. In J. Flood (Ed.), *Reading comprehension*. Newark, DE: International Reading Association, in press.

Moynahan, E. D. Assessment and selection of paired associate strategies: A developmental study. *Journal of Experimental Child Psychology*, 1978, *26*, 257–266.

Nye, W. C., McMannis, D. L., & Haugen, D. M. Training and transfer of categorization by retarded adults. *American Journal of Mental Deficiency*, 1972, *77*, 199–207.

Ornstein, P. A., & Naus, M. J. Rehearsal processes in children's memory. In P. A. Ornstein (Ed.), *Memory development in children*. Hillsdale, NJ: Erlbaum, 1978.

Paivio, A. *Imagery and verbal processes*. New York: Holt, Rinehart & Winston, 1971.

Paivio, A. Strategies in language learning. In M. Pressley & J. R. Levin (Eds.), *Cognitive strategy research: Educational applications*. New York: Springer-Verlag, 1983.

Paivio, A., & Begg, I. *Psychology of language*. Englewood Cliffs, NJ: Prentice-Hall, 1981.

Paivio, A., & Desrochers, A. Effects of an imagery mnemonic on second language recall and comprehension. *Canadian Journal of Psychology*, 1979, *33*, 17–28.

Paris, S. G., & Lindauer, B. K. Constructive aspects of children's comprehension and memory. In R. V. Kail, Jr., & J. W. Hagen (Eds.), *Perspectives on the development of memory and cognition*. Hillsdale, NJ: Erlbaum, 1977.

Peterson, P. L., & Swing, S. R. Problems in classroom implementation of cognitive strategy instruction. In M. Pressley & J. R. Levin (Eds.), *Cognitive strategy research: Educational applications*. New York: Springer-Verlag, 1983.

Piaget, J. Intellectual evolution from adolescence to adulthood. *Human Development*, 1972, *15*, 1–12.

Poon, L. W., Fozard, J. L., Cermak, L. S., Arenberg, D. L., & Thompson, L. W. (Eds.), *New directions in memory and aging*. Hillsdale, NJ: Erlbaum, 1980.

Pressley, M. Imagery and children's learning: Putting the picture in developmental perspective. *Review of Educational Research*, 1977, *47*, 585–622.

Pressley, M. Applying cognitive strategies in the military. (Review of H. F. O'Neil & C. D. Spielberger's *Cognitive and affective learning strategies*.) *Contemporary Psychology*, 1980, *25*, 823–824.

Pressley, M. Elaboration and memory development. *Child Development*, 1982, *53*, 296–309.

Pressley, M., & Dennis-Rounds, J. Transfer of a mnemonic keyword strategy at two age levels. *Journal of Educational Psychology*, 1980, *72*, 575–582.

Pressley, M., Heisel, B. E., McCormick, C. G., & Nakamura, G. V. Memory strategy instruction. In C. J. Brainerd & M. Pressley (Eds.), *Verbal processes in children*. New York: Springer-Verlag, 1982.

Pressley, M., & Levin, J. R. Developmental differences in subjects' associative learning strategies and performances: Assessing a hypothesis. *Journal of Experimental Child Psychology*, 1977, *24*, 431–439. (a)

Pressley, M., & Levin, J. R. Task parameters affecting the efficacy of a visual imagery learning strategy in younger and older children. *Journal of Experimental Child Psychology*, 1977, *24*, 53–59. (b)

Pressley, M., & Levin, J. R. Developmental constraints associated with children's use of the keyword method of foreign language vocabulary learning. *Journal of Experimental Child Psychology*, 1978, *26*, 359–372.

Pressley, M., Levin, J. R., & Delaney, H. D. The mnemonic keyword method. *Review of Educational Research*, 1982, *52*, 61–92.

Pressley, M., Levin, J. R., Kuiper, N. A., Bryant, S. L., & Michener, S. Mnemonic versus nonmnemonic vocabulary-learning strategies: Additional comparisons. *Journal of Educational Psychology*, in press.

Pressley, M., Levin, J. R., & Miller, G. E. The keyword method compared to alternative vocabulary-learning strategies. *Contemporary Educational Psychology*, 1982, *7*, 50–60.

Pressley, M., Levin, J. R., Nakamura, G. V., Hope, D. J., Bispo, J. G., & Toye, A. R. The keyword method of foreign vocabulary learning: An investigation of its generalizability. *Journal of Applied Psychology*, 1980, *65*, 635–642.

Pressley, M., Pigott, S., & Bryant, S. L. Picture content and preschoolers' learning from sentences. *Educational Communication and Technology Journal*, in press.

Rohwer, W. D., Jr. Elaboration and learning in childhood and adolescence. In H. W. Reese (Ed.), *Advances in child development and behavior* (Vol. 8). New York: Academic Press, 1973.

Rohwer, W. D., Jr. An introduction to research on individual and developmental differences in learning. In W. K. Estes (Ed.), *Handbook of learning and cognitive processes* (Vol. 3). New York: Wiley, 1976.

Rohwer, W. D., Jr. An elaborative conception of learner differences. In R. E. Snow, P. A. Frederico, & W. E. Montague (Eds.), *Aptitude, learning, and instruction*. Hillsdale, NJ: Erlbaum, 1980.

Rohwer, W. D., Jr., & Bean, J. P. Sentence effects and noun-pair learning: A developmental interaction during adolescence. *Journal of Experimental Child Psychology*, 1973, *15*, 521–533.

Rohwer, W. D., Jr., Raines, J. M., Eoff, J., & Wagner, M. The development of elaborative propensity during adolescence. *Journal of Experimental Child Psychology*, 1977, *23*, 472–492.

Royer, J. M. Theories of the transfer of learning. *Educational Psychologist*, 1979, *14*, 53–69.

Rumelhart, D. E. Schemata: The building blocks of cognition. In R. J. Spiro, B. C. Bruce, & W. F. Brewer (Eds.), *Theoretical issues in reading comprehension*. Hillsdale, NJ: Erlbaum, 1980.

Schallert, D. L. The role of illustrations in reading comprehension. In R. J. Spiro, B. C. Bruce, & W. F. Brewer (Eds.), *Theoretical issues in reading comprehension research: Perspectives from cognitive psychology, linguistics, artificial intelligence, and education*. Hillsdale, NJ: Erlbaum, 1980.

Schmeck, R. R., Ribich, F., & Ramanaiah, N. Development of a self-report inventory for assessing individual differences in learning processes. *Applied Psychological Measurement,* 1977, *1*, 413–431.

Shriberg, L. K., Levin, J. R., McCormick, C. B., & Pressley, M. Learning about "famous" people via the keyword method. *Journal of Educational Psychology*, 1982, *74*, 238–247.

Spiro, R. J. Constructive processes in prose comprehension and recall. In R. J. Spiro, B. C. Bruce, & W. F. Brewer (Eds.), *Theoretical issues in reading comprehension*. Hillsdale, NJ: Erlbaum, 1980.

Trabasso, T., & Nicholas, D. W. Memory and inferences in the comprehension of narratives. In F. Wilkening, J. Becker, & T. Trabasso (Eds.), *Information integration by children*. Hillsdale, NJ: Erlbaum, 1980.

Tulving, E., & Donaldson, W. (Eds.). *Organization of memory*. New York: Academic Press, 1972.

Turnbull, A. P. Teaching retarded persons to rehearse through cumulative overt labeling. *American Journal of Mental Deficiency*, 1974, *79*, 331–337.

Wanshura, P. B., & Borkowski, J. G. The development and transfer of mediational strategies by retarded children in paired-associate learning. *American Journal of Mental Deficiency*, 1974, *78*, 631–639.

Wanshura, P. B., & Borkowski, J. G. Long-term transfer of a mediation strategy by moderately retarded children. *American Journal of Mental Deficiency*, 1975, *80*, 323–333.

Weinstein, C. E., Underwood, V. L., Wicker, F. W., & Cubberly, W. E. Cognitive learning strategies: Verbal and imaginal elaboration. In H. F. O'Neil, Jr., & C. D. Spielberger (Eds.), *Cognitive and affective learning strategies*. New York: Academic Press, 1979.

Wolff, P., & Levin, J. R. The role of overt activity in children's imagery production. *Child Development*, 1972, *43*, 537–547.

Yuille, J. C., & Catchpole, M. J. Associative learning and imagery training in young children. *Journal of Experimental Child Psychology*, 1973, *16*, 403–412.

Yuille, J. C., & Catchpole, M. J. The effects of delay and imagery training on the recall and recognition of object pairs. *Journal of Experimental Child Psychology*, 1974, *17*, 474–481.

3. Mnemonic-Device Instruction with Adults

Francis S. Bellezza

The use of special learning techniques for memorizing information is not a new phenomenon. Greek and Roman orators used a memorizing technique called the method of loci to memorize their speeches, and medieval academics used the commonplace method for remembering all the knowledge that they would need for scholarly disputation (Yates, 1966). The first book in the English language devoted entirely to applied psychology was on memory techniques (Laver, 1977). Many people in the United States today use the memory aids "spring forward" and "fall back" to remember how to change their clocks in April and October. Mnemonic devices have existed in Western culture for a long time, and interest in them has always been fairly high.

Recent research has demonstrated the usefulness of mnemonic procedures as aids in vocabulary development and the study of geography, history, and related areas (Higbee, 1979; Levin, 1981a; Paivio, 1983; Paivio & Desrochers, 1981; Pressley, Levin, & Delaney, 1981). Yet the question may be raised why the use of mnemonic devices is not more widespread. One commonly accepted reason is that the literacy rate is now so high in Western culture that people not being tested in school or in other situations can simply write what they wish to remember (Baddeley, 1976). Purely mental mnemonic devices are not needed. In earlier times, when the average person could not read and write, information (such as religious teachings) was conveyed by means of visual aids and symbols in order to make what was taught more memorable (Roberts & Weisberg, 1976; Yates, 1966).

A second possible reason why mnemonic devices are not used is that our educational policy has been to emphasize the comprehension of information rather than its memorization. In a provocative study, however, Hayes-Roth and Walker (1979)

Carlyle Campbell Library
Meredith College

instructed one group of college students to try to remember the contents of a passage and then tested them without allowing them to refer to the passage. A second group was instructed simply to become familiar with the passage and to refer to it when answering the test questions. They found that the students who had to rely solely on memory performed better than those students who could refer to the text when answering the questions. Hayes-Roth and Walker suggest that memorizing individual facts may be a necessary precursor to a thorough understanding of the relations among the facts. Later in this chapter information will be considered that shows that comprehension does not automatically result in remembering.

A third reason mnemonics may not be used is that people are unaware of their existence. Mnemonic techniques found to be of general usefulness may have to be taught in the schools in order to become widely used. Just what mnemonic devices fall into this category is a question that is still being investigated.

A fourth reason that mnemonic devices are not more widely used is that they often require practice and training. A basic question about any specialized learning technique is not only whether it is superior to other traditional procedures of learning, but whether this superiority is worth the time and effort needed to learn to use the mnemonic effectively.

Many of the criticisms that have been made of mnemonic techniques are not justified. Higbee (1978) summarizes a number of arguments that have been used against mnemonics that simply are not true. These include the arguments that mnemonics are never practical, do not help understanding, are memory crutches, and are tricks.

The Scope of the Chapter

This chapter reviews some issues that I believe are important in the evaluation of memorization techniques and in the development of training procedures to instruct adults in these techniques. Because of limitations of space, only one or two studies relevant to each issue will be mentioned. Most of these experiments will deal with free-recall performance, rather than recognition or cued recall, as the response measure. A free-recall measure of retention is often very sensitive to the effects of learning with a mnemonic technique. Free recall occurs under minimal cuing conditions. Therefore, the cognitive cuing structures—that is, the mental cues created by an organizational mnemonic—have an opportunity to be maximally effective (Bellezza, 1981).

The usefulness of many mnemonic techniques is still being debated, so it is not surprising that there are many more experiments focused on the evaluation of techniques rather than on the development of effective training procedures. Somewhat more comprehensive discussions of research with mnemonic devices can be found in Bellezza (1981), Gruneberg, Morris, and Sykes (1978), Higbee (1977), Norman (1976), Paivio (1971), Pressley et al. (1982), and other chapters in this volume.

This chapter is divided into two parts. The first part focuses on memory techniques used to memorize lists of words, and the second part deals with memorization techniques used for prose materials. Many of the techniques used for words lists are also used for text, so the issues raised concerning list-learning techniques and the methods for evaluating them are also relevant to the learning of textual material.

In the course of the chapter two main points are emphasized. The first point is that in any mnemonic technique the characteristics of the memory structure representing the remembered information are very important if the information is to be retained in memory. This emphasis on cognitive representation is the primary difference between learning by using a mnemonic device and the more traditional and behaviorally oriented learning procedures (see also Cook & Mayer, 1983). Investigators should not only assess memory performance based on what material was presented but should also try to assess and to understand the nature of the cognitive representation of this information. For example, verbal material may be stored in memory as visual images (Paivio, 1971; 1983), yet often the nature or even existence of these images is not assessed when a learning procedure is evaluated. The memory representations for prose material often involve subjects' knowledge structures, so some discussion of schema theory will be presented (again, Cook & Mayer, 1983, take up this problem).

The second recurring theme of this chapter is that the use of a mnemonic technique is a skill that involves instruction, training, and practice on the part of the user. The effectiveness of a mnemonic technique cannot be assessed unless the person using it has atained some minimum skill. Yet on the debit side, it may be possible that the investment of time, effort, and other resources used in teaching and learning these skills sometimes may not be worth the gain in learning efficiency.

Mnemonic Techniques and Memory Strategies

In this chapter a *mnemonic technique* or a *mnemonic device* is considered to be a particular procedure that an individual can use to memorize a particular set of materials under a specific set of conditions. This memorization takes place by creating a cognitive representation of that material in memory. In some instances the procedure is familiar to the learner and chosen by him or her. In other instances the experimenter instructs the person in the use of the technique; tells him or her when to use it; or provides memory aids, such as pictures. In distinction to a mnemonic technique, a *memory strategy* is considered to be a more complex and higher level set of skills. If an individual has a memorizing strategy, it can be assumed that he or she has available a number of alternative mnemonic techniques, as well as rules for deciding which technique to use when faced with a particular set of materials and a particular set of learning conditions. Most of the discussion in the chapter centers on mnemonic techniques rather than on memory strategies. Some research has been done investigating the operation of memory strategies in normal adults (Blick, Buonassissi, & Boltwood, 1972; Gruneberg, 1978; Harris, 1980). Training subjects on a particular mnemonic technique and then determining whether they will choose this technique in some other situation is an example of investigating the use of a memory strategy rather than a memory technique. Peterson and Swing (1983) and chapters 1, 2, and 5 of this volume all take up transfer of mnemonic techniques in more detail.

The memorization of information so that it can be recalled after at least a few minutes of other mental activity unrelated to the learning task has been called *long-term memory* (Atkinson & Shiffrin, 1968). *Short-term memory* strategies typically involve the process of rehearsal, by which information is remembered by continuous subvocal repetition (Atkinson & Shiffrin, 1968). The information is quickly forgotten if the learner's rehearsal activity is interrupted by some other task. Those investigators interested in the memory training of the young and mentally retarded have extensively researched short-term memory strategies and assessed their generalization after training (Brown & Barclay, 1976; Flavell, 1970). This chapter is concerned with long-term memory strategies. It is assumed that normal adults typically have available effective short-term memory strategies involving rehearsal and other attentional processes. (See Worden, Chapter 6, for more on the distinctions made in this paragraph.)

List-Learning Techniques

Visual-Imagery Mediation

Visual-imagery mediation is a process that seems to be basic to the operation of traditional mnemonic devices (Bellezza, 1981; Paivio, 1971; 1983). When two words are associated or related by the use of visual-imagery mediation, a visual image or mental picture is formed of familiar objects interacting in some way. These images represent the referents or high associates of the words. Later, when the image is recalled, perhaps after being cued by one of the words, the image can be decoded into the original verbal information. When subjects form visual images, they "chunk," or unitize, the presented words into a single pictorial representation. Simply forming two separate images of words will not result in the words' becoming associated (Bower, 1972).

Source of Visual Images. An important question in any mediated learning concerns the mental processes that create the mediators. With respect to visual imagery, questions can be raised concerning where visual images come from and how they are created. Are they created from experienced components so basic that the images are not recognized by the imager? The imager may not recognize the image as a perception previously experienced. The argument made here is that images are retrieved from memory in fairly large pieces and represent prior perceptual knowledge that somehow fits the information presented. In an unpublished experiment by the author, both the vividness of images formed from pairs of concrete nouns and the familiarity of these images with regard to prior experiences were rated by 24 subjects on 7-point scales. Correlating these two sets of ratings for each subject resulted in a mean correlation coefficient of .75. It seems that when subjects form visual images, they retrieve from memory a perceptual unit that is fairly intact (familiar), yet fits the information to be imaged. The more intact—that is, familiar—the image seems to be, the greater the vividness rating. Later, if one word of the pair is presented, the image is again retrieved and acts as an effective cue for the second word (Paivio, 1971).

Results reported by Bugelski (1977) also support the notion that visual images are intact and are based on previous experience. He asked bilinguals to form visual images in response to single concrete nouns. If the presented noun (such as *latte*) was in the language the bilingual used as a child, then the image created would be based on a childhood experience. If the word presented (such as *milk*) was from the language currently used, then the image was one that the subject recognized as having been more recently experienced.

Training in Imagery. It seems that if people practice using visual imagery and visual-imagery mediation, they become more proficient at it. Whether this is true for *most* people is unclear at this time. Wallace, Turner, and Perkins (cited in Miller, Galanter, & Pribram, 1960) found that in a paired-associate learning task practiced subjects using visual imagery could remember 95% of the 700 pairs of words presented to them. Bugelski (1977) reported improvement in subjects who used the link mnemonic. When using the link mnemonic, a subject memorizes a word list by forming a visual image for each successive pair of words. Bugelski found that subjects were soon able to remember lists of 30–40 words. Perhaps the most amazing data on the effects of practice on the development of visual imagery has been reported by Hatano, Miyake, and Binks (1977). Many Japanese abacus masters are able to calculate faster and more accurately by using the visual image of an abacus than by using the abacus itself. Use of the visual image eliminates the need for finger movements and the physical movements of the beads.

Transformation of Abstract Material. Because many mnemonic techniques depend on the use of visual-imagery mediation, techniques have been developed for transforming verbal material that is low in imagery into words that are more imageable and hence more associable (Bellezza, 1981). Abstract words may be transformed into words representing concrete objects. This is done by using either phonetically similar substitute words or semantically related substitute words (Bugelski, 1970). For example, the abstract low-imagery word *origin* can be transformed into the more concrete word *orange* based on phonetic similarity. Alternatively, it can be transformed into the concrete word *egg* by using semantic similarity.

To remember numbers, a subject can encode each digit into a consonant, and redundant vowels can be added to create meaningful words and phrases. This digit-consonant mnemonic was proposed by Winckelman in 1648 (Hunter, 1956). The techniques of transforming abstract words and numbers into more imageable representations are discussed in most books on mnemonic devices (Bellezza, 1982a; Higbee, 1977; Lorayne & Lucas, 1974). However, very little experimental work has been done on encoding mnemonics (Bellezza, 1981), with the exception of the special case of the keyword mnemonic to be discussed later.

The Method of Loci and the Pegword Mnemonic

The method of loci has been found to be a very effective list-learning mnemonic (Ross & Lawrence, 1968). Before using the method of loci the learner must first memorize the visual images of a sequence of places, such as a series of rooms in a building. Later, when a list of words is to be memorized, a visual image is formed of each list word in one of the locations in the building. When the words are to be recalled, each successive location is visualized and the object that was mentally placed there earlier is "seen" and recalled. The same loci can be used over and over again for different lists of words. The most recent list is easily recalled, but earlier lists learned with the same loci are much less retrievable (Bower & Reitman, 1972).

When using the pegword mnemonic, a subject invokes as cues visual images of objects rather than of locations. A common example is the rhyming pegword mnemonic (Miller et al., 1960), in which the following simple rhyme is first memorized: "One is a bun, two is a shoe, three is a tree, four is a door, five is a hive, six is sticks, seven is heaven, eight is a gate, nine is a line, and ten is a hen." The mnemonist can then associate the visual images of the objects bun, shoe, tree, door, and so on with the words that he or she wishes to memorize. Later, upon reciting the rhyme, the mnemonist can recall the images of the pegwords, along with the information associated with them. The method of loci and pegword mnemonic are very similar in their operation (Bellezza, 1981; Bower & Reitman, 1972). Paivio and Desrochers (1979; 1981) have developed a novel use of the pegword mnemonic in which new second-language vocabulary words can be remembered and practiced. (See Paivio, 1983, and Roberts, Chapter 4 in this volume, both of whom provide additional evaluative insights about the operation of these mnemonics.)

Use of Graphic Locations. In the history of mnemonic devices, arranging words in two-dimensional space, as on a sheet of paper, so that they can be remembered has been an influential and much-used technique (Ong, 1958; Yates, 1966). This type of mnemonic procedure, however, has played a relatively small role in contemporary mnemonic research.

To better understand these techniques, a distinction should be made between a formal representation of information and a cognitive representation. A formal representation may be considered as some logical arrangement of the verbal items from a list in some two-dimensional manner. On the other hand, a cognitive representation of information exists in memory and allows the person to retrieve and recall information from it in a systematic way. Of course, a formal representation may closely parallel a cognitive representation. For example, a list learned by using the method of loci may both be represented in memory and be diagrammed on paper as a series of connected loci, each with a list word attached to it. But a formal representation may not be an effective cognitive or mnemonic one. A matrix of abstract words arranged on a sheet of paper by word length may represent a formal organization but not an effective cognitive one. To commit the list to memory, the learner may have to transform each word and mnemonically organize the list by using a technique such as the method of loci or the link mnemonic.

Nevertheless, it has been found that primarily formal representations of information can facilitate recall performance. Schulman (Note 1) had subjects associate pairs of pronounceable nonwords under various learning conditions. In one condition the words were presented as pairs that represented the names of provinces and their capital cities in a fictitious country. In another condition these province names and capital cities were displayed on a map contrived by the experimenter. Schulman found that presenting the province names on the map resulted in better recall of the capital cities than presenting only the province names.

The Keyword Mnemonic

One of the most extensively tested mnemonic techniques is the keyword mnemonic (Atkinson, 1975). Atkinson and Raugh (1975) first used the keyword technique to teach second-language vocabulary words to college students, but since then a number of other uses have been found and tested with grade school children (Paivio, 1983; Pressley et al. 1982; Chapters 2 and 4 in this volume). The keyword method has also been used to help college students to learn new English vocabulary (Pressley, Levin, & Miller, 1981, 1982; Sweeney & Bellezza, 1982), the names of Chinese ideographs (Higbee, 1977), and to associate faces and names (McCarty, 1980). In general, the results of most studies indicate a substantial advantage of the keyword technique over the other study procedures tested with it.

The keyword mnemonic is a way of associating a familiar verbal response with a new, often complex, verbal stimulus. This association is formed in two steps made up of a phonetic link and an imagery link (Atkinson, 1975). For example, Pressley and Dennis-Rounds (1980) taught junior high and high school students to use the keyword method to associate the names of cities with the names of their products. For an item such as "Deerfield–wheat," the keyword used with the city name *Deerfield* might be *deer*. The keyword is usually a word similar in pronunciation to the cue word and representing an imageable object. Going from *Deerfield* to *deer* is the phonetic link. The second step is to form a visual image connecting deer to wheat. The learner may form a mental picture of a deer eating wheat. This second link is the imagery link. Hence, the keyword acts as a mediator enabling the verbal stimulus to become associated with the verbal response in a manner more memorable than would be the formation of a rote association.

The keyword mnemonic has recently been used by military researchers in a number of learning tasks (Griffith, Note 2), and a manual has been developed to help technical writers utilize mnemonic procedures in training materials (Braby, Kincaid, & Aagard, Note 3). The keyword method has been employed in associating names to visual symbols, as in the learning of the meaning of Navy signal flags (Braby et al., Note 3) and military symbols (Griffith, Note 2). Griffith (Note 2) reviews the results of many of these studies.

Although implementation of the keyword method is taking place in the military, evaluation of its effectiveness has produced mixed results. Griffith (Note 4) found that the keyword method is more effective in learning Korean vocabulary words than more traditional procedures. Ainsworth (Note 5) found that the keyword method enabled trainees to more accurately transmit the Morse code early in train-ing, but showed no superiority over the usual training procedures after four to five weeks. Griffith and Actkinson (Note 6) found no differences between the keyword mnemonic and a control in the learning of international road signs.

Some Issues in Evaluating List-Learning Mnemonic Techniques

Evaluation and Training. The evaluation of a mnemonic technique is partly depen-dent on how well the investigator can train subjects to use the technique. For ex-ample, most studies evaluating the method of loci simply instruct subjects in its use, yet it has usually been found that the method of loci results in recall superior to control procedures (Bellezza, 1981). In many studies, however, the effectiveness of the mnemonic may have been underestimated because not enough training was provided. Weinstein, Cubberly, Wicker, Underwood, Roney, and Duty (1981) found that subjects provided with instructions, practice, and feedback in using the method of loci performed substantially better than subjects merely given instruc-tions. In their experiment the instructions-only group performed no better than a control group allowed to study the words in any manner. The latter result, however, is at variance with the results of most other studies, which have shown that instruc-tions without training in the method of loci result in enhanced recall performance.

Questions sometimes arise as to whether subjects were using the mnemonic tech-nique that they were supposed to use. Pash and Blick (1970) found that only 25% of their college student subjects used the mnemonic device they were instructed to use, and Persensky and Senter (1970) found only 66% following instructions. Sometimes additional information can be collected in an experiment to determine whether subjects are following instructions. For example, when the keyword mne-monic is used to remember information, first the keyword and then the desired ver-bal response must be recalled. Sweeney and Bellezza (1982) instructed subjects to use the keyword mnemonic to learn the meanings of English vocabulary words. They found that individuals in the keyword condition recalled a mean of 59% of the keywords and 35% of the definitions. This type of result was expected because only one link had to be recalled in order to remember the keyword, whereas two links had to be remembered in order to recall the definition. In another experiment, however, Hall, Wilson, and Patterson (1981) reported that subjects were able to recall more definition words than they were able to recall keywords. In this experi-ment the keywords provided were probably not functioning as mediators to the extent that they should have been, and the subjects were using some alternative learning procedure.

Essential to the fair evaluation of a mnemonic technique is the availability of individuals who can use it with some skill. Mnemonic devices evolved for use by those with some minimum level of skill, just as did devices such as the abacus. Giv-ing naive subjects a half hour of training on the abacus may not allow us to con-clude that the abacus is an effective calculating instrument; but it is known that with numbers of any size, abacus operators can add and subtract twice as fast as someone using an electronic calculator (Hunter, 1979).

Chase and Ericsson (1981) gave one of their subjects hundreds of hours of practice in recalling strings of digits. During this subject's first 100 hours of practice he developed his own mnemonic technique for remembering long sequences of digit strings based on his knowledge of the times of track events. However, his performance continued to improve even after 250 hours of practice. Knowing how to use a mnemonic technique is important, but performance continues to improve with practice.

Of course, there is another side to this issue. The emphasis on using skilled subjects when evaluating a mnemonic technique raises the question of cost-effectiveness. The abacus is an effective calculating instrument, but it is not generally used in the United States because too much time is required for training. The expense and relative slowness of the electronic calculator is less of a debit than the training and practice needed for effective use of an abacus. A similar argument can be made with regard to mnemonic techniques. Is the gain in memorizing capability worth the cost of training and practice? This question cannot yet be answered for most mnemonic techniques. Peterson and Swing (1983) also consider cost-effectiveness issues.

Individual Differences. There seem to be differences among people with regard to whether they experience what are described as visual images, and these differences seem to be independent of intellectual abilities (Galton, 1883). The learner not experiencing visual imagery can use verbal mediation to create a cognitive representation of the new information (Paivio, 1971). Two words can be associated by using them in a meaningful phrase or sentence. DiVesta and Sunshine (1974) found that subjects low in visual imagery made fewer errors using verbal mediation, and subjects assessed as high imagers made fewer errors using visual-imagery mediation.

There is also ample evidence that subjects differ greatly in achievement level after being instructed in the use of a mnemonic device. Bellezza (1982b) instructed subjects and provided some training in the use of the simple link mnemonic. Performance ranged from 55% to 97% recalled compared to a range of 29-95% recalled in a control group. Instructing subjects in the use of the link mnemonic reduced individual differences in performance but did not eliminate them. The implications of these differences among subjects are not clear at this time. Should different subjects use different learning procedures because of different abilities (Cronbach & Snow, 1977)? Or do the same techniques work for all people, with different training techniques being appropriate for different individuals because of differences in the level of development of their basic skills?

Griffith and Actkinson (1978) found that only individuals scoring high on the Army's General-Technical (GT) test performed better when using the pegword mnemonic compared to a control procedure. For those individuals with medium and low GT scores there were no differences in the performance of the mnemonic and control groups. In a later experiment, Griffith (Note 4) tested the keyword mnemonic against a control procedure for learning Korean vocabulary words and again used individuals classified as having scored low, medium, or high on the GT test. In this study learning was self-paced, and the keyword mnemonic was shown to be superior to the control procedure for all three ability levels. Griffith's results indicated, however, that the low-ability learners needed more time. On the first trial of List 1, low-GT subjects studied each item for a mean of 16.67 seconds, whereas the high-GT subjects studied each item for a mean of 12.67 seconds. By the third trial these means were 13.00 and 8.00 seconds, respectively. Griffith suggests that the 8 seconds used in the Griffith and Actkinson (1978) experiment discussed earlier may have been too fast for the low-ability subjects to implement the pegword mnemonic. To conclude that the pegword mnemonic is not effective when using low-ability learners may be erroneous.

Memory Representations as Cognitive Structures. In much of the traditional research on learning techniques the emphasis has been on the learner's performing a prescribed series of operations when presented with the information to be learned (Rothkopf, 1970). The assumption has been that once these operations have taken place, later recall performance will be successful. A further development has been the use of information processing models in which the operation of internal mental processes is assumed (Simon, 1979). These internal processes are assumed to be able to operate on internal representations of knowledge (Anderson, 1976). The information processing approach, however, has emphasized process or procedural knowledge to the extent that declarative or structural knowledge has been somewhat ignored.

It is important to add to the typical stage analysis of a learning technique a concern with the manner in which information is represented in memory at each particular stage. This emphasis on the nature of the mental representation of the newly learned information has always been a characteristic of learning with a mnemonic device. This emphasis has been discussed in detail by Bellezza (1981), where these structures are termed *cognitive cuing structures.* Often the memory representation of the original information is metaphorical or analogical in nature and must have certain characteristics, such as constructability, associability, discriminability, and invertibility (see Bellezza, 1981, for discussion of these properties). One impetus for concern about memory representations has been the strong and widespread interest among many learning theorists in visual-imagery representation (Paivio, 1971). The nature of the memory representation of newly learned information is important because at recall the learner does not go through precisely the same set of operations as he or she did when the information was encoded. The storage and retrieval operations in most mnemonic techniques are related but not identical. The storage operations create a representation of the presented material in memory, often using visual imagery and verbal elaboration. The mental representations remain stored in memory for some period of time. Retrieval operations later decode this representation into a form similar to the original information. The retrieval processes operate on the memory structures created by the storage or encoding operations.

This emphasis on memory representations has important implications for research on mnemonic techniques. The learner is not using a particular mnemonic technique unless he or she is creating the type of memory representations prescribed by that procedure. To monitor this process, subjects can be asked to draw or describe their visual images (Paivio & Foth, 1970), to recall not only the response word but also the keyword and mnemonic sentence used for each item (Sweeney & Bellezza, 1982), or to create overt verbal elaborations (Bobrow & Bower, 1969). In a multistage learning procedure, such as the use of the method of loci, some monitoring may be necessary at every stage. For example, the prememorized loci must be remembered both during study and during test. Visual images must be formed by the learner in which the loci or pegs interact with the words to be learned.

Mnemonic Techniques for Prose Materials

Memory Schemata

Mnemonic techniques used to ensure the later free recall of prose materials are similar to the techniques used for memorizing word lists. In a number of mnemonic procedures, prose material is memorized by reducing it to lists of important words from the text. There is, however, an important difference between memorizing lists of unrelated words and memorizing words from a text. A text is designed by the writer to be comprehended and organized in memory by using a variety of natural memory processes and structures that make extensive use of the subjects' prior knowledge (Kintsch, 1974). It will be assumed here that an important part of the comprehension process consists of the activation of memory schemata and of the instantiation or assimilation of the presented prose information into these schemata. This notion is currently a widely accepted one and seems a reasonable way to describe the interaction between new information and prior knowledge in memory by which recognition, comprehension, and understanding can take place (Anderson, 1978; Cook & Mayer, 1983; Minsky, 1975; Rumelhart, 1980; Rumelhart & Ortony, 1977; Schank & Abelson, 1977). It seems reasonable that any mnemonic technique used for prose memorization must acknowledge that the more fundamental processes of schema activation and assimilation are also taking place.

The activation of a memory schema enables information presented in a passage to be interpreted or instantiated (Anderson, Pichert, Goetz, Schallert, Stevens, & Trollip, 1976) such that it becomes associated with or bound to an activated schema in memory. This process of instantiation or assimilation underlies the process of comprehension and remembering. The schema provides an ideational scaffold (Anderson, Spiro, & Anderson, 1978) or a cognitive cuing strategy (Bellezza & Bower, 1982) for the new information. Schema-based comprehension, however, does not automatically result in perfect recall performance. Similarly, perfect recall may not imply earlier perfect comprehension, although schema instantiation may play a major role in each. For example, one may engage in and perfectly understand a great deal of small talk, but be unable to recall much of what was said. On the other hand we may remember the nonsense verse of Lewis Carroll and Edward Lear even though we do not understand all of it (Ortony, 1978).

Mnemonic Devices Supplement Memory Schemata. The degree to which comprehension of a text should be supplemented by mnemonic procedures depends on a number of factors. One factor is the ability of the learner. Some people seem to remember very well what they comprehend, especially if they already have a great deal of knowledge about the topic being discussed (Smith, Adams, & Schorr, 1978). A second factor is the goal of the learner. Using a version of the method of loci (*memoria verborum*), classical orators could memorize their speeches word for word (Yates, 1966). This degree of literal memorization, however, is usually not desired. A third factor is the conditions under which the material is to be learned. Occasionally, the information will be available for so short a time that the use of a deliberate mnemonic procedure is not possible. Finally, the nature of the material is important. Some text is easy to remember and some is difficult.

There are a number of kinds of textual material with which a mnemonic device might be used to supplement schema-based memory (Levin, in press). One case is a passage that can be comprehended and organized by a few higher order schemata, but where many of the details in the passage cannot be assimilated and therefore cannot be remembered. A passage describing the eating of a large meal in a restaurant might be perfectly understood (Schank & Abelson, 1977), but all the particular foods and drinks mentioned might not be remembered. Similarly, one might comprehend the description of a supermarket shopping trip but not be able to recall all the items purchased (Anderson, Reynolds, Schallert, & Goetz, 1978).

A second case where a mnemonic can be helpful is when simple, easily understood descriptions are given of a great many objects or people. In this case interference may occur because one has trouble remembering what feature belonged to what object (Schultz & DiVesta, 1972).

The third and perhaps most common case in which a mnemonic device can be useful occurs when a text has a higher level structure, but it is not simple, familiar, or well defined to the degree that the learner can use the text's schematic structure as an effective retrieval scheme. For example, the classical orator used the method of loci to remember the contents of speeches he himself may have composed. The mnemonic device enabled him to remember the main points of the oration in their correct order. The hierarchical structure of any text, even a simple story (Thorndyke, 1977), can be quite complex and variable. Consequently, a mnemonic procedure can be used to build up a retrieval scheme to supplement recall based on the schematic representation of the text in memory. At recall the learner can use both the activated memory schemata and the mnemonic to reconstruct the contents of the text.

Stages in Remembering Prose Passages

In using a mnemonic technique to aid in remembering a prose passage, it seems that four rather general cognitive steps are necessary (Bellezza, 1982a, chap. 9). These four steps seem to encompass the steps in all methods proposed for remembering prose material, although the details may vary from one method to another, and the different methods may each emphasize one step more than any of the others. First, the learner has to *understand* the passage. Second, some information in the passage must be *selected* to be remembered by means of the mnemonic procedure. Often, this material represents information that the learner believes would not be otherwise remembered, or it might be information that acts as an effective cue for other information in the text (Brown & Campione, 1978). Third, the learner has to *encode* the selected information so that a representation can be formed in memory. These encoding operations may include visual imagery (Levin & Divine-Hawkins, 1974), paraphrasing and verbal elaboration (Weinstein, 1978; Wittrock, 1974), making abstract words more concrete (Levin, 1981b), or encoding numbers (Bellezza, 1981). The fourth step is *organization*—that is, the integration of the various memory representations into a unified, organized, retrievable whole (Shimmerlik, 1978). The process of organization is the process of creating a retrieval scheme, and sometimes list-learning techniques such as the method of loci can be used here. (See Cook and Mayer, 1983, for an alternative conceptualization of memory for prose.)

The Method of Loci

Several studies have been done that use the method of loci or the pegword mnemonic to aid in the recall of a prose passage. Snowman, Krebs, and Lockhart (1980) taught a 14-week course in study skills to 72 freshmen. Half the subjects were taught traditional study skills and half were taught to identify idea units in the material they studied and then to interrelate them by using a tree structure. They were also taught to create visual images for these idea units and then to use the method of loci when serial recall of the ideas was necessary. At the end of the course the mnemonic subjects were able to recall 50% more ideas from a 2200-word passage than were the control subjects.

In a related study, Krebs, Snowman, and Smith (1978) taught students to recognize central themes and information units in the materials they studied and to use the method of loci to organize these themes in memory. They obtained large differences when comparing the recall performance of subjects in the mnemonic and control conditions.

Maps as Recall Aids

Kulhavy and his associates (e.g., Schwartz & Kulhavy, 1981) have found that the use of a map as a memory aid facilitates recall of information from a passage about an imaginary country called Dani. Subjects forced to first label parts of a relevant map recalled more than subjects who simply had a labeled map available to them or had no map (Dean & Kulhavy, 1981). Recall performance was superior for subjects forced to label the map, but only for that information in the passage associated with features on the map. Recall of information in the passage unrelated to the map's features was the same for all three groups. Unlike the Schulman (Note 1) experiment discussed earlier, the map was not available to the subjects during testing, so the subjects who processed the map information must have had available some imagelike representation of it. The map itself contained no information that could help subjects answer any of the questions asked later in a cued-recall test, so it was not merely a pictorial representation of the information in the passage (Levin & Lesgold, 1978). If the subjects forced to study the map formed a visual representation of it in memory, then during recall, features of the map functioned as cues for information in the passage related to those features. The loci of the map, though more graphic and more symbolic than real locations, nevertheless seemed to act as prompts, much like the loci in the method of loci. The representation of the map in memory may have acted as a cognitive cuing structure (Bellezza, 1981).

Formal Representations of Text

Holley, Dansereau, McDonald, Garland, and Collins (1979) used a hierarchical mapping technique to transform scientific and technical text into node (concept) and link (relations) networks. This representation would be an effective one if network models of long-term memory represent the cognitive organization of information (Anderson & Bower, 1973; Rumelhart, Lindsay, & Norman, 1972). Unlike the texts containing easily imaged information used by many other investigators (Levin, 1981b), Holley et al. used material from a geology textbook in which many of the terms and relations were abstract. Holley et al. found better free recall of main ideas for subjects using this procedure compared to subjects using traditional study techniques. Their two groups, however, did not differ in the recall of details of the text. Recall of details was measured by using multiple-choice and short-answer tests. However, the effects of organization are best detected when using a free-recall measure. Thus, the primary effect of networking may be to organize the information into higher order units.

One procedure not used in organization by networking (see also Dansereau, Collins, McDonald, Holley, Garland, Diekhoff, & Evans, 1979) was to have subjects transform or encode the abstract words into more concrete and imageable words in order to better interrelate them in memory. If the formal representation did not result in a good cognitive representation, then transformational encoding could further enhance recall performance.

Pictures as Recall Aids

Pictures may redundantly represent information from a passage in a manner easier to understand than the corresponding verbal representation (Levin & Lesgold, 1978; Schallert, 1980). From the point of view taken here, pictures may activate memory schemata relevant to the context of the text more easily or more effectively than words. This is the representational or interpretive function of pictures (Levin, 1981b). This function, however, is not what we usually have in mind when discussing pictures as mnemonic aids. Levin (1981b, in press) discusses the importance of pictures in transforming and organizing information from a text. In an experiment by Levin, Shriberg, and Berry (Note 7), eighth graders were presented with short passages, each containing the name of a city and some important facts about it. A city named Fostoria may be known for its considerable wealth, abundant natural resources, advances in technology, and growing population. Levin et al. found that subjects recalled best when each passage was presented along with a picture in which each attribute was concretized; that is, a picture of money represented wealth, an oil well represented natural resources, and so on. It was also necessary for these pictured concretizations to be assembled into one composite picture and not presented as four separate pictures. Finally, the picture had to contain some keyword or substitute word for the name of the city. For example, *Fostoria* could be incorporated into the picture by covering objects with frost. It is worthwhile to note that the pictures used by Levin et al. represent three of the four general cognitive steps mentioned as being necessary for prose retention: selection, encoding, and organization (Bellezza, 1982a, chap. 9). Understanding (the first step) was achieved by reading the passage. The attributes of each city were selected and then encoded by using semantic associations such as money for wealth. The name of the city was encoded by using phonetic substitution, such as using the word *frost* for Fostoria. Finally, the picture organized all these components into a unified whole.

Pictures versus Images. A recurring question in memory research concerns the difference between presenting pictures as memory aids versus instructing the learner to create a mental picture from the verbal material presented. Related questions arise as to what procedure is better in light of the type of material and the nature of the subjects (Levin, 1981a; Rohwer, 1970). Of course, these issues cannot be settled here or even discussed in detail. However, some of the problems connected with using pictures and imagery in facilitating comprehension and memory may be better understood if we ask what pictures and visual images have to do with the activation of schemata in memory. For easily comprehended and remembered passages pictures may not be necessary for, nor effective in, improving comprehension or recall performance. However, when subjects are young children (Pressley, 1977) or the material is difficult to understand (Bransford & Johnson, 1972), a picture may help because it activates in memory an appropriate schema, which instantiates or assimilates the information (Friedman, 1979; Mandler & Johnson, 1976).

It is assumed here that pictures have their main effect by activating organized sets of prior knowledge stored as memory schema and not by contributing entirely new visual information to memory. Picture aids can be best characterized as activating the appropriate schemata in memory, but in addition, as sometimes providing a new arrangement of a small number of familiar components. However, this arrangement itself is not haphazard, but in some way conforms to a higher order schema. For example, in the picture used by Bransford and Johnson (1972) a loudspeaker was held in the air by balloons. Most subjects had never seen a loudspeaker held in the air by balloons, but they knew that some balloons are able to lift physical objects into the air and that loudspeakers are physical objects.

Gombrich (1969) makes an eloquent case for assuming that most visual representations make extensive use of the viewer's perceptual schema, some of which have been learned in the process of being exposed to the culture's style of visual representation. A good example of representations that are effective but do not truly depict what is perceived are caricatures of faces (Gombrich, 1969, chap. 10).

If pictures aid in the activation of the appropriate memory schema, then what do visual images do? Perhaps the formation of a visual image is a phenomenal response indicating that a schema subsuming the presented information has been successfully activated. The image then is an indicator of schema activation and represents the visual-perceptual information associated with that schema. As mentioned in the discussion of the role of visual-imagery mediation in learning lists of words, the visual image or the verbal mediator unifies or chunks the two separate words presented; that is, the separate components are subsumed by one activated schema (Halff, 1981).

Other Techniques for Recalling Prose

Limitations of space do not allow for a full discussion of the many other techniques that have been developed to improve the recall of prose material. However, a few of these are mentioned here, and an attempt is made to classify them according to their use of the four cognitive steps mentioned earlier: understanding, selection, encoding, and organization. (See also Cook & Mayer, 1983; Forrest-Pressley & Gillies, 1983.)

Underlining is primarily a selection process, whereas outlining both selects material and arranges information into a hierarchical and verbal arrangement. The organization created by outlining may be a verbal and primarily formal one; that is, no attempt is made in the process to encode and concretize abstract words or to use some technique to further interrelate the components of the outline in memory so that it can be later retrieved. Therefore, outlining may not always result in an effective mnemonic representation.

Instructions to use visual imagery to better remember prose material seems to have a positive effect (Levin & Divine-Hawkins, 1974), although the effect is typically small (see Levin, 1981b). The learner probably tries to understand, select, and visualize events in the text that appear to be important. Thus, understanding, selection, and encoding may be occurring. The weakness in this approach may be that the learner does not have a technique for organizing and interrelating the various images so that they can later be retrieved (Bellezza, Cheesman, & Reddy, 1977). Unless the passage material itself is well organized to begin with, and unless the visual images themselves become interrelated as a result of this organization, some learner-imposed retrieval scheme for the images may be necessary. Visual imagery coupled with a retrieval system, such as the method of loci, may enhance free-recall performance (Krebs et al., 1978; Snowman et al., 1980).

The use of advance organizers (Ausubel, 1968) can help the learner select and organize material from the text. The organization that occurs seems to be the result of the verbal statements provided before presentation of the material activating the relevant schemata and enabling assimilation to occur (Mayer, 1979). For a passage that is particularly difficult to understand, a simple cue such as "washing clothes" can improve recall considerably (Bransford & Johnson, 1972, 1973). Of course, the schemata activated by the advance organizers may not be available in the memories of all the learners and may not subsume all the information desired in recall. As mentioned earlier, memory schemata sufficient for comprehension may be inadequate as a basis for detailed recall. Even with advance organizers, supplementary steps of encoding and organization may be necessary.

Summary

In this limited review of research involving mnemonic device training with adults, the issues discussed were chosen because they now seem to be of particular importance in this area. The performance measure focused on was free recall, because the unique characteristic of most mnemonic devices is that they provide a means of organizing in memory the information to be learned. The organization of information in memory is of maximal importance in a free-recall situation. In the absence of external recall cues the cognitive cuing structure created by the mnemonic provides a set of organized mental cues by which information can be retrieved (Bellezza, 1981).

The approach taken here is a cognitive one. It is suggested that research on all learning techniques must assess to a greater degree than in the past the nature of the memory representation of the learned material (Gagne & White, 1978). This has been the traditional emphasis in learning with mnemonic devices. Both encoding procedures and organizing procedures deal directly with the problem of creating cognitive representations of new information that are retrievable from memory. The memory representation deliberately created by the learning procedure, be it a visual image or a verbal elaboration, is a mediational structure. At recall, the learner retrieves from memory not the original information but the mediating representation from which the original information is decoded. The representation of information in memory forms a signifying system from which the original information must be reconstructed.

Mnemonic techniques are cognitive skills, and as in the case of any skill, the two problems of evaluating their effectiveness and training people to use them can be interrelated and complex. It seems that evaluation cannot occur without adequate training of the users, and of course adequate training procedures are based on knowing a good deal about the technique. The notion of cost-effectiveness of mnemonic techniques may become important in the future if teachers have to decide whether the costs of mnemonic training are matched by corresponding increases in memorizing ability.

The knowledge structures based on prior experience that are activated during the comprehension of prose are memory schemata, and the study of prose recall involves understanding the function of memory schemata. Many of the specialized learning techniques used for prose memorization provide for recall that supplements recall based on naturally activated memory schemata. The importance of these memory schemata is evidenced by the fact that recall of prose material is often greatly different in surface structure from the presented text. Also, inferences are often added that were not part of the original text.

In the process of prose memorization, four basic cognitive steps seem to occur; schema-based understanding, selection, encoding, and organization. Mnemonic techniques that can effectively supplement schema-based recall must include procedures to ensure that selection, encoding, and organization effectively occur. The distinction between formal and cognitive organization is one that should be recognized if prose recall performance is to be optimized.

Acknowledgments. This research was supported in part by a grant from the Field-Wiltsie Foundation. The author thanks John Day and Wendy Schweigert for their helpful comments on an earlier draft of the manuscript. Thanks also go to Ohio University Computer Services for making computer time and their facilities available.

Reference Notes

1. Schulman, A. I. *Beyond the method of loci: The role of place in the memorability of events.* Paper presented at the meeting of the Southern Society for Philosophy and Psychology, 1981.
2. Griffith, D. *A review of the literature on memory enhancement: The potential and relevance of mnemotechnics for military training* (ARI Tech. Paper 436). Alexandria, VA: U.S. Army Research Institute for the Behavioral and Social Sciences, December 1979.
3. Braby, R., Kincaid, J. P., & Aagard, J. A. *Use of mnemonics in training materials: A guide for technical writers* (TAEG Rep. No. 60). Orlando, FL: Training Analysis and Evaluation Group, July 1978.
4. Griffith, D. *The keyword method of vocabulary acquisition: An experimental evaluation* (ARI Tech. Paper 439). Alexandria, VA: U.S. Army Research Institute for the Behavioral and Social Sciences, January 1980.
5. Ainsworth, J. S. *Symbol learning in Navy technical training: An evaluation of strategies and mnemonics* (TAEG Rep. No. 66). Orlando, FL: Training Analysis and Evaluation Group, January 1979.
6. Griffith, D., & Actkinson, T. R. *International road signs: Interpretability and training techniques* (Research Rep. 1202). Alexandria, VA: U.S. Army Research Institute for the Behavioral and Social Sciences, September 1978.
7. Levin, J. R., Shriberg, L. K., & Berry, J. K. *A concrete strategy for remembering abstract prose* (Working Paper No. 314). Madison, WI: Wisconsin Center for Education Research, December 1981.

References

Anderson, J. R. *Language, memory, and thought.* Hillsdale, NJ: Erlbaum, 1976.
Anderson, J. R., & Bower, G. H. *Human associative memory.* Washington, DC: Winston, 1973.

Anderson, R. C. Schema-directed processes in language comprehension. In A. Lesgold, J. Pellegrino, S. Fokkema, & R. Glaser (Eds.), *Cognitive psychology and instruction*. New York: Plenum, 1978.

Anderson, R. C., Pichert, J. W., Goetz, E. T., Schallert, D. L., Stevens, K. V., & Trollip, S. R. Instantiation of general terms. *Journal of Verbal Learning and Verbal Behavior,* 1976, *15,* 667–679.

Anderson, R. C., Reynolds, R. E., Schallert, D. L., & Goetz, E. T. Frameworks for comprehending discourse. *American Educational Research Journal,* 1977, *14,* 367–381.

Anderson, R. C., Spiro, R. J. & Anderson, M. C. Schemata as scaffolding for the representation of information in connected discourse. *American Educational Research Journal,* 1978, *15,* 433–440.

Atkinson, R. C. Mnemotechnics in second-language learning. *American Psychologist,* 1975, *30,* 821–828.

Atkinson, R. C., & Raugh, M. R. An application of the mnemonic keyword method to the acquisition of a Russian vocabulary. *Journal of Experimental Psychology: Human Learning and Memory,* 1975, *1,* 126–133.

Atkinson, R. C., & Shiffrin, R. M. Human memory: A proposed system and its control processes. In K. W. Spence & J. T. Spence (Eds.), *The psychology of learning and motivation: Advances in research and theory* (Vol 2). New York: Academic Press, 1968.

Ausubel, D. P. *Educational psychology: A cognitive approach.* New York: Holt, Rinehart & Winston, 1968.

Baddeley, A. D. *The psychology of memory.* New York: Basic Books, 1976.

Bellezza, F. S. Mnemonic devices: Classification, characteristics, and criteria. *Review of Educational Research,* 1981, *51,* 247–275.

Bellezza, F. S. *Improve your memory skills.* Englewood Cliffs, NJ: Prentice-Hall, 1982. (a)

Bellezza, F. S. Updating memory using mnemonic devices. *Cognitive Psychology,* 1982, *14,* 301–327. (b)

Bellezza, F. S., & Bower, G. H. Remembering script-based text. *Poetics,* 1982, *11,* 1–23.

Bellezza, F. S., Cheesman, F. L., & Reddy, B. G. Organization and semantic elaboration in free recall. *Journal of Experimental Psychology: Human Learning and Memory,* 1977, *3,* 539–559.

Blick, K. A., Buonassissi, J. V., & Boltwood, C. E. Mnemonic techniques used by college students in serial learning. *Psychological Reports,* 1972, *31,* 983-986.

Bobrow, S. A., & Bower, G. H. Comprehension and recall of sentences. *Journal of Experimental Psychology,* 1969, *80,* 455–461.

Bower, G. H. Mental imagery and associative learning. In L. W. Gregg (Ed.), *Cognition in learning and memory.* New York: Wiley, 1972.

Bower, G. H., & Reitman, J. S. Mnemonic elaboration in multilist learning. *Journal of Verbal Learning and Verbal Behavior,* 1972, *11,* 478–485.

Bransford, J. D., & Johnson, M. K. Contextual prerequisites for understanding: Some investigations of comprehension and recall. *Journal of Verbal Learning and Verbal Behavior,* 1972, *11,* 717–726.

Bransford, J. D., & Johnson, M. K. Considerations of some problems of comprehension. In W. C. Chase (Ed.), *Visual information processing.* New York: Academic Press, 1973.

Brown, A. L., & Barclay, C. R. The effect of training specific mnemonics on the metamnemonic efficiency of retarded children. *Child Development*, 1976, *47*, 71–80.

Brown, A. L., & Campione, J. C. The effects of knowledge and experience on the formation of retrieval plans for studying from texts. In M. M. Gruneberg, P. E. Morris, & R. N. Sykes (Eds.), *Practical aspects of memory*. London: Academic Press, 1978.

Bugelski, B. R. Words and things and images. *American Psychologist*, 1970, *25*, 1002–1012.

Bugelski, B. R. The association of images. In J. M. Nichols (Ed.), *Images, perception, and knowledge*. Boston: D. Reidel, 1977.

Chase, W. C., & Ericsson, K. A. Skilled memory. In J. R. Anderson (Ed.), *Cognitive skills and their application*. Hillsdale, NJ: Erlbaum, 1981.

Cook, L. K., & Mayer, R. E. Reading strategies training for meaningful learning from prose. In M. Pressley & J. R. Levin (Eds.), *Cognitive strategy research: Educational applications*. New York: Springer-Verlag, 1983.

Cronbach, L. J., & Snow, R. E. *Aptitudes and instructional methods*. New York: Irvington, 1977.

Dansereau, D. F., Collins, K. W., McDonald, B. A., Holley, C. D., Garland, J., Diekhoff, G., & Evans, S. H. Development and evaluation of a learning strategy training program. *Journal of Educational Psychology*, 1979, *71*, 64–73.

Dean, R. S., & Kulhavy, R. W. Influence of spatial organization in prose learning. *Journal of Educational Psychology*, 1981, *73*, 57–64.

DiVesta, F. J., & Sunshine, P. M. The retrieval of abstract and concrete materials as functions of imagery, mediation, and mnemonic aids. *Memory & Cognition*, 1974, *2*, 340–344.

Flavell, J. H. Developmental studies of mediated memory. In L. C. Lipsitt & H. W. Reese (Eds.), *Advances in child development and behavior* (Vol 5). New York: Academic Press, 1970.

Forrest-Pressley, D. L., & Gillies, L. A. Children's flexible use of strategies during reading. In M. Pressley & J. R. Levin (Eds.), *Cognitive strategy research: Educational applications*. New York: Springer-Verlag, 1983.

Friedman, A. Framing pictures: The role of knowledge in automatized encoding and memory for gist. *Journal of Experimental Psychology: General*, 1979, *108*, 316–355.

Gagne, R. M., & White, R. T. Memory structures and learning outcomes. *Review of Educational Research*, 1978, *48*, 187–222.

Galton, F. *Inquiries into human faculty and its development* (1st ed.) London: Macmillan, 1883.

Gombrich, E. H. *Art and illusion*. Princeton, NJ: Princeton University Press, 1969.

Griffith, D., & Actkinson, T. R. Mental aptitude and mnemonic enhancement. *Bulletin of the Psychonomic Society*, 1978, *12*, 347–348.

Gruneberg, M. M. The feeling of knowing, memory blocks and memory aids. In M. M. Gruneberg & P. Morris (Eds.), *Aspects of memory*. London. Methuen, 1978.

Gruneberg, M. M., Morris, P. E., & Sykes, R. N. (Eds.). *Practical aspects of memory*. New York: Academic Press, 1978.

Halff, H. M. Discussion: Process analysis of learning and problem solving. In R. E.

Snow, P. Frederico, & W. E. Montague (Eds.), *Aptitude, learning, and instruction.* Hillsdale, NJ: Erlbaum, 1981.

Hall, J. P., Wilson, K. P., & Patterson, R. J. Mnemotechnics: Some limitations of the mnemonic keyword method for the study of foreign language vocabulary. *Journal of Educational Psychology,* 1981, *73,* 345–357.

Harris, J. E. Memory aids people use: Two interview studies. *Memory & Cognition,* 1980, *8,* 31–38.

Hatano, G., Miyake, Y., & Binks, M. G. Performance of expert abacus operators. *Cognition,* 1977, *5,* 57–71.

Hayes-Roth, B., & Walker, C. Configural effects in human memory: The superiority of memory over external information sources as a basis for inference verification. *Cognitive Science,* 1979, *3,* 119–140.

Higbee, K. L. *Your memory: How it works and how to improve it.* Englewood Cliffs, NJ: Prentice-Hall, 1977.

Higbee, K. L. Some pseudo-limitations of mnemonics. In M. M. Gruneberg, P. E. Morris, & R. N. Sykes (Eds.), *Practical aspects of memory.* New York: Academic Press, 1978.

Higbee, K. L. Recent research on visual mnemonics: Historical roots and educational fruits. *Review of Educational Research,* 1979, *49,* 611–629.

Holley, C. D., Dansereau, D. F., McDonald, B. A., Garland, J. C., & Collins, K. W. Evaluation of a hierarchical mapping technique as an aid to prose processing. *Contemporary Educational Psychology,* 1979, *4,* 227–237.

Hunter, I. M. L. Mnemonic systems and devices. *Sciences News,* 1956, *39,* 75–97.

Hunter, I. M. L. Memory in everyday life. In M. M. Gruneberg & P. E. Morris (Eds.), *Applied problems in memory.* New York: Academic Press, 1979.

Kintsch, W. *The representation of meaning in memory.* New York: Wiley, 1974.

Krebs, E. W., Snowman, J., & Smith, S. H. Teaching new dogs old tricks: Facilitating prose learning through mnemonic training. *Journal of Instructional Psychology,* 1978, *5,* 33–39.

Laver, A. B. Essay review: Robert Copland's Art of Memory (c. 1545). *Journal of the History of the Behavioral Sciences,* 1977, *13,* 82–93.

Levin, J. R. The mnemonic '80s: Keywords in the classroom. *Educational Psychologist,* 1981, *16,* 65–82. (a)

Levin, J. R. On functions of pictures in prose. In F. J. Pirozzolo & M. C. Wittrock (Eds.), *Neuropsychological and cognitive processes in reading.* New York: Academic Press, 1981. (b)

Levin, J. R. Pictures as prose-learning devices. In A. Flammer & W. Kintsch (Eds.), *Discourse processing.* Amsterdam: North-Holland, in press.

Levin, J. R., & Divine-Hawkins, P. Visual imagery as a prose learning process. *Journal of Reading Behavior,* 1974, *6,* 23–30.

Levin, J. R., & Lesgold, A. M. On pictures in prose. *Educational Communication and Technology,* 1978, *26,* 233–243.

Lorayne, H., & Lucas, J. *The memory book.* New York: Ballantine, 1974.

Mandler, J. M., & Johnson, N. S. Some of the thousand words a picture is worth. *Journal of Experimental Psychology: Human Learning and Memory,* 1976, *2,* 529–540.

Mayer, R. E. Twenty years of research on advance organizers: Assimilation theory is still the best predictor of results. *Instructional Science,* 1979, *8,* 133–167.

McCarty, D. L. Investigation of a visual imagery mnemonic device for acquiring face-name associations. *Journal of Experimental Psychology: Human Learning and Memory*, 1980, *6*, 145–155.

Miller, G. A., Galanter, E., & Pribram, K. H. *Plans and the structure of behavior.* New York: Holt, Rinehart & Winston, 1960.

Minsky, M. A framework for representing knowledge. In P. H. Winston (Ed.), *The psychology of computer vision.* New York: McGraw-Hill, 1975.

Norman, D. A. *Memory and attention* (2nd ed.). New York: Wiley, 1976.

Ong, W. J. *Ramus: Method and the decay of dialogue.* Cambridge, MA: Harvard University Press, 1958.

Ortony, A. Remembering, understanding, and representation. *Cognitive Science*, 1978, *2*, 53–69.

Paivio, A. *Imagery and verbal processes.* New York: Holt, Rinehart & Winston, 1971.

Paivio, A. Strategies in language learning. In M. Pressley & J. R. Levin (Eds.), *Cognitive strategy research: Educational applications.* New York: Springer-Verlag, 1983.

Paivio, A., & Desrochers, A. Effects of an imagery mnemonic on second language recall and comprehension. *Canadian Journal of Psychology*, 1979, *33*, 17–28.

Paivio, A., & Desrochers, A. Mnemonic techniques and second-language learning. *Journal of Educational Psychology*, 1981, *73*, 780–795.

Paivio, A., & Foth, D. Imaginal and verbal mediators and noun concreteness in paired-associate learning: The elusive interaction. *Journal of Verbal Learning and Verbal Behavior*, 1970, *9*, 384–390.

Pash, J. R., & Blick, K. A. The effect of a mnemonic device on retention of verbal material. *Psychonomic Science*, 1970, *19*, 203–204.

Persensky, J. J., & Senter, R. J. The effect of subjects conforming to mnemonic instructions. *Journal of Psychology*, 1970, *74*, 15–20.

Peterson, P. L., & Swing, S. R. Problems in classroom implementation of cognitive strategy instruction. In M. Pressley & J. R. Levin (Eds.), *Cognitive strategy research: Educational applications.* New York: Springer-Verlag, 1983.

Pressley, M. Imagery and children's learning: Putting the picture in developmental perspective. *Review of Educational Research*, 1977, *47*, 585–622.

Pressley, M., & Dennis-Rounds, J. Transfer of a mnemonic keyword strategy at two age levels. *Journal of Educational Psychology*, 1980, *72*, 575–582.

Pressley, M., Levin, J. R., & Delaney, H. D. The mnemonic keyword method. *Review of Educational Research*, 1982, *52*, 61–91.

Pressley, M., Levin, J. R., & Miller, G. E. How does the keyword method affect vocabulary comprehension and usage? *Reading Research Quarterly*, 1981, *16*, 213–226.

Pressley, M., Levin, J. R., & Miller, G. E. The keyword method compared to alternative vocabulary-learning strategies. *Contemporary Educational Psychology*, 1982, *7*, 50–60.

Roberts, K. H., & Weisberg, R. Medieval drawing and the arts of memory. *Coranto*, 1976, *10*, 28–42.

Rohwer, W. D., Jr. Images and pictures in children's learning: Research results and educational implications. *Psychological Bulletin*, 1970, *73*, 393–403.

Ross, J., & Lawrence, K. A. Some observations on memory artifice. *Psychonomic Science*, 1968, *13*, 107–108.

Rothkopf, E. Z. The concept of mathemagenic activities. *Review of Educational Research*, 1970, *40*, 325–336.

Rumelhart, D. E. Schemata: The building blocks of cognition. In R. Spiro, B. Bruce, & W. Brewer (Eds.), *Theoretical issues in reading comprehension*. Hillsdale, NJ: Erlbaum, 1980.

Rumelhart, D. E., Lindsay, P. H., & Norman, D. A. A process model for long-term memory. In E. Tulving & W. Donaldson (Eds.), *Organization of memory*. New York: Academic Press, 1972.

Rumelhart, D. E., & Ortony, A. The representation of knowledge in memory. In R. C. Anderson, R. J. Spiro, & W. E. Montague (Eds.), *Schooling and the acquisition of knowledge*. Hillsdale, NJ: Erlbaum, 1977.

Schallert, D. L. The role of illustrations in reading comprehension. In R. J. Spiro, B. C. Bruce, & W. F. Brewer (Eds.), *Theoretical issues in reading comprehension*. Hillsdale, NJ: Erlbaum, 1980.

Schank, R., & Abelson, R. *Scripts, plans, goals, and understanding: An inquiry into human knowledge and structures*. Hillsdale, NJ: Erlbaum, 1977.

Schultz, C. B., & DiVesta, F. J. Effects of passage organization and note taking on the selection of clustering strategies and on recall of textual materials. *Journal of Education Psychology*, 1972, *63*, 244–252.

Schwartz, N. H., & Kulhavy, R. W. Map features and the recall of discourse. *Contemporary Educational Psychology*, 1981, *6*, 151–158.

Shimmerlik, S. M. Organization theory and memory for prose: A review of the literature. *Review of Educational Research*, 1978, *48*, 103–120.

Simon, H. A. Information processing models of cognition. *Annual Review of Psychology*, 1979, *30*, 363–396.

Smith, E. E., Adams, N., & Schorr, D. Fact retrieval and the paradox of interference. *Cognitive Psychology*, 1978, *10*, 438–464.

Snowman, J., Krebs, E. U., & Lockhart, L. Improving recall of information from prose in high-risk students through learning strategy training. *Journal of Instructional Psychology*, 1980, *7*, 35–40.

Sweeney, C. A., & Bellezza, F. S. Use of the keyword mnemonic for learning English vocabulary. *Human Learning*, 1982, *1*, 155–163.

Thorndyke, P. W. Cognitive structures in comprehension and memory of narrative discourse. *Cognitive Psychology*, 1977, *9*, 77–110.

Weinstein, C. E. Elaboration skills as a learning strategy. In H. F. O'Neil, Jr. (Ed.), *Learning strategies*. New York: Academic Press, 1978.

Weinstein, C. E., Cubberly, W. E., Wicker, F. W., Underwood, V. L., Roney, L. K., & Duty, D. C. Training versus instruction in the acquisition of cognitive learning strategies. *Contemporary Educational Psychology*, 1981, *6*, 159–166.

Wittrock, M. C. Learning as a generative process. *Educational Psychologist*, 1974, *11*, 87–95.

Yates, F. A. *The art of memory*. London: Routledge & Kegan Paul, 1966.

4. Memory Strategy Instruction with the Elderly: What *Should* Memory Training Be the Training Of?

Pamela Roberts

The research literature on providing memory strategies for the elderly is very new and incomplete. Most of the research on memory functioning in the elderly has focused on the explanation and locus of memory decline with age. Although a large body of literature on memory functioning in late adulthood now exists, issues concerning the extent, cause, and prevention of the decline are still vigorously debated (see Poon, Fozard, Cermak, Arenberg, & Thompson, 1980). Thus, one impediment in this research area has been the question: What *should* memory training be the training of (and can it work)?

An important change in research strategy relating to general cognitive decline with age occurred in the mid-1970s. Schaie, Baltes, and their colleagues argued that the existing knowledge about cognitive change with age was seriously flawed as a result of reliance on frequently employed research practices, which included cross-sectional research designs and the use of tests constructed for young adults and children (Baltes & Labouvie, 1973; Baltes & Schaie, 1974; 1976; Labouvie-Vief, 1976; 1977; Schaie, 1974; 1978; Schaie & Baltes, 1977). They suggested that instead of expending the total research resources on possibly uninterpretable cross-sectional comparisons, some examination should be made of the range and plasticity of abilities in the elderly. One proposed method for studying this range of abilities was the cognitive training study. Schaie and colleagues suggested that cognitive training studies could accomplish several goals, including:

1. providing information on the noncognitive factors that affect the performance of the elderly;
2. fostering the remediation of possibly age-related decrements; and
3. contributing to general theories of cognitive development.

Most of the initial cognitive training studies involved practice in and strategies for taking traditional and fluid intelligence tests (Sterns & Sanders, 1980). Closely following this general call for cognitive training studies came a symposium on intervention programs for memory problems in old age (Arenberg, 1978). Research stemming from this new interest area and earlier pioneer efforts will be the core of this chapter.

The research on memory strategy instruction with the elderly does not exist in a vacuum. It is closely tied to current trends in research on memory and the existing knowledge of memory abilities in old age. The outline of this chapter reflects those relationships. First, a brief description of the traditional beliefs about memory change with age is given. The main part of the chapter provides a review of memory training studies, which are grouped by type of strategy employed. Studies that exemplify each training type are highlighted. The third section includes samples of new information on memory in the elderly gathered from less traditional memory tasks. The final section summarizes the chapter and provides an outline for promising future directions of research.

Memory Decline in Old Age

Self-Reports

The evidence for a decline in memory with age comes from several sources, one of the most compelling being reports by the elderly themselves. A large community survey on mental health indicated that approximately one half of persons over 60 years of age perceive that they have serious memory problems (Lowenthal et al., 1967). In my laboratory, as part of our general demographic questionnaire, all subjects in memory research are asked whether they have any memory problems, and to name them. The combined data from three separate studies indicate that 6% of the young subjects (aged 20–39), 12% of the middle-aged subjects (aged 40–59), and 46% of the older subjects (aged 60 and above) state that they have some memory problems. Thus, even active, healthy, community-dwelling elderly volunteers mention memory difficulties with greater frequency than do younger volunteers.

There are several possible explanations for this reported increase in memory difficulties with age. The most obvious explanation is that there is indeed a change in memory capability, and that older people simply notice the change. The research data examining that possibility are summarized below.

A second explanation for the reported increase in memory problems emphasizes the stereotype of memory decline in old age and the possibility of a self-fulfilling prophecy (Kahn, 1971; Kahn, Zarit, Hilbert, & Niederehe, 1975). Kahn suggests that memory difficulties that occur in persons of all ages may be emphasized more in the elderly (by themselves and others) and attributed to the inevitable decline of aging. This attribution may then cause the aged individual to have less confidence in his or her abilities and to report memory problems more often to others.

Laboratory Studies

Most of the recent research on memory in old age has been conducted within an information processing framework, with cross-sectional comparisons between adult age groups used as an indication of the change or stability in each component. The inference of memory change with age based on cross-sectional findings may be inappropriate because of several possible cohort differences, including educational level, cautiousness, experience with testing procedures, motivation, health, and fatigue (see Baltes & Labouvie, 1973, for review). This caveat should be seriously considered while examining this review, which is based almost solely on cross-sectional findings. The common age groups studied have been the young (aged 18–39), the old (aged 60+), and less frequently, the middle-aged (ages 40–59). Deviations from these definitions will be noted. The largest body of research has been conducted with verbal materials; therefore, the study of memory for non-verbal stimuli will rarely be discussed. This brief review is included only to provide a basic background to the strategy instruction studies. Recent detailed reviews can be found in Craik (1977), Poon et al. (1980), and other sources.

An information processing framework divides memory functioning into several components: sensory, primary, secondary, tertiary, and sometimes working-memory stores. For ease of discussion, the literature on memory decline in old age can be further separated into two areas: memory capacity and speed of memory processes. The speed of processing in each memory store appears to decrease with age (Fozard, 1980). Because slowing occurs in all components of memory, it will not be discussed unless it is important to the information on capacity.

Experimental studies suggest a decline in sensory memory with age. Walsh and Thompson (1978) found a slowing effect, in which older adults required more time to identify a single letter than did young adults. Cerella, Poon, and Fozard (reported in Fozard, 1980) presented four to seven unrelated letters to young and old adults and found that old adults identified fewer letters than the young, regardless of stimulus duration. Other investigations support these studies in concluding that speed (and possibly capacity) of sensory memory is impaired in the elderly.

Primary memory, the short-term store, is generally measured with strings of digits, letters, or words to be reproduced in serial order. Most experimental studies have found no decline or minimal decline in the capacity of primary memory with age (Craik, 1977).

Secondary memory, the store for recently learned information, has been studied most often in the aging-of-memory literature. Recall of information in secondary memory appears to be more adversely affected by aging than is recognition, although in both types of tasks a memory decline with age is generally found (Craik, 1977). The extent of the decrement reported on performance in recall and recognition tasks appears to be dependent on several factors, including stimulus pacing, task meaningfulness, task difficulty, and subject variables such as autonomic arousal and cautiousness (Botwinick, 1978). Canestrari (1963) and others have found that self-pacing increases recall performance in the elderly. Monge and Hultsch (1971) varied inspection and anticipation intervals for both old and young subjects, and found that the old benefited more than the young from an increased anticipation interval. Investigations employing long anticipation intervals, however, generally report continued evidence for an age-related decline in responding.

Strength of association in a paired-associate task also affects the extent of memory decrement displayed. Although Botwinick and Storandt (1974) found no difference in recall for high-association pairs (e.g., ocean–water) among young, middle-aged, and older adults, there was an age difference for both medium- and low-association pairs, with a steeper age decline for the low-association stimuli. Subject variables that appear with greater frequency in older subjects than in the young also may affect recall and recognition from secondary memory. Powell, Eisdorfer, and Bogdonoff (1964) found that older subjects displayed greater autonomic arousal (which is associated with depressed memory) during a serial learning task than did the young. A decrease in this arousal through drug administration increased the performance of the elderly (Eisdorfer, Nowlin, & Wilkie, 1970). Also, the elderly may be more cautious in their responding (see Botwinick, 1978).

Tertiary memory is a long-term storehouse. It is more difficult to study than secondary memory because it requires longitudinal methods or access to information about a subject's previously stored memories. Because of these dilemmas, tertiary memory has not often been studied in the elderly. The few studies investigating individual subjects' prior knowledge have utilized tasks such as recall and recognition of names and faces from a high school yearbook. The results of these investigations indicate a greater decrement in recall than recognition, but some decline in both with age. The extent of the decline, however, is small considering the length of the memories (Bahrick, Bahrick, & Wittlinger, 1975; Schonfield, 1972; see Craik, 1977, for review). Other investigations have examined memories accumulated throughout the life span by testing recall and recognition for common knowledge about different decades (e.g., movies, sports, current events). Lachman and Lachman (1980) reported that total knowledge increased with age and that efficiency of remembering remained constant across age. Thus, the limited existing research suggests fairly good retention of long-term memories.

The information presented thus far indicates a general slowing effect across memory stores and a decline in the capacity of sensory and secondary memory. The change in secondary memory functioning has been most frequently investigated, with some researchers attributing the deficit to encoding processes, some to retrieval processes, and some to both (Craik, 1977). Regardless of its origin, secondary memory decline has been the target of memory-training studies with the elderly.

Memory Strategy Instruction Research

As detailed above, most traditional experimental studies report a decline in secondary memory capacity with age, and that older individuals frequently complain of memory problems (Fozard, 1980). Thus, like general cognitive training research, memory-training studies may (1) increase memory functioning and possibly self-esteem in the elderly; (2) provide data on the remediation of memory decline; and (3) contribute to the understanding of the locus of memory decline. Studies reviewed in the following section will be categorized by the type of strategy instruction employed.

Practice

Labouvie-Vief and colleagues have argued that the proposed decrement found in the performance by the elderly on cognitive tasks may, in part, be related to diminished intellectual stimulation in the older person's environment (Labouvie-Vief, 1976; 1977; Labouvie-Vief & Gonda, 1976). Thus, part of the decline with age may be a lack of practice on intellectual tasks, causing slowed responses, lack of confidence, and general strategy breakdown.

Providing the aged with simple practice on cognitive tasks has greatly increased their performance in several cognitive training studies. Labouvie-Vief and Gonda (1976) placed elderly subjects in either one of two conditions involving practice on fluid intelligence materials (cognitive strategy training or no-feedback practice) or a no-contact control condition. A fluid intelligence measure was administered twice after treatment. While the first posttest revealed the superiority of the cognitive strategy training group, both the no-feedback practice and the no-contact control groups displayed extensive improvement at the second testing, and the no-feedback practice group performed significantly better than both others. Labouvie-Vief and Gonda concluded that practice allowed older learners to select a strategy that was most efficient for them, while experimenter-imposed strategies often did not adequately fit subjects' needs. Plemons, Willis, and Baltes (1978) conducted a short-term longitudinal training study on fluid intelligence measures in which training group subjects were given eight detailed strategy instruction sessions and control subjects received no contact with fluid intelligence tasks. Subjects were given three posttests on several intelligence measures. Although the training group subjects performed significantly better than controls on two measures in the first posttest, control subjects improved more than the trained subjects on the second posttest, narrowing the difference in performance on one measure and eliminating the previous group difference on the other. Although the cognitive training provided had been quite detailed, the second posttest scores of controls were similar to the first posttest scores of the trained subjects. It appears that simple practice in test taking was an important component in their cognitive training. Finally, Hofland (Note 1) gave elderly subjects fluid intelligence measures eight times without feedback over a 4-week period. He found steady improvement in performance, with no asymptote.

The use of only elderly subjects in the foregoing studies could provoke a legitimate criticism. Although it is clear that practice enhances their performance, there is no test of the assumption that the older person's unstimulating environment creates a deficit in performance. If environmental deprivation causes cognitive decline, it would be expected that older persons would improve more than younger persons given the same practice opportunities.

Practice on memory tasks has been examined by several researchers in gerontology (Erber, 1976; Gladis, 1964; Hultsch, 1974; Monge, 1969; Taub, 1973; Taub & Long, 1972). The memory research has generally included younger subjects, allowing for an examination of the environmental deprivation suggestion. Consistent with the fluid intelligence test training studies mentioned earlier, all studies have found an increase in performance by the elderly. However, most studies have found either a greater practice effect for the young, or equal improvement for the young and old. A study by Hultsch (1974) will be described as an example of this research area.

Hultsch (1974) gave two successive multitrial free-recall tasks to young, middle-aged, young-old, and old-old women. Two lists of unrelated nouns were presented 10 times each, with the second list following completion of the first-list trials. At the end of each presentation, subjects were tested for recall. Hultsch examined improvement over trials for each list and learning to learn across lists. He also measured organization patterns of recall for all trials. His results indicated that all groups improved individual list recall over trials. Young subjects performed better on List 2 than on List 1 at every trial, showing increased acquisition efficiency. The comparison of performance on List 2 to that on List 1 for the old-old subjects revealed a different pattern of response. In the early trials, old-old subjects performed worse on List 2 than on List 1, then reversed this trend in later trials. Hultsch found that the older the subject, the more likely it was that she displayed this pattern of response. Thus, older subjects increased performance with practice, but did not display increased acquisition efficiency at the introduction of a new list. Although older subjects benefited from practice, they did not gain more than the young. Organization measures indicated that all age groups increased over time; however, the young organized more at each trial than did the old.

The Hultsch study and others demonstrate that older adults better their memory performance through practice and appear to employ more efficient strategies over time, but they do not gain more than younger subjects. Simply providing practice, then, will not decrease the difference in memory performance between the old and the young. Therefore, a strict environmental deficiency hypothesis should be ruled out. One significant variable that appears often in this literature is the difference in organization between age groups, which will be examined next.

General Organization

Studies by Hultsch and others have promoted the hypothesis that there are adult age differences in both the quality and quantity of organization of incoming information (Denney, 1974; Erber, 1976; Hultsch, 1971b; 1974; Mueller, Ranklin, & Carlomusto, 1979; Sanders, Murphy, Schmitt, & Walsh, 1980; Smith, 1979). Hultsch has suggested that as age increases, less organization of material takes place, and what organization does occur is often different from that of the younger adult. Although some studies have not found an age difference in organization (e.g., Laurence, 1966; Wright, 1982), the assertion that a difference exists, and that it may create the deficit exhibited in memory performance of older adults, has generated some interesting research. (See Chapter 1 of this volume for more on organizational effects on memory.)

Hultsch (1969) gave adolescent (aged 16–19), young adult (aged 30–39), and middle-aged (aged 45–54) male subjects a free-recall task. Subjects were assigned to one of three organizational groups that received either standard instructions, instructions to organize the stimuli in some meaningful fashion, or the suggestion to organize the words alphabetically. In addition to examining the effects of instructional set, Hultsch also assessed the verbal facility of the subjects. He found no significant differences by age or instructional set for the high-verbal-facility subjects. Low-verbal-facility subjects displayed a significant decrement in responding with each increasing age group for the first two conditions. Subjects in the alphabetical organization condition showed no age decrement. Thus, at least for low-verbal-facility individuals, the provision of a simple strategy for recall eliminated the age decrement found in the other conditions.

Hultsch (1971a) gave young, middle-aged, and older subjects a free-recall task under one of two experimental conditions. One half of the subjects physically sorted 52 unrelated nouns into subject-generated categories. This procedure was repeated until two successive identical sorts were achieved. Control subjects were yolked to experimental subjects, receiving the same number of trials to inspect (but not categorize) the words that their experimental counterpart took to reach criterion. Hultsch examined six measures of sorting behavior for the experimental subjects: (1) number of trials to criterion, (2) total time to criterion, (3) number of errors to criterion, (4) number of categories used in the criterion trial, (5) stereotypy of category content, and (6) category size range. No differences were found between age groups on category usage in the sorting task. In the sorting condition, young subjects recalled significantly more words than did the elderly subjects, with the middle-aged subjects not significantly different from either age group. In the control condition, young subjects recalled significantly more words than did either the middle-aged or elderly subjects. There was no significant difference between the two older groups in performance. The two older groups were affected more by condition than were the young. Although the interaction was not statistically significant, both the middle-aged and the old groups appeared to recall an average of 5 more words under sorting than under control instructions, whereas the young gained only about 1.5 words under sorting instructions (present author's extrapolation from graph). Hultsch concludes that as age increases, memory performance declines more under conditions that minimize the opportunity for meaningful organization than under conditions that maximize that opportunity. He does not provide an adequate explanation for the finding that there were no age differences in sorting behavior but consistent differences in recall. Although organization cues help the middle-aged and older individual to remember, some other problem must be addressed in order to fully remediate the difficulty.

The final study of this type that I will discuss here was reported by Schmitt, Murphy, and Sanders (in press). In a follow-up of a previous study in which it was found that older adults rehearsed and clustered free-recall items less than did young adults (Sanders et al., 1980), Schmitt et al. assigned elderly subjects to conditions varying in rehearsal activity and strategy type for a multilist free-recall task. All subjects were given five practice lists before actual testing. Prior to practice, subjects were instructed to verbalize everything they thought as they studied, and after the first practice list they were urged to continue overt verbalizations. Control subjects received no further instructions. Before the second practice list, activity and strategy subjects were instructed to be active in studying, to think about as many list items as possible, and to continue to verbalize their thoughts. In addition, strategy subjects were told (prior to the third practice list) to organize the incoming words and rehearse them that way. Thus, the experimental design allowed for an examination of the effect of active rehearsal and organizational strategy instructions on the performance of elderly subjects. Schmitt et al. conducted a detailed analysis of clustering differences, number of rehearsals, and other measures; but for the purposes of the present chapter, only recall accuracy will be examined. Strategy-instructed subjects recalled a significantly greater number of words than did subjects in the other two groups. Performance by subjects in the activity and control groups was not significantly different. Therefore, providing instructions to study the stimuli actively did not better the subjects' performance, whereas adding the organizational strategy did increase recall. Schmitt et al. do not provide data on younger subjects, so it is not known how closely the older subjects performed to a young adult level. Schmitt et al. did compare their results to those of Sanders et al.'s (1980) young adult subjects, and reported that for the same high-strength lists, the percentage correct for the strategy-trained older adults and the nontrained young adults was almost identical. However, it is difficult to interpret this comparison, because the young adults in the Sanders et al. study were not given training.

The three studies just outlined illustrate memory instruction through providing general organizational strategies, such as categorization. They are based on a literature that suggests that older adults do not organize incoming information as extensively as do the young. Each study provides some confirmation that older adults can improve their memory performance when given strategies of organization. The extent of this improvement, the relationship to young adult performance, and the need for providing such strategies appears to be dependent on task difficulty and individual subject variables that have not been adequately explored in the literature.

Visual Imagery

Imagery instruction in the elderly has most often been studied in the context of paired-associate learning. (See Paivio, 1983, and Chapters 2 and 3 in this volume for more on imagery.) Although the details of the imagery instructions have varied from study to study, subjects usually have been told to use elaborative imagery to learn noun pairings. An imagery elaboration for the paired associates *truck–cloud* could be a picture of a truck loaded with a cloud or a self-generated image of a truck driving through a cloud. The results of associative memory, and particularly of elaborative imagery, research in the elderly have been very consistent.

In general, associative learning is lower in elderly adults than in younger adults in both no-strategy control conditions and elaboration conditions (e.g., Canestrari, 1968; Hulicka & Grossman, 1967; Poon & Walsh-Sweeney, 1981; Roberts & Pressley, Note 2, Note 3; Roberts, Pressley, O'Hanlon, Hance, Hans, & Bailey, Note 4). When exceptions to this generalization have occurred, the studies have been suspect because of either ceiling effects (e.g., Treat, Poon, & Fozard, 1981) or extremely small sample sizes (e.g., Treat & Reese, 1976). Imagery elaboration (whether provided or self-generated) generally has produced enhanced learning over that observed in control conditions (e.g., Canestrari, 1968; Hulicka & Grossman, 1967; Poon & Walsh-Sweeney, 1981; Roberts & Pressley, Note 3; Roberts et al., Note 4). The only widely cited exception to this generalization occurred in a study by Treat and Reese (1976) under conditions in which to-be-learned materials were presented at an extremely rapid rate. Finally, the mechanism for enhanced learning has been examined in a few of these studies. It appears that the interactive component is more important than the imagery component, for generally there have not been memory differences between verbal versus imagery elaboration (e.g., Canestrari, 1968; Hulicka & Grossman, 1967), a result consistent with data obtained at other developmental levels (Pressley, 1977).

In addition to the work previously mentioned, a few studies have examined more complex imagery mnemonics and situations that are more demanding than immediate use of the mnemonic on the training task. Mason and Smith (1977), in their first experiment, provided elderly, middle-aged, and young adults with either the pegword mnemonic system (i.e., "One is a bun, two is a shoe, . . .") or control instructions. Subjects were then exposed to four 10-item lists that varied in item concreteness. Recall was assessed during a 90-second response interval immediately after the presentation of each list. An age effect was found in both conditions, with the young recalling significantly more than the middle-aged, who recalled more than the older subjects. The pegword system facilitated recall for the young adults only. Studies employing a longer response interval and more extensive strategy practice may yield different results.

One of the difficulties with the pegword system is the necessity of learning the system prior to its effective usage. Robertson-Tchabo, Hausman, and Arenberg (1976) suggested that having to memorize a separate system as complicated as the pegwords in addition to the material to be learned might overload an older person's memory. To avoid this, they taught older adults the method of loci, involving 16 locations in their own home. In a small initial study, five older individuals were given first a free-recall task of 16 nouns; then three training sessions on the method of loci, in which they memorized and were tested on other 16-item lists. Finally, a fifth session was conducted in which a 16-item list was produced for memorization, but no mention of the method of loci was made. Robertson-Tchabo et al. found that subjects were able to use the method and improve their recall scores, but that they did not transfer use of the method to the final list unless they were cued. A second, larger study was then conducted in the same manner, except for the following changes: (1) a control group was added, which took imaginary trips through their houses, but did not use the trips to aid recall; and (2) during the fifth session, one strategy group was provided with a verbal tour of their homes and asked at each location what noun had been placed there; the other was not given such explicit clues, but was told to use the method that they had been using all week. No difference was found between the two strategy groups for the first four sessions. Subjects in the strategy groups recalled significantly more than the control group during each session, and also improved more over time. In the fifth session, subjects who were given a verbal tour of their homes recalled more words than did the other strategy subjects. Thus, Robertson-Tchabo et al. found that the elderly can use the method of loci to improve memory performance, but optimal performance is achieved only through explicitly cuing them in its continued usage.

Three age groups were compared on their ability to utilize a modified method of loci by Rose and Yesavage (Note 4). All subjects were given three group training sessions (for a total duration of 2.5 hours), in which they were instructed in the traditional method of loci. In addition, subjects were requested to make a judgment of the pleasantness of each image association they constructed; a supplementary elaboration which had improved the performance of elderly subjects in a previous study (Note 5). Pretest–posttest comparisons revealed that young, middle-aged and old subjects displayed significantly better recall after than prior to training. However, as age of the subjects increased, effectiveness of the mnemonic decreased. Thus, in accordance with the research on imagery elaboration with paired-associates, older adults were able to learn the method of loci, but utilization of the mnemonic did not allow them to perform at young adult levels.

The lasting effects of training, including transfer of skills to other tasks, has rarely been examined in the literature. Only one of the studies located for this review has been published. Treat et al. (1981) placed young and old adults in various imagery and control groups and tested them three times (once every 2 weeks) on lists of 10 paired associates. Subjects were tested on two lists in each session, the first given under control conditions, and the second presented after imagery instructions for the experimental groups. Treat et al. found that maintenance of the strategy (measured by List 1 performance in Sessions 2 and 3) was minimal for the elderly subjects, even though there was a significant effect of experimental condition (measured by List 2 performance in Sessions 1 and 2) for this age group. After the first trial in Session 1, performance by the young was uniformly high throughout, indicating that the young did maintain the strategy.

Poon, Walsh-Sweeney, and Fozard (1980) cite two studies that address continued usage of imagery strategies: Thomas and Ruben (Note 7) and DeLeon (Note 8). Thomas and Ruben placed young, middle-aged, and old subjects in imagery or control conditions, and tested them on a paired-associate task 1 hour and 4, 8, and 16 months after learning to criterion. Although there was a substantial loss in retention, elderly imagery subjects continually performed better than controls and equaled the performance of the young imagery subjects. Poon et al. (1980) cautioned that generalization from this study may be limited, because it employed only 12 paired associates of three letters per word, which were arranged in sequential alphabetical order (e.g., *ace–boy, cow–dog*). Thus the task may have been much easier than those employed in other memory investigations. DeLeon (Note 8) provided groups of elderly subjects with a variety of paired-associate learning strategies. Although all groups improved their performance over a 5-day training period, DeLeon found no generalization of training to three practical memory tasks: recall of (1) a personal narrative, (2) a grocery list, and (3) the names and occupations of photographed people.

A recently completed study (Roberts et al., Note 6) utilized methodology from the child memory literature (see Pressley & Dennis-Rounds, 1980) to examine the amount of instruction necessary for strategy transfer. Young, middle-aged, and old subjects received two lists of paired associates: a list of cities and their products, and a list of unfamiliar Old English words and their meanings. Subjects were assigned to one of four groups:

1. Specific instructions, in which the subjects received directions to abstract "keywords" (see Paivio, 1983; Chapters 2 and 3 of this volume) from the pairs and create an interacting image of the keywords; subjects received these instructions for both lists.
2. General instructions, where specific instructions were given for the first list, but vague instructions to utilize "what you have used before" were provided for the second list.
3. No instructions, where specific instructions were given for the first list, but standard control instructions were given for the second.
4. Control, where instructions were given to "try hard to remember" the pairs.

Roberts et al. hypothesized that imagery instructions would increase the performance of all age groups on the training task, but that as age increased, more specific instructions would be required for strategy transfer to the second list. On both tasks, there were significant age and condition effects. The young performed best, and the old obtained the worst scores on both training and transfer tasks. Each of the three experimental conditions performed significantly better than control subjects on both tasks, with no significant differences among the experimental conditions. The technique employed, the keyword method, is slightly more complex than traditional imagery elaboration instructions because it involves the extra step of finding keywords. The complexity of the method, however, did not appear to affect its utilization by older adults, who displayed a pattern of responding similar to that achieved under standard imagery instructions in other studies. Generalization of the technique from one list to another was found for all experimental groups regardless of subject age.

In summary, studies of visual imagery strategies with the elderly have been conducted primarily with standard instructions to create an interactive visual image between two paired items. Most of those studies found significantly better performance by the elderly in imagery conditions than in control conditions. The one study that found no improvement by the elderly after training involved use of the pegword method, which contains a complex extra step that may be too cumbersome for quick training procedures (see Cermak, 1980, for discussion). The method of loci, which utilizes real-world overlearned material, appeared to facilitate memory performance in the elderly, but was not employed unless specific cues to do so were provided. The keyword method, although involving the extra step of finding keywords, improved memory performance in the elderly, and usage was generalized to a second list. Finally, transfer of training across time and tasks has rarely been examined, and only one study that employed an atypical task reported transfer across sessions. Transfer of training should be a very fertile area of research in the future.

The studies reviewed in this section utilize visual instruction strategies with the elderly. As indicated, older adults do not report using visual imagery as frequently as do young adults. Some researchers suggest that this is adaptive, and reflects the steeper decline in memory for nonverbal information than for verbal information found in the aging literature (see Winograd & Simon, 1980). Thus, a program to provide practical memory training for the elderly in particular may not want to rely solely on the use of visual imagery, at least until other data have been accumulated.

Memory-Training Programs

In addition to studies of instruction in quite specific processes, there have also been more ambitious approaches to memory strategy instruction involving packages of strategies and multiple tasks. Zarit, Cole, and Guider (1981) utilized a package of several memory-training techniques with the healthy elderly. After pretesting all subjects for memory performance and complaints, they gave one group of subjects four separate training sessions, testing recall for the material at the beginning and at the end of each session as well as at the completion of the total study. In the first session, subjects were given a list of grocery items or daily activities that could be grouped into categories. Subjects were taught to organize the items into appropriate groups. During the second session, pictures of individuals and names were paired, and the subjects were taught to create a meaningful connection between the name and some feature of the face. Unrelated lists of items, given with the instruction to create novel visual images associating the words, were presented in Session 3. In Session 4 subjects read a long paragraph and were instructed to use the previous techniques (e.g., categorization, meaningful association, and visual imagery) to recall the material. In a final session subjects were given different forms of each of the four tasks administered in Sessions 1-4. In Experiment 1, control subjects participated in current events groups for four meetings of the same length as experimental sessions. Current events subjects were told that their participation in the group would help improve memory performance, although they did not receive any memory strategy training and simply discussed recent news. They were given all of the same tests presented to the experimental group. In Experiment 2, the control subjects consisted of persons on a waiting list who were tested prior to and after training was completed.

In Experiment 1, trained subjects recalled significantly more material than did the current events group on two of the four tasks (related items and unrelated items) given at the completion of the study. There was more improvement, however, on the tests given at the end of each session (immediately after instructions had been provided) than on the tests given during the final session. The largest group difference was found on the unrelated-items task.

Experiment 2 compared similarly trained subjects with a no-contact control group on both recognition and recall tasks. In this experiment, paragraph retention was examined by multiple-choice measures instead of the recall measures used in Experiment 1. Trained subjects improved on all three recall measures: related items, names and faces, and unrelated items. Most of the improvement occurred on tests immediately following specific instructions. Trained subjects recalled significantly more information than did controls on all recall tasks. Both groups performed at comparably high levels on the recognition tasks.

Zarit et al. (1981) found that providing general organizational structure, elaboration, and visual imagery improved the performance of experimental subjects over no-contact and unrelated practice controls. Recall performance was especially improved for the more standard laboratory tasks—unrelated and related lists—but was not changed for paragraph retention. Consistent with the literature, there was a trend suggesting that experimental subjects use the trained strategies more effectively immediately after receiving strategy instructions than when study and testing are delayed.

Carroll and Gray (1981) described a memory improvement program for the mentally impaired elderly living in a long-term care setting. The program is based on the findings of memory research and incorporates the following goals: reducing anxiety about memory loss, maintaining or relearning previously acquired information, and promoting continuing learning in an institutional setting. The authors discuss various uses of cues to facilitate memory and to allow for more reliance on recognition memory, which is less affected by age than recall. Carroll and Gray emphasize the importance of practice on memory ability, and discuss factors that may affect motivation, such as arousal, meaning of the material, and intentional versus incidental learning. No evaluation of the program is given; however, the article is a useful translation of memory research into practical intervention in a long-term care setting.

Important New Developments

Treat, Poon, Fozard, and Popkin (1978) noted that there are four components that should be involved in an effective memory improvement program for the elderly:

1. Techniques that improve the encoding and retrieval of information must be adapted for the aged.
2. Appropriate reinforcers to motivate the elderly must be identified. Extra motivation is necessary if program participants are to attend better to important material, modify memorization methods, and practice mnemonic techniques over a long period.
3. Individual differences in personality, learning ability, and cognitive style must be incorporated into the design of a memory skills program.
4. Memory skill training should be integrated with medical and psychiatric care when needed.

Most of the existing training literature addresses the initial phase of the first component listed. The primary purpose of this research has been to discover training strategies that will improve the memory performance of the aged. Training strategies and memory tasks have rarely been adapted for the elderly, but rather have been borrowed intact from research with other age groups. Motivational factors and individual differences, although mentioned in most papers, have been infrequently and inadequately examined. Finally, the full integration of memory skills training into a comprehensive treatment plan has not been possible because of the limits in existing knowledge (Poon, Fozard, & Treat, 1978). Some practical applications of current research findings for a long-term care facility are listed in Carroll and Gray (1981).

According to the Treat et al. (1978) suggestions, many of the components important to memory improvement in the elderly have not been examined in the training literature. Examination of the variables in the four components listed may provide important future directions for training research. A few studies exemplifying notable related research areas are outlined in the following subsections.

Motivation

One of the purposes of memory training is to increase memory functioning and self-esteem in the elderly. A change in self-esteem requires the motivation to reassess one's functioning in the world. It is possible that the involvement in memory-training programs may enhance this motivation. In a previously discussed study, Zarit et al. (1981) examined both memory functioning and subjective memory complaints in older subjects. Although specific training increased memory performance over that of the current events group, the subjective memory complaints of both groups declined throughout the study, and were not significantly different. In Experiment 2, subjective memory complaints declined for the training group and increased slightly for the no-contact control group. The opportunity to participate in groups that reportedly would help memory performance decreased subjective memory complaints, although discussing current events did not facilitate actual recall. Thus, the participation in a memory improvement group apparently enhanced the self-perception of memory, even when it did not change actual recall ability.

Langer, Rodin, Beck, Weinman, and Spitzer (1979) varied the motivation for memory improvement in older adults by manipulating self-disclosure and environmental contingencies for remembering. In Study 1, high-functioning nursing home residents were assigned to one of the following conditions: (1) high self-disclosure, (2) low self-disclosure, and (3) no-contact control. Subjects in the experimental conditions were visited by a college student four times in 6 weeks, for approximately 30 minutes a session. Students talked with the elderly in either a highly self-disclosing or a question-asking manner, and at the end of the session suggested several topics to think about for discussion in the following session. Langer et al. suggested that practice in thinking about discussion topics might increase the memory performance of the elderly. However, the power of the suggestion and the likelihood of implementation would vary with the characteristics of the visitor. It was hypothesized that visitors who revealed more personal information would exhibit more power over the subject, and therefore the high-disclosure group would exhibit the best performance.

Memory performance was assessed prior to and after treatment on two measures of secondary memory: pattern recall, and a paired-associate names-and-faces task. In addition, a questionnaire on subject social factors (e.g., happiness, sociability, activity) was given to the nurses before and after treatment. All ratings were "blind" with respect to subjects' conditions. Langer et al. found that the high-self-disclosure group performed significantly better than the other groups on both memory assessments. There was no difference in performance between the low-self-disclosure group and controls. Nurses' ratings revealed greater positive changes in social factors for the high-self-disclosure group than for the other two, which were not significantly different. Langer et al. suggested that high-self-disclosing visitors might increase the likelihood that practice on cognitive tasks would be initiated, and that such practice would enhance memory performance. Inasmuch as cognitive practice was not directly measured in any way, however, other interpretations of these findings could be made. However, Langer et al.'s contention that interpersonal activities can affect cognitive functioning does seem compelling.

In Experiment 2, Langer et al. assigned alert institutionalized elderly subjects to one of three conditions: contingency, noncontingency, and no-contact control. Subjects in the two experimental conditions were visited nine times in 3 weeks, and asked a variety of questions in each session. Questions that the subject could not immediately answer were asked again at the end of the session, with the suggestion that the subject find out the answer in the time between visits. Subjects in the contingency condition were presented with poker chips for answers to questions, whereas noncontingency subjects were given an equal number of poker chips without a contingency. Differences among conditions were examined on the following measures: (1) responses to questions asked during visits, (2) questions about their interaction with the visitor, (3) a probe-recall test, (4) memory for remote events, and (5) records of medical condition. The contingent group answered significantly more questions during visits than did the noncontingent group. Contingent group subjects also had better recall of the names of their visitor, although this difference was not statistically significant. Thus, the effect of visits varied with the experimental condition. Results of both memory tests indicated that the contingent group performed significantly better than the other two groups, which did not differ from one another. Finally, "blind" analyses of medical chart data revealed that the contingency group received significantly better social adjustment comments and voiced more complaints about physical comfort than did noncontingency and control subjects, who did not differ. Langer et al. felt that the complaints were a positive sign of the belief that one has control over one's environment. Thus, providing contingencies for remembering appeared to increase memory performance and interaction with the environment.

The studies just described indicate that environmental manipulations affect both subjective memory complaints and objective memory performance by the elderly. Simply being in a group labeled "memory training" may provide the motivation for finding oneself less impaired. The provision of interpersonal and practical incentives for cognitive activity appears to increase memory performance. Further exploration of motivational variables and their inclusion in strategy instruction research could provide important information on remediation, and possibly lessen the difference in performance between the young and old on various recall tasks.

Alternative Tasks

Concern over the use of traditional academic tasks to test the cognitive abilities of the elderly has frequently been voiced (e.g., Schaie, 1978). The argument is presented that the elderly are disadvantaged in two ways when taking academic tests. First, they are out of practice for such tests. It may take the elderly longer to revive their former skills than the warm-up period generally given. The second point is that because the elderly are less familiar with such tasks at the time of test taking, they may not be motivated to expend the effort required to do well. Therefore, some researchers have attempted to utilize more ecologically valid tests on which the young and the old should be equally practiced and motivated.

The search for real-world alternatives to laboratory tests provides some difficult problems. One problem involves the laboratory distinction among stages of memory, and the emphasis that has been placed on the study of secondary memory. Attempts to find tasks in which older people have experience often include tertiary memory functions.

Several studies have examined recognition and recall of remote and present events in the elderly and the young. One difficulty with such measurement is that memory is highly dependent on original learning. In an attempt to control for this problem, several researchers have asked common knowledge questions from various decades. Botwinick and Storandt (1974) asked young, middle-aged, and older subjects six recall questions from each 20-year period from the 1890s to the 1960s. The questions dealt with historical events, such as the assassination of President John F. Kennedy. Perlmutter (1978) utilized the same questions with young and old adults. Poon, Fozard, Paulshock, and Thomas (1979) gave adult males 108 common knowledge recognition questions from the six decades between 1911 and 1970. Finally, Lachman and Lachman (1980) gave adults 95 questions based on common knowledge (e.g., the Bible, geography) and events that had occurred within the past 10 years (e.g., movies, sports, world events). These questions were presented in the laboratory, and a shorter list was presented in a telephone survey. Questions were first given in a recall format, and later those not answered were presented as recognition questions.

In each study cited above, common knowledge increased with age. In no study did the elderly recall or recognize fewer recent events than did the young. Some, like Perlmutter (1978), reported that fact recall and recognition improved with age. Thus, recall of common knowledge may not be impaired in the elderly, as implied in some earlier and less technically sophisticated studies (e.g., Squire, 1974; Warrington & Sanders, 1971; Warrington & Silberstein, 1970). This is certainly an area worth further exploration.

The search for ecologically valid tasks has led some researchers to the study of text and discourse memory. A well-designed study of fable recall by Labouvie-Vief, Schell, and Weaverdyck (Note 9) is a good example of this type of work and will be examined in the next section.

Memory for common knowledge has been cited as a more ecologically valid task than standard recall procedures. However, problems with this technique include a shift to the study of tertiary memory and reliance on the assumption that the material was known at one time. Another problem with the use of more ecologically valid tasks involves the use of memory aids. Outside of academic test taking and some work situations, most tasks allow the rememberer to use retrieval aids, such as note writing. Thus, performance on such tasks may be dependent on the efficient use of aids, rather than on actual memory capacity. These tasks, however, may provide a greater understanding of the capabilities with which the elderly face real-world demands.

A study of this type was reported by Poon (Note 10). Poon and Schaffer recruited young and elderly subjects for a 3-week telephone task. In a situation analogous to checking up on a sick relative, subjects were required to make telephone calls to the experimenters at predetermined times. Contingencies for making the calls varied among the three experimental groups, which were asked to (1) participate in the project, (2) receive a flat fee for calling (regardless of accuracy), or (3) be paid contingent on their performance. Because the literature suggests that the elderly often complain about forgetting appointments, Poon and Schaffer hypothesized that the young would perform better on the task.

Preliminary analyses, however, indicated that the elderly subjects remembered to make significantly more calls than did the young. When the calls were made, the elderly called significantly closer to the target time than did the young (old mean deviation = 10 minutes, young mean deviation = 55 minutes). Older subjects remained close to the targeted time throughout the 3-week period, whereas the young became more negligent as the study progressed. Poon and Schaffer recruited both working and nonworking subjects in each age group, which means that the differences found are probably not due to a simple availability factor. A final age difference was found in the responsiveness to contingencies. Older adults deviated from targeted calling time by an average of 0 minutes for the contingency group, 4 minutes for the flat-fee group, and 25 minutes for the no-pay group. There was no effect of experimental condition among the young adults. Amount of payment and subject resources were not stated in this report, so it is possible that older subjects were simply more needy and therefore had greater motivation to perform the task.

The study reported by Poon (Note 10) does not utilize a methodology that corresponds well to standard laboratory tasks. Therefore, it is difficult to incorporate the findings into the general memory literature. It is unclear why the older adults performed better than the young: greater motivation, more interest in the task, more time available, or some other variable. Despite the number of possible confounds, it is an important step toward examining performance on ecologically valid tasks. The results of this study, combined with the findings on common knowledge, suggest that there may be many areas of memory in which the elderly continue to function at a high level. Those tasks that most closely approximate real-world demands appear to be the tests at which the aged perform best. Further research employing ecologically valid tests is necessary to discern whether the elderly actually have real-world difficulties that need remediating.

Style Differences

A fairly frequent theme in theories of adult development is the assertion that different styles of perceiving and acting on the world develop with age (see Neugarten, 1977, for review). In addition to the studies outlined earlier in the training section of this chapter, new research on memory derived from this hypothesis includes age-related differences in interpretation of what studying and learning entail.

Murphy, Sanders, Gabriesheski, and Schmitt (1981) first asked young and old adults to estimate their memory span on a serial-recall task (a metamemory assessment). This estimate was compared to their actual tested span as a measure of accuracy. In a second phase, subjects were given self-paced recall tests using three list lengths: subspan, span, and supraspan. List lengths were determined individually for each subject. Both accuracy and study time for each list were assessed. Murphy et al. found that the young had a larger memory span than the old. Estimates of memory span were equally accurate for both groups; however, errors were in opposite directions. In general, the young underestimated, while the old overestimated, their memory span. This finding is the inverse of that found in the literature on memory in young children (e.g., Levin, Yussen, DeRose, & Pressley, 1977). Recall of span and supraspan lists was greater for the young than the old. Most important for the present discussion is that at all list lengths, the old spent less time studying than did the young; and when list difficulty increased, the old did not extend their study time as much as the young.

In a second experiment, Murphy et al. (1981) examined possible causes for the age differences in study time and recall. Elderly subjects were assigned to one of three conditions: (1) instruction control, in which subjects received instructions similar to those given in Experiment 1, except that accuracy was stressed; (2) strategy training, which added the suggestion that chunking and rehearsal would improve recall; (3) forced time, in which subjects were told that a minimum study time was necessary in order to do well on the task and that the experimenter would indicate when that time was past. List recall was assessed as it was in Experiment 1. All groups performed at significantly different levels, with the forced-time group recalling the most, and the control group recalling the least, information. A comparison with Experiment 1 results indicated that controls performed in a manner similar to the elderly subjects, whereas the forced-time group responded much like the young. Therefore, with task difficulty equated by span, accuracy for the young and old was equal when the old were forced to study as much as the young. In that condition subjective perceptions of what is sufficient study were eliminated for the elderly—they could not quit when they normally would have. Thus, the monitoring of cognitive processes during memorization may decline over time. The inability to monitor the current state of memory processing may prevent older adults from effectively utilizing techniques learned in memory training.

There are other possible style changes with age. A well-executed study that argues for this type of age difference was reported by Labouvie-Vief et al. (Note 9). Young and elderly subjects listened to a tape-recorded fable and subsequently were asked to recall under one of three conditions: (1) summary, in which subjects were asked to provide a summary of the study; (2) recall, in which subjects were directed to recall as much of the story as they possibly could; and (3) verification, in which multiple-choice questions were asked about the story. Thus, two recall conditions and one recognition condition were utilized.

The structure of the fable was analyzed into 18 consistent propositions, some of which were relevant to the gist of the story and others that could be considered details. Summary and recall protocols were scored for inclusion of these propositions. Verification questions were constructed from the 18 story propositions and were scored according to the frequency of correct gist and detail answers. The performance levels of the young were comparably high in all three conditions. The old performed as well as the young under the recall and verification instructions, but not in the summary conditions. Recall of detail by elderly subjects was significantly lowered under summary instructions, and gist recall showed a similar, but non-significant, trend. Thus, Labouvie-Vief et al. found similar performances by old and young on a recognition task and on a recall task when both were instructed to recall as much as possible. The lack of age differences in recall is a finding at variance with the more standard laboratory task research results.

Labouvie-Vief et al. (Note 9) also reported qualitative age differences in addition to the quantitative changes just described. Older subjects appeared to focus less on specific story propositions and instead often provided a moral to the fable. One third of the elderly subjects provided a moral as a mode of summarizing the fable, whereas none of the younger subjects furnished a moral in their summary. These qualitative age variations appear to account for some of the quantitative differences found in gist for the summary condition.

Labouvie-Vief et al. suggest that the resulting qualitative differences in summarization originate in the different encoding styles employed by the young and old. They report that in debriefing, many elderly subjects indicated that they were less interested in story detail than in story coherence. Labouvie-Vief et al. stress that the elderly were flexible and responsive to experimental instructions but showed a common stylistic tendency that was qualitatively different from that of the young. The old went beyond the text and related the information to real-world knowledge, whereas the young attempted to give verbatim accounts of the story. The cause of this difference in style is unclear. Labouvie-Vief et al. mention a range of possibilities, including age-related qualitative shifts in the mnemonic system, and a deficit in processing mechanisms that may force the elderly to look for alternative methods to incorporate incoming information. Regardless of the cause, the existence of age- or cohort-related individual differences adds another important variable to the interpretation of reported age differences in memory.

The optimistic tone of Labouvie-Vief et al. has not been echoed by all prose-learning researchers. However, the other prose-learning research with the elderly in many ways seems impoverished relative to Labouvie-Vief's study. Other authors have emphasized accelerated reading of text (e.g., Cohen, 1981), which is known to debilitate performance in the elderly (e.g., Pezdek & Miceli, 1982); have included very abstract materials that might appear meaningless to the elderly (Cohen, 1979, 1981; Gordon & Clark, 1974); and have focused on recall of only the text and low-level inferences rather than on the type of rich, higher order inferences recorded by Labouvie-Vief et al. (e.g., Meyer & Rice, 1981). More research varying context, content, and specific dependent variables is needed to fully understand the variety of findings reported in the literature on prose learning in the elderly.

Summary and Conclusions

In this chapter, a brief account has been given of the existing knowledge about memory decline, memory-training programs and their success, and future directions for memory strategy instruction with the elderly. Self-reports of memory difficulties were shown to be more frequent in the elderly than in the young. Self-reports were confirmed by standard memory research, which indicated a general slowing and a decline in secondary memory capacity with age. The extent of the decrement found appeared to be dependent on various task parameters and subject variables.

Memory-training studies were examined by the type of strategy employed: simple practice, general organization, visual imagery, and composite programs. Although simple practice improved performance on memory tasks, it did not reduce the performance difference between the young and the old. General organizational strategies often provided more help to older individuals, but did not raise their performance to young adult levels. Visual imagery was the most frequently used memory-training strategy. Most studies found that visual imagery training enhanced the performance of older adults, but did not bring it up to young adult standards. Thus, the elderly can learn to better their performance on memory tasks, but in general their improved performance is worse than that of similarly trained young adults. Most of the training described did not fully remediate the problem of decline in memory with age.

It is possible that strategy training did not equalize the performance of the young and elderly because the training did not take into account all the necessary variables. In the third section of the chapter, new information on motivation, alternative task performance, and style differences with age was examined. It was shown that interpersonal and contingent rewards could affect memory performance in the elderly, and that subjective memory complaints could be reduced by holding group discussions. More ecologically valid tasks, such as those measuring tertiary memory, remembering to telephone, and recalling stories, revealed no decline in memory with age under many instructional conditions. Finally, differences in memory monitoring and task interpretation between age groups were suggested as important areas of further research. It was proposed that a memory-monitoring decline in the elderly would hamper the ability to utilize memory-enhancing techniques. Group-related style differences might lead to an inaccurate judgment of decline instead of a simple difference in encoding style preference.

The study of memory in the elderly is fairly recent, and future directions for research seem limitless. It appears that the elderly can learn memory strategies, but that providing these techniques does not eliminate the difference in performance between the young and the old. Therefore, a fruitful line of inquiry may involve a more thorough examination of training strategies and their effects on the elderly. For example, studies comparing training length and strategy type for older adults could clearly contribute to the existing literature. When effective memory strategies and training methods are found for the elderly, the issue of generalization across tasks and time should be addressed. The experimental design used in the 1982 study by Roberts et al. (Note 6) could easily be changed to a multitrial, multitask procedure in order to study generalization.

Following up on the foregoing suggestions would contribute to the existing memory literature. However, I believe that such studies would be less interesting and, in the long run, less important to the goals of memory research with the elderly than the ideas that follow. Although it is possible to refine the existing memory strategy research as suggested, another tactic is to step back and ask: What *should* memory training be the training of? or, Where is the deficit? If one incorporates the new research on alternative task performance and style differences into a conceptualization of memory in old age, the deficit question becomes fairly difficult to answer.

In an early section of this chapter, it was stated that the goals for memory-training studies include (1) increasing memory functioning and, possibly, self-esteem, in the elderly; (2) providing data on the remediation of memory decline; and (3) contributing to the understanding of the locus of memory deficit. These goals depend largely on the notion of memory decline, which is apparent in data from traditional laboratory paradigms but has recently seemed to vanish in studies that include more meaningful materials (e.g., Labouvie-Vief et al., Note 9).

Thus, I propose that there is a more fruitful way to study memory in the elderly than has prevailed in research to date. I think more attention should be given to memory of materials that are important to the elderly and frequently encountered by them. Comparison of younger and older adult performance on everyday memory tasks, with an examination of variables such as age-related style differences, will yield important information about memory processes. There are several possible answers to the question: What *should* memory training be the training of? I suggest that it should be the training of psychologists to remember that explaining behavior in the real world is an important goal, and that differences are not always deficits.

Reference Notes

1. Hofland, B. *Intraindividual variability and retest effects in fluid intelligence.* Paper presented at the Gerontological Society Annual Meeting, Dallas, November 1978.
2. Roberts, P., & Pressley, M. *Imagery and the aged: The effects of age and in-*

struction. Unpublished manuscript, State University of New York, Plattsburgh 1980.

3. Roberts, P., & Pressley, M. *The effect of stimulus type on imagery usage in adults.* Paper presented at the annual American Psychological Association meetings, Washington, DC, August 1982.

4. Rose, T. L., & Yesavage, J. A. *Differential effects of a list-learning mnemonic in three age groups.* Unpublished manuscript.

5. Yesavage, J. A. & Rose, T. L. *Semantic elaboration and the method of loci: A new trip for older learners.* Unpublished manuscript.

6. Roberts, P., Pressley, M., O'Hanlon, A., Hance, J., Hans, T., & Bailey, S. *Generalization of mnemonic use in three adult age groups.* Manuscript in preparation, 1982.

7. Thomas, J. C., & Ruben, H. *Age and mnemonic techniques in paired associate learning.* Paper presented at the annual meeting of the Gerontological Society, Miami, 1973.

8. DeLeon, J. M. *Effects of training in repetition and mediation on paired associate learning and practical memory in the aged.* Unpublished Ph.D. dissertation, Department of Psychology, University of Hawaii, 1974.

9. Labouvie-Vief, G., Schell, D. A., & Weaverdyck, S. E. *Recall deficit in the aged: A fable recalled.* Unpublished manuscript, Wayne State University, 1981.

10. Poon, L. W. *New directions in memory and aging research.* Paper presented at the International Congress of Gerontology, Hamburg, Germany, July 1981.

References

Arenberg, D. Introduction to a symposium: Toward comprehensive intervention programs for memory problems among the aged. *Experimental Aging Research,* 1978, *4,* 233–234.

Bahrick, H. P., Bahrick, P. O., & Wittlinger, R. P. Fifty years of memory for names and faces: A cross-sectional approach. *Journal of Experimental Psychology: General.* 1975, *104,* 54–75.

Baltes, P. B., & Labouvie, V. Adult development of intellectual performance: Description, explanation, and modification. In C. Eisdorfer & M. P. Lawton (Eds.), *The psychology of adult development and aging.* Washington, DC: American Psychological Association, 1973.

Baltes, P. B., & Schaie, K. W. Aging and IQ: The myth of the twilight years. *Psychology Today,* 1974, *7,* 35–40.

Baltes, P. B., & Schaie, K. W. On the plasticity of intelligence: Where Horn and Donaldson fail. *American Psychologist,* 1976, *31,* 720–725.

Botwinick, J. *Aging and behavior: A comprehehsive integration of research findings.* New York: Springer-Verlag, 1978.

Botwinick, J., & Storandt, M. *Memory, related functions and age.* Springfield, IL: Charles C Thomas, 1974.

Canestrari, R. E. Paced and self-paced learning in young and elderly adults. *Journal of Gerontology,* 1963, *18,* 165–168.

Canestrari, R. E. Age changes in acquisition. In G. A. Talland (Ed.), *Human aging and behavior.* New York: Academic Press, 1968.

Carroll, K., & Gray, K. Memory development: An approach to the mentally impaired elderly in the long-term care setting. *International Journal of Aging and Human Development,* 1981, *13,* 15–35.

Cermak, L. S. Comments on imagery as a therapeutic mnemonic. In L. W. Poon et al. (Eds.), *New directions in memory and aging: Proceedings of the George A. Talland Memorial Conference.* Hillsdale, NJ: Erlbaum, 1980.

Cohen, G. Language comprehension in old age. *Cognitive Psychology,* 1979, *11,* 412–429.

Cohen, G. Inferential reasoning in old age. *Cognition,* 1981, *9,* 59–72.

Craik, F. I. M. Age differences in human memory. In J. E. Birren & K. W. Schaie (Eds.), *Handbook of the psychology of aging.* New York: Van Nostrand Reinhold, 1977.

Denney, N. W. Clustering in middle and old age. *Developmental Psychology,* 1974, *10,* 471–475.

Eisdorfer, C., Nowlin, J., & Wilkie, F. Improvement of learning in the aged by modification of autonomic nervous system activity. *Science,* 1970, *170,* 1327–1329.

Erber, J. T. Age differences in learning and memory on a digit-symbol substitution task. *Experimental Aging Research,* 1976, *2,* 45–53.

Fozard, J. L. The time for remembering. In L. W. Poon (Ed.), *Aging in the 1980s: Psychological issues.* Washington, DC: American Psychological Association, 1980.

Gladis, M. Age differences in repeated learning tasks in schizophrenic subjects. *Journal of Abnormal and Social Psychology,* 1964, *68,* 437–441.

Gordon, S. K., & Clark, W. C. Application of signal detection theory to prose recall and recognition in elderly and young adults. *Journal of Gerontology,* 1974, *29,* 64–72.

Hulicka, I. M., & Grossman, J. L. Age group comparisons for the use of mediators in paired-associate learning. *Journal of Gerontology,* 1967, *22,* 46–51.

Hultsch, D. F. Adult age differences in the organization of free recall. *Developmental Psychology,* 1969, *1,* 673–678.

Hultsch, D. F. Organization and memory in adulthood. *Human Development,* 1971, *14,* 16–29. (a)

Hultsch, D. F. Adult age differences in free classification and free recall. *Developmental Psychology,* 1971, *4,* 338–342. (b)

Hultsch, D. F. Learning to learn in adulthood. *Journal of Gerontology,* 1974, *29,* 302–308.

Kahn, R. L. Psychological aspects of aging. In I. Rossman (Ed.), *Clinical geriatrics.* Philadelphia: Lippincott; 1971.

Kahn, R. L., Zarit, S. H., Hilbert, N. M., & Niederche, G. Memory complaint and impairment in the aged: The effects of depression and altered brain function. *Archives of General Psychiatry,* 1975, *32,* 1569–1573.

Labouvie-Vief, G. Toward optimizing cognitive competence in later life. *Educational Gerontology,* 1976, *1,* 75–92.

Labouvie-Vief, G. Adult cognitive development: In search of alternative interpretations. *Merrill-Palmer Quarterly,* 1977, *23,* 227–263.

Labouvie-Vief, G., & Gonda, J. N. Cognitive strategy training and intellectual performance in the elderly. *Journal of Gerontology,* 1976, *31,* 327–332.

Lachman, J. L., & Lachman, R. Age and actualization of world knowledge. In L. W. Poon et al. (Eds.), *New directions in memory and aging: Proceedings of the George A. Talland Memorial Conference.* Hillsdale, NJ: Erlbaum, 1980.

Langer, E. J., Rodin, J., Beck, P., Weinman, C., & Spitzer, L. Environmental determinants of memory improvement in late adulthood. *Journal of Personality and Social Psychology*, 1979, *37*, 2003–2013.

Laurence, M. W. Age differences in performance and subjective organization in the free recall of pictorial material. *Canadian Journal of Psychology*, 1966, *20*, 388–399.

Levin, J. R., Yussen, S. R., DeRose, T. M., & Pressley, M. Developmental changes in assessing recall and recognition memory. *Developmental Psychology*, 1977, *13*, 608–615.

Lowenthal, M. F., Berkman, P. L., Buehler, J. A., Pierce, R. C., Robinson, B. C., & Trier, M. L. *Aging and mental disorder in San Francisco*. San Francisco: Jossey-Bass, 1967.

Mason, S. E., & Smith, A. D. Imagery in the aged. *Experimental Aging Research*, 1977, *3*, 17–32.

Meyer, B. J. F., & Rice, G. E. Information recalled from prose by young, middle, and old adult readers. *Experimental Aging Research*, 1981, 7, 253–268.

Monge, R. H. Learning in the adult years: Set or rigidity. *Human Development*, 1969, *12*, 131–140.

Monge, R. H., & Hultsch, D. F. Paired-associate learning as a function of adult age and the length of the anticipation and inspection intervals. *Journal of Gerontology*, 1971, *26*, 157–162.

Mueller, H., Ranklin, J. L., & Carlomusto, M. Adult age differences in free recall as a function of basis of organization and method of presentation. *Journal of Gerontology*, 1979, *34*, 375–380.

Murphy, M. D., Sanders, R. E., Gabriesheski, A. S., & Schmitt, F. A. Metamemory in the aged. *Journal of Gerontology*, 1981, *36*, 185–193.

Neugarten, B. L. Personality and aging. In J. E. Birren & K. W. Schaie (Eds.), *Handbook of the psychology of aging*. New York: Van Nostrand Reinhold, 1977.

Paivio, A. Strategies in language learning. In M. Pressley & J. R. Levin (Eds.), *Cognitive strategy research: Educational applications*. New York: Springer-Verlag, 1983.

Perlmutter, M. What is memory aging the aging of? *Developmental Psychology*, 1978, *14*, 330–345.

Pezdek, K., & Miceli, L. Life-span differences in memory integration as a function of processing time. *Developmental Psychology*, 1982, *18*, 485–490.

Plemons, J. K., Willis, S. L., & Baltes, P. B. Modifiability of fluid intelligence in aging: A short-term longitudinal training approach. *Journal of Gerontology*, 1978, *33*, 711–717.

Poon, L. W., Fozard, J. L., Cermak, L. S., Arenberg, D., & Thompson, L. W. (Eds.), *New directions in memory and aging: Proceedings of the George A. Talland Memorial Conference*. Hillsdale, NJ: Erlbaum, 1980.

Poon, L. W., Fozard, J. L., Paulshock, D., & Thomas, J. C. A questionnaire assessment of age differences in retention of recent and remote events. *Experimental Aging Research*, 1979, *5*, 401–411.

Poon, L. W., Fozard, J. L., & Treat, N. J. From clinical and research findings on memory to intervention programs. *Experimental Aging Research*, 1978, *4*, 235–255.

Poon, L. W., & Walsh-Sweeney, L. Effects of bizarre and interacting imagery on learning and retrieval of the aged. *Experimental Aging Research,* 1981, *7,* 65–70.

Poon, L. W., Walsh-Sweeney, L., & Fozard, J. L. Memory skill training for the elderly: Salient issues on the use of imagery mnemonics. In L. W. Poon et al. (Eds.), *New directions in memory and aging: Proceedings of the George A. Talland Memorial Conference.* Hillsdale, NJ: Erlbaum, 1980, 461–484.

Powell, A. H., Jr., Eisdorfer, C., & Bogdonoff, M. D. Physiologic response patterns observed in a learning task. *Archives of General Psychiatry,* 1964, *10,* 192–195.

Pressley, M. Imagery and children's learning: Putting the picture in developmental perspective. *Review of Educational Research,* 1977, *47,* 585–622.

Pressley, M., & Dennis-Rounds, J. Transfer of a mnemonic keyword strategy at two age levels. *Journal of Educational Psychology,* 1980, *72,* 575–582.

Robertson-Tchabo, E. A., Hausman, C. P., & Arenberg, D. A classical mnemonic for older learners: A trip that works! *Educational Gerontology,* 1976, *1,* 215–226.

Sanders, R. E., Murphy, M. D., Schmitt, F. A., & Walsh, K. K. Age differences in free recall rehearsal strategies. *Journal of Gerontology,* 1980, *35,* 550–558.

Schaie, K. W. Translations in gerontology—from lab to life, intellectual functioning. *American Psychologist,* 1974, *29,* 802–807.

Schaie, K. W. External validity in the assessment of intellectual development in adulthood. *Journal of Gerontology,* 1978, *33,* 691–701.

Schaie, K. W., & Baltes, P. B. Some faith helps to see the forest: A final comment on the Horn and Donaldson myth of the Baltes-Schaie position on adult intelligence. *American Psychologist,* 1977, *32,* 1118–1120.

Schmitt, F. A., Murphy, M. D., & Sanders, R. E. Training older adult free recall rehearsal strategies. *Journal of Gerontology,* in press.

Schonfield, D. Theoretical nuances and practical old questions: The psychology of aging. *Canadian Psychologist,* 1972, *13,* 252–266.

Smith, A. D. The interaction between age and list length in free recall. *Journal of Gerontology,* 1979, *34,* 381–387.

Squire, L. R. Remote memory as affected by aging. *Neuropsychologia,* 1974, *12,* 429–435.

Sterns, H. L., & Sanders, R. E. Training and education of the elderly. In R. R. Turner & H. W. Reese (Eds.), *Life-span developmental psychology/intervention.* New York: Academic Press, 1980.

Taub, H. A. Memory span, practice and aging. *Journal of Gerontology,* 1973, *28,* 335–338.

Taub, H. A., & Long, M. K. The effects of practice on short-term memory of young and old subjects. *Journal of Gerontology,* 1972, *27,* 494–499.

Treat, N. J., Poon, L. W., & Fozard, J. L. Age, imagery, and practice in paired-associate learning. *Experimental Aging Research,* 1981, *7,* 337–342.

Treat, N. J., Poon, L. W., Fozard, J. L., & Popkin, S. J. Toward applying cognitive skill training to memory problems. *Experimental Aging Research,* 1978, *4,* 305–320.

Treat, N. J., & Reese, H. W. Age, pacing and imagery in paired-associate learning. *Developmental Psychology,* 1976, *12,* 119–124.

Walsh, D. A., & Thompson, L. W. Age differences in visual sensory memory. *Journal of Gerontology,* 1978, *33,* 383–387.

Warrington, E. K., & Sanders, H. The fate of old memories. *Quarterly Journal of Experimental Psychology,* 1971, *23,* 432–442.

Warrington, E. K., & Silberstein, M. A questionnaire technique for investigating very long term memory. *Quarterly Journal of Experimental Psychology,* 1970, *22,* 508–512.

Winograd, E., & Simon, E. W. Visual memory and imagery in the aged. In L. W. Poon et al. (Eds.), *New directions in memory and aging: Proceedings of the George A. Talland Memorial Conference.* Hillsdale, NJ: Erlbaum, 1980.

Wright, R. E. Adult age similarities in free recall output order and strategies. *Journal of Gerontology,* 1982, *37,* 76–79.

Zarit, S. H., Cole, K. D., & Guider, R. L. Memory training strategies and subjective complaints of memory in the aged. *The Gerontologist,* 1981, *21,* 158–164.

Part II
Cognitive Strategies
and Special Populations

There has been a rapid growth in knowledge in recent years about the psychological lives of retarded and learning disabled children, with concomitant increases in understanding about how to devise strategies that will aid these types of children. Borkowski and Büchel, Worden, and Day present here the most recent thinking on the use of strategies with the intellectually handicapped. In doing so, they survey a broad range of theory that has been offered about cognitive functioning in the intellectually handicapped, presenting evaluative commentary about potential directions that follow from these theories.

Borkowski and Büchel discuss research efforts aimed at producing durable and general memory skills in the retarded, noting that efforts to date have generally failed. The authors offer a compelling critique of traditional research approaches to the use of strategies by the retarded, arguing that previous studies have not been very analytical and were often poorly controlled. On a more optimistic note, they review recent research that has been more successful in promoting strategy maintenance and generalization. Borkowski and Büchel discuss a number of studies that suggest that knowledge about strategies is related to continued strategy use by retardates. Transfer research in a variety of areas—mathematics, prose comprehension, vocational training, and language acquisition—is discussed in order to emphasize the importance of determining how to produce generalizable strategies.

Worden's discussion of strategy usage by learning-disabled children begins with a review of the definitions of learning disability, and then proceeds to review studies of learning disabled children's perceptual and linguistic skills, selective attention, short-term memory, long-term memory, and metamemory. Worden concludes that the memory deficits of learning-disabled children are often due to short-term memory disabilities. She makes the case that a critical task for memory researchers during the next decade will be to determine the nature of short-term memory deficits (e.g., metastrategic versus structural). Worden also discusses how memory strategy research may help to reveal more about these short-term problems.

Day outlines a Soviet-based perspective on children with learning problems. With a little help from another person, a child can often do more than (s)he could do without assistance. Vygotsky has argued that what a child can do today with assistance (defined as the "zone of proximal development") is a good indication of tomorrow's accomplishments by the child. According to this Soviet perspective, measures of the zone reflect the intellectual potential of a child better than any measure based solely on the child's unassisted performance. Day considers how zone ideas might be useful in assessing retarded and learning-disabled children. She considers research that has already been conducted within a zone framework, and she also makes suggestions for additional work that is needed to validate zone-of-proximal-development notions. In doing this, she makes many suggestions about potential evaluations of Vygotsky's theory of cognitive development, which is based on social interactions and their internalization as the foundation of intelligence.

5. Learning and Memory Strategies in the Mentally Retarded

John G. Borkowski and Fredi P. Büchel

The development and use of strategic skills may well be the most researched topic in the broad areas of learning and memory in the mentally retarded (see Detterman, 1979; Ellis, 1979). Interest in control processing in the retarded was spurred by the theoretical insights of Norman Ellis (1970). Having pioneered work on structural deficits in retarded learning (Ellis, 1963), he began to shift his research focus in the late 1960s to rehearsal processes as key factors in explaining the memory failures of retarded children. Ellis (1970) concluded that differential performance of mentally retarded and nonretarded individuals on memory tasks was due to the former's failure to use active rehearsal strategies. For instance, retarded individuals recalled as many items as nonretarded individuals on the last few positions of a serial list, but significantly fewer items on the early positions of the list. It is important to note that the earlier items require active rehearsal processing for good recall. Since an increase in exposure time did not noticeably enhance memory for earlier items for retarded individuals, Ellis (1970) concluded that rehearsal deficiencies characterized the encoding processes of the mentally retarded.

A flurry of research activity on strategic behavior in the retarded followed Ellis's 1970 paper. Research was stimulated by a study showing dramatic improvement in memory performance following the integrated training of encoding and decoding strategies on a serial probe task (Butterfield, Wambold, & Belmont, 1973). The overall research orientation was directed by multistage models of memory (cf. Atkinson & Shiffrin, 1968); the objective was to improve memory in the retarded by improving control processing. Summaries of the early research programs on rehearsal strategies, categorization, imagery, metacognition, and executive functioning in the retarded can be found in recent texts (Ellis, 1979; Brooks, Sperber, & McCauley, in press) and chapters (Borkowski, Peck, & Damberg, in press; Campione & Brown, 1977; Sternberg, 1981a).

The optimism of the 1970s, reflecting the hope that learning disabilities might be ameliorated through strategy training, has diminished in recent years. Several interrelated factors account for this decline:

1. Attempts at producing durable and general skills that improve retarded learning have proven time-consuming and difficult to achieve (Borkowski & Cavanaugh, 1979).
2. Theoretical speculation about the nature of mental retardation has returned to the search for structural deficits, especially in isolating elementary information processing components linked to retardation (see Borys, Spitz, & Dorans, 1982; Clark & Detterman, 1981).
3. Instructional research has not resulted in dramatic applied nor theoretical achievements. Basic research has often been theoretically shallow, simply demonstrating that learning will improve following strategy training (e.g., Borkowski & Cavanaugh, 1979). More applied programs, aimed at remediating learning handicaps in the retarded, have not produced large-scale general improvements in cognitive or academic skills (e.g., Page & Grandon, 1981).

Although these developments have tended to diminish the quantity of research on learning problems in the mentally retarded, we contend that the instructional approach to strategy training has much to offer in augmenting our understanding of the nature of mental retardation and its amelioration through education (Sternberg, 1981a). A hiatus in research momentum prompts our reflection on what has been accomplished in recent years and on the directions that research on strategy training might take in the next decade.

In the remainder of this chapter, we will reflect on the adequacy of research designs for studying strategic behavior in the mentally retarded; use this perspective to analyze recent research reflecting concerns about strategy generalization, metacognitive processes, and applied issues in strategy-training research; discuss theoretical aspects of the strategy-training paradigm, especially its relationship to aptitude-by-treatment interactions and to models of cognition; and finally, describe a broader methodological and theoretical framework in which instructional research might find renewal.

Toward a Paradigm for Strategy-Training Research

Paris, Newman, and McVey (in press) have characterized the typical instructional design used to teach strategies to young children. During an initial session, a child is asked to remember a series of words or pictures. No strategy instructions are given. Only spontaneous strategic behaviors are recorded. During a second session, the child is instructed to label, rehearse, sort, imagine, or use some other experimenter-selected strategy. The control group learns the same material without the aid of instructions. Shortly after training, a maintenance task is given and the use and the effectiveness of the instructed strategy are reassessed. For both normal and handicapped learners, this standard strategy-training paradigm has a number of inadequacies if the research is aimed at gaining meaningful insights about learning and memory deficiencies.

A strategy, by definition, must be goal directed (Paris et al., in press). That is, a strategy is always used to enhance performance on a particular task or set of tasks. Merely copying the strategies of an experimenter without understanding the reasons for the strategies is neither intelligent nor effective in the long run. Parroting the teacher or trainer represents a fundamental failure—a failure in understanding the cause-and-effect relationship between a learning goal and the choice of an effective strategy (Flavell, 1979). The newly learned strategy will be neither durable nor general. In this regard, Paris and his colleagues have provided a useful methodological suggestion, one missing in most training studies: Assess the child's perceptions of and knowledge about mnemonically relevant actions. In short, it is essential to measure a child's metacognitions (i.e., her knowledge about strategies and control processes) and beliefs about a strategy's usefulness, in addition to obtaining traditional process and performance measurements (Belmont & Butterfield, 1977).

Often there are difficulties in interpreting the precise instructional effects that occur in "minimal-training" designs. Few published studies have isolated the precise components of instructional packages so as to allow a determination of the factors critical in producing behavioral changes. The majority of instructional studies reviewed by Borkowski and Cavanaugh (1979) contained multiple components in their respective strategy-training packages, any component of which might have contributed to the posttreatment outcome.

One reservation should be noted here in arguing for the decomposition of elements in a training package. At times, the analyses of isolated components is theoretically meaningless. That is, when two components are functionally related, then the manipulation of only one of them may change the phenomenon, rendering it uninterpretable. Theory needs to guide the analysis of the effectiveness of the individual components in a training package.

Often control groups have not been used wisely, resulting in designs that reveal simply that some training is better than none. O'Leary and Borkovec's (1978) insightful suggestions about the use of the "best available treatment" as an effective control condition have generally been ignored in instructional research. Training packages designed to teach a specific learning strategy result in side effects such as increased attention or renewed motivation because they inevitably involve "special" handling or produce "special" behavioral effects, which in turn influence behavioral outcomes. Side effects are probably responsible for a sizable portion of most treatment-related gains. We simply are unaware of the exact portion given the usual methodologies employed in strategy training with the retarded (Borkowski & Cavanaugh, 1979).

A major weakness in strategy-training research conducted in the early 1970s has recently been altered—a failure to use transfer tests to assess strategy durability and generalization (see Borkowski & Cavanaugh, 1979). Although methodologies and research designs have improved immensely in recent years (Burger, Blackman, Clark, & Reis, 1982), few new theoretical insights have been generated to inspire research hypotheses about processes underlying strategy transfer. For example, if Flavell's (1979) theoretical position is tenable—that training effects will not prove durable if a child lacks understanding of why the trained strategy should be employed—then components of "awareness" and "understanding" need to be taught and assessed as standard features of strategy-training paradigms (Borkowski, Reid, & Kurtz, in press; Peterson & Swing, 1983, see Chapters 1 and 2 of this volume for additional commentary on generalization).

In summary, we have suggested that strategy-training research should be analyzed from the following perspectives:

1. What specific components of a training package were functional? How are these components to be theoretically interpreted?
2. Was the control condition adequate? Did it motivate the child to attend and learn to the same extent as the treatment condition?
3. Were strategy durability (i.e., the maintenance of the strategy on a task identical to the training task) and strategy generality (i.e., the use of the strategy on a new task) assessed? Was the common underlying process in the training and transfer tasks camoflaged by surface dissimilarities (Borkowski & Cavanaugh, 1979)?
4. Has knowledge about specific and general strategies, and beliefs about their utility, been assessed prior to and following the training routine? Was information about the strategy's value included as an essential component in the training package, and did prior knowledge about other types of strategic behavior account for individual differences in the transfer of the newly acquired strategy?

These perspectives provide a framework for analyzing recent research on strategy training with the mentally retarded and help point the way to new research issues and directions.

Research on Strategy Acquisition and Transfer

Strategy-training studies with the mentally retarded can be classified into two general types: (1) those studies using active strategy-inducing training procedures in which the child is explicitly taught strategies, perhaps given knowledge about their usefulness, and encouraged to use them on laboratory and/or academic tasks; and (2) those studies using passive teaching procedures in which a mnemonic aid is demonstrated by the experimenter but in which the child neither actively manipulates the strategy on practice tasks nor is taught the long-run utility of the strategy. A number of studies suggest that retention and transfer of passively instructed strategies will be minimal for mentally retarded individuals (e.g., Mar & Glidden, 1977). In contrast, there are reports of long-term retention and transfer of strategies following active meaningful training (e.g., Wanschura & Borkowski, 1975). It is to the search for evidence about processes that produce strategy generalization in the retarded that we now direct attention in a review of the most relevant literature.

Searching for Strategy Generalization

Strategy generalization, with both normal and retarded children, is difficult to achieve (see Borkowski & Cavanaugh, 1979). Only a handful of studies have reported durable transsituational strategy transfer. In this section we discuss a variety of training studies in the area of mental retardation. The aim is to isolate the essential aspects of training that influence successful strategy generalization. We begin with an important study by Earl Butterfield and John Belmont that achieved remarkable improvements in deliberate strategic memory following thorough strategy training.

Butterfield et al. (1973) found large individual differences in memory processes and performance between mentally retarded and chronological age (CA) -matched adolescents. By extensive systematic instruction about both rehearsal and retrieval strategies, pretraining memory deficits in the retarded were ameliorated following strategy training. In fact, trained subjects actually performed better than their untrained CA-matched normal counterparts on a self-paced, six-item single-exposure recall task. Butterfield et al. (1973) suggested that mentally retarded individuals not only suffer from a rehearsal deficit, but additionally fail to properly sequence rehearsal and retrieval techniques. Typically, they fail to coordinate multiple retrieval strategies and integrate retrieval strategies with acquisition strategies. Given these processing deficiencies, it seems clear that one objective for training research is the enhancement of executive mechanisms so that selecting, sequencing, and coordinating of rehearsal and retrieval strategies are synchronized in order to improve retention.

Bilsky, Whittemore, and Walker (1982) assessed the effectiveness of a multi-session training approach, teaching mentally retarded adolescents to discover and utilize categorical list structure. As in the Butterfield et al. (1973) study, both en-coding and retrieval components of categorization were trained. A fading technique was used to transfer strategy use from experimenter to subject. Strategy-trained subjects achieved the recall criterion at transfer in fewer trials than untrained control subjects. In addition, more trained than control subjects eventually mas-tered the 24-word list, allowing the conclusion that multisession training of a complex strategy, including both categorical encoding and retrieval components, facilitated the acquisition of a new word list. Training sensitized the retarded subjects to employ category-based organization and induced many of them to use category names deliberately to aid recall. When trained retarded adolescents were compared with nonretarded peers, two interesting differences emerged: (1) Re-tarded subjects were markedly slower than normal subjects in reaching the recall criterion, and (2) normal subjects appeared to be using a variety of strategies in combination with categorical grouping, whereas retarded subjects relied exclusively on categorization. Normal subjects were able to master the list rapidly by coordinating several strategic approaches. Retarded subjects learned more slowly with what appeared to be a single type of strategic approach, categorization. On the whole, the findings of Bilsky et al. (1982) are consistent with a principle of organization and learning in which categorical organization facilitates memory processing but is not essential to memory performance. Categorization is most beneficial to those retarded persons who do not possess a variety of alternative strategies, any one of which would be effective in solving the task at hand.

Wanschura and Borkowski (1975) compared different groups of moderately retarded children on a paired-associate task in which prepositional mediators (*in*, *on*, or *under*) were provided for some, all, or none of the pairs. Results demonstrated unusually large individual differences, especially on an uninstructed transfer task designed to assess the maintenance of the acquired strategy. Those subjects trained to use the mediational strategy showed two types of transfer: 100% strategy maintenance or 0% maintenance on the nonprompted transfer test. It was concluded that individual differences in knowledge about a strategy's potential applications and its utility must be carefully monitored when training the mentally retarded. Simply using a strategy during acquisition may not be sufficient if the aim is for the child to apply it spontaneously during transfer.

A study by Reichhart, Cody, and Borkowski (1975) showed the importance of carefully monitoring individual differences when training retarded subjects to use learning strategies. In one of the few studies that compared a variety of study strategies, Reichhart et al. (1975) assessed the effects of clustering instructions, cumulative rehearsal, and a combined cumulative-clustering strategy on learning a nine-item categorized list of pictures. Subjects were assigned to one of two experimental groups (cumulative rehearsal or cumulative-clustering rehearsal) or to control groups (uninstructed or instructed in the use of clustering), with the groups balanced for higher functioning (mean IQ = 55) and lower functioning (mean IQ = 40) mentally retarded adolescents. On the immediate transfer test, the best recall was found in the cumulative rehearsal condition. On the short-term transfer test, both experimental groups learned more rapidly than the control groups. Further analyses revealed that the overall results were due to dramatically different processing abilities in the two retarded subgroups. Lower functioning individuals failed to transfer the strategy in either rehearsal condition, even immediately after training, whereas retarded individuals with IQs of about 50 used the cumulative-rehearsal strategy with good efficiency. These findings suggest that individual differences among mentally retarded subjects must be fully understood and assessed if we are to explain the extreme variability in strategy transfer demonstrated by Reichhart et al. (1975), Wanschura and Borkowski (1975), Butterfield et al. (1973), and Belmont, Ferretti, and Mitchell (in press). It is clear that retarded people bring vastly different learning histories to a training experience. These histories are themselves causal factors in strategy generalization (Borkowski & Kurtz, in press).

Production deficiencies are commonplace in research on control processes in the mentally retarded. The concept refers to the failure to use a mediational strategy that is known to be part of the learner's repertoire of skills. Turnure, Buium, and Thurlow (1976) posited that production deficiencies are not viable descriptions of learning difficulties in the retarded, especially if "deficient" children can easily be taught to use more appropriate strategies. Mentally retarded children were presented with an interrogative strategy to aid paired-associate learning. Interrogative cues provided an opportunity for greater semantic analysis; consequently, recall was improved. Similarly, Kendall, Borkowski, and Cavanaugh (1980) found transfer of an acquired, self-generated interrogative strategy to a nonprompted maintenance task by educable mentally retarded (EMR) children. These two sets of findings question the conceptual utility of "production deficiencies." If adequate instruction can elevate memory performance and maintain that performance on a transfer test at some later point in time, the outcome is due more to a failure in the teacher's full and complete instructions than a "flaw" in the child's mental apparatus.

Burger, Blackman, Holmes, and Zetlin (1978) showed that mentally retarded children, given explicit training on a sorting strategy for lists of pictures, performed comparably to nonretarded children 1 year above the retarded group in mental age (MA). Retention of the sorting strategy occurred on a transfer test 3 weeks following training. Once again, it appears that explicit training resulted in improved performance by retarded individuals, a result consistent with findings by Turner et al. (1976) and Kendall et al. (1980). More recently, Burger and her colleagues trained a self-managed verbal abstraction strategy, in which children were taught to use attributes of pictures as abstract representations and to "check out" the abstractions across a set of three exemplars for their appropriateness. In addition to trained and untrained EMR subjects, single and multiple formats were included in an effort to enhance strategy generalization. Although the training program with both formats produced "near" generalization (on a verbal dyads task), no "far" generalization (on a multiple-classification task) was observed. The reason that far generalization did not occur may be that an element was missing in training—that is, one of the components necessary to solve the multiple-classification task was not included in the training package. Two components required for the solution of the multiple-classification task are verbal abstracting and detecting simultaneity of similarity; the latter refers to the possibility that a particular stimulus may contain attributes characteristic of more than one conceptual category (Burger et al., 1982). For example, a knife can be both "found in a kitchen" and "a weapon." The verbal abstraction component was trained to a high level of proficiency; the detecting of the simultaneity of similarity component was not trained. Burger et al. (1982) concluded that reliable generalization effects for mentally retarded people will be obtained only if all required strategy components are initially trained and only if the subjects are able to perceive the applicability of the trained strategy in the new task setting. We find in the work of Burger and her colleagues a theme consistent with other statements in recent retardation research: a learner must come to understand the limitations of the processing advantage conveyed by a specific strategy. This simple insight provides an important perspective from which to initiate strategy-training research.

Brown, Campione, and Barclay (1979) taught mentally retarded children to make recall-readiness estimations of their own memory capacities, a self-monitoring process. One year following original training on a list of items, older EMR children (mean MA = 8) not only maintained the recall-readiness strategy but also showed evidence for its generalization to gist recall of prose passages. Although this remarkable finding needs to be replicated and extended, Brown et al. (1979) have demonstrated that a general process, recall readiness, can be taught so as to induce retarded children to implement the strategy actively on a far transfer test.

Borys et al. (1982) tested institutionalized mentally retarded young adults and nonretarded 6-, 7-, 8-, and 10-year-olds on the Tower of Hanoi problem. These investigators were interested in assessing individual differences in problem solving as a function of the number of moves required for solution on the Tower of Hanoi problem. All subjects had difficulty in solving the standard seven-move problem, but showed dramatic improvements on the six-move problem. The investigators attributed this result to the fact that the seven-move problem requires a three-level depth of search, whereas the six-move problem requires only a one-level depth of search. Borys and her colleagues found that mentally retarded subjects generally had a limited search capacity, responsible for a maturational lag of about 1½ years. The maturational lag was most pronounced on the seven-move problem, and dissipated, probably as a result of ceiling effects, on the five-move problem for educable and borderline groups, and on the three-move problem for a trainable group of retarded adolescents. Additionally, subjects spontaneously solved problems in a easy-to-hard progression (e.g., first solving an experimenter-guided six-move problem and then applying the strategies to the seven-move problem). Borys et al. (1982) suggested that the use of superior strategies by the more mature groups is related to greater depth-of-search capacities, and that the limited search capacity of the mentally retarded is largely responsible for the pronounced maturational lag. The extent to which strategy instructions can be successfully applied to this deficit in problem solving is unknown, although Spitz would likely hypothesize that training attempts would prove futile given capacity limitations.

Along the lines of the Borys et al. study (1982), McCauley, Kellas, Dugas, and Devillis (1976) and Clark and Detterman (1981) have suggested that deficits in processes or structures other than rehearsal might be responsible for poorer short-term memory performance in mentally retarded individuals. For instance, Clark and Detterman (1981) found evidence supporting the view that architectural differences in capacity account for memory deficits observed when rehearsal has been eliminated. If architectural deficits underlie and determine a large portion of control processes, performance differences will not be easy to remediate through strategy training (Campione & Brown, 1978).

In summary, it appears that mentally retarded individuals typically have deficits in a wide range of strategy behaviors. However, a growing number of successful training studies, in which attention has been paid to both study strategies and coordinated retrieval techniques, suggests that deficits in memory may be reduced by providing the mentally retarded with adequate cognitive instructions—especially if explicit hints are given about how and when to generalize strategies to novel tasks (see Chapter 2 in this volume). It should be emphasized, however, that all of the training studies reviewed in this section, and in the early literature on strategy training (Borkowski & Cavanaugh, 1979), failed to meet the methodological and theoretical standards of the ideal instructional paradigm discussed earlier. Problems inherent in existing research designs include the following:

1. failure to use control conditions that increase attention and motivation to the same degree as in the treatment condition;
2. failure, in most cases, to use the "best available alternative" treatment as an additional baseline for judging the size and theoretical importance of treatment effects;
3. incomplete task analyses that often result in vague statements about the similarities in processing requirements of the training and transfer tasks;
4. neglect of the individual characteristics that each child brings to the training setting, such as metamemorial knowledge, beliefs about the importance of strategic effort and learning success, and the quality of superordinate executive skills.

It is to the latter issues that we now turn our attention in an attempt to understand more about the phenomenon of strategy generalization.

Feedback, Metacognition, and Executive Skills

Is explicit feedback about a strategy's usefulness a necessary component of strategy-training packages? Is it essential that knowledge about a wide variety of strategies and their respective utilities be part of a child's metamemory before a new strategy can be successfully taught? Is it critical that executive skills, such as strategy monitoring and revision, be trained in order to produce strategy generalization? Recent strategy-training research on feedback, metacognition, and executive functions leads us to answer affirmatively to all three questions.

In the late 1970s, two studies were conducted that provide interesting insights into the importance of metamemory, or knowledge about metamemory processes (Flavell, 1979), as both precursor and consequence of effective strategy use (cf. Burger et al., 1978; Kendall & Borkowski, Note 1). Both studies are instances of failures in strategy generalization with retarded children. What is instructive is that these failures occurred in the face of exceptionally thorough, prolonged strategy training and followed good strategy maintenance. We argue that an absence of mature metamemorial knowledge prior to training, in concert with an absence of explicit feedback about the general utility of the instructed strategies during training, were two important factors leading to the failures in strategy generalization.

Burger et al. (1978) taught a categorical sorting and retrieval strategy to normal and retarded adolescents during three sessions. Sizable training effects were found on a transfer test in terms of both performance and process measures. Six months later three tests were given: strategy maintenance; near generalization (a free-recall task similar to that used during maintenance except that the mode of presentation was switched from visual to auditory); and far generalization (a word elicitation task in which the subjects were told to generate three words that would go with a stimulus word). Although evidence of strategy maintenance was found after 6 months, no near or far generalization occurred. It appeared that the strategy had become "welded" to a specific task (Brown, 1978). In a subsequent study, training using multiple exemplars also failed to produce generalization (Burger et al., 1982). Prior knowledge about the use of superordinate processes as guides for strategy selection, modification, and invention—together with specific feedback about the utility of the strategy, its range of applicability, and its similarity to existing strategies—appear necessary for producing generalization.

In an attempt to shed light on the generalization problem, Kendall and Borkowski (Note 1) studied strategy transfer in EMR children after they had received traditional strategy training or self-instructional training. In both conditions, the basic strategies were identical: (1) an anticipation strategy for use on a serial-recall task with pictures (Brown & Barclay, 1976), and (2) a paraphrase strategy for use on a gist-recall task for sentences (Wark, 1968). Built into both strategies was a monitoring component, self-testing for recall readiness (Brown & Barclay, 1976). Maintenance tests were given 1 and 3 weeks following training. Generalization tests used by Brown et al. (1979)—gist recall for stories—were administered by a different experimenter each afternoon following the morning training or maintenance sessions.

Self-instructional routines, such as Meichenbaum's (1977), involve teaching the child to produce covert verbalizations concerning the following behaviors: (1) task definitions together with an inquiry about how to approach the task (e.g., "What do I do here? How do I do it?"); (2) behavioral or strategic guidance (e.g., "I do this first. . . . Now I do . . ."); (3) self-evaluation and coping (e.g., "That's okay, I'll try again"); and (4) self-reinforcement (e.g., "Very good! I'm really doing well!"). Self-instructional procedures not only force strategic awareness and conscious control over processing, but also provide an executive-oriented approach to learning, an approach applicable to many different memory and problem-solving situations. Given the paucity of successful strategy generalization studies, it was assumed that self-instruction training would be useful in producing generalization in that the self-instructional routines would equip the child with higher order processes such as strategy selection, monitoring, and modification. (See Chapters 10 and 11 of this volume, for additional descriptions of self-instructional approaches.)

Three weeks after training, Kendall and Borkowski (Note 1) found no differences between the traditional and self-instructional conditions, but both were dramatically superior to an uninstructed control condition. In contrast to strategy maintenance were the generalization data. No differences in recall or strategy use were found between the two strategy-trained groups and the control group on four of five generalization tests. Trained children generally failed to recognize that story recall could be enhanced by using the anticipation and paraphrasing strategies that existed in their repertoires of learning skills. The failures in long-term generalization by EMR adolescents may be understood in terms of two factors: immature metacognitive states and the absence of feedback about using superordinate processes to coordinate strategy use. In the sub-section that follows we will consider these factors in greater depth, focusing on the role of feedback in enhancing strategy transfer, metacognitive correlates of strategy use, and the training of executive skills in order to provide new perspectives on the problem of strategy generalization in mentally retarded individuals.

Feedback and Strategy Generalization. Feedback refers to information supplied to an individual concerning the accuracy of performance or the efficacy of a strategy. In cognitive-instructional research with normal children, the purpose of feedback is to increase the likelihood of strategy utilization during maintenance and generalization tests. For instance, Kennedy and Miller (1976) reported that verbal feedback following training of a rehearsal strategy significantly improved strategy maintenance. Borkowski, Levers, and Gruenenfelder (1976) found that a brief film depicting the correct use of an active mediational strategy preceding training enhanced strategy maintenance for first-grade children. Cavanaugh and Borkowski (1979) showed that feedback concerning a strategy's efficacy, administered following a maintenance task, improved task-specific metamemory. Asarnow and Meichenbaum (1979) included feedback in a self-instruction training package designed to teach a repetition-rehearsal strategy; impressive strategy maintenance was achieved and production deficiencies were eliminated. We believe that the role of feedback in instructional research is to enhance metamemorial knowledge about a strategy's utility. Feedback heightens metamemory by emphasizing the match between task demands, strategic actions, and successful performance, including the experience of doing well on a difficult task.

Belmont, Butterfield, and Borkowski (1978) successfully trained retarded adolescents to generalize a memorization method across a variety of similar memory tasks. On each of 50 trials subjects paced themselves through a list of seven different random letters, viewing each for 0.6 second in a separate window. No letter was repeated in a list, and no list was repeated in the series. The child was free to pause however long he or she wished before exposing each letter in sequence. Immediately after viewing the last letter in a list, the child attempted to execute whatever recall requirements were currently in force. We used four different recall requirements. The three/four circular recall task required the child to recall the last three letters in their order of presentation, followed by the first four in their proper order. The four/three circular task required the child to recall the last four letters and then the first three. The two/five task asked the subject to recall the last two and then the first five. In the position probe task, the child saw a probe letter immediately following the disappearance of the final letter that remained until he or she responded. Instead of verbally recalling letters, the child simply pushed the window where the last letter was thought to have appeared. Strategy training (a fast-finish study strategy for the last few letters in a series and cumulative rehearsal for the first set of letters) was provided for the first two tasks that required three/four or four/three circular recall. (This strategy is described in additional detail in Chapter 2.) A unique aspect of training was intensive feedback. On each training trial the child was shown how to evaluate the effectiveness of the fast-finish, cumulative rehearsal method on recall during the previous test trial. Following training, generalization of the strategy was assessed on two/five circular recall and position probe tests.

The combination of careful attention to the specific components of the strategy, coupled with ample feedback on the effectiveness of the trainee's efforts, led to immediate strategy generalization and to the frequent use of the strategy on a new task presented 2 weeks following training. It is interesting to note that generalization was more apparent on later than on early trials during the final test. Apparently, the reinstatement of the acquired strategy took time to incorporate into the learning process because of changes in task demands.

Another approach to feedback research is to embellish the strategy with related information prior to training. A test of the importance of preliminary information on the potential utility of a strategy was conducted by Lawson and Flueloep (1980). Two groups of retarded adults were trained to use a cumulative rehearsal strategy with a serial-recall task. One of the groups was given additional information prior to training: "In this remembering task we will tell you a way to remember better. We will give you a rule and this rule will help you to remember more and more pictures. You can use the rule to help you remember other lists of things." Note that these preliminary instructions contained two elements: (1) a statement about the value of the strategy for the task at hand and (2) a suggestion about the applicability of the strategy with new tasks. Those children who received the setting instructions showed significantly better recall performance after 1 week than those children who simply received strategy training. Although it is surprising that minimal setting information, such as that provided by Lawson and Flueloep (1980), would produce sizable recall differences, similar results were obtained by Kennedy and Miller (1976), who found improvements in recall following a few brief sentences about the value of the strategy. Information about a strategy's effectiveness—whether given prior to or following strategy training—is an important factor in producing strategy maintenance.

A somewhat contradictory set of findings was provided by Kramer and Engle (1981). They failed to find facilitating effects from awareness-inducing instructions with EMR children. Instructions informed the subjects that they would learn "to break a list into smaller pieces and practice saying the names of items over and over." In addition, feedback about the relationship between strategy use and good recall was given following training. It should be noted, however, that rehearsal and awareness training produced significantly longer study times on a recognition test for strategy generalization, even though maintenance recall was not different for rehearsal-only and rehearsal-awareness conditions (Kramer & Engle, 1981).

Taken together, studies with young normal children and retarded adolescents lead us to conclude that feedback influences strategy durability by increasing the child's knowledge about, and understanding of, a strategy's value in improving learning. Feedback enhances metamemory, increasing a child's tendency to be strategic and effortful in future problem-solving endeavors.

Metamemory and Strategy Use. Engle and Nagle (1979) suggested that two factors responsible for memory problems in retarded children are deficits in the amount and complexity of knowledge that the retarded child has about memory processes and the number of automatically elicited access routes to this information. Flavell (1979) has labeled this special kind of knowledge *metamemory*. We shall return to the issue of automatic access when we discuss theoretical issues related to strategy-training research. It is to the former consideration, metamemory in the mentally retarded, that we now turn our attention.

We have hypothesized that feedback has its effect on transfer by enriching metamemory (Borkowski & Kurtz, in press). As an initial step in documenting the importance of prior metamemory knowledge on subsequent strategy training, we assessed the validity of the concept by examining metamemory-strategy-recall connections with EMR children in transfer contexts (Kendall et al., 1980). Our hypothesis was that metamemorial knowledge would predict the maintenance and generalization of an acquired interrogative strategy on paired-associate tasks. During training, children learned pairs of unrelated items by posing questions about them, then answering the inquiries with semantic elaborations associating the main attributes of each item together. For example, if the to-be-learned pair was *nurse-toaster,* the child might say, "Why is the *nurse* holding the *toaster*?" Eventually, a relationship might be formed: "The *nurse* is holding the *toaster* so she can make toast for the sick people."

Two groups of EMR children (mean MA = 6 and 8) participated in pretest and posttest metamemory assessments, the Story-List, Study Plan, and Preparation-Object items from the Kreutzer, Leonard, and Flavell (1975) questionnaire; four training sessions in which a four-part self-instructional study strategy was taught; a long-term test for retention of the pairs learned during the final training session; a strategy maintenance test with a new paired-associate task (and new experimenter); and a strategy generalization test involving lists of word triads. Metamemory data were quantified as in an earlier study by Cavanaugh and Borkowski (1980). An index of strategy use, based on probe tests at transfer, assessed the extent of the elaborations for each pair immediately after recall trials.

The most important results were the significant correlations relating quality of elaborations at strategy transfer to metamemory pretest ($r = .50$) and to metamemory posttest ($r = .46$). Metamemory was related to both recall performance and strategy use during transfer but not during strategy acquisition. The point to emphasize is that individual differences in prior levels of memory knowledge among a group of EMR children predicted subsequent differences in strategy use at transfer. One of the more interesting questions concerning metamemory theory arises out of these correlational data: Is metamemory a prerequisite for problem solving guided by superordinate and subordinate processes? These basic research questions may eventually have implications for using cognitive theory as an aid in remediating learning and memory problems in the mentally retarded.

Executive Skills. The concept of executive functioning is operationally defined to be "when the subject spontaneously changes a control process or sequence of control processes as a reasonable response to an objective change in an information processing task" (Butterfield & Belmont, 1977, p. 284). In other words, if strategy A is used with task X, and if task Y is then introduced, the subject is said to employ executive functioning if strategy B replaces A. Or if strategy A is replaced by strategy B during the course of problem solving, the substitution is an instance of executive functioning. In a sense, a transfer test is indirectly a test of the adequacy of the executive system.

Belmont et al. (in press) have recently completed a study on executive functioning in the mentally retarded. Forty untrained mildly retarded and 32 untrained nonretarded adolescent subjects were given eight trials of practice on a self-paced memory problem with lists of letters or words. Subjects were required to order their recall, first giving terminal list items, then the initial items. Subgroups of solvers and nonsolvers were identified at each IQ level on the basis of recall accuracy. Interestingly, direct measures of mnemonic activity showed that solvers at both IQ levels increasingly fit a theoretically ideal memorization method. Solvers invented the "best" input strategy to meet the demands of ordered recall over trials. That is, on early trials for both IQ levels, fit to the ideal strategy was uncorrelated with recall accuracy. On late trials, however, strategy fit and recall were highly correlated at each IQ level and across levels. At neither IQ level did nonsolvers show mature strategic inventions. The results support a problem-solving explanation of individual differences in the memory performance of retarded and nonretarded people. Large individual differences in strategy selection and invention were found in both samples. Some retarded adolescents were extremely successful in their use of executive skills to create an encoding strategy sufficient to meet the demands of the recall requirements without explicit aid from the experimenter (Belmont et al., in press). These findings suggest that executive skills are important to efficient and effective learning in the retarded.

Applied Research on Strategy Transfer

At the time of our 1978 review of strategy-training research with the mentally retarded, only a few applied studies had been conducted (Borkowski & Cavanaugh, 1979). Since then, a number of new projects have been undertaken and several older research programs have continued to produce important results. In this section we selectively review research on strategy training in the following areas: mathematics, comprehension, vocational training, language learning, and instrumental enrichment.

Mathematics. Johnston, Whitman, and Johnson (1980) used a multiple baseline-across-subjects design to analyze the effects of two self-instructional training packages on rate and accuracy of mathematics problem solving. Following baseline assessments, three EMR children were given self-instructions for addition problems requiring regrouping. The training sequence focused on (1) asking questions about the specific demands of each task, (2) listing the steps necessary to complete all of the components of the problem, (3) self-control statements directing attention and monitoring speed, (4) coping statements to handle errors, and (5) self-reinforcement to maintain task persistence. Table 5-1 contains one example of the self-instruction sequence for addition. Following the addition phase, self-instructional training for subtraction problems with regrouping was introduced for each child.

All three children increased their efficiency on addition and subtraction problems requiring regrouping during training. Less pronounced improvements in accuracy were also found. According to the teacher's reports, the children showed

Table 5-1 Example of Self-instruction Training Sequence for Addition with Regrouping

	36
	+47

Q. What kind of a problem is this?

A. It's an add problem. I can tell by the sign.

Q. What do I do?

A. I start with the top number in the one's column and I add. Six and 7 (the child points to the 6 on the number line and counts down 7 spaces) is 13. Thirteen has two digits. That means I have to carry. This is hard so I go slowly. I put the 3 in the one's column (the child writes the 3 in the one's column in the answer) and the 1 in the ten's column (the child writes the 1 above the top number in the ten's column in the problem).

Q. Now what do I do?

A. I start with the top number in the ten's column. One add 3 (the child points to the 1 on the number line and counts down 3 spaces) is 4. Four add 4 (the child counts down 4 more spaces) is 8 (the child writes the 8 in the ten's column in the answer).

Q. I want to get it right so I check it. How do I check it?

A. I cover up my answer (the child covers the answer with a small piece of paper) and add again starting with the bottom number in the one's column. Seven add 6 (the child points to the 7 on the number line and counts down 6 spaces) is 13 (the child slides the piece of paper to the left and uncovers the 3; the child sees the 1 which he/she has written over the top number in the ten's column in the problem). Got it right. Four add 3 (the child points to the 4 on the number line and counts down 3 spaces) is 7. Seven add 1 (the child counts down 1 more space) is 8 (the child removes the small piece of paper so that the entire answer is visible). I got it right so I'm doing well. (If, by checking his/her work, the child finds an error, he/she says, "I got it wrong. I can fix it if I go slowly." The child then repeats the self-instruction sequence starting from the beginning.

Note. From "Teaching Addition and Subtraction to Mentally Retarded Children: A Self-Instructional Program" by M. B. Johnston, T. L. Whitman, and M. Johnson, *Applied Research in Mental Retardation,* 1980, *1,* 141–160. Copyright 1980 by Pergamon Press. Reprinted by permission.

noticeable improvements in math computation skills in the classroom. There is an important advantage to training math skills via a self-instructional approach: The teacher receives ongoing feedback from the child which allows rapid diagnosis of the child's specific points of difficulty (Johnston et al., 1980). We expect to see greater use of self-instructional procedures to teach mathematics skills.

Comprehension. Peleg and Moore (1982) studied the effectiveness of an advance organizer on written or orally presented prose passages with 96 EMR adolescents. With written passages the advance organizer improved recall. With oral presentation, however, the advance organizer produced a negative effect. Apparently, the organizer caused an added drain on memory in the oral condition where repetition of information was impossible. When presentation rate could be adjusted, as in the written condition, the advance organizer aided recall. Research on various types of teacher-supplied and self-generated organizers is desirable if we are to make inroads on the comprehension problems of the retarded.

Vocational Training and Metaknowledge. In a recent study of mentally retarded adults, knowledge of various learning principles and teaching techniques, such as the value of feedback, was assessed in the context of a simulated vocational training problem. Grover and Wight-Felske (Note 2) found that individual preferences about training modes interacted with treatment conditions. Preferences were assessed during an interview that followed a videotape depicting alternative teaching and learning techniques. Those subjects who selected visual demonstration plus verbal instruction and who were then instructed on a simulated vocational task (assembling a mechanical pulley) required fewer prompts than subjects who chose visual demonstration or verbal instruction alone. It should be noted that only 35% of the retarded adults realized that the combined instructions were optimal. Metamemorial awareness was also low in other areas. For instance, only 45% knew that repeating an instruction following an error was better than presenting it only once. These findings suggest that successful vocational training is dependent, in part, on a person's prior knowledge about learning techniques. Since this type of knowledge can be altered through systematic training, it can be determined whether the modification of prior knowledge states about learning processes will lead to more efficient vocational rehabilitation practices.

Language Acquisition and Cognitive Training. In one of the more provocative projects in the area of language learning with severely and profoundly retarded people, Kahn (1977) suggested that the training of cognitive skills, specifically object permanence, can lead to more rapid language acquisition. In the most recent update of this "cognitive readiness" project, Kahn (Note 3) continued to find dramatic gains in language learning for profoundly retarded nonspeech children who received object permanence training prior to their admission to a language-training program. Slightly less improvement was noted for subjects receiving training in means-end analysis. These recent data, based on eight subjects per group, support the hypothesis that referential speech does not develop until Stage 6 of the sensorimotor period has been achieved.

Instrumental Enrichment. Feuerstein (1980) has developed in Israel an elaborate training program—instrumental enrichment—designed to remediate the poor cognitive habits of retarded adolescents. For a variety of reasons, Feuerstein claims that "mediated learning" is deficient in the retarded. In mediated learning, parents and teachers help children interpret their encounters with problem-solving tasks by inducing rules of thought and applying these rules to new settings. Instrumental enrichment is targeted at mediational deficiencies, attempting to build basic processes of thought. Educational programs based on the techniques of instrumental enrichment are currently being tested in the United States on classes of EMR adolescents. One such program administered over a 2-year period to adolescents in special education classes has yielded increases, in contrast to gains shown by control students, in cognitive functioning, IQ, some areas of school achievement, reasoning, spatial relations, and intrinsic motivation (Haywood & Arbitman-Smith, in press). The Feuerstein method holds promise for improving the education of mentally handicapped youth by remediating basic cognitive and motivational deficiencies.

In this section we have shown that recent instructional research with the retarded is characterized by two trends: (1) As regards the search for a broader theoretical base in which to house the strategy-training paradigm, new or revised constructs such as metamemory (Kendall et al., 1980), feedback (Lawson & Flueloep, 1980), and executive skills (Belmont et al., in press) enlarge the framework for studying control processes. (2) The applied focus of strategy-training research has expanded into the new areas such as mathematics (Johnston et al., 1980), language acquisition (Kahn, Note 3), and classroom performance (Feuerstein, 1980). In at least one instance, a theoretical shift, integrating the concept of metacognition into the strategy-training paradigm, was carried out on an applied problem, vocational training (Grover & Wight-Felske, Note 2). Continuing with this theme, we turn next to a consideration of the theoretical underpinnings of the strategy-training paradigm.

Theory and Strategy-Training Research

As stated earlier, much of the research on strategy training in the mentally retarded has been conducted within multistage models of memory (see Atkinson & Shiffrin, 1968). These models rely heavily on rehearsal as a principal process in memory. In recent years, however, a number of alternative perspectives have emerged that cast research on strategy transfer in new theoretical contexts. We consider three perspectives that have applicability in furthering our understanding of the interrelationship of theory and the instructional research paradigm for both retarded and normal children: strategy training and aptitude-by-treatment interactions (ATIs); strategy use and automaticity; and strategy transfer and elementary cognitive processes.

Strategy Training and ATIs

Aptitude has been defined as "any characteristic of a person that forecasts his or her probability of success under a given treatment" (Cronbach & Snow, 1977, p. 6). The theory of aptitudes often focuses on the differential effectiveness of educational programs for different characteristics of a group of learners. For instance, Pascarella and Pflaum (1981) found an interaction between the locus of children's attributions (internal vs. external) and their control over the determination of errors (either student or teacher determined). Students initially high in internal control benefited more under a condition in which they were encouraged to determine the correctness of their responses; those low in internal control benefited more from teacher-determined errors. Locus of attribution was a setting condition for determining the effectiveness of a remedial intervention program for improving reading.

The search for ATIs can be found in the strategy-training literature. Schleser, Meyers, and Cohen (1981) have tested the interaction of type of training package (e.g., specific self-instructions, general self-instructions, specific didactic control, and general didactic control) with children's cognitive operativity (preoperational vs. concrete operational). The objective of training was to improve problem-solving skills. Children in the general self-instructions condition showed gains in performance on a perspective-taking transfer task; however, the extent of the improvement was not different for children differing in level of cognitive growth. More recent research from the Memphis State group indicates that concrete-operational children seem to benefit more at generalization than preoperational children when training is couched in a dialogue framework requiring the discovery of the study skills.

We have argued that metamemory is an important aptitude that both normal and retarded children possess prior to training. High aptitude for metamemory determines the efficacy of an acquired strategy. Children who know about their minds are more likely to show strategy maintenance and generalization than children low in metamemorial knowledge (Cavanaugh & Borkowski, 1979; Kendall et al., 1980). From this perspective, metamemory is a personal characteristic—much like an aptitude—that accounts for large individual differences in strategy transfer within a group of children who have received identical forms of strategy training.

Strategy Use and Automaticity

Engle and Nagle (1979) made an interesting observation to account for transfer data gathered following the training of a semantic encoding strategy: Retarded children may have deficits in the number of associations that are automatically elicited when an item is presented. That is, the retarded appear to have a less rich and less automatically activated semantic network. Similarly, Davies, Sperber, and McCauley (1981) demonstrated that the speed of retrieval for familiar information is much slower in retarded than in normal individuals. The suggestion here is that a deficit characteristic of retardation is the delayed development of automatic processing skills.

Data from free-recall learning studies can also be interpreted in terms of delays in automatic activation of semantic memories in low-IQ subjects (cf. Büchel, 1978). Sixty-four mentally retarded children (average MA = 8.5) were presented with categorized word lists together with category cues and with noncued lists. The analysis of subsequent free-recall learning revealed a significant correlation between MA and amount of recall and between IQ and recall but only for cued recall. Furthermore, it was found that children with MAs > 8.5 had profited from category cues, but children with MAs < 8.5 had not. It seems that retarded children with higher MAs had a richer semantic network, with more extended concepts. For these children a category name elicited more associations with category membership (Büchel, 1978).

Since trained strategies, like other types of information, take on representations in semantic memory, it may be that the retarded need to allocate more conscious attention to the activation of their memories, including their metamemorial systems. Domains that are unfamiliar, such as metamemory, in which one has little expertise, require a great deal of attention and effort to activate. The retarded child may be preoccupied with the implementation of a strategy, having few resources available with which to perform other cognitive activities such as strategy monitoring or strategy revision. From this perspective, the retarded child is not simply strategically deficient, but rather is deficient in the process of making formerly conscious routines effortless through automization. What does this view mean for strategy-training research? Perhaps it implies that the actual use of a strategy is only the initial step in training. Other objectives might include a clear specification of when the strategy would be useful and when not, followed by extensive practice in some of the former instances. In a sense, this is a distinction between a strategy and its format. This perspective fits well with our early discussion of the importance of feedback in instructional research. Feedback builds a comfortable format for the strategy and speeds up the automization process in a mature learner. It should be noted that an emphasis on automaticity and learning efficiency fits well with Sternberg's (1981b) most recent version of the metacomponential theory of intelligence.

Strategy Transfer and Elementary Cognitive Processes

Although it is a subtle point not widely recognized, *strategies* are not synonymous with *processes*. Strategies are techniques useful for initiating or enhancing the operation of theoretically based processes. They are observed behaviors such as sorting scores (Cavanaugh & Borkowski, 1980), think-aloud protocols (Ericsson & Simon, Note 4), retrospective verbal reports (Büchel, 1982; Ericsson & Simon, Note 5), or pause-time patterns (Belmont & Butterfield, 1977). From this perspective, strategies are defined as planned, controlled, self-instructed sequences used by a learner to initiate or control processing efficiency. The distinction between a strategy and a theoretical process or component has implications for our understanding of generalization failures.

A strategy is planned and carried out for a concrete purpose—to solve a problem. The problem or task can be theoretically defined by the process necessary for its successful completion. For any task, different theories may postulate unique components or processes. For example, Sternberg (1979) has emphasized specific components of acquisition, retention, and transfer, acting in concert with metacomponents to account for a wide variety of intellectual behaviors. Carroll (1981) has used the notions of elementary task analyses and corresponding mental operations to reveal individual differences in cognitive performance. In fact, regression analyses can be used to test which theory and its components best account for individual differences in task performance. For our purposes, we will simply draw on Carroll's analysis as an aid in presenting an alternative perspective on the relationship of strategy use to underlying cognitive processes.

Given that a theory specifies the essential elements or processes for solving a set of similar tasks, predictions can be made about the impact of a trained strategy on improving original learning as well as on transfer. The extent to which a strategy maps onto essential processes and the extent to which a learner is deficient in executing these processes determine its potential influence in remediating learning and memory deficits. In addition, transfer tasks often involve processes different from those of the training tasks. Processes required to solve the transfer test are often more complex than the processes of training (see Borkowski & Cavanaugh, 1979). If all of the processes of transfer are not encompassed by the trained strategy, or are not included in the learner's repertoire of other skills, then transfer performance should be poor. The strategy will be less likely to be used, and if used, it will be less effective in improving performance. An example in which we explain strategy generalization on the basis of alterations in underlying processes will be helpful in clarifying the strategy-versus-process distinction. It will also be useful in understanding the interrelationship of the training paradigm with more elementary cognitive theory.

Carroll (1981) lists 10 fundamental cognitive processes, several of which are deficient in the retarded (see Detterman, 1979): monitoring, attending apprehension, perceptual integration, encoding, comparison, corepresentation formation, corepresentation retrieval, transformation, and response execution. Any task, whether used during training or transfer, can be understood theoretically in terms of a hierarchy of its essential underlying processes. To the extent that the strategy enhances one or more essential processes, improvements in performance are to be anticipated. For instance, Kendall et al. (1980) found that a verbal elaboration strategy aided paired-associate learning for EMR children on transfer tests some 2 weeks after strategy training. Using Carroll's framework, the following processes were likely augmented by the self-generated elaboration strategy: (1) the encoding process (forming a mental representation of the stimulus and its attributes); (2) the corepresentation formation (establishing a new representation in memory in association with one having a longer history); and (3) the corepresentation retrieval (finding in memory a representation in association with another representation on the basis of a rule). In the Kendall et al. (1980) study, transfer performance reflected a 100% gain in the trained group in contrast to the control group, presumably due to improved functioning in basic processes: encoding, corepresentation formation, and corepresentation retrieval processes.

The advantage of conceptualizing strategies in terms of elementary processes that are hypothesized to be enhanced by the implementation of a strategy include the following:

1. The necessary analysis of a task into its component processes yields a more intelligent basis for the selection of a strategy.
2. Near and far transfer can be defined in terms of the number of processes shared with the training task.
3. Strategy generalization will occur only if processes necessary for solving the transfer task are part of the original strategy or are part of the existing repertoire of skills possessed by the learner. To the extent that the generalization task introduces new components not included in the strategy or unfamiliar to the learner, generalization failures should occur.

When viewed from this perspective, it seems useful to couch strategy-training research in one or more models of information processing. To date, this approach has not been characteristic of research on strategic learning in the retarded. We advocate additional reflection and debate about the merits of the strategy-versus-process distinction in the remediation of learning deficiencies.

New Directions for Strategy-Training Research

We conclude this review with some suggestions for strategy-training research with the mentally retarded. The first recommendation concerns the goals of strategy-training programs. Should we continue to train lower order subordinate strategies in the hope of elevating performance for the retarded? Should we instead shift attention to instructing children about superordinate executive processes? Or should we assess the knowledge base that contains information about subordinate and superordinate processes and build on that base, if necessary, before commencing strategy training? We argue that research programs should continue in all three directions. In addition, research should be planned that coordinates elements from all three orientations within the same design. This would mean that each child's knowledge about subordinate and superordinate processes would be initially assessed as a prerequisite to strategy training; this step is required if the ATI framework is to be applied to instructional research. Next we would intentionally build on the knowledge base, emphasizing the value of strategic behavior through the use of concrete examples. Finally, we would train subordinate and/or superordinate strategies, eventually testing for their range of generalization and for the inventiveness that might flow from the total training experience in concert with initial differences in metamemorial states.

A second research recommendation centers on children's motivation to employ strategies. Balla and Zigler (1979) have reviewed the literature on social deprivation, wariness, expectancies of failure, outerdirectedness, self-concept, and anxiety as they influence the performance of retarded people. Extensive differences can be found between retarded and nonretarded individuals in varied aspects of personality and motivational functioning. These findings suggest a need to integrate theories of motivation into the cognitive training paradigm if the intention is to alter strategic processing across time and settings. One possible candidate for incorporation into strategy-training research is attribution theory (Weiner, 1974, 1980).

The relevance of attribution theory for research on strategy training and metacognitive training with the retarded is as follows: We cannot presume to train strategies for long-term generalization by simply teaching subordinate or superordinate processes in combination with their corresponding metacognitive states. Missing are the affective, the personal, and the motivational domains. While some in the field of mental retardation have not ignored these phenomena (Balla & Zigler, 1979; Haywood, in press), others have omitted an analysis of attributional and motivational histories, proceeding directly to cognitive or metacognitive training.

The implications of the neglect of motivational and attributional factors are twofold: (1) Metacognitive states are not only knowledge states. In addition to cognitive components, they have affective and motivational components that energize or delay the occurrence of a strategy or skill. Most likely the concept of metacognition is tied in intricate ways to notions about self-esteem and self-control. More complex theoretical treatments of the dynamic interactions between strategy-training programs and prior, as well as subsequent, motivational states are sorely needed. (2) Attributional retraining can be integrated easily into the strategy-training paradigm. For instance, Short and Ryan (Note 6) have outlined a procedure for creating more effective attributions in less skilled readers as a part of a complex strategy-training package designed to improve reading comprehension. Attribution retraining was aimed at teaching poor readers the merits of strategic effort and undoing the damage created by self-descriptions that ascribe failure to a lack of ability. The integration of strategy training and attribution retraining holds great potential for producing more generalizable skills in the mentally retarded.

These recommendations and suggestions for new directions in instructional research with the retarded require greater sophistication, both methodologically and theoretically, for their successful implementation. Methodologically, we can expect to find increased use of structural equational procedures to test dynamic, multicausal, bidirectional, longitudinal models of strategy transfer (see Paris et al., in press). Theoretically, instructional research will need to build new bridges with key concepts in personality and motivational psychology. It is a hopeful sign that some of these trends are already apparent (Haywood, Meyers, & Switzky, 1982).

Although new theoretical insights and more complex designs will undoubtedly enhance the quality of strategy-training research, paradoxically these trends will result in a diminution of the pace of research in this area. The era of the quick, simple training study has come to an end. We begin a period in which considerable thought will need to be devoted to the design and execution of training research in order to ensure that the high costs inherent in this approach—in subject time, experimental efforts, and support funds—are justified. More important is the need to respect, in a theoretical sense, the full complexities of the minds that we attempt to modify. Research on strategy training has tended to ignore this complexity. Integrative scholarship is needed to meaningfully advance our understanding of strategic behavior in the mentally retarded.

Acknowledgments. The writing of this chapter was made possible, in part, by NIE Grant G-81-0134 and by Swiss National Foundation Grants 79FR10 and 4.323.0.79.10.

Reference Notes

1. Kendall, C., & Borkowski, J. G. *Training generalized strategies in retarded children.* Paper presented at the 12th Annual Gatlinburg Conference on Mental Retardation, Gulf Shores, AL, March 1979.

2. Grover, S. C., & Wight-Felske, A. *The developmental handicapped adults' concept of self as learner.* Paper presented at the Sixth International Congress on the Scientific Study of Mental Deficiency, Toronto, August 1982.
3. Kahn, J. *Cognitive and language training with profoundly retarded children.* Paper presented at the Sixth Biennial Meeting of the International Society for the Study of Behavioral Development, Toronto, August 1981.
4. Ericsson, K. A., & Simon, H. A. *Thinking-aloud protocols as data* (C. I. P. Working Paper 397). Pittsburgh, PA: Carnegie-Mellon University, 1979.
5. Ericsson, K. A., & Simon, H. A. Retrospective verbal reports as data (C. I. P. Working Paper 388). Pittsburgh, PA: Carnegie-Mellon University, 1978.
6. Short, E. J., & Ryan, E. B. Remediating poor readers' comprehension failures with a story grammar strategy. Paper presented at the Gatlinburg Conference on Retardation, Gatlinburg, Tenn., April, 1982.

References

Asarnow, J. R., & Meichenbaum, D. Verbal rehearsal and serial recall: The mediational training of kindergarten children. *Child Development,* 1979, *50,* 1173–1177.

Atkinson, R. C., & Shiffrin, R. M. Human memory: A proposed system and its control processes. In K. W. Spence & J. T. Spence (Eds.), *The psychology of learning and motivation.* New York: Academic Press, 1968.

Balla, D., & Zigler, E. Personality development in retarded persons. In N. R. Ellis (Ed.), *Handbook of mental deficiency* (2nd ed.). Hillsdale, NJ: Erlbaum, 1979.

Belmont, J. M., & Butterfield, E. C. The instructional approach to developmental cognitive research. In R. Kail & J. Hagen (Eds.), *Perspectives on the development of memory and cognition.* Hillsdale, NJ: Erlbaum, 1977.

Belmont, J. M., Butterfield, E. C., & Borkowski, J. G. Training retarded people to generalize memorization methods across memory tasks. In M. M. Gruneberg, P. E. Morris, & R. N. Sykes (Eds.), *Practical aspects of memory.* London: Academic Press, 1978.

Belmont, J. M., Ferretti, R. P., & Mitchell, D. W. Memorizing: A test of untrained mildly retarded children's problem solving. *American Journal of Mental Deficiency,* in press.

Bilsky, L. H., Whittemore, C. L., & Walker, N. Strategies in the recall of clusterable lists. *Intelligence,* 1982, *6,* 23–35.

Borkowski, J. B., & Cavanaugh, J. C. Maintenance and generalization of skills and strategies by the retarded. In N. R. Ellis (Ed.), *Handbook of mental deficiency* (2nd ed.). Hillsdale, NJ: Erlbaum, 1979.

Borkowski, J. G., & Kurtz, B. Metacognition and special children. In J. B. Gholson & T. L. Rosenthal (Eds.), *Applications of cognitive developmental theory.* New York: Academic Press, in press.

Borkowski, J. G., Levers, S. R., & Gruenenfelder, T. M. Transfer of mediational strategies in children: The role of activity and awareness during strategy acquisition. *Child Development,* 1976, *47,* 779–786.

Borkowski, J. G., Peck, V. A., & Damburg, P. R. Attention, memory, and cognition in the retarded. In J. L. Matson & J. A. Mulick (Eds.), *Comprehensive handbook of mental retardation.* Elmsford, NY: Pergamon, in press.

Borkowski, J. G., Reid, M. K., & Kurtz, B. Metacognition and retardation: Paradigmatic, theoretical, and applied perspectives. In P. Brooks, R. Sperber, & C. McCauley (Eds.), *Learning and cognition in the mentally retarded.* Hillsdale, N.J.: Erlbaum, in press.

Borys, S. V., Spitz, H. H., & Dorans, B. A. Tower of Hanoi performance of retarded young adults and non-retarded children as a function of solution length and goal state. *Journal of Experimental Child Psychology,* 1982, *33,* 87–110.

Brooks, P., Sperber, R., & McCauley, C. *Learning and cognition in the mentally retarded.* Hillsdale, N.J.: Erlbaum, in press.

Brown, A. L. Knowing when, and how to remember: A problem of metacognition. In R. Glaser (Ed.), *Advances in instructional psychology* (Vol. 1). Hillsdale, NJ: Erlbaum, 1978.

Brown, A. L., & Barclay, C. R. The effect of training specific mnemonics on the metamnemonic efficiency of retarded children. *Child Development,* 1976, *47,* 71–80.

Brown, A. L., Campione, J. C., & Barclay, C. R. Training self-checking routines for estimating test readiness: Generalization from list learning to prose recall. *Child Development,* 1979, *50,* 501–512.

Büchel, F. P. *Gedachtnis und Lernen bein geistigbekinderten Kind.* Weinheim: Beltz, 1978.

Büchel, F. P. Metacognitive variables in the learning of written text. In A. Flammer & W. Kintsch (Eds.), *Discourse processing.* Amsterdam: North-Holland, 1982.

Burger, A. L., Blackman, L. S., Clark, H. T., & Reis, E. The effects of hypothesis testing and variable format training on the generalization of a verbal abstraction strategy in EMR learners. *American Journal of Mental Deficiency,* 1982, *86,* 405–413.

Burger, A. L., Blackman, L. S., Holmes, M., & Zetlin, A. Use of active sorting and retrieval strategies as a facilitator of recall, clustering, and sorting by EMR children. *American Journal of Mental Deficiency,* 1978, *83,* 253–261.

Butterfield, E. C., & Belmont, J. M. Assessing and improving the cognitive functions of mentally retarded people. In I. Bialer & M. Sternlicht (Eds.), *The psychology of mental retardation: Issues and approaches.* New York: Psychological Dimensions, 1977.

Butterfield, E. C., Wambold, C., & Belmont, J. M. On the theory and practice of improving short-term memory. *American Journal of Mental Deficiency,* 1973, *77,* 654–669.

Carroll, J. B. Ability and task difficulty in cognitive psychology. *Educational Researcher,* 1981, *10,* 11–19.

Campione, J. C., & Brown, A. L. Memory and metamemory development in educable retarded children. In R. V. Kail & J. W. Hagen (Eds.), *Perspectives on the development of memory and cognition.* Hillsdale, NJ: Erlbaum, 1977.

Campione, J. C., & Brown, A. L. Toward a theory of intelligence: Contributions from research with retarded children. *Intelligence,* 1978, *2,* 279–304.

Cavanaugh, J. C., & Borkowski, J. G. The metamemory-memory "connection": Effects of strategy training and maintenance. *Journal of General Psychology,* 1979, *101,* 161–174.

Cavanaugh, J. C., & Borkowski, J. G. Searching for metamemory-memory connections: A developmental study. *Child Development,* 1980, *16,* 441–453.

Clark, P. A., & Detterman, D. K. Performance of mentally retarded and nonretarded persons on a lifted-weight task with strategies reduced or eliminated. *American Journal of Mental Deficiency,* 1981, *85,* 530–538.

Cronbach, L. J., & Snow, R. E. *Aptitudes and instructional methods: A handbook for research on interactions.* New York: Irvington, 1977.

Davies, D., Sperber, R. D., & McCauley, C. Intelligence-related differences in semantic processing speed. *Journal of Experimental Child Psychology,* 1981, *31,* 387–402.

Detterman, D. K. Memory in the mentally retarded. In N. R. Ellis (Ed.), *Handbook of mental deficiency* (2nd ed.). Hillsdale, NJ: Erlbaum, 1979.

Ellis, N. R. The stimulus trace and behavioral inadequacy. In N. R. Ellis (Ed.), *Handbook of mental deficiency.* New York: McGraw-Hill, 1963.

Ellis, N. R. Memory processes in retardates and normals. In N. R. Ellis (Ed.), *International review of research in mental retardation* (Vol. 4). New York: Academic Press, 1970.

Ellis, N. R. *Handbook of mental deficiency* (2nd ed.). Hillsdale, NJ: Erlbaum, 1979.

Engle, R. W., & Nagle, R. J. Strategy training and semantic encoding in mildly retarded children. *Intelligence,* 1979, *3,* 17–30.

Feuerstein, R. *Instrumental enrichment: An intervention program for cognitive modifiability.* Baltimore: University Park Press, 1980.

Flavell, J. Metacognition and cognitive monitoring: A new area of cognitive-developmental inquiry. *American Psychologist,* 1979, *34,* 906–911.

Haywood, C. Motivation and learning: Let's change what we can. In P. Brooks, R. Sperber, & C. McCauley (Eds.), *Learning and cognition in the mentally retarded.* Hillsdale, N.J.: Erlbaum, in press.

Haywood, H. C., & Arbitman-Smith, R. Modification of cognitive functions in slow-learning adolescents. In P. Mittler (Ed.), *Frontiers of knowledge in mental retardation: Social, education, and behavioral aspects.* Baltimore, University Park Press, in press.

Haywood, H. C., Meyers, C. E., & Switzky, H. N. Mental retardation. *Annual Review of Psychology,* 1982, *33,* 309–342.

Johnston, M. B., Whitman, T. L., & Johnson, M. Teaching addition and subtraction to mentally retarded children: A self-instructional program. *Applied Research in Mental Retardation,* 1980, *1,* 141–160.

Kahn, J. V. Cognitive training of severely and profoundly retarded children. In M. A. Thomas (Ed.), *Developing skills in severely and profoundly handicapped children.* Reston, VA: Council for Exceptional Children, 1977.

Kendall, C. R., Borkowski, J. G., & Cavanaugh, J. C. Metamemory and the transfer of an interrogative strategy by EMR children. *Intelligence,* 1980, *4,* 255–270.

Kennedy, B. A., & Miller, D. Persistent use of verbal rehearsal as a function of information about its value. *Child Development,* 1976, *47,* 566–569.

Kramer, J. J., & Engle, R. W. Teaching awareness of strategic behavior in combination with strategy training: Effects on children's memory performance. *Journal of Experimental Child Psychology,* 1981, *32,* 513–520.

Kreutzer, M. A., Leonard, C., & Flavell, J. H. An interview study of children's knowledge about memory. *Monographs of the Society of Research in Child Development,* 1975, *40*(1, Serial No. 159).

Lawson, M. J., & Flueloep, S. Understanding the purpose of strategy training. *British Journal of Educational Psychology,* 1980, *50,* 175–180.

Mar, H. H., & Glidden, L. M. Semantic and acoustic processing in free and cued recall by educable mentally retarded adolescents. *Intelligence,* 1977, *1,* 298–309.

McCauley, C., Kellas, G., Dugas, J., & Devillis, R. F. Effects of serial rehearsal training on memory search. *Journal of Educational Psychology,* 1976, *68,* 474–481.

Meichenbaum, D. *Cognitive-behavior modification: An integrative approach.* New York: Plenum, 1977.

O'Leary, K. D., & Borkovec, T. D. Conceptual, methodological, and ethical problems of placebo groups in psychotherapy research. *American Psychologist,* 1978, *33,* 821–830.

Page, E. B., & Grandon, G. M. Massive intervention and child intelligence. *Journal of Special Education,* 1981, *15,* 239–256.

Paris, S. G., Newman, R. S., & McVey, K. A. Learning the functional significance of mnemonic actions: A microgenetic study of strategy acquisition. *Journal of Experimental Child Psychology,* in press.

Pascarella, E. T., & Pflaum, S. W. The interaction of children's attribution and level of control over error correction in reading instruction. *Journal of Educational Psychology,* 1981, *73,* 533–540.

Peleg, Z. R., & Moore, R. F. Effects of the advanced organizer with oral and written presentation on recall and inference of EMR adolescents. *American Journal of Mental Deficiency,* 1982, *86,* 621–626.

Peterson, P. L., & Swing, S. R. Problems in classroom implementation of cognitive strategy instruction. In M. Pressley & J. R. Levin (Eds.), *Cognitive strategy research: Educational applications.* New York: Springer-Verlag, 1983.

Reichart, G. J., Cody, W. J., & Borkowski, J. G. Training and transfer of clustering and cumulative rehearsal strategies in retarded individuals. *American Journal of Mental Deficiency,* 1975, *79,* 648–658.

Schleser, R., Meyers, A. W., & Cohen, R. Generalization of self-instructions: Effects of general versus specific contrast, active rehearsal, and cognitive level. *Child Development,* 1981, *52,* 335–340.

Sternberg, R. J. The nature of mental abilities. *American Psychologist,* 1979, *34,* 214–230.

Sternberg, R. J. Cognitive-behavioral approaches to the training of intelligence in the retarded. *Journal of Special Education,* 1981, *15,* 165–183. (a)

Sternberg, R. J. The evaluation of theories of intelligence. *Intelligence,* 1981, *5,* 209–230. (b)

Turnure, J. E., Buium, N., & Thurlow, M. L. The effectiveness of interrogatives for promoting verbal elaboration productivity in young children. *Child Development,* 1976, *47,* 851–855.

Wanschura, P. B., & Borkowski, J. G. Long-term transfer of a mediational strategy by moderately retarded children. *American Journal of Mental Deficiency,* 1975, *80,* 323–333.

Wark, D. Reading comprehension as implicit verbal behavior. *Seventeenth Yearbook of the National Reading Conference,* 1968, *17,* 192–198.

Weiner, B. *Achievement motivation and attribution theory.* Morristown, NJ: General Learning Press, 1974.

Weiner, B. *Human motivation.* New York: Holt, Rinehart & Winston, 1980.

6. Memory Strategy Instruction with the Learning Disabled

Patricia E. Worden

In any consideration of the various applications of memory strategy instruction in special populations, the learning disabled constitute an especially appropriate target group. Because of an uneven pattern of abilities (i.e., a specific deficit in processing letters, numbers, sounds, or word meanings, while showing normal performance in other intellectual areas), the learning-disabled child experiences repeated failure in the classroom and the learning-disabled adult suffers restricted socioeconomic opportunity. In a culture where universal literacy is expected and universal schooling is required, a person who nevertheless fails to achieve literacy is disadvantaged indeed. Moreover, the learning-disabled population contains an overrepresentation of minority individuals (Rosner, Abrams, Daniels, & Schiffman, 1981). In the sense that they are multiply disadvantaged, the failure of the American educational system to serve the needs of learning disabled individuals is a serious problem.

Thus, the study of learning disabilities should represent a major area of educational and psychological research. Sadly, this is not the case. There is relatively little legitimate empirical research on the causes of learning disabilities. Researchers who study the underlying cognitive deficits have only recently been very active. Research on memory strategy instruction represents only a handful of studies at present. Because of this state of affairs, it is premature to undertake a major review of research on strategy instruction with the learning disabled at this time. Instead, this chapter will focus on a description of the disorder, will briefly review the existing research on the cognitive deficits of learning disabilities, and will present a number of studies that seem to have direct relevance to the question of memory strategy instruction. It will conclude with an outline of future directions, because the important research on memory strategy instruction in the learning disabled has yet to be conducted.

Definition of Learning Disabilities

In discussing the question of how many learning-disabled children there are, Helmer Myklebust has said, "Tell me how many you want to find and I'll write you a definition that will find that many" (Algozzine & Sutherland, 1977, p. 91).

The field of learning disabilities is characterized by a lack of consensus between researchers and practitioners as to how a learning-disabled individual should be identified. As a result, the incidence of learning disabilities has not been firmly established, nor are the demographic characteristics of this special population precisely known, except that males outnumber females by at least four to one (Money, 1966; Owen, Adams, Forrest, Stolz, & Fisher, 1971). Official estimates identify approximately 2–3% of the school-aged population as being learning disabled (e.g., Public Law 94-142), but with the use of some definitions, it can rise as high as 30% (Eisenberg, 1966). However, the National Advisory Committee on Handicapped Children (1968) has established a working definition of learning disabilities that is accepted by most educators and researchers:

> Children with special learning disabilities exhibit a disorder in one or more of the basic psychological processes involved in understanding or in using spoken or written languages. These may be manifested in writing, spelling, or arithmetic. They include conditions which have been referred to as perceptual handicaps, brain injury, minimal brain dysfunction, dyslexia, developmental aphasia, etc. They do not include learning problems which are due primarily to visual, hearing, or motor handicaps, to mental retardation, emotional disturbance or to environmental disadvantage.

A learning-disabled child is almost always "diagnosed" initially in the classroom; a large survey by Owen et al. (1971) reported that 67% are between 8 and 11 years of age (see also Koppitz, 1972). Typically the teacher notices that the child is lagging behind the class in one or more subjects; failure to learn to read is a common source of concern. The child may also have earned the teacher's attention by displaying an unusually high activity level. The child is referred for psychological testing, and often a pediatric examination is given as well. Stimulant drugs are frequently prescribed because (paradoxically) they are often effective in reducing the child's hyperactivity. Contrary to earlier claims, it is now recognized that although such drugs improve school behavioral problems, the effects on learning are restricted to certain tasks only. Furthermore, dose-response curves and state-dependent learning effects qualify any simple assertion that stimulant drugs also improve learning (Swanson & Kinsbourne, 1979).

A major component of the psychological exam is the administration of an intelligence test, typically the Wechsler Intelligence Scale for Children-Revised (WISC-R). Theoretically, if the child scores uniformly low he or she will be identified as retarded. The designation *learning disabled* is reserved for children who show a lag on only one or more of the subscales, with normal levels of performance in the other areas. This use of WISC-R profile "scatter" for placement in special programs assumes that the profiles of normal children will be relatively homogeneous, an assumption that has come under much criticism lately (e.g., Kaufman, 1981). It is easy to see how the child's chance of being labeled "normal," "learning disabled," or "retarded" will depend on school policies and psychological practice in setting criteria for evaluating IQ test profiles.

It is quite appropriate, then, to ask who qualifies as a learning-disabled subject, since researchers as well as educators have had to cope with these definitional problems (see Hammill, 1976; Rosner et al., 1981). Increasingly, the importance of reporting test scores and cutoff criteria is recognized in order to assure comparability of studies, but it is often difficult or impossible to obtain such scores for the comparison population as well. In addition, the reliance upon the triad of school problems, behavioral disturbance, and IQ test profiles has resulted in the exclusion of children known to have brain injury, or aphasia from the typical research study of learning-disabled children (contrary to their inclusion in the National Advisory Committee definition quoted above). In practice, most researchers rely on a "readymade" population by selecting subjects from a special program or class. Poor reading performance is often the criterion for subject selection; in describing such studies of good and poor readers, we will use the term *learning disabled* to refer to the poor readers, since only studies of seriously disabled readers will be reviewed. The widespread use of these undoubtedly heterogeneous groups of subjects is troubling, as is recognized by serious researchers in this field. A promising trend is the search for distinct subtypes of learning disabilities (i.e., learning disabled in reading, in writing, in mathematics, etc.). To the extent that such subgroups can be reliably distinguished, research questions can be focused more precisely, thus enabling training in specifically appropriate cognitive strategies. Some examples will be discussed later.

A word or two should be said about current theories of the causes of learning disabilities. Two major views exist, neither of which is necessarily incompatible with the other, and neither of which provides a particularly precise explanation of the etiology of the disorder. (Although readers should see Chapter 7 of this volume for a new approach.) Adherents to the "minimal brain dysfunction" theory observe that many of the symptoms that can accompany learning disabilities (e.g., hyperactivity, distractibility, poor motor control, short attention span, and impulsivity) seem to be "mild" versions of symptoms typically observed in victims of frank brain damage (see Benton, 1973). Unfortunately for this theory, however, no direct measure of minimal brain dysfunction exists as yet that reliably discriminates learning-disabled from normal individuals (Freeman, 1967; Harris, 1979; Hughes, 1976; Owen et al., 1971). The minimal brain dysfunction view is characteristically related to the association of hyperactivity with learning problems, and one variation holds that the brain dysfunction is structural and/or functional in nature (i.e., it is permanent).

A second theory is that the problem lies in the rate of development only. Thus, it is very common for researchers to speak of a "developmental lag" when describing learning disabled individuals (e.g., Satz & van Nostrand, 1973), especially when disabled learners who do not exhibit hyperactivity are studied. Evidence for developmental delay comes from the finding that learning-disabled subjects resemble younger normal subjects on a wide variety of research tasks. In this view, cognitive development is seen only as slower than normal, not different in any fundamental way. Development will progress through the same stages and milestones that produce qualitative and quantitative growth in normal children, but at a slower rate. Thus the learning disabled child may eventually outgrow one kind of problem (e.g., in identifying individual symbols), only to exhibit another deficit at the next stage of development (e.g., in assigning meaning to words). Effective learning strategies will have to be appropriate for particular developmental stages. This view seems to imply that learning disabled individuals will someday "catch up" to their faster progressing peers and may eventually achieve adult status (Rourke, 1976; Satz & Friel, 1973). On the other hand, evidence for "sustained" (i.e., permanent and persisting) deficits on specific IQ subtests has been found, such that the same profiles were found for learning disabled adolescents (Ackerman, Dykman, & Peters, 1977) and young adults (Cordoni, O'Donnell, Ramaniah, Kurtz, & Rosenshein, 1981) as are typically exhibited by children.

Finally, neither the theory of minimal brain dysfunction nor the developmental lag view has much to say about the cause of the disorder. Current theories of causation range from the reasonable to the incredible: learning disabilities have been attributed to genetic factors (Silver, 1971), incomplete hemispheric lateralization (see Harris, 1979), environmental and nutritional deprivation (Cravioto & DeLicardie, 1975), biochemical anomalies (Wender, 1976), food allergies, vitamin deficiencies, children's TV, fluorescent lights, cigarette smoke, and aerosol sprays (Schrag & Divoky, 1976).

The problems, then, are that it is difficult to say precisely who is learning disabled, how he or she got that way, and what should be the best course of instruction. The permanent deficit view suggests that learning-disabled children should receive training in compensatory learning and memory strategies; the developmental lag view suggests that the specific deficits themselves should be treated, in order to increase their rate of development. As will be seen in the brief review that follows, specific deficits may be perceptual, linguistic, attentional, memorial, and/or metacognitive, and are most typically revealed through reading problems. Research on strategy instruction in each of these areas is needed, but it is quite outside the scope of this chapter to cover all deficit areas comprehensively. Those interested in the topic of reading are referred to the appropriate chapters in this volume. Here we will focus on memory, since the retention of information is the ultimate goal in most learning situations.

Studies of Cognitive Disabilities

Perceptual and Linguistic Skills

Learning disabled children have been found to exhibit language deficits that interfere in particular with the acquisition of reading skills. White, Pascarella, and Pflaum (1981) reviewed a number of studies showing that learning disabled children typically are deficient in awareness of syntactical rules. This, coupled with problems in isolating and manipulating phonetic sounds in words, often interferes with young children's ability to associate words, letters, and sounds for reading purposes. Individual letters may even be perceived incorrectly; in particular, reversals of mirror-image letters and words have been the basis of a theory of impaired perceptual processing.

However, it is a matter of some controversy whether defective perceptual processing is a fundamental component of learning disabilities (especially of reading problems, or dyslexia). In support of this position, Kavale (1982) recently conducted a meta-analysis of 161 studies and concluded that visual perceptual skills are important correlates of reading achievement; breakdowns by grade level suggested that visual-perceptual skills were more important in preschool and primary grades than in "intermediate" grades. This finding agrees with the suggestion (e.g., Benton, 1975; Satz & Fletcher, in press) that perceptual problems may only be a factor in learning disabilities for younger children. However, an examination of the tasks commonly used to measure perceptual deficits often implicates higher order conceptual components, rather than purely perceptual skills (Jorm, 1979; Vellutino, Steger, Moyer, Harding, & Niles, 1977). Indeed, Orton (1937) was one of the first to speculate that "this disorder is not one of sensory reception but rather of memory" (p. 145). This hypothesis was given more recent support by Morrison, Giordani, and Nagy (1977), who compared disabled and normal learners' visual perception by using the partial report technique: Recognition accuracy for visually presented symbols did not differ for delay intervals between 0 and 300 msec (the duration of the purely perceptual visual information store). Normal subjects performed significantly better than disabled subjects at delays of 300–2000 msec, when information undergoes active coding and transfer to short-term memory. Based on such findings, current research has concentrated on cognitive rather than perceptual deficits, and may be roughly divided into studies of selective attention, short-term memory, long-term memory, and metamemory.

Selective Attention

One of the important elements of information processing is the application of attentional processes. Because of basic capacity limitations, successful learning requires the ability to attend directly to relevant information, with extraneous information undergoing only superficial monitoring. Tarver and Hallahan (1974) reviewed a large number of studies and concluded that learning disabled children do have difficulty in distinguishing between relevant and irrelevant aspects of a stimulus situation. Hagen (1967) developed a central-incidental task, based on Broadbent's (1958) stimulus filter theory, that compares performance on a primary short-term memory task with the learning of incidental information presented simultaneously. This paradigm has been tested in a variety of experimental settings (Drucker & Hagen, 1969; Hagen & Sabo, 1967; Hallahan, Kauffman, & Ball, 1974) and with various special populations (Hagen & Huntsman, 1971; Hallahan, Stainback, Ball, & Kauffman, 1973). It is not surprising to find that learning-disabled subjects perform poorly on Hagen's task (as reviewed by Hallahan, 1975; Hallahan

& Reeve, 1980). The nature of their poor performance is an alleged failure to filter out incidental information, as shown by a lower proportion of central information as a function of overall recall (compared to normal age-mates).

Recently, however, this interpretation has been seriously criticized (Douglas & Peters, 1979; Tarver, 1981), because typically the amount of incidental recall does not differ in disabled and nondisabled learners; only intentional recall is actually deficient in learning disabled subjects. In fact, Douglas and Peters (1979) reviewed the literature on distractibility and concluded that disabled learners are *not* more susceptible to distraction than their nondisabled peers. Accordingly, they suggest that the central-incidental task is merely a standard short-term serial-recall task plus distraction (which affects disabled and nondisabled children alike), rather than a measure of attention per se.

Similarly, several authors (Bauer, 1977, 1979; Pehlam, 1979; Tarver, 1981) point out that the tasks traditionally used to measure attention (e.g., detection of weak stimuli, recall of irrelevant information, sustained performance over relatively long periods, perception of figure-ground relationships) place a variety of complex demands on subjects. Attributing poor performance to lack of attention may be simplistic and unjustified. In fact, there is a growing body of research indicating that specific deficits in learning may be more strategic than attentional in nature, as shown in studies of short-term memory.

Short-Term Memory

Short-term memory refers to a hypothetical buffer in the information processing system where incoming stimuli (e.g., visual symbols) are held momentarily for purposes of decoding (retrieval and assignment of phonological and/or semantic representations) and further processing (necessary for storage in long-term memory). Short-term memory is limited in size, and information therein undergoes rapid decay unless processed further.

Short-term memory is considered by some to be the main "bottleneck" in the process of comprehending and retaining prose materials (Lesgold & Perfetti, 1978; Perfetti & Lesgold, 1978). The size of short-term memory is not the critical variable; Chi (1976) has shown that short-term memory *capacity* does not increase between the ages of 5 and adulthood. Further, short-term memory for digits does not differ in good and poor readers (Cohen & Netley, 1978; Jackson & McClelland, 1975; Perfetti & Goldman, 1976; but see also Torgesen & Houck, 1980). Rather than inherent size, procedures for making use of short-term capacity are critical (Case, 1974; Huttenlocher & Burke, 1976).

Consider Bauer's (1977, 1979) studies of short-term recall of words. With a 1-second delay after presentation, recall of all but the first few items was similar in learning disabled and normal children. Neither the reduced short-term capacity nor the attentional deficit hypothesis is compatible with this result. However, as the delay between presentation and retrieval was increased, recall declined much more rapidly in children with learning disabilities. Torgesen and Houck (1980) found similar results when they varied the rate of presentation of digits to be recalled in sequence. Performance of the learning disabled subjects declined more dramatically at slower rates of presentation. In addition, the effects of interference on short-term memory were shown to be greater for learning disabled children than for normals when the interfering items were phonetically or semantically similar to the items to be remembered (Cermak, Goldberg-Warter, DeLuca, Cermak, & Drake, 1981). These results suggest that the learning disabled children were not processing the items as thoroughly as normals; they may not have been rehearsing or engaging in elaborative encoding. Rehearsal and elaboration are necessary to maintain the kinds of information lost by learning disabled subjects: (a) primacy items, (b) information presented more slowly or held over a delay period, and (c) information that must be distinguished from similar distractors. Similarly, learning disabled children were found to perform considerably worse than normal controls on a probed serial-recall task involving lists that exceeded the children's short-term memory span (Cohen & Netley, 1978), and the difference between learning disabled and normal adults' short-term recall of simple sentences increased dramatically as a function of sentence length (Kee, Worden, & Gardner, Note 1). Consistent with such findings, Cohen and Netley proposed that "the inability of the memory system to cope with overload is a central feature" in learning disabilities (p. 733). Considered together, these studies suggest greater spontaneous usage of rehearsal and elaborative encoding strategies in normals than in learning disabled individuals. That is, voluntary control processes for strategic encoding may distinguish the short-term memory performance of the two ability groups.

However, others have suggested various structural deficiencies that could also diminish the efficiency of short-term encoding in disabled learners. As discussed by Torgesen and Houck (1980), an increased rate of decay of the stimulus trace, or a particular difficulty coding information about the order of items, could account for the poor short-term memory performance of learning disabled individuals (but a recent study by Manis & Morrison, 1982, casts doubt on the latter hypothesis). In the case of text comprehension, Perfetti and Lesgold (1978) have proposed that the learning disabled are not able to encode stimuli into meaningful representations as quickly as can normals. It is known that less skilled readers are slower at retrieving semantic information in response to words and wordlike stimuli (Frederiksen, 1978; Perfetti & Hogaboam, 1975). Further, Perfetti and Lesgold propose that clausal boundaries in sentences are important for processing discourse in short-term memory. Information is held in working memory until a clausal boundary is encountered, at which time the meaning of the clause is processed for long-term storage. The faster such clause integration takes place, the more information is stored. The reduced speed of verbal coding results in what Perfetti and Lesgold called the "double whammy" effect. As sentences are read into short-term memory, poor readers take longer to retrieve verbal codes for individual words. This delay in turn impairs their ability to hold information about larger linguistic units (clauses, sentences) for integration purposes. A study of probed short-term sentence recall showed that less skilled readers had particular difficulty encoding sentences containing more than one clause (Perfetti & Lesgold, 1978).

In summary, information processing in short-term memory is deficient in learning disabled individuals. The deficiency is not simply due to lack of attention, nor is it the case that the absolute capacity of the short-term store is reduced. Two possible explanations have been reviewed. The first is that the learning disabled fail spontaneously to engage in rehearsal or elaborative encoding necessary for the maintenance of memory traces over time. To the extent that strategy instruction elevates performance to normal levels, the rehearsal deficit could be metacognitive in origin (e.g., a production deficiency). On the other hand, to the extent that the *rate* of encoding is limited, a second view is that the deficit may be a more permanent structural feature of the information processing system (e.g., a mediation deficiency). Although the effects of slower encoding speed have typically been investigated in the context of linguistic tasks, such as word naming and sentence comprehension, researchers have recently begun to study other tasks, such as the central-incidental paradigm (Tarver, 1981), looking for effects of hypothesized structural deficits. (Peterson & Swing, 1983, consider the implications of slow short-term processing for classroom use of cognitive strategies.)

Long-Term Memory for Lists of Words and/or Pictures

Whereas short-term memory is evanescent and capacity limited, long-term memory is typically viewed as potentially unlimited in capacity and length. Semantic memory is an organized store (hypothetically permanent) of word and event meanings, loosely characterized as knowledge. Episodic memory describes our memory for specific events, which remain accessible in long-term memory from several minutes to a lifetime. The semantic organization of long-term memory determines, to a great extent, the efficiency of storage and retrieval of such information. However, the effectiveness of processing during the short-term memory stage is also critical for long-term storage of episodic memories. Therefore, the demonstration that learning disabled subjects recall less than normals on long-term memory tasks does not necessarily implicate semantic memory as deficient in and of itself. It is necessary to show that the long-term memory decrement is not simply a product of inefficient short-term encoding, known to be a critical problem in learning disabilities.

A number of studies have found reduced long-term recall for learning disabled subjects in free-recall tasks requiring memory for lists of words (Bauer, 1979; Dallago & Moely, 1980; Torgesen, 1977; Wong, Wong, & Foth, 1977), as well as in memory for prose materials (Smiley, Oakley, Worthen, Campione, & Brown, 1977; Worden, Malmgren, & Gabourie, 1982). In their search for the locus of the problem, however, researchers have consistently concluded that the organization of long-term semantic memory is *not* deficient in learning disabled individuals. Faulty encoding is indirectly implicated in most studies; an important task for future researchers is to develop a way to separate more directly the effects of short-term encoding vs. long-term semantic organization.

Torgesen (1977) found that although learning disabled children recalled significantly less than normals, clustering scores (a measure of organization in recall) of the two ability groups did not differ. He attributed their poor performance to inefficient study of the items, since learning disabled children were significantly less likely than normals to form category groups of the items during study. A similar study by Dallago and Moely (1980) replicated the finding of lower recall in spite of equivalent levels of clustering. Although study behaviors (distraction, looking at and/or touching items, self-testing) did not differ, learning disabled children studied for less time, and their recall was notably improved by a manipulation that induced their use of category organization in study and recall. Dallago and Moely concluded that structural factors in long-term organization did not appear to exist, but rather that the spontaneous employment of organized study strategies was deficient.

Unfortunately, results do not consistently support the argument that long-term memory organization is intact because recall deficits are found in spite of normal levels of clustering. Other studies (Bauer, 1979; Wong, Wong, & Foth, 1977) have found both recall and clustering to be significantly lower in learning disabled children, compared to normal subjects. The relationship between clustering and recall probably depends on the task.

A stronger demonstration that long-term memory performance is likely dependent on short-term deficits was provided by Bauer (1979). He also found that long-term memory was inferior to that of normal children, but when the lists were adjusted to take into account the short-term encoding ability of each child individually, acquisition of both ability groups was similar. Furthermore, when memory was tested after a 24-hour interval, the two goups did not differ in percentage retention. Encoding strategy rather than long-term organization per se was further implicated in a self-paced study task, where (similar to Dallago & Moely's, 1980, findings) learning disabled subjects studied for less time, and as a result, took more trials to learn the list to criterion. Normals apparently used the study time to practice clustering items and rehearsing. Bauer concluded that although learning disabled subjects did not completely fail to use elaborative encoding strategies (since the clustering of learning disabled children reached normal levels in some conditions), nevertheless deficient encoding seems to be the major cause of poor long-term memory in these subjects.

Next, two studies by Ceci and associates provided important converging evidence for the intact nature of long-term semantic structure in learning disabilities. Ceci, Lea, and Ringstrom (1980) separated learning disabled children into those with specific visual deficits, specific auditory deficits, and those with deficits in both areas. This study is exemplary, in that it is one of the very few that did not ignore the heterogeneous nature of the learning disabled population. The approach paid off: In a cued-recall task, learning disabled children showed the same pattern of cue effectiveness as normal children, but only if the modality of presentation was one in which they had no diagnosed learning deficit. The results again suggested that semantic memory as such is not impaired, in that the deficiency was modality specific. Incidentally, children who were impaired in both auditory and visual processing showed the worst performance of all, consistent with the finding of a survey by Koppitz (1972) that the severity of learning disabilities is correlated with the number of specific deficits.

Ceci (in press) used a clever primed-naming task to show that 10-year-old learning disabled children do not differ from normal age-mates in automoatic semantic processing, but resemble 4-year-olds in purposive (strategic) processing. That is, when an appropriate strategy was available for anticipating the items to be named, the learning disabled children failed to use it; when no strategy was necessary, both groups of children performed alike. The results suggested a limited capacity for purposive processing. Once again, basic semantic memory appeared unimpaired.

Long-Term Memory for Prose

Studies of processing and recall are beginning to show the extent to which short-term encoding deficits affect memory for textual materials of more educational relevance. For example, memory for narrative materials in learning disabled adult college students was assessed by Worden et al. (1982). The story grammar of Mandler and Johnson (1977) was used to create a set of stimulus stories, much the way that sentences are derived from generative grammars of syntax. The stories were composed of a number of propositional nodes, corresponding to the proposed canonical structure of well-formed stories, mentally represented as the "story schema" (see Pressley, 1983). If learning disabled adults showed a pattern of nodal recall that differed from that of normal adults and children, we would have evidence that the structure of long-term memory might differ in some fundamental way. A preliminary experiment showed that the learning disabled adults' overall recall of stories was similar to that of normal third graders. However, even though recall was dramatically depressed vis-à-vis that of other adults, the learning disabled subjects' *pattern* of nodal recall was essentially intact (i.e., their recall was reduced by a constant amount across the various story constituents). Thus, the use of grammatically structured stories enabled rejection of the hypothesis of a structural deficiency in the organization of the story schema in long-term memory. Other measures of the quality of recall (distortions, deletions, or additions to the stimulus stories in recall) showed no differences among the subject groups (see also Hansen, 1978). Once again, the short-term memory "bottleneck" was implicated; while the deficit reduces a constant proportion of the information at each story node, what *is* stored is of good quality.

Several studies, all based on the same paradigm (i.e., Brown & Smiley, 1977), have investigated sensitivity of disabled learners to the relative importance of ideas in prose passages. Children (Hansen, 1978), adolescents (Smiley et al., 1977), and college students (Worden & Nakamura, 1982) have all been investigated. In two of these studies (Hansen, 1978; Smiley et al., 1977) disabled learners recalled considerably fewer of the most important propositions of narrative stories, when compared to normal subjects. In fact, Smiley et al. had to test subjects as young as first grade to find normal children who showed the same pattern of results as the disabled seventh graders! However, subjects in these studies received only one presentation of the stimulus stories. An important exception was the experiment by Worden and Nakamura (1982), who had their subjects rate the stimulus stories— a complex and repetitive analytic task—prior to recall. Their results showed that although learning disabled college students were significantly less sensitive to degrees of importance in the rating task, they nevertheless remembered main ideas better than less important parts, to the same degree as normals. In striking contrast to the other prose-recall studies, learning disabled adults' overall recall was equal to that of normal college students. Worden and Nakamura suggested that the repeated exposure afforded by the rating task may have elevated recall to normal levels.

In summary, no evidence exists that the schematic structure of long-term memory differs, but learning disabled subjects who have had only one exposure to prose materials recall quantitatively less than normal age-mates. In addition, the ability of learning disabled subjects to evaluate and recall story propositions as a function of importance level suffers when they have had only one presentation of the materials to remember. This general result is important, since students in educational settings may be expected to remember their lessons after reading them only once. However, the finding of normal performance in both (a) the overall amount of recall, and (b) the tendency to recall propositions of higher importance, after learning disabled subjects performed a repetitious and analytic rating task, suggests that strategy instruction should have important educational benefits in the area of prose recall.

Metamemory

Metamemory could be characterized as cognition about memory in general (see Forrest-Pressley & Gillies, 1983). It has also been conceived as specific knowledge about the workings of one's own memory. The study of metamemory may yield information relevant to the view of the learning disabled child as an inactive learner (Torgesen, 1980), whose major problem is only that he or she is less prone to employ the strategic memory behaviors that normal children spontaneously execute. However, although the study of metamemory in normal children has recently blossomed to almost unmanageable proportions, very little is known about learning-disabled children's awareness of the workings of their memory. Douglass (Note 2) gave children aged 8–11 a number of metamemory problems developed by Kreutzer, Leonard, and Flavell (1975). Disabled learners and normal controls showed equally good awareness of questions about the effects of memory ability, immediate versus delayed recall, study time, and preparation for remembering objects and events; knowledge of serial position effects was equally poor for both groups. In contrast, learning disabled children showed significantly lower awareness than normal controls about serial-recall and internal storage strategies (see also Haines & Torgesen, 1979; Torgesen & Goldman, 1977). In other words, a certain congruence appears to exist between disabled learners' memory deficits and metamemory in those deficit areas.

However, reported awareness may have no relation to use of a given strategy. For instance, even though learning disabled subjects reported awareness of study time as important for memory in Douglass's survey, we have already reviewed studies showing the tendency for disabled learners to spend *less* time than normals studying for memory tasks (Bauer, 1979; Dallago & Moely, 1980). Perhaps they are aware of study time as important in the abstract, but lack awareness of how much study time is appropriate for themselves or for various tasks. For example, Owings,

Petersen, Bransford, Morris, and Stein (1980) found that although "less successful" fifth graders spent as much time overall as "more successful" peers studying prose materials, they did not regulate their study time according to story difficulty.

Wong (1982) has recently reported the first systematic investigation of disabled learners' strategies in studying prose. Using stories developed by Brown and Smiley (1977), subjects read through 59 story units (each representing a separate event or idea) and selected 12 to serve as potential retrieval cues. Disabled learners were compared to normal and gifted children. An analysis of cue selection behavior showed that although the learning-disabled children were *not* less organized or planful, they were less exhaustive in their consideration of the story cues, and they showed less tendency to check their cue selections. Wong and Wilson (Note 3) studied fifth- and sixth-grade children's awareness of organization in prose materials by giving them organized versus scrambled expository passages to study. When asked "How are the two passages different?" normal children were able to give an adequate answer (after being given specific probe questions). In contrast, learning disabled children were significantly more likely to be unable to identify the differences, even when very explicit probe questions were asked. Moreover, in a subsequent sorting task, normal children reorganized a disorganized passage much more successfully than did learning disabled children. This deficiency in organizing the textual materials was quite easily overcome by a brief training procedure, however. Considered together, Wong's studies show that important differences exist between normal and disabled learners' awareness of the structure of prose, as well as their knowledge of how to study prose efficiently. See research discussed by Forrest-Pressley and Gillies (1983) for more on this theme.

Unfortunately, little more is known at this time about metamemory in the learning disabled. Reported awareness of memory strategies, as well as knowledge about when and in what tasks certain strategies are most appropriately applied, should be verified with more direct behavioral indices of strategy usage. Most critically, further research is needed before the direction of causation in memory-metamemory connections is understood. For example, is the poor serial memory of learning disabled children a cause or an effect of their metamemory deficiency in serial recall, or are both a result of some other factor(s)?

Research on Memory Strategy Instruction

We are now ready to review investigations of memory strategies. The prevailing procedure in this research has been that the investigator selects a deficit area (e.g., short-term serial recall) and trains subjects in a strategy (such as cumulative rehearsal) designed to overcome the deficit. A demonstration of the strategy's effectiveness is provided if the strategy-instructed group performs significantly better than a comparable group of uninstructed subjects. A more educationally meaningful question is whether the learning disabled strategy group achieves a *normal* level of performance. That is, if strategy-instructed disabled learners perform as well as normal controls (assuming that no ceiling effects exist), a production deficiency for that strategy can be inferred. However, if the strategy helps both groups, it cannot be assumed to be the only factor distinguishing learning disabled from normal subjects (but may be a worthy strategy nevertheless). If the strategy is ineffective, a mediation deficiency may be suspected, but further research is needed to discover whether the strategy was too weak, too difficult, or inappropriate in some other respect. What should be noted in this approach is the emphasis on very specific strategies for very specific tasks. Little research exists at present on the utility of general strategies, or on the generalization of strategies from one situation to another. Again, Forrest-Pressley and Gillies (1983) provide additional commentary on this point.

Strategies for Short-Term Memory

Torgesen and Goldman (1977) asked learning-disabled second graders to learn the sequence in which the experimenter pointed to a series of pictures. A 15-second delay period was used to observe any evidence of rehearsing, such as lip movements or whispered words. The learning disabled children showed less evidence of rehearsal and recalled less than their normal peers. Training in the use of rehearsal eliminated the recall difference between the two ability groups. This study was partially replicated by Haines and Torgesen (1979), who studied the effects of reward on short-term serial recall. Although this was not a training study per se, the findings were exciting because they suggested that disabled learners may be able to generate their own strategies spontaneously, if only given an incentive to perform better. When given a penny for each correctly recalled item, children from both ability groups rehearsed more and recalled more. The number of learning disabled children who reported the use of rehearsal improved significantly from 28% (no incentive) to 70% in the incentive condition. Thus, both reported awareness and actual use of the rehearsal strategy were increased in learning disabled children, even though no particular strategy instruction was given. However, because the rewards improved recall performance for learning disabled and normal children to the same degree, Haines and Torgesen (1979) pointed out that motivation could not be the only difference between the two ability groups: "Although incentives may help to eliminate some of the performance deficiencies of poor readers, it may also be necessary to provide them with specific training and practice in the efficient use of appropriate task strategies" (p. 53). Moreover, in a study where disabled learners were separated into groups defined by normal versus poor digit-span peformance, the latter group was not able to improve when given rewards for better performance (Torgesen & Houck, 1980).

The combined effects of rewards and strategy instruction were studied by Dawson, Hallahan, Reeve, and Ball (1980), using the central incidental task. We have already noted that this task, once thought to measure selective attention, is now viewed as a short-term serial-recall task complicated by the presentation of irrelevant stimuli (see Douglas & Peters, 1979; Tarver, 1981). Following an earlier study by Tarver, Hallahan, Kauffman, and Ball (1976), Dawson et al. (1980)

trained learning disabled children to use a cumulative rehearsal strategy that significantly improved their performance. To rule out the possibility that the strategy merely increased performance via increased motivation, Dawson et al. also employed a reinforcement manipulation in which the children were awarded a prize for every correct answer on the central task. Although reinforcement plus rehearsal training resulted in the best performance, the reinforcement-only condition did not differ from the standard control condition (contrary to the result of Haines & Torgesen, 1979, for short-term serial recall). Both rehearsal only and rehearsal plus reinforcement significantly improved performance. Dawson et al. concluded that incentives are only effective when subjects are also provided with the strategy that they lack. Although neither the Tarver et al. (1976) nor the Dawson et al. (1980) study directly compared the effects of rehearsal strategy instruction on learning disabled versus normal children, evidence that rehearsal may be the critical variable came from the finding of improved recall on primacy items in the trained learning-disabled subjects. A reduced primacy effect in this task is a result that most characteristically distinguishes learning disabled from normal subjects.

In contrast, Ford, Pelham, and Ross (Note 4) trained learning disabled and normal children to use a cumulative rehearsal strategy in both the central-incidental task and on a standard serial-recall task. Both ability groups benefited equally, suggesting that lack of rehearsal is not the *only* critical variable distinguishing learning disabled subjects from normals in short-term memory. Similarly, Torgesen and Houck (1980) found equal benefits of induced cumulative rehearsal for learning disabled and normal subjects. Another strategy, experimenter-imposed temporal chunking of the items, also improved peformance equally. Based on these results, Torgesen and Houck made the strong statement that "such control processes as cumulative rehearsal and chunking could not have been responsible for performance differences among groups" (p. 158).

Findings such as by Ford et al. (Note 4) and by Torgesen and Houck (1980) suggest the existence of one or more basic structural deficits that may (a) inhibit the spontaneous use of the rehearsal strategy and (b) limit its effectiveness for disabled learners relative to normals when both groups have been strategy instructed. If speed of processing is an important variable, as Perfetti and Lesgold (1978) and others (see Tarver, 1981) have suggested, the reduced rate of information processing in short-term memory could account for both kinds of results. Nevertheless, although much further reserach is needed to pinpoint the true locus of the deficit, it is safe to conclude that short-term memory can be improved in the learning disabled via instruction in strategies such as temporal chunking and cumulative rehearsal.

Strategies for Long-Term Memory
for Lists of Words and/or Pictures

As we have seen, no evidence exists at present that the structure of long-term memory is deficient in the learning disabled. Rather, inefficient encoding is suspected to be the cause of poor long-term memory performance of learning-disabled subjects. Consequently, an obvious research strategy would be to focus on inducing the active use of a particular organizational strategy during study. Typically, however, a shotgun approach has been used to search for effective strategies. For instance, Wong et al. (1977) and Wong (1978) found that recall of categorical words was improved by a combination of (a) presenting items in categories, (b) instructing subjects to learn conceptually related items together, and (c) presenting category cues at recall (compared to a random-presentation uncued recall). Since there were no groups X conditions interactions in these studies, learning disabled and normal children appeared to benefit equally from these manipulations. A similar study by Dallago and Moely (1980) used a more direct strategy manipulation, wherein subjects were required to sort 25 items into five categories prior to recall. Three sorting strategies were compared: semantic (subjects sorted into conceptual categories), formal (color categories were required), and self-determined (a free-sort condition). Both the semantic-sort and free-sort strategies significantly improved recall, and once again the improvement was similar for both learning disabled and normal children.

Torgesen (1977) employed an even stronger approach. He trained learning-disabled and normal children to sort 24 pictures into four conceptual categories and also trained them to recall in category blocks, using a cuing chart. The strategy thus induced organized encoding and also provided categorical support at retrieval. Memory was dramatically improved for both ability groups, and the strategy may even have elevated the learning disabled group to the normal level. Unfortunately, performance in the strategy-trained groups was so good that ceiling effects likely existed.

Ceci et al. (1980, Experiment II) trained learning disabled and normal subjects to sort into semantic categories (perceptual-sort and no-sorting control groups were also included). The mode of presentation was either visual (color categories) or auditory (words were presented in different voices). This was important because Ceci et al. studied separate groups of learning disabled children whose deficits were exclusively visual, auditory, or both. Ceci et al. found that semantic sorting was effective in eliminating differences between learning disabled and normal subjects, but only when the mode of presentation did *not* match the deficits exhibited by a particular learning disabled group. That is, semantic sorting of visually presented items aided the aurally deficient subjects, and semantic sorting of aurally presented items aided the visually deficient subjects, when performance was compared to that of the no-sorting subjects. Subjects who were deficient in both modalities did not benefit from semantic sorting as much as the other groups. Nevertheless, with use of the semantic sorting strategy, the groups with exclusively auditory or visual deficits performed at normal levels for both cued and uncued recall, where no ceiling effect existed. Cuing substantially improved recall for everybody, suggesting that output deficiencies do not distinguish learning disabled subjects from normals. The results of this study show that active organization induced by sorting may be effective in erasing recall differences between ability groups, as long as processing does not take place in the impaired modality.

Finally, a movement toward studying the permanency and transferability of trained memory strategies has just begun. Consider an unpublished study by Cort, Shepherd, and Frank (Note 5, reported in Fleischner & Shepherd, Note 6) comparing three different training procedures. In the "instructional" condition, children were taught to sort items into categories, to study the pictures by groups, and to recall the pictures by group. In the "cued-inferential" condition, the experimenter progressively blocked the pictures into categories across several trials (it was thought that if this procedure led the children to discover the sorting strategy themselves, more lasting effects might be obtained than with direct instruction—this turned out to be false). A "practice" condition simply gave subjects more exposure to the task. Results of a 1-day posttest and a 1-month retest showed that direct instruction was associated with significantly higher sorting, clustering, and recall scores in both learning disabled and non-learning-disabled children, compared with the cued-inferential and practice conditions. Thus, preliminary research gives hope that benefits of strategy training might persist for at least a month after instruction.

Before considering the role of strategy instruction in memory for prose materials, we should reflect upon the questions raised in the word- and/or picture-recall studies just reviewed. Researchers have consistently found benefits of strategies designed to promote the use of organization in study, especially when modality-specific deficits are taken into consideration. However, because of conflicting results, it is premature to conclude that "brief training in the use of strategies . . . essentially eliminates performance differences between learning disabled and normal children" (Torgesen, 1980, p. 24). In some studies it does, but in others the strategy instruction benefited the normal subjects as well. When this occurs, it is necessary to examine the degree of benefit; even though learning disabled performance does not match that of normal strategy-instructed subjects, it could be that learning disabled subjects have improved to a greater degree, relative to their initially lower level of performance. In such a case it could be said that the strategy benefited the disabled learners more than normals, but that there still are other factors responsible for the remaining performance discrepancy. Thus, as in studies of short-term memory, it is not possible to decide at present that poor long-term recall is entirely the result of a production deficiency in the spontaneous application of appropriate study strategies. It is also possible that there could be a basic structural deficit, such as in the speed of information processing, that interferes with the successful execution of organized study strategies and thereby reduces long-term memory.

Moreover, because researchers have designed strategy manipulations that vary several factors at once, it is not possible to identify which strategy components are most responsible for memory improvement in learning disabled children. Well-designed parametric studies are needed to tease apart, for example, the effects of blocked versus random presentation, category naming versus active sorting, and use of cues versus category-constrained recall. The task should be designed so that the effects of a given strategy on normals can be measured without ceiling effects.

If researchers eventually identify a critical strategy (or strategies) in which learning disabled subjects are deficient, it will become appropriate to investigate the reasons behind failure to exhibit the strategy under standard conditions. A good suggestion (Torgesen, 1980) is that "the basic skills necessary for the execution of a strategy must be firmly established and practiced before they can become organized and used as a aid in learning" (p. 24). Torgesen suggests that even though learning disabled children may have the skills to use memory strategies when instructed, they have not had the relevant strategies in their repertoire of cognitive skills long enough (because of a developmental lag) to be invoked automatically in appropriate situations. This suggestion could be tested in future research by including (in addition to normal age-mates) a comparison group of normal children at least 2 years younger than the learning disabled subjects.

Finally, although the identification of a specific strategy that distinguishes learning disabled from normal children on long-term memory tasks will contribute significantly to theoreticians' understanding of learning disabilities, little pedagogical progress will be made until studies of the transferability and generalization of memory strategies are conducted. One study has found that learning disabled subjects who were taught to sort categorical stimuli prior to recall derived benefits that lasted at least a month. Other questions, however, remain unanswered at present. Will subjects who successfully sort categorical stimuli be able to form a sorting organization of more difficult semantically unrelated items? If so, will the sorting strategy aid recall of unrelated items to the same degree as it does for categorical materials? Should strategies learned for one kind of materials (such as word lists) generalize to other materials (e.g., prose)?

Strategies for Long-Term Memory for Prose

Worden et al. (1982) studied two strategies designed to help learning disabled college students remember more from stories for which their level of recall had previously been found to be at the third-grade level. First, a repetition strategy simply entailed reading the story three times, and was based on the short-term memory bottleneck view (due to reduced speed of processing) of learning disabilities. That is, rote repetition was designed to give subjects more than one opportunity to process information that was not successfully encoded on the first pass. The second strategy was designed to increase the subjects' awareness of the schematic organization of the materials to be remembered. The subjects were instructed in the story grammar on which the stories were based (i.e., Mandler & Johnson, 1977), and became proficient at constructing grammatical stories from a scrambled set of story propositions. In essence, this "construction" strategy was analogous to the strategy of sorting words into a categorical structure; in this case the elements were the propositions and the structure was the story schema. Surprisingly, although the repetition strategy resulted in a striking improvement in performance, there was no difference between the construction and the standard conditions. It was concluded that the analytic activity required in story construction interfered with the storage of the actual content of the propositions.

The benefits of repetition were also indirectly suggested in a study that required learning-disabled college students to rate the importance level of story propositions prior to recall (Worden & Nakamura, 1982). Following a similar procedure by

Brown, Smiley, and Lawton (1978; see also Wong, 1982), the subjects were required to select 12 propositions to serve as potential retrieval cues. Although recall was not actually cued, the effects of retrieval cue selection as a study strategy were compared in groups that selected cues before recall versus after recall. Normal subjects' recall benefited from cue selection prior to recall; learning disabled subjects' performance did not. In fact, it was only the learning-disabled subjects who selected cues after recall whose performance was equivalent to that of normal adults, and this good performance was thought to result from the repetitious exposure afforded by the story-rating task. On the other hand, the poor performance of learning disabled subjects who selected cues immediately prior to recall seems to have been caused by the very analytic activity that boosted performance in the normal group. That is, the activity of searching for 12 propositions to serve as potential retrieval cues seems to have interfered with memory for the actual story content.

These failures of certain analytic study strategies to improve story recall (i.e., the construction task in Worden et al., 1982, and the cue selection task in Worden & Nakamura, 1982) do not rule out the possibility that other such strategies may improve recall. Thus far, researchers have been only partially successful, however. Wong (1979) also used the Brown and Smiley (1977) materials to investigate the effects of a questioning strategy on story recall. Wong designed a series of questions based on the most important propositions from these stories. Half the children were given a question about a target paragraph prior to hearing that section of the story. In the no-questions condition the usual finding that normal children recalled more story propositions than learning-disabled children was obtained. In the questions condition, however, the two ability groups did not differ, and ceiling effects were not in evidence. A groups × questions × importance level interaction showed that the use of questions substantially and differentially increased the disabled learners' recall of the most important story propositions. However, this result raises the possibility that the questions, because they were based on the most important propositions, constituted a repeated input for those items. Thus, although Wong's research suggests that a study strategy based on prior questions may improve retention, the effects of repeated exposure cannot be ruled out as a possible explanation.

The possibility that learner-generated questions might improve recall of prose materials in learning disabled adolescents was investigated by Wong and Jones (Note 7). Subjects were trained to underline the main ideas in short paragraphs and to formulate questions based on the underlined ideas. As a result, the disabled learners' awareness of important textual elements improved substantially, and their performance on a subsequent comprehension test (essentially, cued recall) was facilitated. Significantly, however, their free recall of the paragraphs was not improved to normal levels by this method. The results suggest that although self-generated questions may be useful for enhancing storage of prose information, as tested by cued recall, this method may not be a useful strategy for improving retrieval of information from textual materials.

In spite of this single promising result, the overall impression one gets is that there is no consistent finding as yet that strategies promoting the use of organization in study improve the retention of prose materials. Moreover, future studies of organizational strategies will need to rule out the potential benefit of simple repetition, since at least one study has shown dramatic effects of providing repeated exposure to stories. Finally, as in the word-recall area, studies of the transfer and generalization of effective study strategies must also be conducted if this research is to have any meaningful educational application (see also Chapters 1, 2, and 5 of this volume).

Future Directions for Memory Strategy Instruction

Our consideration of the research on memory deficits in disabled learners has identified short-term memory as the locus of inefficient information processing. The general problem can be characterized in the following oversimplified fashion. Perceptual information is initially intact—although opinions vary, this is the current consensus view. At the other end of the information processing chain, researchers agree that there does not seem to be anything deficient about the structure of long-term semantic memory. Rather, memory problems are due to inefficient and incomplete processing in short-term memory. Deciding whether short-term memory deficits are strategic and/or metamemorial in character, or whether they are based on structural deficiencies (such as slower decoding, faster rate of decay, or inability to keep track of order information) will be one of the main tasks for researchers over the next several years.

Research on strategy instruction has been used to defend both the strategic deficit and the structural deficit view. Indeed, sometimes the same researcher has advocated both views (cf. Torgesen & Houck, 1980, with Torgesen, 1980)! The strategy deficit view is supported in studies in which strategy-instructed disabled learners achieve performance equal to normal controls (but critics warn that ceiling effects can compromise these findings). The structural deficit view is supported whenever both ability groups benefit from strategy instruction (but critics can argue that the optimal strategy was not taught). Because both types of results have been obtained, it is clear that either (a) one finding will predominate over the long run, and its associated theory will be supported by the weight of accumulated studies; or (b) some other research approach will have to be found to pit the strategy deficit against the structural deficit hypothesis more directly.

Ironically, the outcome may have great theoretical importance and little educational impact. Educators will probably emphasize strategy instruction even if the main problem in learning disabilities proves to be structural in nature. Happily, researchers have identified several strategies that significantly improve memory for disabled learners. The list of potential strategies has not been exhausted by any means. For example, recognition memory, of obvious relevance to performance on multiple-choice tests, has not been studied. Paired-associate studies are also needed to investigate whether strategies known to help normal students (such as elaborative imagery or the keyword method) will also aid disabled learners (Paivio, 1983;

Pressley, 1983; Chapter 2 in this volume). Much further research on prose recall is also needed, particularly with expository materials that more closely approximate educational texts.

Studies that separate learning disabled groups into distinct subtypes such as groups with visual versus auditory deficits (e.g., Ceci et al., 1980; Cohen & Netley, 1978) or with digit-span deficiencies (Torgesen & Houck, 1980) promise to provide information enabling the design of specific strategies for specific problems. In addition, the role of incentives in improving memory performance should be investigated further. The expectation of success may provide normal learners with intrinsic motivation in learning tasks; repeated failure may lead to a lack of intrinsic motivation for learning disabled students. The application of strategy instruction plus extrinsic rewards may prove a powerful combination for improving their performance.

Finally, much more research is needed on the application of memory strategies in real-world settings. Since learning disabilities are now known to persist into adulthood, efforts should be made to train students to apply memory strategies in everyday tasks, as well as in educational settings. Serial recall, for instance, is relevant for remembering a series of bus transfers or the correct execution of a recipe. List-recall techniques can be valuable in shopping. Techniques for improving prose recall are valuable for remembering information gleaned from books, magazines, and newspapers. Associative learning strategies are useful for recall of names and dates such as appointments, birthdays, and anniversaries; the keyword method aids memory for paired information, such as states and capitals, or foreign-language and English vocabulary (see other chapters in this volume). At present it is simply not known whether strategy techniques developed for disabled learners in laboratory tasks will transfer to similar real-world memory problems.

A good start has been made. The next several years should yield many exciting new developments that will enrich the educational experience of disabled learners, improve their self confidence, and lead to greater success in overcoming their memory difficulties in everyday life.

Acknowledgments. I would like to thank several important researchers in this field who forwarded preprints and unpublished manuscripts to me: Richard Bauer, Steve Ceci, Daniel Hallahan, Margaret Jo Shepherd, Sara Tarver, Joseph Torgesen, and Bernice Wong.

Reference Notes

1. Kee, D. W., Worden, P. E., and Gardner, B. *Sentence demonstration ability in learning disabled and normal college students: Analysis of presentation mode, sentence length, and syntactic violation effects.* Paper presented at the annual meeting of the American Educational Research Association, New York, March 1982.

2. Douglass, L. C. *Metamemory in learning disabled children: A clue to memory*

deficiencies. Paper presented at the biennial meeting of the Society for Research in Child Development, Boston 1981.

3. Wong, B. Y. L., & Wilson, M. *Investigating awareness of and teaching passage organization.* Unpublished manuscript, 1981.
4. Ford, C. E., Pelham, W. E., & Ross, A. O. *The role of selective attention and rehearsal in the auditory short-term memory task performance of poor and normal readers.* Unpublished manuscript, 1978.
5. Cort, R. Shepherd, M. J., & Frank, B. *The effects of instruction on learning disabled and nondisabled children's use of an organization strategy to aid recall.* Unpublished manuscript, The Research Institute for the Study of Learning Disabilities. New York: Teachers College, Columbia University, 1980.
6. Fleischner, J., & Shepherd, M. J. *Improving the performance of children with learning disabilities: Instruction matters.* Unpublished manuscript, 1980.
7. Wong, B. Y. L., & Jones, W. *Increasing metacomprehension in learning-disabled and normally-achieving students through self-questioning training.* Unpublished manuscript, 1982.

References

Ackerman, P., Dykman, R. A., & Peters, J. E. Learning disabled boys as adolescents. *Journal of the American Academy of Child Psychiatry,* 1977, *16,* 293–313.

Algozzine, R., & Sutherland, J. Non-psychoeducational foundations of learning disabilities. *Journal of Special Education,* 1977, *11,* 91–98.

Bauer, R. H. Memory processes in children with learning disabilities: Evidence for deficient rehearsal. *Journal of Experimental Child Psychology,* 1977, *24,* 415–430.

Bauer, R. H. Memory, acquisition, and category clustering in learning disabled children. *Journal of Experimental Child Psychology,* 1979, *27,* 365–383.

Benton, A. L. Minimal brain dysfunction from a neuropsychological point of view. *Annals of the New York Academy of Sciences,* 1973, *205,* 29–37.

Benton, A. L. Developmental dyslexia: Neurological aspects. In W. J. Friedlander (Ed.), *Advances in Neurology* (Vol. 7). New York: Raven Press, 1975.

Broadbent, D. E. *Perception and communication.* New York: Pergamon, 1958.

Brown, A. L., & Smiley, S. S. Rating the importance of structural units of prose passages: A problem of metacognitive development. *Child Development,* 1977, *48,* 1–8.

Brown, A. L., Smiley, S. S., & Lawton, S. Q. C. The effects of experience on the selection of suitable retrieval cues for studying texts. *Child Development,* 1978, *49,* 829–835.

Case, R. Structures and strictures: Some functional limitations on the course of cognitive growth. *Cognitive Psychology,* 1974, *6,* 544–573.

Ceci, S. J. An investigation of the semantic processing characteristics of normal and language/learning-disabled children (L/LDs). *Developmental Psychology,* in press.

Ceci, S. J., Lea, S. E. G., & Ringstrom, M. D. Coding characteristics of normal and learning-disabled 10-year-olds: Evidence for dual pathways to the cognitive system. *Journal of Experimental Psychology: Human Learning and Memory,* 1980, *6,* 785–797.

Cermak, L. S., Goldberg-Warter, J., DeLuca, D., Cermak, S., & Drake, C. The role of interference in the verbal retention ability of learning disabled children. *Journal of Learning Disabilities*, 1981, *14*, 291–295.

Chi, M. T. H. Short-term memory limitations in children: Capacity or processing deficits? *Memory & Cognition*, 1976, *4*, 559–572.

Cohen, R. L., & Netley, C. Cognitive deficits, learning disabilities, and WISC verbal-performance consistency. *Developmental Psychology*, 1978, *14*, 624–634.

Cordoni, B. K., O' Donnell, J. P., Ramaniah, N. B., Kurtz, J., & Rosenshein, K. Wechsler adult intelligence score patterns for learning disabled young adults. *Journal of Learning Disabilities*, 1981, *14*, 404–407.

Cravioto, J., & DeLicardie, E. R. Environmental and nutritional deprivation in children with learning disabilities. In W. M. Cruickshank & D. P. Hallahan (Eds.), *Perceptual and learning disabilities in children* (Vol. 2, *Research and theory*). Syracuse: Syracuse University Press, 1975.

Dallago, M. L. P., & Moely, B. E. Free recall in boys of normal and poor reading levels as a function of task manipulations. *Journal of Experimental Child Psychology*, 1980, *30*, 62–78.

Dawson, M. M., Hallahan, D. P., Reeve, R. E., & Ball, D. W. The effect of reinforcement and verbal rehearsal on selective attention in learning-disabled children. *Journal of Abnormal Child Psychology*, 1980, *8*, 133–144.

Douglas, V. I., & Peters, K. G. Toward a clearer definition of the attentional deficit of hyperactive children. In G. A. Hale & M. Lewis (Eds.), *Attention and cognitive development*. New York: Plenum, 1979.

Drucker, J. F., & Hagen, J. W. Developmental trends in the processing of task relevant and task irrelevant information. *Child Development*, 1969, *40*, 371–382.

Eisenberg, L. The epidemiology of reading retardation and a program of preventive intervention. In J. Money (Ed.), *The disabled reader: Education of the dyslexic child*. Baltimore: Johns Hopkins Press, 1966.

Forrest-Pressley, D. L., & Gillies, L. A. Children's flexible use of strategies during reading. In M. Pressley & J. R. Levin (Eds.), *Cognitive strategy research: Educational applications*. New York: Springer-Verlag, 1983.

Frederiksen, J. R. Assessment of perceptual, decoding, and lexical skills and their relation to reading proficiency. In A. M. Lesgold, J. W. Pellegrino, S. D. Fokkema, & R. Glaser (Eds.), *Cognitive psychology and instruction*. New York: Plenum, 1978.

Freeman, R. D. Special education and the electroencephalogram: Marriage of convenience. *The Journal of Special Education*, 1967, *2*, 61–73.

Hagen, J. W. The effects of distraction on selective attention. *Child Development*, 1967, *38*, 658–668.

Hagen, J. W., & Huntsman, N. J. Selective attention in mental retardates. *Developmental Psychology*, 1971, *5*, 151–160.

Hagen, J. W., & Sabo, R. A developmental study of selective attention. *Merrill-Palmer Quarterly*, 1967, *13*, 159–172.

Haines, D. J., & Torgensen, J. K. The effects of incentives on rehearsal and short-term memory in children with reading problems. *Learning Disabilities Quarterly*, 1979, *2*, 48–55.

Hallahan, D. P. Distractibility in the learning disabled child. In W. M. Cruickshank & D. P. Hallahan (Eds.), *Perceptual and learning disabilities in children* (Vol. 2, *Research and theory*). Syracuse: Syracuse University Press, 1975.

Hallahan, D. P., Kauffman, J. M., & Ball, D. W. Developmental trends in recall of central and incidental auditory materials. *Journal of Experimental Child Psychology*, 1974, *17*, 409–421.

Hallahan, D. P., Stainback, S., Ball, D. W., & Kauffman, J. M. Selective attention in cerebral palsied and normal children. *Journal of Abnormal Child Psychology*, 1973, *1*, 280–291.

Hallahan, D. P., & Reeve, R. E. Selective attention and distractibility. In B. K. Keogh (Ed.), *Advances in special education* (Vol. 1, *Basic constructs and theoretical orientations*). Greenwich, CT: JAI Press, 1980.

Hammill, D. D. Defining "LD" for programmatic purposes. *Academic Therapy*, 1976, *12*, 29–37.

Hansen, C. L. Story retelling used with average and learning disabled readers as a measure of reading comprehension. *Learning Disability Quarterly*, 1978, *1*, 62–69.

Harris, A. J. Lateral dominance and reading disability. *Journal of Learning Disabilities*, 1979, *12*, 57–63.

Hughes, J. R. Biochemical and electroencephalographic correlates in learning disabilities. In R. M. Knights and D. J. Bakker (Eds.), *The neuropsychology of learning disorders*. Baltimore: University Park Press, 1976.

Huttenlocher, J., & Burke, D. Why does memory span increase with age? *Cognitive Psychology*, 1976, *8*, 1–31.

Jackson, M., & McClelland, J. Sensory and cognitive determinants of reading speed. *Journal of Verbal Learning and Verbal Behavior*, 1975, *14*, 565–574.

Jorm, A. J. The cognitive and neurological basis of developmental dyslexia: A theoretical framework and review. *Cognition*, 1979, *7*, 19–33.

Kaufman, A. S. The WISC-R and learning disabilities assessment: State of the art. *Journal of Learning Disabilities*, 1981, *14*, 520–526.

Kavale, K. Meta-analysis of the relationship between visual perceptual skills and reading achievement. *Journal of Learning Disabilities*, 1982, *15*, 42–51.

Koppitz, E. M. Special class pupils with learning disabilities: A five-year follow-up study. *Academic Therapy*, 1972, *8*, 133–153.

Kreutzer, M. A., Leonard, C., & Flavell, J. H. An interview study of children's knowledge about memory. *Monographs of the Society for Research in Child Development*, 1975, *40*(1, Serial No. 159).

Lesgold, A. M., & Perfetti, C. A. Interactive processes in reading comprehension. *Discourse Processes*, 1978, *1*, 323–336.

Mandler, J. M., & Johnson, N. S. Remembrance of things parsed: Story structure and recall. *Cognitive Psychology*, 1977, *9*, 111–151.

Manis, F. R., & Morrison, F. J. Processing of identity and position information in normal and disabled readers. *Journal of Experimental Child Psychology*, 1982, *33*, 74–86.

Money, J. On learning and not learning to read. In J. Money (Ed.), *The disabled reader: Education of the dyslexic child*. Baltimore: Johns Hopkins Press, 1966.

Morrison, F. J., Giordani, B., & Nagy, J. Reading disabilities: An information-processing analysis. *Science*, 1977, *196*, 77–79.

National Advisory Committee on Handicapped Children. *First annual report: Special education for handicapped children*. Washington, DC: U. S. Office of Education, Department of Health, Education, and Welfare, 1968.

Orton, S. T. *Reading, writing, and speech problems in children*. New York: Norton, 1937.

Owen, F. W., Adams, P. A., Forrest, T., Stolz, L. M., & Fisher, S. Learning disorders in children: sibling studies. *Monographs of the Society for Research in Child Development*, 1971, *36*, No. 4 (Serial No. 144).

Owings, R., Petersen, G., Bransford, J. D., Morris, C. D., & Stein, B. S. Spontaneous monitoring and regulation of learning: A comparison of successful and less successful fifth-graders. *Journal of Educational Psychology*, 1980, *72*, 250–256.

Paivio, A. Strategies in language learning. In M. Pressley & J. R. Levin (Eds.), *Cognitive strategy research: Educational applications*. New York: Springer-Verlag, 1983.

Pelham, W. E. Selective attention deficits in poor readers? Dichotic listening, speeded-classification, and auditory and visual central and incidental learning tasks. *Child Development*, 1979, *50*, 1050–1061.

Perfetti, C. A., & Goldman, S. R. Discourse memory and reading comprehension skill. *Journal of Verbal Learning and Verbal Behavior*, 1976, *14*, 33–42.

Perfetti, C. A., & Hogaboam, T. The relationship between single word decoding and reading comprehension skill. *Journal of Educational Psychology*, 1975, *67*, 461–469.

Perfetti, C. A., & Lesgold, A. M. Discourse comprehension and sources of individual differences. In M. Just & P. Carpenter (Eds.), *Cognitive processes in comprehension*. Hillsdale, NJ: Erlbaum, 1978.

Peterson, P. L., & Swing, S. R. Problems in classroom implementation of cognitive strategy instruction. In M. Pressley & J. R. Levin (Eds.), *Cognitive strategy research: Educational applications*. New York: Springer-Verlag, 1983.

Pressley, M. Making meaningful materials easier to learn: Lessons from cognitive strategy research. In M. Pressley & J. R. Levin (Eds.), *Cognitive strategy research: Educational applications*. New York: Springer-Verlag, 1983.

Rosner, S. L., Abrams, J. C., Daniels, P. R., & Schiffman, G. B. Dealing with the reading needs of the learning disabled child. *Journal of Learning Disabilities*, 1981, *14*, 436–448.

Rourke, B. P. Reading retardation in children: Developmental lag or deficit? In R. M. Knights & D. J. Bakker (Eds.), *The neuropsychology of learning disorders*. Baltimore: University Park Press, 1976.

Satz, P., & Fletcher, J. M. Minimal brain dysfunctions: An appraisal of research concepts and methods. In H. Rie & H. Rie (Eds.), *Minimal brain dysfunctions*, in press.

Satz, P., & Friel, J. Some predictive antecedents of specific learning disability: A preliminary one year follow-up. In P. Satz and J. Ross (Eds.), *The disabled learner: Early detection and intervention*. Rotterdam: Rotterdam University Press, 1973.

Satz, P., & van Nostrand, G. K. Developmental dyslexia: An evaluation of a theory. In P. Satz and J. Ross (Eds.), *The disabled learner: Early detection and intervention*. Rotterdam: Rotterdam University Press, 1973.

Schrag, P., & Divoky, D. *The myth of the hyperactive child*. New York: Dell, 1976.

Silver, L. B. Familial patterns in children with neurologically-based learning disabilities. *Journal of Learning Disabilities*, 1971, *4*, 349–358.

Smiley, S. S., Oakley, D. D., Worthen, D., Campione, J. C., & Brown, A. L. Recall of thematically relevant material by adolescent good and poor readers as a function of written versus oral presentation. *Journal of Educational Psychology*, 1977, *69*, 381–389.

Swanson, J. M., & Kinsbourne, M. The cognitive effects of stimulant drugs in hyperactive children. In G. A. Hale and M. Lewis, *Attention and cognitive development,* New York: Plenum, 1979.

Tarver, S. G. Underselective attention in learning-disabled children: Some reconceptualizations of old hypotheses. *Exceptional Education Quarterly,* 1981, *2,* 25-35.

Tarver, S. G., & Hallahan, D. P. Additional deficits in children with learning disabilities: A review. *Journal of Learning Disabilities,* 1974, *7,* 560-569.

Tarver, S. G., Hallahan, D. P., Kauffman, J. M., & Ball, D. W. Verbal rehearsal and selective attention in children with learning disabilities: A developmental lag. *Journal of Experimental Child Psychology,* 1976, *22,* 375-385.

Torgesen, J. K. Memorization processes in reading-disabled children. *Journal of Educational Psychology,* 1977, *79,* 571-578.

Torgesen, J. K. Conceptual and educational implications of the use of efficient task strategies by learning disabled children. *Journal of Learning Disabilities,* 1980, *13,* 19-26.

Torgesen, J. K., & Goldman, T. Verbal and rehearsal and short-term memory in reading disabled children. *Child Development,* 1977, *48,* 56-60.

Torgesen, J. K., & Houck, D. G. Processing deficiencies in children who perform poorly on the digit span test. *Journal of Educational Psychology,* 1980, *72,* 141-160.

Vellutino, F. R., Steger, B. M., Moyer, S. C., Harding, C. J., & Niles, J. A. Has the perceptual deficit hypothesis led us astray? *Journal of Learning Disabilities,* 1977, *10,* 375-385.

Wender, P. H. Hypothesis for a possible biochemical basis of minimal brain dysfunction. In R. M. Knights & D. J. Bakker (Eds.), *The neuropsychology of learning disorders.* Baltimore: University Park Press, 1976.

White, C. V., Pascarella, E. T., & Pflaum, S. W. Effects of training in sentence construction on the comprehension of learning disabled children. *Journal of Educational Psychology,* 1981, *73,* 697-704.

Wong, B. Y. L. The effects of directive cues on the organization of memory and recall in good and poor readers. *Journal of Educational Research,* 1978, *72,* 32-38.

Wong, B. Y. L. Increasing retention of main ideas through questioning strategies. *Learning Disability Quarterly,* 1979, *2,* 42-47.

Wong, B. Y. L. Strategic behavior in selecting retrieval cues in gifted, normal achieving and learning disabled children. *Journal of Learning Disabilities,* 1982, *15,* 33-37.

Wong, B. Y. L., Wong, R., & Foth, D. Recall and clustering of verbal materials among normal and poor readers. *Bulletin of the Psychonomic Society,* 1977, *10,* 375-378.

Worden, P. E., Malmgren, I., & Gabourie, P. Memory for stories in learning disabled adults. *Journal of Learning Disabilities,* 1982, *15,* 145-152.

Worden, P. E., Nakamura, G. V. Story comprehension and recall in learning-disabled vs. normal college students. *Journal of Educational Psychology,* in press.

7. The Zone of Proximal Development

Jeanne D. Day

Children develop within a changing social world. In interaction with others they acquire new ways of responding to the people and things around them. But even as they practice their new skills, their environment changes and so they must learn still other ways of behaving. Thus, children develop in a dialectical fashion.

The dialectical interpretation of development, long accepted in the Soviet Union (e.g., Cole, 1978; Cole & Scribner, 1978; Luria, 1976, 1979; Vygotsky, 1978; Wertsch, 1981; Wozniak, 1975a, 1975b), has recently become more popular in the West (e.g., Meacham, 1972, 1976; Piaget, 1952; Riegel, 1975, 1976). This enthusiasm for a dialectical approach to human development has produced new trends in research. For instance, the number of studies investigating interactions in mother-child (Gardner & Rogoff, 1982; Hood, Feiss, & Aron, 1981; Sameroff, 1975; Wertsch, McNamee, McLane, & Budwig, 1980), father-child (Parke & O'Leary, 1976) and tutor-pupil (Allen & Feldman, 1976; Collins & Stevens, 1981) dyads has grown considerably. Similarly, the dialectical perspective has led to new views about the development (e.g., Campione, Brown, & Ferrara, in press), assessment (e.g., Brown & French, 1979; Feuerstein, 1979), and modifiability (e.g., Feuerstein, 1980; Haywood & Arbitman-Smith, 1981) of intelligence.

This chapter is about one concept that emerges from a dialectical perspective and that is directly related to issues surrounding the development of intelligence and current research on strategy instruction. The concept, developed by the Soviet psychologist Lev Vygotsky, is that of the zone of proximal development. The zone is a theoretical construct that can be defined loosely as the difference between an individual's current level of development and her potential level of development. In other words, the zone is the difference between what a child can do today and what she will be able to do tomorrow. The zone of proximal development has obvious practical, predictive utility—if it can be assessed. For example, measures of the zone might allow us to differentiate children who score poorly on intelligence tests because they are unable to learn from those who have not had the opportunity to learn. Some of these practical implications are drawn out in this chapter. The chapter begins with a brief overview of some of the guiding philosophical tenets in Soviet psychology. Given this background, the zone of proximal development is described and ways to measure it are discussed. Dynamic assessments of intelligence and related research on strategy instruction are described in the following section. Empirical studies of the zone follow next. The final section contains a few suggestions for future research.

Philosophical Background

Soviet psychological theories are explicitly Marxist in nature (Bauer, 1952; Kussman, 1976; Lomov, 1982; McLeish, 1975; Rahmani, 1976; Venable, 1945). They reflect the dialectical materialism of Marx and a genetic perspective. Soviet theorists believe that a real material world exists, and further, that it exists independent of a knowing mind. This world is ultimately "knowable," but our understanding of it is dependent on our physical and social milieu. Moreover, *social* connotes more than interpersonal interactions; it also refers more generally to the cultural and historical aspects of society (Lomov, 1982; Luria, 1928; Vygotsky, 1929, 1978; Wozniak, 1975b; see also Faris, 1961; Tulkin & Konner, 1973).

Our knowledge, socially determined as it is, improves in a dialectical fashion (Rahmani, 1976). In knowing the environment, we alter it. The alterations we effect, in turn, change us as we try to understand further. In this manner, human knowledge becomes increasingly accurate (Luria, 1928). Since a reciprocal interaction exists between the knower and what is known, and since this relationship is constantly changing, the only way to understand a given event or process is to examine it genetically and historically (Vygotsky, 1929, 1978). For example, a psychologist wishing to understand the memory functioning of young adults must look at the origin and development of their memory skills. Only by understanding the genesis of these skills can the psychologist grasp their significance in the life of the individual.

Vygotsky was interested in studying the development of the higher mental functions, such as perception, voluntary attention, and intentional memory. However, he disagreed with his contemporaries' views on the nature of mind (Bauer, 1952). Vygotsky rejected the behaviorists' thesis that higher psychological functions could be reduced to elementary physiological processes and mechanical laws or that human development could be explained as a history of reinforcements. Likewise, he rejected the idealists' view that mind was immaterial, knowable only through introspective methods, and either preformed or simply the result of maturation. He argued that the higher psychological functions were neither preformed nor the consequence of combining more elementary processes through reinforcement.

Vygotsky offers a Marxist resolution to these two conflicting viewpoints. In contrast to behaviorism and idealism, Vygotsky suggests that higher psychological functions differ qualitatively from more elementary processes and that they develop as children interact with other people in their environment. In this way, Vygotsky seeks to preserve the uniqueness of the higher psychological functions and to leave them accessible to study. Vygotsky's (1929, 1962, 1978) suggestion, in general form, is that children come into the world with a tendency to play active roles in their environments. Their propensity for activity makes development possible (Kussmann, 1976). Development begins as children interact with adults and more capable peers. During interactions, older, more capable people serve as mediators. They focus children's attention on relevant dimensions of the environment, supply strategies for dealing with problems, and generally oversee ongoing activities. Individuals in this mediating role provide an indirect link between stimuli and children's responses, and they supply the tools for problem solving (e.g., speech, memory strategies) that children eventually internalize. These socially provided tools, once internalized, continue to serve a mediating function and form the basis of children's independent thought. Vygotsky claims that *all* higher mental functions are developed in interaction with others. All higher psychological functions have a mediated structure and so are qualitatively different in form from elementary psychological processes (Vygotsky, 1929, 1978). Nevertheless, the higher mental functions can be studied empirically because their genesis, which is social, can be traced.

In arguing that the higher mental functions have social origins, Vygotsky stresses the priority of learning in development (Vygotsky, 1978). However, he does not equate learning and development as a behaviorist might. Vygotsky recognizes that other people mediate the environment for children—that adults and more capable peers demonstrate and teach the knowledge and skills of their culture. But Vygotsky also claims that the child's internalization of these skills is a prolonged developmental process in which the learned skills undergo fundamental changes. Once internalized, the skills are no longer governed by the same laws that controlled them externally. They are incorporated into an inner mental system that has its own laws. Thus, internalization *transforms* the skills, producing qualitatively different ones with altered forms and changed guiding principles (Leont'ev, 1961).

According to Vygotsky, the higher psychological functions cannot develop without social input (i.e., learning), but learning and development are not isomorphic processes either. Instead, the true relation between learning and development is that learning precedes development. Internalization is a process that takes time (Wertsch, 1979; Wertsch et al., 1980). Before a given skill is completely internalized, children can carry it out with the assistance of other people. In fact, it is through this interaction that they acquire the skill. Only after the skill is internalized can they carry it out independently. So a gap exists between what children can do in conjunction with other people and what they can do alone. (See Pressley, 1983, for a similar theme concerning children's learning from materials.) Their learning, which occurs in interaction with others, precedes their development. Vygotsky (1978) writes that

> learning awakens a variety of developmental processes that are able to operate only when the child is interacting with people in his environment and in cooperation with peers. Once these processes are internalized, they become part of the child's independent developmental achievement.
>
> From this point of view, learning is not development; however, properly organized learning results in mental development and sets in motion a variety of developmental processes that would be impossible apart from learning. Thus, learning is a necessary and universal aspect of the process of developing culturally organized, specifically human, psychological functions. (p. 90)

Zone of Proximal Development

Vygotsky's analysis of the relationship between learning and development is the basis for his concept of the zone of proximal development. He elaborates on the observation that children can often complete tasks when they are working with other people that they could not possibly manage working in isolation: "What children can do with the assistance of others might be in some sense even more indicative of their mental development than what they can do alone" (Vygotsky, 1978, p. 85). The reasoning is that the abilities children exercise without assistance are those that have already been internalized. They are mature and may have been so for some time. The abilities children cannot exercise at all, even with extensive assistance, are those that have not yet been learned. They may mature later. But the abilities children can demonstrate when given assistance are those that are in the process of becoming internalized. They are not yet mature, but they are maturing. These maturing abilities provide excellent predictive information on how children will perform independently in the near future. Assessment of the soon-to-be mature mental functions provides a prospective measure of performance.

The mental abilities that are already internalized reflect the "actual" developmental level. The abilities that can be carried out with assistance reflect the "potential" development level. Vygotsky defines the zone as the distance between the actual level and the potential level. That is, the difference between what children can do independently and what they can accomplish with aid is a measure of their zone of proximal development. The zone of proximal development might be assessed in the following way. Two children could be asked to sort a set of 20 pictures into four subgroups that "belong together." Neither child is able to do so initially; both sort the pictures into haphazard, nontaxonomically related groups. Thus, the sorting task is beyond their actual level of development. The experimenter then sorts the pictures for the children, explaining why certain pictures go together. The order of the pictures is scrambled once again and the children are asked to sort them. One child benefits from instruction; she now sorts the pictures perfectly. The other child, in contrast, produces another haphazard arrangement. The Soviets would argue that these children have different zones of proximal development. The child who profited from instruction has a wider zone, as assessed by this sorting task, than the child who did not.

Luria (1961) and Vygotsky (1978) define the zone of proximal development, give examples of how it might be assessed, and indicate how information gained from measuring the zone might be useful. For instance, both Luria and Vygotsky claim that intelligence tests like those common in the United States have limited utility, since they tap only mental functions that have completely developed. Intelligence tests do not indicate how a child reached a particular level of performance (e.g., with extensive assistance or with none at all) nor do they reveal how well a child is likely to perform once training is initiated. Yet, the reasons why a child performs at a given level and the prognosis for enhancing her current cognitive skills are critically important variables. Not all children come to the testing situation with equivalent developmental histories. Some are better able to learn than others, even when they test at the same starting level. In particular, the Soviets argue that learning-disabled and mentally retarded children may demonstrate comparably low performance levels when they are asked to work independently, but that learning-disabled children, unlike mentally retarded children, are able to benefit from instruction. (Readers may be interested in comparing these claims with themes raised in Chapters 5 and 6 of this volume.)

The Soviets add a new twist to the arguments against static intelligence tests by claiming that they fail to distinguish between learning-disabled and mentally retarded children. But static measures of intelligence have been criticized before for their inability to provide information on a child's ability to learn (e.g., Bereiter, 1962; Budoff & Corman, 1976; Budoff, Meskin, & Harrison, 1971; Clarke & Clarke, 1978; Feuerstein, 1979; Hamilton & Budoff, 1974; Resnick, 1979; Schucman, 1960). Even some of Vygotsky's specific suggestions for improving the assessment of mental abilities have been made before. Specifically, other researchers have argued for dynamic testing procedures that would include ease of learning measures (Feuerstein, 1979, 1980; Schucman, 1960). The Soviets' approach, however, is intimately tied to their sociocultural theory of dialectical development. Also, their assessment measures are more numerous than those proposed by many other critics. In fact, by combining the suggestions made in several different sources (Brown & French, 1979; Luria, 1961; Sutton, 1980; Vygotsky, 1978; Wozniak, 1975c; Campione & Brown, in press) no fewer than seven different measures of learning potential can be found: (1) how much a child benefits from a particular training intervention; (2) how explicit training must be to raise performance to a certain level; (3) how well the child maintains trained skills; (4) how much additional training is needed to get a child to maintain; (5) how well a child transfers spontaneously; (6) how easily the child transfers with assistance; and (7) how quickly the child acquires a skill over different problem types.

Vygotsky (1978) claims that two dimensions of intellectual functioning, the actual and potential developmental levels, are important in the diagnosis of mental ability. The actual level can be ascertained much as it is on standard intelligence tests. The most difficult task a child can solve when she works independently measures her completed, or actual, level of development. To determine her potential level of development, instruction begins on a task too difficult for her to solve on her own. Instruction can proceed in a couple of different ways. Complete and explicit instruction can be offered and the child's ability to benefit from it measured. The dependent measure is the amount of improvement a child shows. The greater the improvement, the wider the zone of proximal development. Alternatively, the experimenter can supply a series of increasingly explicit prompts to help the child complete the task. In this case, the number of prompts she needs to solve the problem successfully is the measure of her zone of proximal development. The more assistance she requires, the lower her potential developmental level and the smaller her zone of proximal development.

Testing need not stop with one of these two measures. Luria (1961), for example, proposes retesting the child at a later point in time. That is, after some delay the child can be asked to solve a problem very similar to the one she was trained on, but this time without any assistance, so that maintenance can be assessed. A test for maintenance may be a sound idea, since as Luria (1961) points out, two children may start at the same level and may learn equally well during training, but may differ in their ability to maintain what they have been taught. Presumably, a child who continues to perform successfully after a delay has internalized the trained skill and so has a wider zone than a child who fails to maintain. Pursuing this logic a bit further, one could argue for re-initiating training for the child who fails to maintain. In this way, the amount or explicitness of additional assistance that the child needs before she can perform successfully *and* can maintain that high level of performance could serve as a dependent measure of the zone.

In addition to ease of learning and maintenance, transfer can be assessed. A series of tasks increasingly different from the training task can be presented. The child's spontaneous transfer of what she has been taught can be measured. The experimenter might also give hints to facilitate transfer when the child fails to do so spontaneously. So, two more measures of the zone can be obtained: how far the child is able to transfer her learning spontaneously, and how much aid she needs to transfer even farther. A child who spontaneously applies her newly learned skills across a variety of novel tasks has a wider zone than a child who transfers very little or who requires aid to transfer at all.

Finally, Brown and French (1979) report one other method to measure the zone of proximal development. This measure resembles, but is not exactly like, the assessment of maintenance and re-initiating instruction for maintenance. The child is presented with a task too difficult for her to solve on her own and is given a series of increasingly explicit prompts to help her solve it. When she solves that problem another similar problem is presented, and the amount of assistance she needs to solve it is recorded. The amount of aid she requires should decrease over problems. The slope of that decrease is yet another measure of her zone of proximal development. Depending on how closely related each of the problems used in training are, this procedure could be viewed as either training to maintenance or training to transfer, even though all training takes place within one instructional session.

Vygotsky and Luria thus lay out a dynamic testing method that includes several learning and transfer measures. All of the suggested measures tap the child's ability to benefit from instruction. Or, in Vygotsky's terms, the proposed measures assess the child's ability to internalize what she is taught. All measures should, therefore, be useful in predicting the child's future performance and in diagnosing deficits for possible remediation.

Dynamic Assessments of Intelligence

Vygotsky is not the first psychologist to recognize that learning and transfer processes are essential aspects of intellectual functioning. Nor is he the only researcher to argue for dynamic assessments of intelligence. Although few psychologists actually claim to measure the zone of proximal development, many do try to assess learning and transfer in nonstatic ways. Several researchers, for example, include instruction in their assessments of intelligence. They, therefore, gather data on one measure of the zone of proximal development. In this section, research on dynamic assessments of intelligence is described and some of the parallels and contrasts between these studies of dynamic assessment procedures, currently work on strategy instruction, and Vygotsky's ideas are drawn out.

The major difference between Vygotsky and other researchers is that Vygotsky's concept of the zone of proximal development is embedded in his elaborate theory of cognitive development. His thesis is that intellectual functions are internalized from social interactions. The functions that children have encountered and are internalizing are those that they can employ when given assistance. Thus, ease of learning and ability to transfer are two ways to find out what processes are maturing. In contrast to Vygotsky, many of the researchers included in this section do not lay out a general theory of cognitive development. They do not claim to illuminate those mental functions that are in the process of developing. Their goals are somewhat more pragmatic—to show that static intelligence tests are often insensitive to individual differences in the ability to learn.

Budoff is an excellent example of a researcher who had largely practical goals. Budoff was convinced that static, one-session testing procedures provided inadequate information about a students' ability to profit from instruction. He argued that dynamic testing methods that included training components were absolutely essential in order to avoid misclassifying some students as "unable to learn" when, in fact, their poor performance on intelligence tests was due to their having fewer school-preparatory learning experiences. To demonstrate his point, he employed tasks like those found in intelligence tests but used a test-train-test procedure. He evaluated the relationship between students' pretraining and posttraining performance and their independently measured IQ scores. For example, Hamilton and Budoff (1974) used a modified version of Koh's block design test with moderately and severely retarded adolescents. The adolescents' reasoning skills were assessed on the Koh's blocks before and after they received instruction designed to improve their performance. Some children benefited from the instruction (gainers) whereas others did not (nongainers). Moreover, the independently assessed IQ scores did not predict which of the adolescents would benefit most from instruction. Budoff concluded, therefore, that one-session intelligence tests were not accurate predictors of learning potential.

Budoff has bolstered his conclusion in a series of studies using the test-train-test procedure. He has repeatedly demonstrated that learning potential assessments can differentiate those low-IQ children who might benefit from instruction (high scorers and gainers) from those who probably could not (nongainers) (Babad & Budoff, 1974). He has also shown that the learning potential assessment was more accurate than IQ scores in predicting either teacher-rated school achievement (Babad & Budoff, 1974) or students' actual gain from academic instruction (Budoff & Gottlieb, 1976; Budoff et al., 1971).

Budoff's finding that children who perform similarly on intelligence tests may actually differ in their ability to profit from instruction is clearly relevant to Vygotsky's arguments against static measures of ability. Furthermore, Budoff's test-train-test method of assessing learning potential is remarkably similar to Vygotsky's (1978) description of how to measure the zone of proximal development. Budoff can compare how much instruction various children need before they improve to some level or how much improvement each child makes when all children are given equivalent instruction. Some children need less explicit instruction to show gains, and some progress further with what instruction they do get, both conditions implying that some children have higher potential developmental levels than others. The trained skills, in other words, lie within the zones of proximal development for some children and lie outside the zones of others.

Budoff's data are intriguing, although somewhat limited. His arguments would be significantly more convincing if he showed that some low-IQ children gain from instruction *and* maintain that gain across time. This is an important point, since children often fail to maintain the effects of training (e.g., Brown, Campione, & Murphy, 1977; Butterfield & Belmont, 1972; Keeney, Cannizzo, & Flavell, 1967). If children fail to maintain instruction across time, there is little sense in which one can argue that they have really internalized what they have been taught (Luria, 1961).

Fortunately, other researchers interested in strategy instruction have assessed maintenance of training and still found results similar to Budoff's. Indeed, work with mentally retarded children has repeatedly shown that baseline measures of competence may be insensitive to differences in cognitive ability that are revealed when training is instigated (Brown & Barclay, 1976; Brown & Campione, 1978; Chapter 5 in this volume). For example, Brown, Campione, and Barclay (1979), taught educable retarded children whose mental ages (MAs) were 6 and 8 a memory strategy that involved a self-checking component. The two groups of children did not differ in their original performance, but older students responded more quickly to training and they maintained strategy use. Vygotsky would explain that this result, much like Budoff's, was obtained because older subjects were already in the process of internalizing the trained skill. The skill was within their zones of proximal development.

Even more interesting, of course, would be a demonstration by Budoff that some children gain from instruction, maintain that gain across time, *and* transfer the effects of training to similar tasks. Children who maintain and transfer trained skills would indeed seem to have higher potential than children who neither maintain nor transfer. Unfortunately, Budoff does not assess generalization.

Schucman (1960), however, did include tests for spontaneous transfer in her study of learning potential. She employed a test-train-test procedure to evaluate the educability of a group of severely retarded children. She assessed how easily these children learned across a variety of tasks (e.g., imitative abilities, memory, shape and size discriminations) and how well they retained and transferred what they had been taught. She replicated Budoff's finding that learning potential scores were better than pretraining scores in predicting actual classroom achievement. Interestingly, she also found that learning potential scores were more stable over time and tasks than were pretraining scores. Most important to this discussion, however, was her finding that the learning potential measures most sensitive to differences in ability were the transfer and retention scores. The individual's ability to retain and to generalize her newly learned skills predicted classroom learning even better than did the dynamic measure of ease of initial learning.

Schucman's (1960) results are intriguing in light of the fact that generalization is not at all a common outcome of training. As repeatedly demonstrated in strategy instruction research, children often do not transfer skills, even to very closely related tasks (e.g., Brown et al., 1977; Campione & Brown, 1974; Chapters 1 and 2 of this volume). Indeed, researchers have to go to great lengths to induce children to transfer a trained skill (Belmont, Butterfield, & Borkowski, 1979; Borkowski & Cavanaugh, 1979; Borkowski, Levers, & Gruenfelder, 1976; Brown et al., 1979; Kennedy & Miller, 1976). Specifically, researchers desiring generalization effects have to program them directly, for example, by showing children how the trained skill is useful by including general self-monitoring routines in the training package. In other words, metacognitive knowledge and skills seem to be essential in programming transfer. Perhaps those children who spontaneously transfer, as in Schucman's (1960) study, make the most out of training by accessing their metacognitive knowledge and skills without explicit instructions to do so. This tendency to interrelate "new learning" with what is already known may underlie academic success.

That metacognitive processes play important roles in learning, retention, and transfer of training is relevant to the work of another researcher, Reuven Feuerstein. Feuerstein, who has ideas quite similar to Vygotsky's, tries to enhance the academic success of retarded performers by teaching them metacognitive skills. Feuerstein (1979) believes that children learn through direct experience (manipulating objects, etc.) and through mediated experience. Mediated learning experiences are those in which an adult selects, frames, and labels the external world in order to focus a child's attention on those aspects that are most important. These mediated experiences, Feuerstein argues, help to shape specific cognitive abilities such as reflective thought and inner representation. They also result in an orientation or attitude toward thinking and problem solving that is active. Mediated learning experiences are, therefore, critical to the development of high-level cognitive functioning. When children lack such experiences or when their mediated learning experiences are inadequate, their performance on tests of ability may be poor. They may perform at mentally retarded levels on static tests of intelligence. Thus, Feuerstein (1979) argues that mental retardation is sometimes caused by inadequate and insufficient mediated learning experiences.

The cognitive impairments resulting from inadequate mediated learning experiences are, according to Feuerstein, reversible. They can be remediated because the deficient cognitive functions, although underdeveloped, are not lacking entirely. They can be developed through appropriate learning experiences in which the skills employed by active, nonretarded learners are taught. Feuerstein teaches retarded performers such skills as to plan and to be systematic in their exploration of the environment, to recognize when they are faced with a problem, and then to define the problem carefully, to compare objectives and events in order to establish relationships, to organize, to group, and to classify objects, to communicate precisely and accurately, and to provide supportive evidence for answers. Most of these skills are very general ones—they are applicable in a wide variety of settings. Most of these skills are also ones that might be called metacognitive (Brown, 1978; Flavell, 1978).

Before Feuerstein institutes remedial training, he assesses whether a child can benefit from his intervention program and which particular cognitive functions are deficient. Static intelligence tests are inadequate for his purposes, since Feuerstein is interested in finding out how modifiable an individual is, not how much he or she already knows. He therefore uses a dynamic assessment procedure (Feuerstein, 1980; Haywood & Arbitman-Smith, 1981; Haywood, Filler, Shifman, & Chatelanat, 1975; Haywood & Wachs, 1981) in which he measures whether an individual is able to benefit from instruction, how much and what kind of teaching is necessary to bring about improvement, and how well an individual can apply newly acquired skills in different settings. Without stating that he is doing it, Feuerstein measures exactly those dimensions of intellectual functioning that Vygotsky calls the zone of proximal development.

Feuerstein and Vygotsky obviously have several ideas in common. They agree that many cognitive abilities originate in social interactions and that intellectual functioning can best be assessed by using dynamic procedures that include learning and transfer measures. Vygotsky does speak to broader issues. He is interested in normal and abnormal cognitive development; he embeds his theory in the more general dialectical-materialist model; and he discusses the process by which functions initially shared between adults and children become intrapersonal mental processes. Feuerstein is less explicit about these broader concerns, concentrating more on the causes of retarded intellectual performance and the means to remediate it.

In summary, the Soviets' argument that learning and transfer are important dimensions of intellectual functioning that can only be assessed dynamically has been made by others. In fact, the Soviets' claim that dynamic testing procedures provide more sensitive measures of individual differences in the ability to profit from instruction has found empirical support. Other of the Soviets' ideas need further research, however. In particular, the Soviets' claim that learning, maintenance, and transfer measure one underlying construct, the zone of proximal development, needs verification. If all of the suggested measures do tap one unitary construct, and if the variance due to testing methods is relatively slight, then all measures should be highly correlated. Furthermore, these measures should be minimally correlated with independent assessments of other constructs. In other words, the reliability and validity of the zone construct can be assessed through the convergent and discriminant validation procedures suggested by Campbell and Fiske (1959). For example, the Soviets propose two measures of learning: how detailed instruction must be to effect improvement, and how much improvement a child makes given a particular amount of instruction. Although both measures have been employed and have been shown to be sensitive to individual differences in ability, the relationship between the two measures is not demonstrated in one group of children. Although unlikely, it is possible that a child may need very direct and explicit instruction in order to show any improvement at all, but once given that instruction would demonstrate large gains. At any rate, a high positive correlation between the two measures must be demonstrated to substantiate the Soviets' claim that they tap one underlying construct.

The relationship between learning and transfer also needs investigation. Presumably, learning and transfer processes are closely related (e.g., Ferguson, 1954). In conjunction with learning measures, the Soviets propose using transfer measures to assess the zone of proximal development. Yet, related as they may be, learning and transfer are not identical processes. An individual who learns quickly may not necessarily transfer well. The validity of the zone construct, therefore, can be established in another way—by demonstrating the relationship between learning and transfer.

Even if learning and transfer are imperfectly related, both assessments may be informative. Specifically, learning/transfer profiles may be useful in diagnosing various disabilities. For example, learning-disabled children, like educable mentally retarded children, may learn slowly, but unlike retarded children, may transfer well. These differing profiles, if obtained, would support the Soviets' idea that dynamic assessments may differentiate educable mentally retarded and learning-disabled children.

Empirical Studies of the Zone of Proximal Development

Researchers investigating the zone of proximal development have studied the relation between learning, maintenance, and transfer very directly. They have taken multiple measures of learning and of transfer on children from different diagnostic categories (e.g., educable mentally retarded, learning disabled, normally achieving). Then, they have looked at individual learning/transfer profiles to determine how related the various measures were.

Hall and Day (Note 1), for example, studied the zone of proximal development with educable mentally retarded, learning disabled, and normally achieving second-grade children. They employed a balance scale task to take advantage of the extensive task analyses provided by Siegler (1976). Initially, children were pretested to ensure that all could add sums to 15 and that all performed at Siegler's Rule Level 1 (they attended to only one dimension in making judgments about whether the scale would balance, tip right, or tip left). Thus, children were matched on starting competence. Each child then received a series of increasingly explicit hints as needed to progress through the developmental sequence described by Siegler (1976) to an understanding of torque. The number of prompts each child required to solve three successive problems without aid was recorded. Maintenance and transfer were assessed approximately 5 days after training. The balance scale used to test maintenance was the same as that used during pretesting and training. It had 10 pegs on either side of a stationary fulcrum. The weights that hung from these pegs were all equal. In contrast, the two balance scales used to test transfer were structurally dissimilar from the one used during pretesting, training, and maintenance assessment. The near transfer task consisted of nine small, connected balance scales. Each scale had three spaces for equal weights on either side of a stationary fulcrum. The far transfer task was a doll's teeter-totter. Dolls of different sizes and weights sat astride the teeter-totter, which had a movable fulcrum. Thus, both near and far transfer tasks looked different from the training task, but the far transfer task was the only one that involved new "twists"—unequal weights and a movable fulcrum. Each child was tested for spontaneous transfer. If the child failed to transfer, increasingly explicit hints were supplied until transfer was demonstrated.

In terms of initial learning, the three groups did not differ significantly. Although the mean number of prompts required by each group to reach criterion performance was in the predicted order, mentally retarded children did not require significantly more prompts than learning disabled or normally achieving children. Mentally retarded children did need more prompts than other children, however, to generalize their learning on the transfer tasks. Furthermore, their dependence on experimenter assistance was especially marked on the far transfer task. Thus, retarded children, like younger children in other studies (e.g., Pressley & Dennis-Rounds, 1980), needed more encouragement to transfer at all and became increasingly dependent on external aid as the task became less like the training task. Finally, mentally retarded children also maintained less well. Only about half of the retarded children continued to perform at high levels, in comparison to 90% of the learning disabled and 80% of the normally achieving children. Since maintenance is a prerequisite for generalization (Borkowski & Cavanaugh, 1979), the reliable group differences in transfer could have been an artifactual result. However, mentally retarded children needed more aid to show transfer even when the analysis included only those children who did maintain.

To further investigate the relationship between learning and transfer, the median number of hints required for learning was calculated, as was the median number of hints required for transfer. Each child was then classified as a fast learner (one who required fewer than the median number of hints) or as a slow learner (one who required the median number of hints or more). Similarly, each child was classified as a narrow or wide transferer. Three fourths of the subjects had consistent learning/transfer profiles. That is, 75% were either fast learners and wide transferers or slow learners and narrow transferers. However, a significant number of children did not have consistent learning/transfer profiles. For example, 15% of the children learned quickly but did not transfer well (these were called *context-bound children*); 10% were slow learners who were able to transfer well (these were called *reflective children*). Interestingly, none of the retarded children fell into the reflective category and none of the learning disabled children fell into the context-bound category. Thus, the learning/transfer profiles revealed a striking difference between learning-disabled and educable mentally retarded children: Learning disabled children may have learned slowly, but they, unlike mentally retarded children, were able to transfer what they had learned. The Soviets' claim that learning disabled and mentally retarded children would respond differently to instruction even when they had similar starting competencies was, therefore, substantiated.

Wozniak (1975c) also reports evidence supporting the Soviets' claim that differences between the learning disabled and the mentally retarded emerge in dynamic tests of ability. He summarizes several studies conducted in the Soviet Union in which normally achieving, learning disabled, and/or mentally retarded children's zones of proximal development are compared. Interested readers are referred to Wozniak (1975c) for details. Briefly, however, the Soviets find that learning disabled and mentally retarded children perform less well than their normally achieving peers when they work independently (as on a pretest), but when given instruction, learning-disabled children, unlike mentally retarded children, can reach the level of performance demonstrated by untrained normal children. When all groups receive instruction, however, normally achieving children benefit more than learning-disabled children, who in turn benefit more than mentally retarded children. Finally, learning disabled children need more explicit instruction than normally achieving children to show gains.

The studies reported by Wozniak (1975c) and the one conducted by Hall and Day (Note 1) differ in two important respects. First, Hall and Day do not confound children's diagnostic category (learning disabled, mentally retarded, normally achieving) with their starting competence on the training task. Children, regardless of their diagnostic classification, have similar starting skills on the balance scale task. This precaution makes the comparisons of group differences in improvement after instruction more meaningful. Nevertheless, the interactive assessment procedure reveals reliable differences between learning disabled and mentally retarded children. Second, breadth of transfer and individual learning/transfer profiles are not evaluated in the Soviet research reported by Wozniak (1975c); Hall and Day's results indicate that these variables provide valuable information. In fact, like Schucman (1960), Hall and Day's findings suggest that retention and transfer may be more sensitive indicators of intellectual functioning (and the zone of proximal development) than learning measures—at least when starting levels are equal across groups.

In a recent chapter, Campione and Brown (in press) describe several studies they have conducted on the zone of proximal development with mentally retarded, normally achieving, and high-achieving children. In one study, Brown and Ferrara (in press) compared learning and transfer processes in children of average and above-average intelligence. They used a series completion task on which all children performed poorly before instruction. Children received increasingly explicit prompts to help them solve four particular types of series completion problems. They were trained to criterion. Later, retention and transfer were assessed. The transfer tasks varied in how closely related they were to the training task. Thus, how far children could spontaneously transfer was assessed, as well as how much assistance they needed to show broad generalization. They found that average children needed more prompts than above-average children in order to learn to solve the four problem types used in training and to transfer to novel problem types. The learning/transfer profiles were similar to those described by Hall and Day (Note 1). Most children had consistent profiles; they were either fast learners and wide transferers or slow learners and narrow transferers. However, a significant minority—about one third—of the children did demonstrate inconsistent profiles.

In further similar studies, Campione and Brown (in press) have replicated many of their findings using a different task, Raven's progressive matrices. Although various groups of children do not always differ significantly in the ease with which they learn to solve problems, reliable group differences in transfer are always obtained. Mentally retarded children require more assistance to transfer than do average children, who require more aid than above-average children. The majority of children have consistent learning/transfer profiles, although a few have inconsistent ones. Moreover, these individual learning and/or transfer profiles seem to be fairly consistent across the Raven's and series completion tasks. Children classified as fast learners and wide transferers on a series completion task, for example, tend to have the same classification on the Raven's progressive matrices. The few children who show different learning/transfer profiles across the two tasks always maintain their classification on either learning or transfer. That is, no children alter their standing on learning and on transfer assessments.

The issue of across-task consistency in learning/transfer profiles is an interesting one that relates to the reliability issue (Campbell & Fiske, 1959) discussed earlier. From a strict interpretation of Vygotsky (1978), one would not necessarily expect to find consistency except across tasks that demand similar cognitive processes. Learning and transfer are indices of the mental processes that are maturing. Different processes can be in different stages of development. Therefore, a priori, one would expect to find consistent learning/transfer profiles only across tasks that tap the same mental processes or that happen to tap different processes at similar stages of development. Of course, some skills, particularly metacognitive ones, may be transsituationally relevant (e.g., Borkowski & Kurtz, in press; Brown, 1974; Butterfield, 1981). To the extent that these skills are demanded, one might find somewhat more across-task consistency in learning/transfer profiles. Similarly, children who have supportive, responsive environments (Clarke-Stewart, 1973; Yarrow, Rubenstein, & Pedersen, 1975) may have many mediated learning experiences in many different domains including the metacognitive domain. These children may develop several different processes simultaneously and, therefore, may demonstrate fast learning/wide transfer profiles across many different tasks. Nevertheless, if they were faced with a task entailing processes not called for in their environments and one in which metacognitive skills were only minimally involved, these children would not demonstrate the same fast learning/wide transfer profiles. Thus, the reliability of the zone construct is best assessed across highly similar ecologically valid tasks.

In summary, many of the ideas expounded by the Soviets find support in recent research on the zone of proximal development. Dynamic assessments of intellectual functioning do reveal individual differences not apparent on static tests of ability. Children who perform equally poorly when they work alone may differ in how much they benefit from instruction. Learning and transfer processes, although not identical, are related to intelligence. Mentally retarded children tend to learn slowly and transfer only narrowly. Above-average children tend to learn quickly and transfer broadly. Notably, many learning disabled children learn slowly but transfer broadly. Thus, dynamic assessments can prove useful in differentiating learning-disabled and mentally retarded children.

Implications for Future Research

Dynamic assessments of intellectual functioning have both practical and theoretical import. Practically, dynamic tests can reveal individual differences in the ability to learn and in the ability to transfer what is learned that cannot be discerned with static tests. Dynamic testing procedures can therefore be useful in pinpointing specific cognitive impairments. With accurate diagnosis, attempts at remediation can be directed at particular deficient functions, thus making those attempts more successful and less time consuming. Theoretically, dynamic tests can be used to further our understanding of the relationship between intelligence, learning, and transfer (Campione & Brown, in press). Such understanding can lead to more adequate theories of intelligence and of intellectual development (e.g., Campione et al., in press).

Vygotsky's discussion of the zone of proximal development, however, goes beyond a concern with dynamic testing procedures. He proposes a general theory of cognitive development. The zone of proximal development is a logical outgrowth of that more general theory. Vygotsky theorizes that all higher cognitive processes develop in social interaction. Adults and more capable peers mediate the environment for children, supplying the culturally available tools of thought, which children eventually internalize.

Two concepts are central to this theory: internalization and social mediation. Internalization is the process by which interpersonal activities become intrapersonal ones. The process is described by Vygotsky (1929, 1978) and by Wertsch (1979), but it is not explained. Many questions can be asked about internalization: What exactly is internalization? How does it happen? Are all cognitive functions internalized, or do some remain socially bound? What conditions must be met for internalization to occur? Do individuals differ in the speed or efficiency with which they internalize what they are taught? Can internalization be facilitated by particular types of instruction? These are difficult questions that need to be answered.

Social mediation is the process by which cognitive skills are introduced. If mental processes are learned in social interaction, as Vygotsky suggests, then psychologists should be able to trace the ontogeny of various abilities and disabilities. Wertsch (1979, 1981; Wertsch et al., 1980) and Gardner and Rogoff (1982) provide insightful analyses of how mothers regulate their children's learning attempts and teach strategies for problem-solving. For example, Gardner and Rogoff (1982) document how one mother prepared her 8-year-old son for a memory test by teaching a rehearsal strategy and relevant metamemorial knowledge. Had her son been retarded, she might have taught him less, perhaps by omitting the metamemorial component of instruction. Thus, she might have hindered his performance and his development. Comparisons of different parent-child dyads (e.g., mother and learning-disabled daughter, father and gifted son), of how they interact, and of what they say to each other may give us clues to why some children are gifted and others mentally retarded.

Of course, parents are not the only people in the child's world. Teachers, siblings, and friends all interact with the developing child. They, too, teach cognitive skills and help set up supportive or nonsupportive environments. Hood, McDermott, and Cole (1980) give an excellent example of how social environments can be set up to foster displays of *in*competence. They describe how Adam, a learning disabled child, tries to hide his weaknesses by stalling for answers, skirting problems, and covertly seeking outside support. When social pressure is applied, Adam is reduced to failure-avoiding tactics even on tasks that are well within his abilities. In these situations, the social environment supports intellectual incompetence. At other times, the same people support competence. Adam's intellectual abilities and disabilities, like those of other people, are closely linked with the social environment.

The point is that intellectual skills develop and are manifested in ever-changing social settings. Social environments sometimes support certain kinds of cognitive activities over others. The particular intellectual skills that emerge in particular environments are purposeful and "make sense" within those settings. Individuals change and are changed by their social milieu. Theories of cognition and of cognitive development must reflect this nontrivial interaction. (See Chapter 11 in this volume for additional commentary on Soviet theories of cognitive development.)

Acknowledgments. The preparation of this manuscript was supported by NIH Training Grant (HD-07184).

Reference Note

1. Hall, L., & Day, J. D. *Comparison of the zone of proximal development in learning disabled, mentally retarded, and normal children.* Paper presented at the meeting of the American Educational Research Association, New York: 1982.

References

Allen, V., & Feldman, R. Studies on the role of tutor. In V. Allen (Ed.), *Children as teachers: Theory and research on tutoring*. New York: Academic Press, 1976.

Babad, E., & Budoff, M. Sensitivity and validity of learning-potential measurement in three levels of ability. *Journal of Educational Psychology*, 1974, *66*, 439–447.

Bauer, R. *The new man in Soviet psychology*. Cambridge, MA: Harvard University Press, 1952.

Belmont, J., Butterfield, E., & Borkowski, J. Training retarded people to generalize memorization methods across memory tasks. In M. M. Gruneberg, P. E. Morris, & R. N. Sykes (Eds.), *Practical aspects of memory*. London: Academic Press, 1979.

Bereiter, C. Using tests to measure change. *Personnel and Guidance Journal*, 1962, *41*, 6–11.

Borkowski, J., & Cavanaugh, J. Maintenance and generalization of skills and strategies by the retarded. In N. R. Ellis (Ed.), *Handbook of mental deficiency* (2nd ed.). Hillsdale, NJ: Erlbaum, 1979.

Borkowski, J., & Kurtz, B. Metacognition and special children. In J. B. Gholson & T. L. Rosenthal (Eds.), *Applications of cognitive-developmental theory*. New York: Academic Press, in press.

Borkowski, J., Levers, S., & Gruenenfelder, T. Transfer and mediational strategies in children: The role of activity and awareness during strategy acquisition. *Child Development*, 1976, *47*, 779–786.

Brown, A. The role of strategic behavior in retardate memory. In N. T. Ellis (Ed.), *International review of research in mental retardation* (Vol. 7). New York: Academic Press, 1974.

Brown, A. Knowing when, where, and how to remember: A problem of metacognition. In R. Glaser (Ed.), *Advances in instructional psychology*. Hillsdale, NJ: Erlbaum, 1978.

Brown, A., & Barclay, C. The effects of training specific mnemonics on the metamnemonic efficiency of retarded children. *Child Development*, 1976, *47*, 70–80.

Brown, A., & Campione, J. Permissable inferences from the outcome of training studies in cognitive developmental research. *Quarterly Newsletter of the Institute for Comparative Human Development*, 1978, *2*, 46–53.

Brown, A., Campione, J., & Barclay, C. Training self-checking routines for estimating test readiness: Generalization from list learning to prose recall. *Child Development*, 1979, *50*, 501–512.

Brown, A., Campione, J., & Murphy, M. Maintenance and generalization of metamnemonic awareness in educable retarded children. *Journal of Experimental Child Psychology*, 1977, *24*, 191–211.

Brown, A., & Ferrara, R. Diagnosing the zone of proximal development. In J. Wertsch (Ed.), *Culture, communication, and cognition: Vygotskian perspectives*. New York: Academic Press, in press.

Brown, A., & French, L. The zone of potential development: Implications for intelligence testing in the year 2000. *Intelligence*, 1979, *3*, 253–271.

Budoff, M., & Corman, L. Effectiveness of a learning potential procedure in improving problem-solving skills of retarded and non-retarded children. *American Journal of Mental Deficiency*, 1976, *81*, 260–264.

Budoff, M., & Gottlieb, J. Special-class EMR children mainstreamed: A study of an aptitude (learning potential) X treatment interaction. *American Journal of Mental Deficiency,* 1976, *81,* 1–11.

Budoff, M., & Hamilton, J. Optimizing test performance of moderately and severely mentally retarded adolescents and adults. *American Journal of Mental Deficiency,* 1976, *81,* 49–57.

Budoff, M., Meskin, J., & Harrison, R. Educational test of the learning potential hypothesis. *American Journal of Mental Deficiency,* 1971, *76,* 159–169.

Butterfield, E. Instructional techniques that produce generalized improvements in cognition. In P. Mittler (Ed.), *Frontiers of knowledge in mental retardation* (Vol. 1). Baltimore: University Park Press, 1981.

Butterfield, E., & Belmont, J. The role of verbal processes in short-term memory. In R. L. Schiefelbusch (Ed.), *Language research with the mentally retarded.* Baltimore: University Park Press, 1972.

Campbell, D., & Fiske, D. Convergent and discriminant validation by the multitrait-multimethod matrix. *Psychological Bulletin,* 1959, *56,* 81–105.

Campione, J., & Brown, A. The effects of contextual changes and degree of component mastery in transfer of training. In H. W. Reese (Ed.), *Advances in child development and behavior* (Vol. 9). New York: Academic Press, 1974.

Campione, J., & Brown, A. Memory and metamemory development in educable retarded children. In R. V. Kail, Jr., & J. W. Hagen (Eds.), *Perspectives on the development of memory and cognition.* Hillsdale, NJ: Erlbaum, 1977.

Campione, J., & Brown, A. Learning ability and transfer propensity as sources of individual differences in intelligence. In P. H. Brooks, C. McCauley, & R. Sperber (Eds.), *Learning and cognition in the mentally retarded.* Baltimore: University Park Press, in press.

Campione, J., Brown, A., & Ferrara, R. Mental retardation and intelligence. In R. Sternberg (Ed.), *Handbook of intelligence,* New York & London: Cambridge University Press, in press.

Clarke, A. M., & Clarke, A. D. B. Severe subnormality: Capacity and performance. In A. M. Clarke & A. D. B. Clarke (Eds.), *Readings from mental deficiency: The changing outlook.* London: Methuen, 1978.

Clarke-Stewart, K. Interactions between mothers and their young children: Characteristics and consequences. *Monographs of the Society for Research in Child Development,* 1973, *38*(6–7, Serial No. 153).

Cole, M. (Ed.). Introduction. In *The selected writings of A. R. Luria.* White Plains, NY: M. E. Sharpe, 1978.

Cole, M., & Scribner, S. Introduction. In M. Cole, V. John-Steiner, S. Scribner, & E. Souberman (Eds.), *Mind in society: The development of higher psychological processes.* Cambridge, MA: Harvard University Press, 1978.

Collins, A., & Stevens, A. Goals and strategies of inquiry teachers. In R. Glaser (Ed.), *Advances in instructional technology* (Vol. 2). Hillsdale, NJ: Erlbaum, 1981.

Faris, R. E. L. Reflections on the ability dimensions in human society. *American Sociological Review,* 1961, *26,* 835–843.

Ferguson, G. On learning and human ability. *Canadian Journal of Psychology,* 1954, *8,* 95–112.

Feuerstein, R. *The dynamic assessment of retarded performers: The learning potential assessment device, theory, instruments, and techniques.* Baltimore: University Park Press, 1979.

Feuerstein, R. *Instrumental enrichment.* Baltimore: University Park Press, 1980.

Flavell, J. Metacognitive development. In J. M. Scandura & C. J. Brainerd (Eds.), *Structural/process theories of complex human behaviors.* Alphen a.d. Rijn: Sijthoff & Noordhoff, 1978.

Gardner, W., & Rogoff, B. The role of instruction in memory development: Some methodological choices. *Quarterly Newsletter of the Laboratory of Comparative Human Cognition,* 1982, *4,* 6–12.

Hamilton, J., & Budoff, M. Learning potential among the moderately and severely retarded. *Mental Retardation,* 1974, *12,* 33–36.

Haywood, H., & Arbitman-Smith, R. Modification of cognitive functions in slow-learning adolescents. In P. Mittler (Ed.), *Frontiers of knowledge in mental retardation* (Vol. 1). Baltimore: University Park Press, 1981.

Haywood, H., Filler, J., Shifman, M., & Chatelanat, G. Behavioral assessment in mental retardation. In P. McReynolds (Ed.), *Advances in psychological assessment* (Vol. 3). San Francisco: Jossey-Bass, 1975.

Haywood, H., & Wachs, T. Intelligence, cognition and individual differences. In M. Begab, H. Haywood, & H. Garber (Eds.), *Psychosocial influences in retarded performance.* Baltimore: University Park Press, 1981.

Hood, L., Feiss, K., & Aron, J. Growing up explained: Vygotskians look at the language of causality. In C. Brainerd & M. Pressley (Eds.), *Verbal processes in children.* New York: Springer-Verlag, 1981.

Hood, L., McDermott, R., & Cole, M. "Let's try to make it a good day"—Some not so simple ways. *Discourse Processes,* 1980, *3,* 155–168.

Keeney, T., Cannizzo, S., & Flavell, J. Spontaneous and induced rehearsal in a recall task. *Child Development,* 1967, *38,* 953–966.

Kennedy, B., & Miller, D. Persistent use of verbal rehearsal as a function of information about its value. *Child Development,* 1976, *47,* 566–569.

Kussmann, T. The Soviet concept of development and the problem of activity. In K. F. Riegel & J. A. Meacham (Eds.), *The developing individual in a changing world.* Chicago: Aldine, 1976.

Leont'ev, A. N. Learning as a problem in psychology. In N. O'Connor (Ed.), *Recent Soviet psychology.* New York: Van Rees Press, 1961.

Lomov, B. Soviet psychology: Its historical origins and contemporary status. *American Psychologist,* 1982, *37,* 580–586.

Luria, A. The problem of the cultural development of the child. *Journal of Genetic Psychology,* 1928, *35,* 493–506.

Luria, A. R. An objective approach to the study of the abnormal child. *American Journal of Orthopsychiatry,* 1961, *31,* 1–14.

Luria, A. *Cognitive development: Its cultural and social foundations* (M. Cole, Ed.; M. Lopez-Morillas & L. Solotaroff, trans.). Cambridge, MA: Harvard University Press, 1976.

Luria, A. *The making of mind* (M. Cole & S. Cole, Eds.). Cambridge, MA: Harvard University Press, 1979.

McLeish, J. *Soviet psychology: History, theory, content.* London: Methuen, 1975.

Meacham, J. The development of memory abilities in the individual and society. *Human Development,* 1972, *15,* 205–228.

Meacham, J. Continuing the dialogue: Dialectics and remembering. *Human Development*, 1976, *19*, 304–309.

Parke, R., & O'Leary, S. Father-mother-infant interaction in the newborn period: Some findings, some observations, and some unresolved issues. In K. F. Riegel & J. Meacham (Eds.), *The developing individual in a changing world* (Vol. 2, *Social and environmental issues*). The Hague: Mouton, 1976.

Piaget, J. *The origins of intelligence in children.* New York: International Universities Press, 1952.

Pressley, M. Making meaningful materials easier to learn: Lessons from cognitive strategy research. In M. Pressley & J. R. Levin (Eds.), *Cognitive strategy research: Educational applications.* New York: Springer-Verlag, 1983.

Pressley, M., & Dennis-Rounds, J. Transfer of a mnemonic keyword strategy at two age levels. *Journal of Educational Psychology*, 1980, *72*, 575–582.

Rahmani, L. Philosophy and psychology in the Soviet Union. In K. F. Riegel & J. A. Meacham (Eds.), *The developing individual in a changing world.* Chicago: Aldine, 1976.

Resnick, L. The future of IQ testing in education. *Intelligence*, 1979, *3*, 241–253.

Riegel, K. Toward a dialectical theory of development. *Human Development*, 1975, *18*, 50–64.

Riegel, K. The dialectics of human development. *American Psychology*, 1976, *10*, 689–701.

Sameroff, A. Transactional models in early social relations. *Human Development*, 1975, *18*, 65–79.

Schucman, H. Evaluating the educability of the severely mentally retarded child. *Psychological Monographs: General and Applied*, 1960, *74*(14), 1–32.

Siegler, R. Three aspects of cognitive development. *Cognitive Psychology*, 1976, *8*, 481–520.

Sutton, A. Backward children in the USSR: An unfamiliar approach to a familiar problem. In J. Brine, M. Perrie, & A. Sutton (Eds.), *Home, school and leisure in the Soviet Union.* London: George Allen & Unwin, 1980.

Tulkin, S., & Konner, M. Alternative conceptions of intellectual functioning. *Human Development*, 1973, *16*, 33–52.

Venable, V. *Human nature: The Marxian view.* New York: Knopf, 1945.

Vygotsky, L. S. The problem of the cultural development of the child. *Journal of Genetic Psychology*, 1929, *36*, 415–434.

Vygotsky, L. *Thought and language* (E. Haufmann and G. Vakar, Eds. and trans.), Cambridge, MA: MIT Press, 1962.

Vygotsky, L. *Mind in society: The development of higher psychological processes* (M. Cole, V. John-Steiner, S. Scribner, & E. Souberman, Eds.). Cambridge, MA: Harvard University Press, 1978.

Wertsch, J. From social interaction to higher psychological processes: A clarification and application of Vygotsky's theory. *Human Development*, 1979, *22*, 1–22.

Wertsch, J. The concept of activity in Soviet psychology: An introduction. In J. Wertsch (Ed.), *The concept of activity in the Soviet Union.* New York: Sharpe, 1981.

Wertsch, J., McNamee, G., McLane, J., & Budwig, N. The adult-child dyad as a problem-solving system. *Child Development*, 1980, *51*, 1215–1221.

Wozniak, R. H. A dialectical paradigm for psychological research: Implications drawn from the history of psychology in the Soviet Union. *Human Development,* 1975, *18,* 18–34. (a)

Wozniak, R. Dialecticism and structuralism: The philosophical foundation of Soviet psychology and Piagetian cognitive developmental theory. In K. F. Riegel & G. C. Rosenwald (Eds.), *Structure and transformation: Developmental and historical aspects.* New York: Wiley, 1975. (b)

Wozniak, R. Psychology and education of the learning disabled child in the Soviet Union. In W. M. Cruickshank & D. P. Hallahan (Eds.), *Perceptual and learning disabilities in children.* Syracuse: Syracuse University Press, 1975. (c)

Yarrow, L., Rubenstein, J., & Pedersen, F. *Infant and environment.* New York: Halsted Press, 1975.

Part III
Strategies for Attitudinal
and Social-Behavioral Change

This section includes four chapters that are broadly concerned with strategies for attitudinal and social-behavioral change. The first two chapters address strategy manipulations in media, specifically television and advertising. The manipulations reviewed have dramatic effects on both cognitive and behavioral variables. The latter two chapters are concerned with clinical problems and increasing self-control.

In the first chapter of Part III, Collins and Wiens review recent work on children's cognitive processing while they view television. In general, children's memory for televised sequences is often poor and is affected by a number of factors. Structural aspects of programs, such as the temporal proximity of critical segments and the salience of important scenes, exert a powerful influence on children's comprehension. Also, children's general knowledge affects their interpretations of TV content (content either congruent or incongruent with children's schematized knowledge). Collins and Wiens discuss children's selection, encoding, and inferential difficulties with a variety of television content. In light of these difficulties, the authors are able to outline interventions that positively affect children's processing of, and social-behavioral reactions to, television content. They detail interventions designed to moderate directly behaviors and attitudes that occur because of TV viewing. They also consider strategies aimed at increasing understanding and evaluation of television content. Collins and Wiens provide summaries of impressive studies that document that cognitive strategies can increase children's retention of television content, as well as increase and/or improve children's inferences about that content.

Alesandrini summarizes a number of strategies that can be used to create more effective and memorable advertisements. She discusses the criticality of the memorableness of ads, and reviews various visual strategies that can be used to affect buyer preferences. Many of her suggestions, especially those dealing with the concreteness of advertisements, are derived from the more basic research approaches reviewed in other chapters of these volumes (e.g., imagery, dual coding, mnemonic elaboration). Because so little research has been done in the field of advertising, and because advertising affects every segment of the population, this seems to be an area in which many theoretical ideas could be fruitfully applied.

Cognitive therapies are now commonplace in clinical settings. The purposes of the final two chapters of this volume are to trace the roots of cognitive approaches to therapy and to discuss the efficacy of cognitive interventions. Reynolds and Stark provide a plethora of data based on clinical research. They particularly focus on cognitive interventions for the treatment of anxiety and depression. They consider cognitive restructuring techniques, imagery techniques, and combinations of cognitive and behavioral approaches, as well as other clinical strategies. In general, the cognitive-based approaches for the clinical problems of anxiety and depression have proven effective, and a detailed summary of their effects are provided by Reynolds and Stark. The authors also provide a brief history of cognitive behavior modification, with brief overviews of the contributions of Ellis, Meichenbaum, Goldfried, and Beck. In doing so, they contrast the assumptions of cognitive behavior modifiers with the more traditional behavior therapists. Reynolds and Stark also provide a thoughtful summary of methodological issues in cognitive behavior modification research. In particular, they summarize the study-to-study variability in subject populations, treatments, and therapist characteristics, and they provide an overview of problems in assessment, as well as in designing and analyzing cognitive therapy research.

Then, Pressley, Reynolds, Stark, and Gettinger review cognitive self-control strategies, with special attention paid to developmental theories of self-instructional control. They specifically take up Luria's theory of motor control and its implications for strategy instruction. Children's strategy usage in resistance-to-temptation situations is reviewed. The contributions of social-learning theorists and researchers to the development of strategies for reducing behavioral deviation are especially significant. The chapter also considers self-instructional approaches to the modification of impulsivity and hyperactivity. Recent studies by Kendall, which are exemplary efforts in the area, are considered in some detail. The authors conclude that young children certainly have the competence to execute a variety of cognitive strategies. Pressley and his colleagues lament, however, that so much of the research to date on self-control in children has been conducted only in laboratory settings. Taken together, the last two chapters present a balanced review of cognitive strategy research relevant to therapy—both theoretical and practical concerns are covered, both laboratory and clinical studies are reviewed, work with both children and adults is considered, and extensive commentary is offered on issues related to both internal and external validity.

8. Cognitive Processes in Television Viewing: Description and Strategic Implications

W. Andrew Collins and Mary Wiens

Television is now a common feature of the environments of children throughout the world. In the United States the average family operates television sets more than 6 hours per day (Comstock, Chaffee, Katzman, McCombs, & Roberts, 1978); children under the age of 6 view an average of 4–5 hours daily (Roberts & Bachen, 1981). The potential impact of this extensive exposure to television on psychological and behavioral development is now well established (Ball & Bogatz, 1972; Collins, 1982; Comstock et al., 1978; Stein & Friedrich, 1975). Television programs have been found to influence patterns of social behavior and self-regulation in laboratory and field experiments (e.g., Friedrich & Stein, 1973; Leyens, Camino, Parke, & Berkowitz, 1975; Rushton, 1979). Evidence from correlational field studies supports the relationship between viewing preferences and patterns of general behavioral tendencies, which may persist over long periods (e.g., Belson, 1978; Eron, 1982; Eron, Huesmann, Lefkowitz, & Walder, 1973; Huesmann, 1982). In addition, programs produced with a teaching intent, like "Sesame Street" and "The Electric Company," have demonstrated effectiveness and efficiency in teaching certain basic skills of literacy to children who view regularly (Ball & Bogatz, 1972; Watkins, Huston-Stein, & Wright, 1980).

Most research on television and children has been focused on the content of television and the outcomes of viewing. Viewers have typically been seen as passive recipients of salient images. Increasingly, however, child viewers are being perceived as active participants in the viewing process, whose perceptions and interpretations of television images play a significant role in television effects (Collins, 1982). Consequently, television researchers have begun to analyze the ways in which children of varying ages and abilities, with different social and personal histories, perceive and evaluate social portrayals on television. A particular focus is the characteristics of children's processing of the often complex content of typical programs.

The focus of this chapter is current research on the nature of children's cognitive processes in viewing. We will first outline the various aspects or components of the viewing process that have been examined in studies over the past decade. These components will then serve as the basis for discussion of two related research emphases: (1) processes involved in *comprehension* and *evaluation* of typical entertainment programming; and (2) strategies to improve comprehension and/or the social impact of television. Finally, we will discuss the implications of research on viewing and suggest directions for future investigation.

Aspects of the Viewing Process

Two primary themes in recent research on children's viewing of television concern what viewers do, overtly and covertly, in response to what they are watching, and how they represent program content after viewing. These examinations of viewer processing come primarily from studies of comprehension of program content. Among the issues addressed in such research are viewers' *retention* of the content of typical programs and their *inferences* about related information not explicitly depicted or stated in shows; the nature of viewers' *attention* and its role in comprehension; and the *use of general and specific knowledge* in comprehension of new information in programs. The implications of comprehension strategies for viewing have also been addressed. In this section, we attempt to characterize the evidence on these aspects of viewing and the skills required for viewers to comprehend and evaluate programs maturely. (The model of reading proposed by Cook and Mayer, (1983) shares many elements with the approach discussed here.)

Comprehension

Comprehension of programs varies dramatically from childhood to adulthood. In this section we address the nature of program comprehension and its development. Several questions are particularly pertinent: (1) What do children retain from typical programs? (2) How effectively do children infer implicit content from programs? (3) What is the relationship between attention to programs and children's retention of and inferences about the content presented? (4) How do children use their previously acquired general knowledge in understanding and evaluating what they see? In reviewing the information relevant to these questions, we will also attempt to specify the skills that children appear to use in comprehending typical programs.

The Viewing Task. In general, television programs consist of sequences of visual and auditory stimuli organized in particular ways. In children's programs like

"Sesame Street," the organization consists of a series of disconnected brief episodes of one or a few scenes. In dramatic programs produced for general audiences, the sequence of scenes is subordinated to a plot or narrative; the series of discrete scenes implies interrelationships from which coherence must be inferred, including off-screen, implicit events and relationships. For example, there may be an early scene in the plot involving two characters (e.g., a verbal disagreement) and a later scene in which the same two characters are portrayed in somewhat altered circumstances (e.g., one character physically attacks the other). The information that something has occurred to cause a change from the first to the second scene is an implicit linkage that is important for understanding the plot—as in the case of the inference that an early program event *caused* a later event. Furthermore, the particulars of such plots are often subtle, inexplicit, and interspersed with extraneous or tangentially relevant material. Program comprehension involves both (1) attention to and retention of explicitly portrayed plot-essential events, and (2) inferences in which viewers go beyond on-screen events to grasp the relationships among them. The latter task requires *temporal integration* of information from the plot (Collins, 1978).

Developmental Patterns of Retention and Inference. In general, children as old as 8 years retain a relatively small proportion of depicted actions, events, and settings in typical programs. Memory for information particularly important to plots and other primary messages (e.g., commercial appeals) improves dramatically across the grade school to high school age range (Collins, 1978; Collins, Wellman, Keniston, & Westby, 1978; Newcomb & Collins, 1979). These age-related trends have been documented across a range of types of programs produced for general audiences (e.g., action adventure programs, family dramas, situation comedies). Although young viewers attend to information that is obviously salient and informative, their processing of less salient plot-essential information is not as certain.

These difficulties can be illustrated with findings from a representative study (Purdie, Collins, & Westby, Note 1). The program of interest was an edited version of a commercial network action-adventure drama. The plot involved a man searching for his former wife in order to prevent her from presenting damaging testimony against him in a kidnapping case. His intention is discovered by law enforcement officers, who arrest him. The main events of the plot were retained, but some extraneous material and all commercials were deleted. Two versions were created, containing exactly the same material: a *distal-motive version*, in which scenes depicting the character's motives and aggression were separated from each other by a period of 3 minutes; and a *proximal-motive version*, in which the motive scene was contiguous to the aggression. We showed one or the other of the two versions to 200 second- and fifth-grade boys and girls. After viewing, the children completed a recognition-item measure constructed to test their retention of explicitly presented content and their inferences about important implicit information.

As in our studies of other programs, second graders answered correctly an average of only 65% of the explicit-content items that adults had judged to be essential for understanding of the plot. This proportion is significantly lower than the 85%

remembered by fifth graders. Furthermore, younger children were much less likely than older children to infer the implicit content of the program, such as the relationship between motive and aggression scenes. Even when the younger children knew the explicit scenes required to infer implicit content, the conditional probability for correct inferences was .29 for second graders in the distal-motive condition (see Figure 8-1). This amounts to performance at chance level. However, second graders in the proximal-motive condition, in which motive and aggression cues were portrayed in closer proximity, were much more likely to understand the implicit-motive aggression relationship. The conditional probability for correct inferences was .52 in this group. Fifth graders' probabilities were higher and essentially equal in both viewing conditions. As in other studies, both second and fifth graders performed at chance level when only one or neither explicit-premise scene was known.

Thus, by manipulating the temporal placement of central scenes, we improved inference making by younger groups. Still, even with the advantage of a well-structured presentation, age differences persist. Older children comprehended most program information, but even the best performing second graders understood significantly less of the show. Younger children may lack the necessary processing skills to overcome the lack of structure in many television presentations. (The comments of Pressley, 1983, on the amount of structure required in presentations to children may be of interest here.)

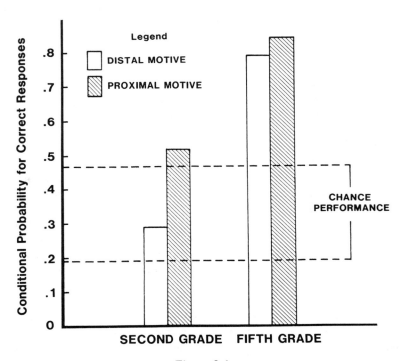

Figure 8-1.

Before examining these skill deficits in more detail, we turn briefly to two general aspects of viewing processes relevant to selection and encoding of content by viewers of different ages, backgrounds, and abilities: amount and use of general knowledge relevant to program content, and the constraints presented by the nature and difficulty of this program.

The Use of General Knowledge in Viewing. Collins (1981) has recently suggested three categories of knowledge that may affect comprehension of and responses to television programs: (1) knowledge about presentation formats (e.g., the structure of stories, commercials); (2) knowledge of media conventions (e.g., formal features, cinematic conventions); and (3) general social or "world" knowledge. Recent reviews (Collins, in press; Rice et al., 1982) have emphasized the first two, with virtually no attention to the role of social knowledge and expectations.

Recent findings indicate, however, that prior knowledge contributes both to developmental differences in comprehension of programs and to individual differences within age groups (refer also to Cook & Mayer, 1983, and to Chapter 3 of this volume). In an investigation of cognitive gains from exposure to "Sesame Street," Salomon (1976) tested Israeli 5- and 7- to 8-year-olds before and after 5 months of twice-weekly exposure to "Sesame Street." The skills tested were of two kinds: (1) particular cognitive skills applicable to the television format (e.g., close-ups, calling upon the skill of relating parts to the whole; and the embedding of messages in long [60-second] sequences, calling upon the skill of freeing one's self from the context of the field); and (2) skills assumed to *supplant* other skills (e.g., the changing angle of the camera, supplanting the skill of moving over to see somebody else's point of view; and the kaleidoscopic pattern, supplanting the tendency to shift rapidly from one issue to another). Children who were initially most skilled benefited most from formats calling on their skills, and showed no improvement where skills were only supplanted. By contrast, less skillful children gained only when skills were supplanted. Salomon concludes from his findings that cognitive effects of media presentations depend on children's initial levels of skill mastery, such that less skillful persons largely imitate and internalize media codes, whereas those who have already mastered the codes can begin to master other skills.

Social knowledge also affects comprehension from viewing. Collins and Wellman (1982) asked children to retell a television narrative so that someone would be able to understand what happened in the program. They found that second, fifth, and eighth graders were equally likely to mention stereotyped, or common, knowledge that occurred in the program; but the older children were much more likely than were second graders to mention knowledge specific to the program as well. Memory differences do not account for this age-related tendency. It may be that older viewers are more adept at integrating their prior world knowledge and experiences with specific program portrayals, while younger viewers are more apt to focus on common behavior and events to the exclusion of new information that does not fit their expectations. In a study of comprehension of plots featuring middle-class or working-class characters, second-grade children's understanding of characters' actions and feelings and of the causes of events was associated with their general familiarity with the types of characters and settings being portrayed (Newcomb &

Collins, 1979). Individual differences in other areas of knowledge and expectations may similarly bias children's processing of television social roles, attitudes, and behaviors.

Program Constraints on Viewing Processes. One factor in young children's poor understanding may be the lack of salience and concreteness with which much information is presented in programs. For example, Calvert, Huston, Watkins, and Wright (1982) have recently documented the influence of high- and low-salience formal features on comprehension. *Formal features* are attributes of television productions that are the result of visual or auditory production techniques. Highly salient features included high action, loud music, visual special effects, and auditory sound effects. Low-salient features were character dialogue and low action. Processing of abstract central content was more difficult when presented through character dialogue, a nonsalient feature, than when presented through a salient feature like action. Salient features probably affect comprehension by drawing attention to central content and by "presenting information through iconic images whose sensory properties parallel early encoding devices of children" (p. 14). Anderson and his colleagues (e.g., Anderson, Alwitt, Lorch, & Levin, 1979) have presented compelling evidence that even very young viewers use formal attributes of programs to guide attention to television.

Comprehension is also affected by the concreteness of event portrayal. In one study (Collins, 1978) the most difficult items of central content for second-grade subjects were those that were especially abstract and/or required multiple inferential steps. Thus, the way in which content is presented places an important constraint upon young viewers' processing. (Work reviewed by Pressley, 1983, and Paivio, 1983, as well as by Bellezza in Chapter 3 of this volume, is consistent with this theme.)

Young children's processing difficulties are not due simply to the length of programs nor to the presence of extraneous intervening information in plots, however. We have recently investigated forgetting and interference effects, using a procedure of interrupting viewing at different points in a program for different subgroups of children. When interrupted, the children are tested on their knowledge of explicit content and inferences in the program to that point. One group of children sees the entire program without interruption in order to provide a check on possible contamination of postinterruption answers in the other three groups. The procedure is diagrammed in Figure 8-2. Children tested on content they had seen only minutes before performed no better than children who were asked the same questions at a much later time (Purdie, Collins, & Westby, Note 1; Collins & Westby, Note 2). In other words, second graders' retention was poorer than fifth and eighth graders', regardless of the point at which they were tested. Similar findings were reported in a study of retention of simpler content from "Sesame Street" (Friedlander, Wetstone, & Scott, 1974). Young viewers appear to select and encode program content inadequately *during viewing,* and this is probably the primary reason they retain essential information so poorly.

Condition	Time Line of the Plot		
I. Before-motive Group:	↓Motive portrayal	Aggressive Action	Consequences
II. Before-action Group:	Motive portrayal	↓Aggressive Action	Consequences
III. After-action Group:	Motive portrayal	Aggressive Action	↓Consequences
IV. No interruption Group:	Motive portrayal	Aggressive Action	Consequences ↓

Figure 8-2. The interruption design: ↓ denotes point of interruption (i.e., points at which initial comprehension and evaluation measures are taken).

Some Processing Difficulties of Child Viewers

Discussion of attentional processes and the role of general knowledge in viewing implies several possible types of difficulties that may enter into young children's poor retention and inference making.

Selection and Encoding Difficulties. One line of evidence indicates that younger children's difficulties in retention may stem from poor selection and encoding of relevant content. For example, while recall of both central and peripheral, or non-essential, content improves linearly with age, central plot-relevant information accounts for an increasingly larger proportion of what is remembered (Collins, 1970; Collins et al., 1978; Calvert, Watkins, & Huston-Stein, Note 3). Indeed, in one study (Collins, 1970), peripheral-content memory bore a curvilinear relationship to age: recognition measure scores increased until early adolescence and declined thereafter. Whether peripheral retention declines among more mature individuals obviously depends on the interest value and difficulty of the presentation (Collins, 1970; Hale, Miller, & Stevenson, 1968; Hawkins, 1973; Calvert et al., Note 3), but diverging central- and peripheral-content curves have been found for a number of different instances of typical programs, including situation comedies, action-adventure dramas, and a cartoon produced for school-age children. The diverging relationship between central and peripheral content has been interpreted as reflecting children's increasingly greater ability to recognize and encode essential content while filtering out extraneous details.

A somewhat different, but consonant perspective (Wright & Vlietstra, 1975; Wright, Watkins, & Huston-Stein, Note 4) is that age differences in dominance of memory for central content reflect a developmental shift from an early tendency for attention to be commanded by highly salient perceptual features of shows (whether essential or peripheral to the plot) to a more mature pattern in which attention is intuitively marshaled in the service of logical search. Wright attributes the shift both to general cognitive development and to increasing television-viewing experience as children grow older. According to his formulation, viewing experience results in habituation to salient perceptual features of presentations and in an induction of the "grammar" of the medium, including the structure of programs generally; in addition, with age there is likely to be greater knowledge of how individual programs and their segments are ordinarily constructed.

Experience with television is clearly an important source of knowledge and skills relevant to processing of subsequent content. Nevertheless, currently available evidence indicates that retention of even the most important features of shows is relatively poor for young grade school children, despite the many hours of viewing in which children typically engage between toddlerhood and the early grade school years. It seems likely that age differences in cognitive processing are based on some general determinants of cognitive performance of the sort outlined in theories of cognitive development. Both the skills acquired through viewing experiences and the cognitive capabilities that enable viewers to find the logic and meaning in presentations contribute to older viewers' more complete representations of programs.

Age differences in use of knowledge may also be a factor in young viewers' relatively poorer retention. Having relatively little basic information in a task impairs incorporation of additional information (Chi, 1978). Younger children are less likely to acquire program specifics and also less likely to have a store of general knowledge that would facilitate remembering the content of narratives. Young viewers may also be less likely to be able to retrieve and use such knowledge, even when they have it. Although the reasons for generally poor selection and encoding of television content are neither simple nor obvious, the resulting limitations on young viewers' retention of plot information are now well established as a characteristic of their typical processing of general entertainment programming (Collins, 1982). (The themes raised in this subsection are very similar to classroom issues addressed by Peterson & Swing, 1983.)

Inferential Difficulties. Young children's poorer recall of central details of typical programs may also impair their abilities to infer important implicit content in programs as well. Moreover, even when knowledge of specific scenes was taken into account in our analyses, younger children were unlikely to make inferences about the linkages among scenes. Thus, it seems that (1) young viewers fail to *recognize*— or recognize to a lesser degree than older individuals—the need to infer relations; and/or (2) they may have difficulty *coordinating* the need to infer relations and the activity of making the inferences in the ongoing comprehension of the plot.

Literate decoding of messages in written, spoken, or audiovisually presented forms involves a process of review and comparison of information with an internal representation of what needs to be known. Psychologists who study children's processing of written and oral discourse (Mandler & Johnson, 1977; Stein & Glenn, 1979) have found that older children, more than younger ones, tried to fill in gaps in their memory of stories with plausible details that fit a common psychological scheme of story structure (Stein & Glenn, 1979). In reading, the comparison process may be somewhat easier for younger children than the analogous process in decoding oral and audiovisual materials. If motivated, children can always go back and fill in gaps in their understanding by reviewing the printed text. By contrast, the sequential format of audiovisual presentations and oral messages requires the decoder to review and compare spontaneously and rather continuously during viewing, a tendency or ability that apparently increases developmentally. The process of television comprehension, then, may be more similar to processing oral speech than to reading and writing, at least in the sense that the latter involve an immediate record that partly externalizes the comparison process, rather than limiting the perceiver to a memorial record, as does the former (Collins, 1978). Peterson & Swing, 1983, consider similar problems in the context of classroom processing.)

Why are inferences so difficult, when the information is at hand? Perhaps young viewers' lower level of knowledge impairs all aspects of making new inferences for which the knowledge is relevant. Or perhaps young viewers, even when they have the relevant information that should facilitate comprehension, apply it less flexibly than older children (Collins and Wellman, 1982). Once information has been instantiated by salient cues (e.g., the label "police," when seeing uniformed characters), younger children may perceive the program in terms of a standard, preset sequence of events that is already familiar to them. As a result, they may fail to notice or may ignore ways in which the program varies from familiar sequences. Consequently, explicit and implicit details of particular events may be short-circuited by rigid expectations of actors and actions (Collins, in press; Schank & Abelson, 1977). More mature or more knowledgeable viewers may be likely to recognize significant departures from expected sequences and to process them as significant aspects of stories that override usual occurrences.

This hypothesis has recently received suggestive support in a study of children's moral judgments of television characters (Collins & Westby, Note 2). In this study, we used the interruption procedure diagrammed in Figure 8-2 to trace the formation of, and change in, evaluations over the course of viewing the program. We also examined emerging evaluations in relation to comprehension of evaluation-relevant cues. The stimulus was the program about the kidnapping suspect searching for his wife to prevent her testifying against him. We interrupted 88 second- and fifth-grade boys and girls at one of the four interruption points and asked them to evaluate the goodness or badness of the character. We also tested their comprehension of the program up to the point of interruption.

We found the usual differences in comprehension between second and fifth graders, as well as parallel differences between the two grades in the degree to which children evaluated the antisocial character as bad. But at the first two interruption points, only about 25% of the second graders and 40% of the fifth graders gave negative evaluations. However, by the third interruption—after the aggressive action—fifth graders' evaluations were overwhelmingly negative (83%), while the proportion of second graders giving negative evaluations did not increase significantly until after the protagonist's arrest at the end of the program.

To examine the role of processing activity in children's evaluations, we compared second graders who eventually changed from positive to negative evaluations of the protagonist with those who remained positive throughout the program (nonchangers). In general, changers and nonchangers did not differ in their knowledge either of the motive scene or of the aggressive action alone; but changers understood the implicit causal links among motives, actions, and consequences scenes better than nonchangers.[1] However, changers and nonchangers gave markedly different *reasons* for their initial evaluation (coded as either positive or negative; interrater agreement = .94). Although participants interrupted for the motive scene gave uniformly positive evaluations, 75% of those who remained positive explicitly justified their initial judgments with incorrect, but positive, interpretations of ambiguous events occurring early in the program (i.e., "He is trying to help the girl" or "He is trying to find her so she won't be scared"). By contrast, children who eventually changed their evaluations often gave initially noncommittal answers (80%), indicating that they did not have reasons for their evaluation. After the program, nonchangers continued to explain evaluations in terms of the positive interpretation of early cues (83%), while changers focused on the negative motives or action (73%).

Thus, changers and nonchangers apparently selected and retained plot information differently as a function of the explicitness of early instantiated expectations about the actor. Nonchangers' initial positive perceptions may have affected retention of some plot events, much as social prototypes or schemata have been found to create confirmatory biases in memory for social information (e.g., Hastie, 1981; Nisbett & Ross, 1980; Schneider, Hastorf, & Ellsworth, 1980). Furthermore, their expectations may well have interfered with recognition of negative consequences of the protagonist. By contrast, changers' less explicit initial assumption, while not facilitating their overall comprehension, may have permitted assimilation of later occurring negative views. In short, young viewers may often foreclose on interpretations of characters and fail to incorporate later inconsistent information during viewing. (Pressley, 1983, makes suggestions about how to modify materials in order to increase the probability of correct inferences by children.)

At this point, many questions remain to be answered about typical cognitive processes in viewing for children of different ages. Clearly, age trends have been documented that reflect attention, encoding, and inferential processes in which viewers "go beyond the information given" to a greater or lesser extent. The particular processes encompassed by these global difficulties are at present poorly understood, however.

Behavioral and Attitudinal Outcomes

The longstanding emphasis of mass media researchers on the content of television programs has yielded a rich and diverse array of evidence of the influence of television on children's social behavior. In general, studies of behavioral and attitudinal outcomes have subscribed to the assumption that the primary social effects of television reflect directly the types of content the medium presents (Collins, in

---

[1] These differences are not attributable to differences in verbal ability, which we had controlled in covariance analyses. Nor did they reflect limitations in acquiring information; children who did not change their evaluations over the course of viewing actually performed better than changers on tests of content that had been presented early in the program, but that was unrelated to the characters' motives.

press). To be sure, postviewing behavior has also sometimes been viewed partly as a function of age and social group variables that heighten or reduce viewers' motivations to adopt the salient social behaviors presented in typical programs (e.g., Comstock et al., 1978; Feshbach & Singer, 1971; Leifer, Gordon, & Graves, 1974; Liebert, Neale, & Graves, 1973; Maccoby, 1964; Siegel, 1975; Stein & Friedrich, 1975). For example, aggressive behavior after viewing a violent program may also be influenced by the results of antecedent social learning (e.g., internalization of social and moral values, previous direct or vicarious experience with the observed behaviors) and by states and circumstances subsequent to viewing (e.g., behavioral opportunities and their circumstances, including instances of provocation, existing or expected performance sanctions, and emotional arousal). In both cases, media effects have been assumed to reflect complex mixtures of external forces.

Additional processes are implied, however, by the findings on plot comprehension and evaluations of social acts described above. In several studies, behavioral differences have been found that are suggestive of links between children's representations of programs and subsequent behavior. For example, Collins, Berndt, and Hess (1974) found that kindergarten and second-grade children who had watched an action-adventure program had difficulty remembering the relations of the motives and consequences cues to the aggressive action. Seeing aggression in the context of negative motives and consequences ordinarily reduces deleterious behavioral effects of observed aggression (Bandura, 1965; Berkowitz & Geen, 1967; Berkowitz & Rawlings, 1963). In this research, however, children remembered the aggressive scene and not its links with the motives and consequences. Collins (1973) reported behavioral outcomes that ostensibly reflect such cognitive processing differences. When commercials were inserted between scenes showing negative motives and negative consequences for aggression and the violent scene itself, third graders' postviewing aggressive tendencies increased, in comparison to the behavior of children who saw the scenes close together in time. Although comprehension was not directly assessed, the task of inferring relations between aggression and the pertinent motive and consequences cues was probably more difficult for the first group than the second, presumably because of the temporal separation imposed by commercials. There was no evidence of behavioral differences among the sixth and tenth graders who saw the same types of programs. Thus, the possible links between comprehension and behavioral influences of typical dramatic television programs may involve the abilities of viewers of different ages to comprehend relevant cues in typical programs. Indeed, how well viewers understand what they see potentially affects their attitudes and behaviors.

One example of research designed to examine more explicitly the intermediate steps in a comprehension-behavior linkage is Purdue et al.'s (Note 1) study of children's comprehension and evaluations of characters. Children's evaluations of the goodness or badness of the aggressor were assessed in relation to their comprehension of the links between motive and aggression scenes in the program. The measurement technique was a variation of the Likert Scale, in which six size-graduated squares were labeled from "very bad" to "very good" (Costanzo, Coie, Grumet, & Farnill, 1973). Participants pointed to the square that showed how good or how bad a character was. Children who answered all three motive-aggression inference questions correctly were significantly more negative in their evaluation of the aggressor than were children who understood two or fewer inferences. Whether motives and aggression were proximally or distally portrayed also affected evaluations. At both grades, distal-motive viewers evaluated the character less negatively than proximal-motive viewers, particularly following portrayal of the aggressive action. Thus, children's inferences about critical links were correlated with their evaluative responses. Such evaluative responses may play an important role in determining children's inclinations to adopt a character's behavior, or other similar actions, in their own experience. Thus, the processing difficulties that cause younger viewers to understand programs less well than older ones may also affect the power of television programs to influence viewers' social behavior.

In summary, evidence now exists of processing difficulties among younger viewers in retention of plot content and inferences about the relationships among explicitly portrayed events. The difficulties may be partly due to characteristics of programs. Many of the more subtle, but nevertheless essential, aspects of plots are not presented saliently and therefore are missed by many preschool and young school-aged viewers. In addition, young viewers' more limited knowledge relevant to understanding programs may exacerbate ineffective or inefficient processing skills. Such deficits and inefficiencies thus contribute to children's cognitive and evaluative responses to content, which in turn affect the behavioral and attitudinal outcomes of viewing.

In the next section, we examine some attempts to devise strategies to supplement young viewers' relatively inadequate skills for comprehending common programs.

Research on Interventions in Viewing

The large body of literature on the effects of television viewing on children's attitudes and behaviors has inspired a number of attempts to devise interventions in the viewing process. These interventions range from informal suggestions to parents who are concerned about deleterious influences of viewing to more formal curricula to teach children generally to be more critical viewers of television fare. Two assumptions underlying the development of such curricula are that (1) the medium of communication is an integral part of the message and (2) there are elements and meanings that are medium specific and can be taught (Anderson, 1980).

In this section we review briefly four types of interventions. The first type concerns interventions designed to directly moderate behavioral and attitudinal effects of viewing. Three other types are designed to accomplish the same goal, but less directly. One type of intervention involves instruction about the medium and the industry; the others, strategies for improving understanding and evaluation of television content. These intervention approaches involve the aspects of viewing described in the first section of the chapter. For example, while attempts to intervene directly to moderate attitudinal and behavioral effects obviously draw on the assumptions and evidence relating to attitudinal and behavioral outcomes of viewing, efforts to teach children about the medium and industry and to improve their understanding of specific programs also implicitly address aspects of the viewing process that are assumed to contribute to attitudinal and behavioral outcomes.

Following the brief overview of general types of interventions in viewing, we will turn to a more detailed account of intervention research addressed to improving children's comprehension during viewing.

Interventions to Moderate Behavioral and Attitudinal Effects

The most obvious type of intervention in children's television viewing involves altering the behavioral consequences that television viewing may produce. In this type of strategy, sources of influence other than the television program are introduced in order to try to counteract potential deleterious effects of televised-modeled behavior. For example, in an early experimental intervention, Hicks (1968) had adult coviewers make evaluative comments while children were watching an aggressive model. Postviewing aggression increased following comments that implied adult positive sanctions for the model's behavior, but decreased following negative statements. These effects persisted over a 6-month period. Other researchers (Horton & Santogrossi, Note 5) have also reported moderating effects of adult coviewers' comments on behavior following aggressive programs. The impact of violence on children's attitudes about stealing and hurting people is also affected by coviewer's attitudes. In one demonstration (Corder-Bolz, 1980), a teacher viewed an episode of "Batman" with young children and made either neutral or explanatory judgmental comments about the portrayal (e.g., "It is bad to fight. It is better to get help"). In a second group, children viewed without the adult's comments. After viewing, children in the mediation condition were less likely to believe that other people typically hit and stole (societal norm) and slightly less likely to say it was all right for them to hit and steal (personal ethic).

Corder-Bolz (1980) also used the same episode of "Batman" to investigate the effectiveness of television itself as a source of mediating information. In the mediation condition, two 60-second spots were substituted for commercials. The spots provided editorial and explanatory comments similar to those provided by adult coviewers, as in the previous study. Children in the TV and coviewer mediation conditions were equally less likely to judge hitting, stealing, and hurting people as acceptable, compared to children who viewed without mediation.

Instruction About the Medium and the Industry

A less direct intervention approach involves teaching children about the techniques of television in hopes of affecting their understanding of the messages television conveys. This approach, sometimes referred to as teaching "visual literacy" (Anderson, 1980), emphasizes practice in understanding symbols, grammar, and techniques of television as a communication medium. For example, Singer, Zuckerman, and Singer (1980) evaluated the effectiveness of eight 40-minute lessons focusing on specific topics: introduction to television, reality and fantasy in television, camera effects and special effects, commercials in the television business, identification with television characters, stereotypes in television, violence and aggression, and how viewers can influence television. Third, fourth, and fifth graders exposed to the lessons increased in understanding of special effects, commercials, and advertising, and also learned more lesson-related vocabulary words than control group children. In a 3-month follow-up test, training group children demonstrated significantly more improvement than children in the control group in identifying camera effects and understanding commercials. An adaptation of this intervention for kindergartners and first and second graders has recently been tested with similar results (Rapaczynski, Singer, & Singer, 1982).

In a different approach, Dorr, Browne-Graves, and Phelps (1980) compared two different approaches to teaching about television. The first condition focused on applying facts about television production and the economic system of the industry to "reasoning about the reality/fantasy of entertainment programming." The second curriculum condition emphasized the availability and use of sources of information other than television portrayals for evaluating television content. A third—control—curriculum was included to teach children general role-taking skills, a general social-cognitive skill that might affect reasoning about television content.

Kindergartners and second and/or third graders subsequently better understood and evaluated television content in terms of the material each curriculum taught. Children who were taught the industry curriculum learned more about television production and industry economics than did children who were taught the other two curricula. Those who were taught the process curriculum learned more about sources for evaluating the realism of television content than did other children. Furthermore, the children were able to use their new knowledge to some extent in discussions of the reality of television. However, they did not demonstrate changes in attitudes toward television that they had been expected to evince after learning about the medium.

Interventions to Facilitate Learning Television Content

Intervention approaches of the third type involve strategies for facilitating children's learning. They include efforts to teach general cognitive skills, reading skills, and consumer information. Two general types of interventions have been attempted: (1) before-viewing instruction, or *sets* for viewing; and (2) provision of additional information during viewing by an adult coviewer.

A prime example of this approach involves programs designed to teach cognitive skills. In the production of "Electric Company," a program aimed at teaching elementary reading skills, auditory and visual techniques are used to direct children's attention to basic elements of reading tasks. Viewing in the classroom enhanced the program's effects on reading, but there were no effects of the show when viewing took place only at home (Ball & Bogatz, 1973). Supplementary materials and an interested coviewing adult appear to be important components in learning program material (Watkins et al., 1980). For example, when a teacher aide made explanatory comments during viewing about the grammatical concepts presented in "Electric Company," higher comprehension scores resulted, at least for children who were not already very familiar with the concept being taught (Corder-Bolz, 1980).

Coviewers may facilitate learning in a variety of ways: by serving as models of attention, interest, or liking; by giving verbal clarifications or labels to events and behaviors; or by making value judgments about behavioral portrayals (Stein & Friedrich, 1975). In one study, Friedrich and Stein (1975) found that stating verbal labels for nonverbal cues improved kindergarten children's retention of visually presented information. In a similar vein, adult coviewers' statements about the nature of program events and their relationship to other parts of the plot led to improved comprehension of explicitly presented content for both kindergartners and third and fourth graders (Watkins et al., 1980).

There have been fewer efforts to improve children's retention by providing previewing instructions or training, and results have been mixed. The primary example is Wackman, Wartella, and Ward's (Note 6) effort to train children in the categories of information about products commonly included in commercials (e.g., what the product looks like, how it works, what it tastes like). The training sessions constituted about 3½ hours over a period of about 2 weeks. When subsequently tested for their memory of specific commercials, the training groups of both kindergartners and third and fourth graders showed significantly better retention of concretely presented product information (e.g., how many items of a product are in a package) than the no-training control group; however, the training program did not affect retention of more abstract kinds of product information (e.g., "requires experience and skill"). In contrast, simply telling children to "try hard to remember as much as possible" from a dramatic program did not lead to greater retention by second graders, even when material incentive was provided (Collins, Karasov, & Westby, Note 7). The authors speculate that the second graders lacked adequate cognitive strategies for improving their comprehension of the program and thus could not remember significantly more only because they knew better performance was desired. Providing labels or statements of implicit information, on the other hand, appears to facilitate children's comprehension by instantiating parts of the comprehension task that children do not or cannot accomplish spontaneously. Once these critical aspects of processing are made available, young viewers may be able to achieve on their own the other activities necessary for accurate representation of content.

The main focus of the interventions described thus far has been on accurate learning from television and evaluation or reinterpretation of explicitly portrayed events in programs. The latter two types of intervention attempts have demonstrated that children can be taught, in a relatively short period, skills that mature television viewers use automatically. In the next section, we address strategies to improve children's *inferences* about the implicit content of programs.

Interventions to Improve Inferences During Viewing

The fourth type of intervention is based on the comprehension processes investigated in research on the cognitive requirements of television viewing. Of central importance is that comprehension of narratives presented on television requires that a viewer go beyond explicit discrete items of information to infer the interrelationships of events and the coherence of the plot. Children as old as second and third graders are less apt to "strain for meaning" than adults would expect (e.g., Collins & Wellman, 1982; Collins et al., 1978). This failure to infer relationships among discrete events seems to be a major impediment to functional literacy in television viewing. Like the other intervention attempts discussed, this type of intervention has as its goal improving children's critical responses to television content in the hopes that deleterious effects will thereby be reduced.

Coviewing Interventions. An intervention strategy to aid children in the process of inferring interrelationships among important scenes in a program was used in a recent study by Collins, Sobol, and Westby (1981). The subjects in this study were second graders, an age group previously found to show markedly poor comprehension (Collins et al., 1978). The stimulus was an edited version of an action-adventure television program. A coviewer made comments at strategic points in the program to induce the children to infer relations among explicit scenes. The comments were made at points in three scenes that were crucial to understanding the relation between motives and the actions to which they were related. In the control condition, the coviewer made neutral comments, which merely described the action taking place during the scenes, at the same points at which facilitative comments were provided in the intervention condition.

Facilitative comments markedly affected children's inferences that were directly related to the adults' statements and those that were less directly related as well. Perhaps coviewers' facilitative statements compensated for the strategic-skill deficits to which second graders' typically poor comprehension has been attributed (Collins et al., 1978). By reducing the extent and complexity of reasoning necessary for inferring related content, coviewers' statements may make it possible for the young viewers to apply more successfully the relatively limited strategic skills available to them. Similar interventions used informally by parents at critical points in a show (e.g., when an important scene is related to events that happened much earlier in the show) may be helpful for young children. Comments such as these can serve as prompts for children to search for meanings and to ask questions that they do not seem to ask spontaneously. In addition, parents can better monitor what their children extract from television programs and can mediate more effectively the potential behavioral and attitudinal outcomes of television viewing. (Pressley, 1983, also takes up the effects of in-the-world comments on children's inferences.)

Program-Relevant Knowledge Interventions. Another intervention strategy currently under investigation (Collins, Westby, & Easter, Note 8) reflects emerging evidence on the role of viewers' existing knowledge in comprehension. Extra-viewing experiences, circumstances, and states have long been recognized as relevant to the prediction of behavior after viewing. Judging from our evidence, these effects may operate partly through their influence on the way in which portrayals are understood and remembered. Children's responses to television content may be dif-

ferentiated not only by the behavioral tendencies attributable to socialization antecedents, but also by the way in which the social knowledge and expectations
acquired in those previous social experiences affect processing of the television
stimulus itself.

An especially detailed account of the role of prior knowledge in understanding
stories is the scripts approach (Cook & Mayer, 1983; Schank & Abelson, 1977;
Chapter 3 in this volume), in which prior knowledge, in the form of stereotypes of
event sequences, enables filling gaps in the linkages between the actions or states of
the story characters. As we have seen, older children are more likely than younger
children to recognize the need to "fill in the gaps" of a portrayal they did not
understand, and often do so with likely or stereotyped events.

In our research, we provided one group of second-grade subjects with a script
that generally described courtroom settings and the types of roles that operate
within them. The subjects later viewed an edited version of an action-adventure
television program. In the plot, which was also used in the study by Purdie et al.
(Note 1), a woman is prepared to be a key witness against her ex-husband at his
trial on kidnapping charges. The woman flees before the trial to seek refuge at her
grandfather's home. The ex-husband pursues and tries to kill the woman in order to
keep her from testifying against him in court. In the end, federal officers arrest the
man as he is shooting at the house where his ex-wife is hiding. Another group of
second graders was provided with the script and answered the comprehension questionnaire without watching the program. This condition was designed to determine
if children could use the script alone to make informed guesses about the questionnaire items. A third group viewed the program without having been exposed to the
script. Comprehension was assessed by a recognition measure.

The results showed that boys, but not girls, in the script-plus-program condition
understood the program better than those in the program-only condition. The boys
apparently made use of the script to comprehend more effectively while viewing
the program. Girls in the script-only condition did as well as girls who saw the program without script training, indicating that the script training per se was effective
for girls, although girls apparently did not use the script to understand the program
better. Girls appear to view the program with a more positive set than boys and
continue to see characters as relatively positive, despite evidence to the contrary.
These positive expectations may have led to misinterpretations of the portrayal, a
hypothesis also suggested in a study by Collins and Westby (Note 2). In the present
script-plus-program condition, in which boys' comprehension was better than girls',
girls rated the main character as more positive than the boys did. These patterns are
currently being examined to specify further the constraints on children's use of
knowledge in understanding televised programs.

One issue little addressed in previous research concerns how extensively children
are able to make use of new understanding to become more critical viewers. Relevant to this issue is a study now in progress at Minnesota. We are interested in how
children extract and use information from several episodes of a program (a situation
comedy, in this case) to better understand another episode of the same program.
Learning from initial exposure to programs in an unfamiliar series will be assessed.

Generalizability of information from these episodes to a new episode will then be examined. Two kinds of information will be assessed: (1) knowledge specific to the program, but common to all episodes of the program (e.g., relationships of characters to each other, typical settings); and (2) knowledge specific to individual episodes (i.e. unique plot information). In this way we hope to gain an understanding of the kinds of information children are able to use to aid comprehension of newly encountered television stimuli.

Implications and Possibilities

In the past decade research on the processing and representation of televised narratives by children of different ages has departed from the historical trend in studies of mass-media effects. The longstanding assumption that television's "dominant images" shape the attitudes and behaviors of a vast viewing audience (Collins, in press), including suggestible children and youth, has been supplemented by emerging evidence on the importance of cognitive processing of content. Grade school and preadolescent children construct representations of typical programs that vary considerably in how accurately and completely they reflect the content of portrayals; and their evaluations of characters and their actions appear to vary concomitantly with comprehension. Although it is impossible to estimate the proportion of variance in postviewing behavioral and attitudinal effects due to incomplete or distorted comprehension, the marked variability of children's comprehension of socially pertinent content and laboratory evidence of concomitant patterns of comprehension and behavior indicate the potential importance of cognitive processing factors.

Interventions based on common deficits in understanding have both provided useful information about cognitive processes relevant to viewing and potential applications of knowledge about these processes to more skilled viewing. To date, the most successful of these applications have been strategies designed to facilitate retention of specific parts of programs and inferences about the relationships among them. These interventions have depended on the presence of adults, either for comments during viewing or for instruction just before viewing; and the assessments of their effects have been immediate, rather than long term. Whether or not children use skills taught in connection with viewing a specific program on their own and whether the intervention of a coviewer affects viewing in other settings are important questions about which no information is available. Nevertheless, the power of the simple interventions thus far attempted demonstrates the potential value of using evidence on the nature of viewing processes as a basis for devising strategic interventions to improve comprehension and evaluation of programs.

A potential strategic application not examined thus far concerns the possible use of knowledge about viewing strategies in the service of traditional educational goals. For example, many commentators on literacy have blamed television for the decline of traditional literacy skills like reading and writing. Little support for this contention exists in the research literature at present (Hornik, 1981). Indeed, in a broader perspective, comprehension of television content demands many skills that are similar to those required for literacy more traditionally defined. Typical television programming requires viewers to use a range of literacy skills that can be elaborated and reinforced in classroom exercises—skills like selective attention to relevant attributes, role taking, empathy, impression formation, and temporal integration of information. Watching and expatiating upon television content can be used to exercise these skills in a way that seems completely pertinent to the development of literacy in traditional terms. For example, children might be induced to engage in the kind of review and comparison processes that are rather unlikely among younger children, but appear important to plot comprehension and other literacy tasks. This approach is similar to traditional literacy training and thus could probably be readily combined with, say, reading comprehension exercises in school curricula. The transfer of training effects from these exercises to writing and reading, speaking and listening, are only speculative at present; but the commonalities in the cognitive processing aspects of these different activities suggest that benefits may generalize. In addition, television may offer the motivation needed to engage children in communicative tasks in the classroom.

The strategic implications of processes involved in viewing thus go well beyond experiences with television per se. Television viewing is an aspect of children's social and cognitive development and as such may parallel or even shape the way in which nontelevision information is processed (McLuhan, 1964). Conversely, a wide range of tasks, including social relations within families and among peers, may be approached differently as a function of expectations derived from common television portrayals. A perspective on television viewing that includes the social and cognitive processes of viewers as a focal consideration may thus prove relevant to understanding the nature of children's functioning in diverse circumstances in ordinary experience.

Acknowledgments. Preparation of this chapter was facilitated by Grant No. 24197 from the National Institute of Mental Health to W. Andrew Collins. The authors thank Sally Westby, Andrea Easter, and Michael Pressley for their helpful comments on an early draft of the chapter.

Reference Notes

1. Purdie, S., Collins, W. A., & Westby, S. *Children's processing of motive information in a televised portrayal.* Unpublished manuscript, Institute of Child Development, University of Minnesota, 1979.
2. Collins, W. A., & Westby, S. *Moral judgments of TV characters as a function of program comprehension.* Paper presented at biennial meeting of the Society for Research in Child Development, Boston, April 1981.
3. Calvert, S. L., Watkins, B. A., & Huston-Stein, A. *Immediate and delayed recall of central and incidental television content as a function of formal features.*

Portions of this paper were presented at the meeting of the Society for Research in Child Development, San Francisco, March 1979.

4. Wright, J. C., Watkins, B. A., & Huston-Stein, A. *Active vs. passive television viewing: A model of the development of television information processing by children.* Unpublished manuscript, University of Kansas, 1979.

5. Horton, R., & Santogrossi, D. *Mitigating the impact of televised violence through concurrent adult commentary.* Paper presented at the annual meeting of the American Psychological Association, Toronto, Canada, August 1978.

6. Wackman, D. B., Wartella, E., & Ward, S. *Children's information processing of television advertising.* Unpublished manuscript, 1979.

7. Collins, W. A., Karasov, R., & Westby, S. *Effects of pre-viewing instructions on children's retention and inferences following a dramatic television program.* Unpublished manuscript, University of Minnesota, 1978.

8. Collins, W. A., Westby, S., & Easter, A. *Effects of script training on comprehension and evaluation in television viewing.* Unpublished manuscript, Institute of Child Development, University of Minnesota, 1982.

References

Anderson, D., Alwitt, L., Lorch, E., & Levin, S. Watching children watch television. In G. Hale & M. Lewis (Eds.), *Attention and cognitive development.* New York: Plenum, 1979.

Anderson, J. The theoretical lineage of critical viewing curricula. *Journal of Communication,* 1980, *30,* 64–70.

Ball, S., & Bogatz, G. Summative research on *Sesame Street:* Implications for the study of preschool children. In A. D. Pick (Ed.), *Minnesota Symposia on Child Psychology* (Vol. 6). Minneapolis: University of Minnesota Press, 1972.

Ball, S., & Bogatz, G. *Reading with television: An evaluation of the Electric Company.* Princeton, N.J.: Educational Testing Service, 1973.

Bandura, A. Influence of models' reinforcement contingencies on the acquisition of imitative responses. *Journal of Personality and Social Psychology,* 1965, *1,* 589–595.

Belson, W. *Television violence and the adolescent boy.* Westmead, England: Saxon House, Teakfield Limited, 1978.

Berkowitz, L., & Geen, R. The stimulus qualities of the target of aggression: A further study. *Journal of Personality and Social Psychology,* 1967, *5,* 364–368.

Berkowitz, L., & Rawlings, E. Effects of film violence on inhibitions against subsequent aggression. *Journal of Abnormal and Social Psychology,* 1963, *66,* 405–412.

Calvert, S., Huston, A., Watkins, B., & Wright, J. The effects of selective attention to television forms on children's comprehension of content. *Child Development,* 1982, *53,* 601–610.

Chi, M. Knowledge structures and memory development. In R. Siegler (Ed.), *Children's thinking: What develops?* Hillsdale, NJ: Erlbaum, 1978.

Collins, W. A. Learning of media content: A developmental study. *Child Development,* 1970, *41*(4), 1133–1142.

Collins, W. A. The effect of temporal separation between motivation, aggression and consequences: A developmental study. *Developmental Psychology*, 1973, *8*(2), 215–221.

Collins, W. A. Developmental aspects of literacy: Communication skills and the specter of television. In R. Beach & P. D. Pearson (Eds.), *Perspectives on literacy*. Minneapolis: National Council of Teachers of English, 1978.

Collins, W. A. Children's comprehension of television content. In E. Wartella (Ed.), *Children communicating: Media and development of thought, speech, understanding*. Beverly Hills, CA: Sage Publications, 1979.

Collins, W. A. Schemata for understanding television. In H. Kelly & H. Gardner (Eds.), *New directions for child development: Viewing children through television*. San Francisco: Jossey-Bass, 1981.

Collins, W. A. Cognitive processing in television viewing. In D. Pearl, L. Bouthilet, & J. Lazar (Eds.), *Television and behavior: Ten years of scientific progress and implications for the 80's* (Vol. 2). Washington, DC: U.S. Government Printing Office, 1982.

Collins, W. A. Social antecedents, cognitive processing, and comprehension of social portrayals on television. In E. T. Higgins, D. Ruble, & W. Hartup (Eds.), *Social cognition and social behavior: Developmental perspectives*. New York & London: Cambridge University Press, in press.

Collins, W. Berndt, T. J., & Hess, V. L. Observational learning of motives and consequences for television aggression: A developmental study. *Child Development*, 1974, *45*. 799–802.

Collins, W. A., Sobol, B., & Westby, S. Effects of adult commentary on children's comprehension and inferences about a televised aggressive portrayal. *Child Development*, 1981, *52*, 158–163.

Collins, W. A., & Wellman, H. Social scripts and developmental changes in representations of televised narratives. *Communication Research*, 1982, *9*, 380–398.

Collins, W. A., Wellman, H., Keniston, A., & Westby, S. Age-related aspects of comprehension of televised social content. *Child Development*, 1978, *49*, 389–399.

Collins, W. A., & Westby, S. Moral judgments of TV characters as a function of program comprehension. Paper presented at biennial meeting of the Society for Research in Child Development, Boston, April 1981.

Comstock, G., Chaffee, S., Katzman, N., McCombs, M., & Roberts, D. *Television and human behavior*. New York: Columbia University Press, 1978.

Cook, L. K., & Mayer, R. E. Reading strategies training for meaningful learning from prose. In M. Pressely & J. R. Levin (Eds.), *Cognitive strategy research: Educational applications*. New York: Springer-Verlag, 1983.

Corder-Bolz, C. Mediation: The role of significant others. *Journal of Communication*, 1980, *30*(3), 106–118.

Costanzo, P. R., Coie, J. D., Grumet, J. F., & Farnill, D. A reexamination of the effects of intent and consequence on children's moral judgments. *Child Development*, 1973, *44*, 154–161.

Dorr, A., Browne-Graves, S., & Phelps, E. Television literacy for young children. *Journal of Communication*, 1980, *30*(3), 71–83.

Eron, L. Parent-child interaction, television violence, and aggression of children. *American Psychologist*, 1982, *37*, 197–211.

Eron, L. D., Huesmann, L. R., Lefkowitz, M. M., and Walder, L. O. Does television violence cause aggression? *American Psychologist*, 1972, *27*, 253–263.

Feshbach, S., & Singer, R. *Television and aggression: An experimental field study.* San Francisco: Jossey-Bass, 1971.

Friedlander, B., Wetstone, H., & Scott, J. Suburban pre-school children's comprehension of an age-appropriate informational television program. *Child Development,* 1974, *45,* 561–565.

Friedrich, L., & Stein, A. H. Aggressive and prosocial television programs and the natural behavior of preschool children. *Monographs of the Society for Research in Child Development,* 1973, *38*(4).

Friedrich, L. K., & Stein, A. H. Prosocial television and young children: The effects of verbal labeling and role playing on learning and behavior. *Child Development,* 1975, *46,* 27–38.

Hale, G., Miller, L., & Stevenson, H. Incidental learning of film content: A developmental study. *Child Development,* 1968, *39,* 69–77.

Hastie, R. Schematic principles in human memory. In E. T. Higgins, C. Sherman, & M. Zanna (Eds.), *The Ontario Symposium on Personality and Social Psychology: Social cognition.* Hillsdale, NJ: Erlbaum, 1981.

Hawkins, R. P. Learning of peripheral content in films: A developmental study. *Child Development,* 1973, *44,* 214–217.

Hicks, D. J. Effects of co-observer's sanction and adult presence on imitative aggression. *Child Development,* 1968, *39*(1), 303–309.

Hornik, R. Out-of-school television and schooling: Hypotheses and methods. *Review of Educational Research,* 1981, *51,* 193–214.

Huesmann, L. R. Television violence and aggressive behavior. In D. Pearl and L. Bouthilet (Eds.), *Television and behavior: Ten years of scientific progress and implications for the 80's.* Washington, DC: U.S. Government Printing Office, 1982.

Leifer, A., Gordon, N., & Graves, S. Children's television: More than mere entertainment. *Harvard Educational Review,* 1974, *44,* 213–245.

Leyens, J., Camino, L., Parke, R., & Berkowitz, L. Effects of movie violence on aggression in a field setting as a function of group dominance and cohesion. *Journal of Personality and Social Psychology,* 1975, *32*(2), 346–360.

Liebert, R., Neale, J., & Davidson, E. *The early window: Effects of television on children and youth.* New York: Pergamon, 1973.

List, J., Collins, W. A., & Westby, S. Comprehension and inferences from traditional and nontraditional sex-role portrayals on television. *Child Development,* in press.

Maccoby, E. Effects of the mass media. In M. Hoffman & L. Hoffman (Eds.), *Review of child development research* (Vol. 1). Chicago: University of Chicago Press, 1964.

Mandler, J., & Johnson, N. Remembrance of things parsed: Story structure and recall. *Cognitive Psychology,* 1977, *9,* 111–151.

McLuhan, M. *Understanding media: The extensions of man.* New York: Signet Books, 1964.

Newcomb, A. F., & Collins, W. A. Children's comprehension of family role portrayals in televised dramas: Effects of socioeconomic status, ethnicity, and age. *Developmental Psychology,* 1979, *15*(4), 417–423.

Nisbett, R., & Ross, L. *Human inference: Strategies and shortcomings of social judgment.* Englewood Cliffs, NJ: Prentice-Hall, 1980.

Paivio, A. Strategies in language learning. In M. Pressley & J. R. Levin (Eds.), *Cogni-*

tive strategy research: Educational applications. New York: Springer-Verlag, 1983.

Peterson, P. L., & Swing, S. R. Problems in classroom implementation of cognitive strategy instruction. In M. Pressley & J. R. Levin (Eds.), *Cognitive strategy research: Educational applications.* New York: Springer-Verlag, 1983.

Pressley, M. Making meaningful materials easier to learn: Lessons from cognitive strategy research. In M. Pressley & J. R. Levin (Eds.), *Cognitive strategy research: Educational applications.* New York: Springer-Verlag, 1983.

Rapaczynski, W., Singer, D., & Singer, J. Teaching television: A curriculum for young children. *Journal of Communication,* 1982, *32,* 46–55.

Rice, M., Huston, A., & Wright, J. The forms and codes of television: Effects on children's attention, comprehension, and social behavior. In D. Pearl, L. Bouthilet, & J. Lazar (Eds.), *Television and behavior: Ten years of scientific progress and implications for the 80's* (Vol. 2). Washington, DC: U.S. Government Printing Office, 1982.

Roberts, D., & Bachen, C. Mass communication effects. *Annual Review of Psychology,* 1981, *32.*

Rushton, J. P. Effects of television and film material on the prosocial behavior of children. In L. Berkowitz (Ed.), *Advances in experimental social psychology.* New York: Academic Press, 1979.

Salomon, G. Cognitive skill learning across cultures. *Journal of Communication,* 1976, *26,* 138–144.

Schank, R., & Abelson, R. *Scripts, plans, goals, and understanding.* Hillsdale, NJ: Erlbaum, 1977.

Schneider, D., Hastorf, A., & Ellsworth, P. *Person perception* (2nd ed.). Reading, MA: Addison-Wesley, 1980.

Siegel, A. Communicating with the next generation. *Journal of Communication,* 1975, *25,* 14–24.

Singer, D., Zuckerman, D., & Singer, J. Helping elementary school children learn about TV. *Journal of Communication,* 1980, *30*(3), 84–93.

Stein, A., & Friedrich, L. Impact of television on children and youth. In E. M. Hetherington (Ed.), *Review of child development research* (Vol. 5). Chicago: University of Chicago Press, 1975.

Stein, N., & Glenn, C. An analysis of story comprehension in elementary school children. In R. Freedle (Ed.), *Advances in discourse processes* (Vol. 2). Hillsdale, NJ: Erlbaum, 1979.

Watkins, B. A., Huston-Stein, A., & Wright, J. C. Effects of educational television. In E. Palmer & A. Dorr (Eds.), *Three faces of children's television.* New York: Academic Press, 1980.

Wright, J. C., & Vlietstra, A. G. The development of selective attention: From perceptual exploration to logical search. In H. W. Reese (Ed.), *Advances in child development and behavior* (Vol. 10). New York: Academic Press, 1975.

9. Cognitive Strategies in Advertising Design

Kathryn Lutz Alesandrini

Issues in Strategy Effectiveness

This chapter focuses on the application of cognitive strategies to advertising design, an area that has received little attention from advertising researchers but is replete with examples of strategy application. The chapter is organized around two main categories of strategies that have been applied in advertising. Visual strategies are emphasized and refer to presenting information graphically and in other concrete ways to elicit mental imagery in the viewer. Organizational strategies are also discussed and refer to techniques that provide a unifying framework for the advertising message. It should be noted that most of the strategy applications within these two broad categories are advertiser provided rather than viewer generated, despite the growing evidence that learner-generated strategies are proving to be more effective in educational settings.

Indicators of Advertising Effectiveness

The application of cognitive strategies in advertising design may be discussed in relation to the type of impact being considered, including (a) cognitive effects, concerned with the viewer's understanding and memory for an ad; (b) attitudinal effects, concerned with the feelings that an ad elicits; and (c) behavioral effects, concerned with the extent to which an ad persuades the viewer to actually purchase. The volume of sales that an advertisement generates is the "bottom line" in determining advertising effectiveness, yet sales volume for a product is the outcome of many variables other than advertising. One approach to assessing behavioral outcomes of advertising short of measuring sales volume has been to assess behavioral intentions rather than actual purchase behavior—that is, to determine whether the advertising results in the consumer's intention to purchase the product. Some researchers have contended that advertising produces a "hierarchy of effects," with cognitive effects subsumed by attitudinal and behavioral effects (Lavidge & Steiner, 1961). The assumption is that cognitions lead to attitude, which leads to behavior (or behavioral intentions). This hierarchy-of-effects model has been criticized by some, however, who claim that the model may be valid only when the consumer is motivated or has "high involvement" with the product, but may not hold for a consumer who has "low involvement" with the product (Ray, 1977). Krugman (1965) has argued that consumers passively view more pictorial advertising (such as TV ads) without involvement and form no attitude or evaluation of the brand until after they initially purchase the product. Therefore, when visual strategies are used in advertisements, it may be more important to determine the impact of those strategies on the viewer's cognitions rather than to assess attitudinal outcomes.

Researchers have tended to overemphasize verbal measures of cognitive responses to advertising, although visual measures may be equally appropriate or perhaps more appropriate for assessing the cognitive impact of advertising messages. In the 1960s, George Gallup instituted a survey to assess the verbal recall of commercials during prime-time TV shows. On the average, only 12% of viewers can verbally recall the average commercial on the following day. However, Krugman (1975) has reported that viewers who are later shown photoscripts of TV commercials weeks after exposure were able to correctly recognize nearly half of the commercials they had seen. These findings are consistent with the psychological literature on the superiority of visual memory. One advertising researcher concluded that consumers have cognitions about products and brands that cannot be verbally reported, so he asked children to draw colored pictures of breakfast cereals in order to investigate the relationship between visual and verbal recall of cereal products (Rossiter, 1976). Children at several age levels included in the drawings a great deal of information and details that were not reported verbally. Rossiter called for greater reliance on visual outcome measures in advertising research based on the results.

Actually, advertising research has used visual recognition as a general indicator of advertising effectiveness since the 1920s, when a leading advertising company named Daniel Starch and Staff began conducting recognition and readership studies for print advertisements. More recently, many studies of advertising effectiveness have used Starch readership scores as the key dependent measures. Starch scores provide the following data for an ad: (1) noted—the percentage of readers who remember seeing the ad (recognition); (2) associated—the percentage of readers who can identify the brand or company name associated with the ad; and (3) read most—the percentage of readers who read more than half of the printed copy in the ad. Most of the research studies using Starch scores have investigated mechanical factors such as page position, size of ad, number of words in the headline, and use of color. A more recent study not only looked at mechanical factors in ads that may affect recognition and readership but also investigated the effectiveness of content and message factors (Holbrook & Lehmann, 1980). One of the best predictors of the Starch scores in that study was a content factor called "creativity." According to the researchers, "an ad is creative to the extent that it conjures up special artistic effects rather than resorts to a conventional, matter-of-fact, or stereotyped style of presentation" (p. 62). It would have been helpful if the researchers had described or included some examples of creative ads. Perhaps the creative ads tended to be more pictorial than the noncreative ones. Unfortunately, the content analysis in the study did not include any categories for the various cognitive strategies that have been applied in advertisements.

In this chapter, cognitive outcomes are broadly defined to include both visual and verbal cognitions about the brand. These cognitions are not limited to beliefs about specific product attributes that can be assessed by verbal rating scales, but can include more holistic and nonverbal cognitions that visual recognition measures may assess.

Applying Strategies Effectively

In order for cognitive strategies to facilitate communication of the advertising message, the strategies must be applied to the most important or critical information. Before the 1971 Federal Trade Commission (FTC) regulation requiring that advertisers substantiate their claims, "information" in an ad generally referred to statements of product performance, attributes, price, quality, components, and so on. Since the FTC ruling, ads have made more "subjective claims," and some critics have described ads as less informative (FTC, 1979). Yet pictorial ads actually provide a great deal of information, although in a different form. Schwartz (1978) discusses a six-page pictorial ad for Marlboro cigarettes that contains very little verbal information:

> We hardly bother to read it [the copy] because we are so affected by the background of sweeping plains, majestic hills and snow capped mountains, rugged cowboys roping cattle, wandering herds, a chuck wagon and campfire at night. A dream of paradise. The copy, of course, says very little. The visuals, exquisite, artful, eye-filling, say a great deal. (p. 7)

It should be noted that the task of this advertisement may be quite different from that of others in the industry, since Marlboro holds the top position in terms of market share. The ad merely reminds the viewer of the brand-benefit association and need not communicate new information.

Regardless of the pictorial or verbal form of an ad, the most critical information in it is the brand-benefit association. The benefit is not verbally stated in the Marlboro ad but the viewer is given pictorial information about the implied benefit —you can come to "Marlboro country" if you smoke Marlboro cigarettes. From a communication perspective, the key objective of an ad is to facilitate learning and memory for the brand name and help the viewer associate the benefit information with that name. The aim of an advertisement for a common laundry detergent, for example, is not to communicate a message about all detergents but to tell about a particular brand of detergent and its associated benefits. In learning terminology, the ad is attempting to facilitate paired-associate learning, where one item of the pair is always the brand or company name and the other item is the product, service, product benefits (implied or stated) or characteristic, and the like. Cognitive strategies should focus on the brand or company name to help viewers remember it, yet many ads apply strategies to less relevant information. How often have you remembered a jingle, phrase, or scene from an ad but could not remember what brand was being advertised? Which brand of margarine (or is it butter?) told you that it's not nice to fool Mother Nature? The following discussion stresses how strategies have been used or could be used to facilitate cognitions about the brand or company name and associations between the name and other information.

Visual Strategies

Pictorial Equivalent

A pictorial equivalent of a word refers to a literal translation of the word into pictorial form. Translating brand names or attribute claims into pictorial equivalents should facilitate memory, but little research has been reported to date on this strategy.

The effect of pictorial equivalents in advertising was investigated in an experiment conducted by the author (Lutz & Lutz, 1977). Pictorial equivalents were among the several types of pictures in ads selected from the Yellow Pages of a metropolitan phone directory. The ads used visual strategies to portray either the brand or company name or the product or service, or both. After seeing the ads, participants in the study recalled more company or brand names that had been pictorially depicted or embellished in the ad. The viewers did not remember brand names as well when the ad showed only a picture of the product or service. Many of the ads portraying only the product or service were visually interesting or amusing, such as the ad for All State Tree Survey (see Figure 9-1), but did not help the viewer remember the brand names; whereas ads showing a pictorial equivalent of the brand name, such as the ad for O'Bear Abrasive Saws (Figure 9-1) resulted in better brand recall. How one translates a brand name such as O'Bear into an equivalent picture is not always obvious, but a literal translation appears to be the most effective strategy. Another example of an effective literal translation is the pictorial equivalent for Arrow Pest Control, which shows an arrow piercing (exterminating) a bug (see Figure 9-1). Companies included in our study that used a pictorial equivalent strategy—some used other strategies as well—for the brand name include Acorn, Arrow, Bird, California (outline of state), Giant Whale, Jack (playing card jack), King, Link (chain links), O'Bear (bear holding the letter O), Pilgrim, Rhino, Rocket, Shamrock, Su (oriental man), Tiger, Tomato, Top Hat, and Top Kat (cat sitting on top of product).

INTERACTIVE IMAGERY

PICTURE INTERACTION

A. Arrow Pest Control

LETTER ACCENTUATION

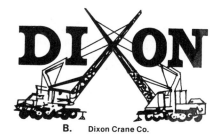

B. Dixon Crane Co.

NON-INTERACTIVE IMAGERY

BRAND OR COMPANY NAME

C. OBear Abrasive Saws

PRODUCT OR SERVICE

D. All State Tree Surgery

Figure 9-1. Examples of types of imagery mediating the brand-product pairs.

No studies have investigated the effects of pictorial equivalents on remembering product claims or product attributes, but there are numerous applications of this strategy in advertisements. Perhaps the most effective application of a pictorial equivalent strategy in advertising is a picture that simultaneously communicates the brand name and the desired product attributes. Consider the ad for Bird Carpet Company (see Figure 9-2), which shows birds saying "Cheap, cheap, cheap" to convey the low price of the product. The automobile industry offers several examples of this type of application, including the television ads for Audi Fox and Ford Mustang. Those ads show the pictorial equivalent of the name (fox and mustang) and superimpose the animal over the car as both move, thereby communicating the name of the car as well as its salient attributes, such as speed, power, and maneuverability.

One problem with applying a pictorial equivalent strategy to the recall of brand names is that many names are impossible to depict visually (although some strategies are subsequently discussed that may be useful). However, according to my recent survey of company names listed in a major metropolitan Yellow Page directory, most company names are proper nouns, which may be particularly difficult

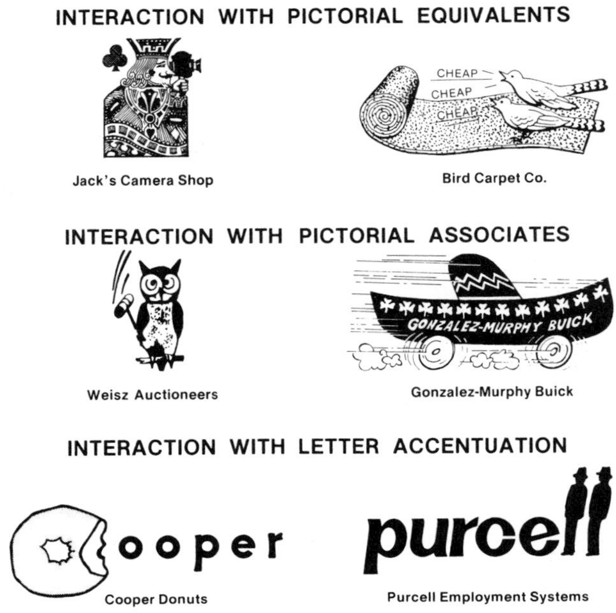

INTERACTION WITH PICTORIAL EQUIVALENTS

Jack's Camera Shop   Bird Carpet Co.

INTERACTION WITH PICTORIAL ASSOCIATES

Weisz Auctioneers   Gonzalez-Murphy Buick

INTERACTION WITH LETTER ACCENTUATION

Cooper Donuts   Purcell Employment Systems

Figure 9-2. Examples of interactive imagery for brand-product pairs.

to visually portray. We randomly sampled 5% of the pages in the directory and then counted the total company names on each page and the number of companies with proper nouns as names. The majority of the names could be classified as proper nouns, and many other companies used initials, abbreviations, or other nonword names. Some of these companies can use a pictorial associate strategy if there is no pictorial equivalent for the name.

Pictorial Associate

Not all companies have the kind of name that readily lends itself to pictorial depiction. Some names are more concrete and easily pictured, whereas others are more abstract and difficult to portray directly. Companies using proper nouns or abstract words may use a picture strategy by showing a pictorial associate rather than a pictorial equivalent of the name. For example, the ad for Weisz Auctioneers uses an owl as a pictorial associate of *wise*, a word that sounds like the company name (see Figure 9-2). Companies in our study used the pictorial associates indicated in parentheses to depict the brand or company name: Gonzales-Murphy (sombrero with clover leaves), King (crown), Leo (lion), Weisz (owl), and Western (cactus cowboy). An interesting question for research is whether pictures that are equivalent to their verbal counterparts facilitate memory for the company name better than pictures that are indirectly associated with the name. A dual-code model of memory (Paivio, 1971) predicts that pictorial equivalents would be more effective because the brand would be encoded in two memory systems—visual and verbal—instead of one, whereas a depth-of-processing framework (Craik & Lockhard, 1972) favors the use of pictorial associates because viewers may have to process the information to a greater depth in order to see the link between the picture and the brand name.

According to recent findings, pictorial associates can be used to better communicate product attributes. Mitchell and Olson (1981) compared the effectiveness of pictorial and verbal strategies to communicate the attribute of "softness" in hypothetical brands of facial tissues (Brands I, J, L, and R). The ad for Brand I communicated the attribute by using the verbal headline "Brand I Facial Tissues are Soft." The ad for Brand J communicated the attribute by presenting a half-page colored photograph of a fluffy kitten, a pictorial associate for softness, using only the brand name as the headline. The two other brands used half-page colored photographs that were conceptually irrelevant to the product attributes, but one (a sunset) was presumed to elicit positive attitudes, while the other (an abstract painting) was presumably neutral. The effects of repetition were also investigated in the study by presenting each ad either 2, 4, 6, or 8 times. After the ads were presented, viewers completed rating scales that reflected their belief strength about various product attributes, including softness; their attitude toward the brand; and their intentions to purchase the brand. Results indicate that viewers had stronger beliefs that Brand J was soft compared to their softness ratings of the other brands, regardless of the number of times that the other ads had been presented. This result suggests that a pictorial strategy is more effective than verbal repetition even when the verbal message is repeated two and three times more often than the visual message. Use of the pictorial associate in the Mitchell and Olsen study also resulted in more favorable attitudes toward the brand than did the use of a verbal claim. One of the other pictorial conditions also enhanced attitudes: Showing a beautiful sunset in the ad resulted in more favorable attitudes toward the brand. But it seems obvious that a relevant picture is the better choice, since it facilitates both learning and attitude.

Picture Interaction

When both the brand and the product are pictorially presented, the two can be united in one integral picture showing some mutual or reciprocal action. The strategy of picture interaction in ads was also tested in the Lutz and Lutz (1977) study. Participants in the study who saw the interactive pictures recalled significantly more company names than those who viewed the noninteractive pictures. The interactive ads integrated the brand and product in one picture, while noninteractive ads showed the brand and product separately. Figure 9-1 gives examples of interactive and noninteractive pictures in ads.

According to our study, a picture interaction strategy appears to be the most effective strategy, and it can be used by companies with portrayable names (although it may require some ingenuity to create a pictorial associate or equivalent for some names). Picture interaction ads unite a depiction of the brand along with a picture of the product or service in one picture. The brand name may be portrayed via either a pictorial equivalent or a pictorial associate. Two of the examples in Figure 9-2 use a pictorial equivalent strategy to depict the brand name in the picture interaction ads. One ad is for Jack's Camera Shop and shows a playing-card jack (pictorial equivalent of the brand name) holding a movie camera to his eye (a pictorial depiction of the product). The other is for the Bird Carpet Company and shows several birds sitting on a roll of carpet as they chirp "Cheap." The other two picture interaction items shown in Figure 9-2 use a pictorial associate strategy to depict the brand name. Weisz Auctioneers uses an owl as a pictorial associate for its name and the ad shows the owl pounding an auctioneer's gavel. Finally, the picture interaction item for Gonzales-Murphy Buick automotive dealer uses a sombrero with a row of shamrocks as pictorial associates for Gonzales and Murphy, respectively. The ad then puts the sombrero on wheels so that it looks like a car (Buick). (This work relates well to the keyword method; see, e.g., Paivio, 1983, and Chapters 2 and 3 in this volume.)

Letter Accentuation

Some company or brand names cannot be represented by either a pictorial equivalent or a pictorial associate, but may still benefit from an interactive visual strategy by the conversion of one or more of the letters in the name to a picture conveying the product or service, as shown in Figures 9-1 and 9-2. A letter accentuation strategy is typically applied to the first letter of the name, as in the example for Cooper Donut Shop, in which the *C* in *Cooper* looks like a doughnut with a bite out of it. Letter accentuation can also be applied to middle or ending letters. Dixon Crane Company uses this strategy by replacing the *X* in *Dixon* with the top of two cranes crossing.

As with brand names, either a pictorial equivalent or a pictorial associate may be used in portraying the product or service. The preceding products (doughnuts and cranes) used pictorial equivalents in their letter accentuation strategies. Products can also be represented by a pictorial associate. For example, Purcell Employment Agency uses a pictorial associate for its letter accentuation strategy that shows two workers standing in line as the *LL* in *Purcell.*

A letter accentuation strategy can also be used to communicate other information about the brand or company. Ford Motor Company, for example, has used a letter accentuation strategy to convey their company slogan that "Ford has a better idea." Their ads replace the *o* in *Ford* with a light bulb that illuminates, the visual symbol in this culture for having a good idea.

Another type of letter accentuation, called inclusion, refers to incorporating a critical characteristic of the product into the letters (often shown as block letters) of the brand or company name. Letter inclusion is used in the logo for Mullin Lumber Company, which depicts the letters of *Mullin* as woodgrained boards arranged as letters.

The interactive picture group in the Lutz and Lutz (1977) study actually saw two types of logos, including picture interaction logos and letter accentuation logos (see Figure 9-1). Participants in the study recalled more company names with accompanying picture interaction logos than companies using letter accentuation logos. However, both types of interactive logos—completely pictorial interactions and letter accentuations—facilitated brand name memory more than the all-verbal control condition. Thus, companies with names that have no pictorial equivalent or associate can still capitalize on interactive imagery benefits by using a letter accentuation logo to show the brand name and product together.

Modeling and Demonstration

These two pictorial techniques are frequently used in television advertising and may quickly and effectively convey more complicated concepts and information. For example, a television ad for the Plymouth Camp (an automobile) on the West Coast used a pictorial demonstration to show that the car has high gas mileage. The ad demonstrated a car starting in Los Angeles with 10 gallons of gasoline, driving through Santa Barbara, and arriving in San Francisco, having traveled a distance of 434 miles on the 10 gallons of gasoline.

Research on modeling and demonstration in advertising indicates that such techniques can affect the behavior of the viewers. Wright (1979) attempted to increase the reading of warning labels on over-the-counter drugs (antacids) by visually showing and concretely describing such behavior in ads for the drugs. To do this, Wright modified several ads for antacid products by adding 5-second messages about reading warning labels to the end of several 30-second commercials. The 5-second messages showed either the product or a consumer reading the label on the product while a verbal message (which was either general or concrete) told the viewer to read the warning on the product's label. Viewers who saw ads with the concrete message and the demonstration of a person actually reading the warning subsequently spent more time reading in-store warnings and package labels of antacids before buying them compared with viewers who had not seen the demonstrations in the ads. The demonstrations affected only viewers who shopped immediately after seeing the ads and not viewers who delayed shopping for 40 minutes or more after exposure to the ads. Nevertheless, the results are noteworthy because the pictorial strategy was so short in duration (5 seconds), yet affected behavior.

Other Pictorial Techniques

The effect that a picture has on the viewer may depend on the physical characteristics of the picture, such as size and color, as well as on the function that the picture serves relative to cognition and attitude. We reviewed the application of a physical and a functional taxonomy of pictures to advertising and concluded that the effectiveness of pictorial strategies in advertising can depend on such physical factors as color, and realism as well as on how well the picture functions to satisfy viewer needs (Alesandrini & Sheikh, in press).

Color is one technique that has long been recognized as an important visual strategy in advertising. The effect of color on cognition and attitude was investigated in a study of color versus black and white television commercials by Burke Marketing Research (1960). Viewers in their study who saw the commercials in color gave them higher ratings and tended to watch the entire commercial. In addition, the viewers recalled more details from the color commercials. In another study, the effect of colored ads on subsequent sales volume was investigated by Sparkman and Austin (1980), who found that one-color (green) versions of newspaper ads generated 41% more sales volume than matched black and white versions of the ads. Hendon (1973) discusses some of the research on color and other mechanical variables, such as size, and then concludes that larger colored ads are generally preferable to smaller black and white advertisements.

Concreteness

The strategy of concreteness refers to using words, phrases, and stories that arouse sensory images. Several reviewers have discussed the use of this technique in advertising and recommended that for optimal communication messages in ads should be concrete rather than abstract (Alesandrini, in press; Alesandrini & Sheikh, in press; Percy, 1982; Rossiter, 1982). After considering the evidence concerning the effectiveness of a concreteness strategy, the FTC Task Force on Consumer Information Remedies suggested that abstract warning messages such as "This product could be hazardous to your health" be changed to more concrete warnings such as "Consuming this product will increase the user's chance of death by 5%" (FTC, 1979).

Although it has not been empirically tested, one application of concreteness to advertising is to base brand names strategy on concrete nouns rather than on an abstract noun, proper noun, abbreviation, adjective, or verb. Although adjectives may be a poorer choice for a brand name from a concreteness perspective, they are often used and can be effective if used in combination with a concrete noun, as in the brand Green Giant (vegetables). Using adjectives as brand names is somewhat popular because of the assumption that important characteristics about the product are being communicated by the adjective. Consider, for example, the intended messages behind Kool cigarettes and Arid deodorant.

One of the more effective strategies for the advertiser, as mentioned earlier in this chapter, is probably to select a concrete noun that has desirable associated attributes. The implications of concrete names such as Audi Fox and Ford Mustang are clear compared to more abstract names such as Chevy Citation and Oldsmobile Omega.

Another approach to applying a concreteness strategy to advertising is to use action verbs rather than linking verbs, since action verbs are more concrete. The more effective ad may tell what the product *does* (its usage benefits) rather than what the product *is* (its attributes). However, evidence indicates that ads tend to give more information about product characteristics and attributes than about product performance (Stern, Krugman, & Resnik, 1981).

Two studies have attempted to investigate the use of concrete language in advertising. Unfortunately, both studies appear to have confounded concreteness with amount of information. Wright (1979) conducted a study, discussed in an earlier section, that varied the wording of a message about reading the warnings on drug labels before purchasing the drug. According to Wright, the verbal message given in the ad was either more abstract, "Read the package warnings," or more concrete, "In the store, before buying, read the package warnings." Comparing the two messages reveals that the two versions of the message differ in terms of amount of information rather than on the dimension of concreteness versus abstractness. There was no main effect for the message manipulation in the study, although the combination of the longer message and the pictorial demonstration of the action did result in the consumers' spending more time reading drug labels. The other study in the field is fraught with similar problems. Rossiter and Percy (1978) originally described their study as an investigation of abstract and concrete messages in a print ad for a hypothetical beer. Abstract messages in the ad included claims such as "affordably priced" and "great taste." Concrete versions of these messages were "Affordably priced at $1.79 per six pack of 12-oz. bottles" and "Winner of 5 out of 5 taste tests in the U.S. against all major American beers and leading imports." Obviously, these messages differ more on the factor of amount of information than on the concreteness-abstractness dimension. In a later version of the report, the researchers referred to the manipulation as explicitly stated claims and implicitly stated claims, which correspond to the concrete and abstract conditions, respectively (Rossiter & Percy, 1980). The explicit claims fostered more favorable attitudes toward the hypothetical brand than did the ad versions with the implicit claims. The most effective version was a combination of the explicit verbal claims and a larger picture of the product.

The effects of concrete and vivid stories in advertising have also not been empirically investigated, but the implication of this research is that vivid, concrete stories and scenarios will be more memorable than abstract descriptions or stories. An FTC Task Force (1979) notes the effectiveness of beer commercials that "show the actors participating in some Herculean sports event which brings on a 'good sweat', and ultimately, a beer. This is likely to make the viewer think of the last episode in his or her life where s/he worked up a good sweat, and either had, or would have liked to have had an ice-cold beer" (p. 103). (Related concreteness effects are taken up by Pressley, 1983, and by Bellezza in Chapter 3 of this book.)

Imagery Instructions

Another visual memory strategy is to give instructions or other prompts to create mental visualizations or images that relate to the content of the ad. One approach is to tell consumers to picture themselves using the product. Mowen (1980) tested this strategy in an advertising context by showing consumers an ad for a hypothetical brand of shampoo that either included instructions to imagine themselves using the product or contained no such instructions. Viewers who were given the imagery instructions later repeated no stronger intentions to try the product than viewers who had not seen the imagery instructions. However, the imagery instructions may have been too contrived and overstated to elicit a positive response from the viewers.

Another application of this technique is to ask consumers to picture themselves in a situation with such questions as, "What if this happened to you?" The ad campaign by a life insurance company instructing readers to "imagine yourself *out* of the picture" is a variant of this approach.

Organizational Strategies

Imagery strategies are only one general class of strategies that are relevant in the advertising context. Organizational strategies have also been applied to advertising (see review by Alesandrini, in press). Organizational strategies serve to coordinate the parts of an information presentation into a meaningful whole.

Chunking

Chunking may be the most important strategy in promoting advertising effectiveness, especially when combined with visual strategies. Brand names, slogans, logos, and jingles can all be powerful chunks that communicate a great many "bits" of information. The brand can serve as a chunk for a number of pieces of information that the advertiser wishes to communicate. The FTC realized that a brand name can summarize a number of qualities about a product, some of which may be deceptive. Based on the realization that Listerine mouthwash ads created the impression that the product had medicinal qualities, the Commission required corrective advertisements that explicitly stated that Listerine is not an effective treatment for colds and sore throats. The Commission also realizes that corrective disclosures may be needed for products with similar brand names, such as Listermint mouthwash or Listerine throat lozenges, since consumers chunk beliefs about medicinal qualities with the name (FTC, 1979). When consumers have beliefs embedded in a holistic chunk about a product, it may be difficult to correct misconceptions, however.

Slogans and jingles have been used as another approach to chunking information for consumers. Budweiser's slogan summarizes its campaign and tries to create a chunk of the brand name: "When you've said 'Bud,' you've said it all." Similarly, many advertisers end an ad by telling the viewers that all they need to think of is the brand name rather than the many attributes.

The use of the proper visual strategy or logo can also be a way to chunk information and promote memory. The interactive pictures discussed earlier are good examples of effective chunking strategies. For example, the logo for Arrow Pest Control Company shows a bug killed by an arrow. In one chunk of information, the logo communicates the brand name (Arrow) as well as the service (extermination).

Advance Organizers

Although the use of advance organizers in advertising should help organize the information and thereby result in better memory, listeners or readers of the ad could "turn off" to the ad if the topic and introduction were not of interest to them. Therefore, this strategy is used sparingly, with only those organizers that can hold the viewer's attention beyond the introduction. Verbal advance organizers in ads may include catchy titles for the ad such as "Free" or "Find Out How to Win Money." Commercials can also use visual advance organizers. For example, the ad can cue the viewers and capture their attention by posing a situation that the viewers want to know about, such as a problem that can be solved or a positive situation that can be achieved by watching the ad. An ad that uses this technique is a commercial for heavy duty trash bags, which begins by showing how other brands of garbage bags break and spill their contents, a situation that can be avoided by watching the commercial to learn about the advertised brand.

Analogies

The use of analogies in advertising campaigns is common, although no studies have tested the effectiveness of this strategy in an advertising context. Many brand names are selected to suggest an analogy between the product and familiar referents with desirable characteristics. There are many examples in the area of car names in which an object or animal name is selected because it is associated with speed, power, surefootedness, and the like. Such brands include Mustang, Cougar, Pinto, and Rabbit. Some product names are based on adjectives, in order to suggest an analogy between the product and a particular attribute rather than an analogous object. A few examples are Sure deodorant, Gleam toothpaste, Long 'n' Silky hair products, Kool cigarettes, and Downy fabric softener. Products named after an analogous object rather than an attribute are more easily portrayed.

The FTC has sometimes required disclosures in ads where the product name suggests an analogy that gives a false impression about the product. For example, Manchurian Linseed Oil had to be labeled as "not imported"[1] and makers of Cashmora had to list their constituent materials, which did not include cashmere,[2] conspicuously.

Advertisements can also communicate abstract information more effectively by using analogies. An ad for a leading brand of cereal makes the analogy that having a bowl of this cereal with milk is like eating a bacon and egg breakfast, communicating the idea that the product is high in protein and nutritional value. Another example is the ad for a savings and loan institution that uses a visual analogy in its newspaper ad for home equity loans. The ad campaign slogan is "Tap your assets" and the visual analogy shows a faucet pouring money out of a house. Using an analogy is probably a very effective strategy for communicating information.

[1] FTC v. Consol. Oil Co., 1 F.T.C. 285 (1918).
[2] Elliot Knotwear, Inc. v. FTC, 226 F, 226F.2d 787 (2d Cir. 1959).

Context

Advertisers make use of the context strategy when they show a cigarette smoker in front of a waterfall or out on the open plains rather than in a hot, stuffy, smoke-filled room. The kind of visual context in which a product is shown probably has major effects on what the viewer learns and remembers from the message. Since no studies have tested the effects of an ad's visual context, such as a cigarette smoker in a refreshing setting, we do not know how much influence the context has. The FTC has acknowledged the potential impact that visual context can have on beliefs and attitudes toward the product. For example, the Commission is questioning whether the ad for Belair cigarettes, showing a happy couple frolicking in the surf, communicates the message that Belairs will make the user healthy and happy, a message that might be considered deceptive if stated verbally in the ad (Crock, 1978).

Conclusion

Advertisements that use visual and organizational strategies to communicate the intended message are probably more effective than ads that do not, in terms of the impact on consumers' cognitions, attitudes, and purchase behaviors or purchase intentions. Research in the area is rather sparse, with advertising designers relying on their own intuitions or drawing directly on research findings from the learning literature. Governmental policy concerning advertising regulation relative to cognitive strategies appears to be lagging behind the advertising industry's use of visual and organizational strategies. The use of visual strategies has increased since the 1971 ruling that product claims in advertising must be substantiated. But as has been pointed out, public policy on affirmative disclosure, nutrient labeling, and substantiation of claims rests on the notion that information is verbal and that consumers' responses to information are verbal (Lutz & Lutz, 1978). The FTC has more recently acknowledged the need to identify the message communicated by pictorial information in advertisements so that the commission can determine if the message is deceptive or may result in consumer injury. One approach that the FTC has considered is to conduct surveys to determine what meaning the consumer actually derives from the total advertisement, including the nonverbal elements of the ad (FTC, 1979).

Advertising researchers can borrow techniques from psycholinguistics to analyze the content of advertising messages. The verbal information in an ad can be broken up into component propositions by a procedure such as the one proposed by Rumelhart (1975). Such procedure was used by Gordon, Munro, Rigney, and Lutz (Note 1, p. 29) and can be applied to both the verbal and pictorial content of a commercial. For example, the propositional analysis was applied to the verbal information contained in a Ford Motor Company ad, with the resultant propositions presented in Table 9-1. The same componential analysis can be applied to

Table 9-1 Propositional Analysis of Verbal Ad Content

Verbal Information

Ford Motor Company hates rust. To fight rust, they do a lot of testing. Test cars get humidified for 22 hours. [Test cars are] sprayed and splashed with salt water. [Test cars are] splattered with salt and mud and humidified again. Then, except for the mud, they do it all over again 60 times. That's what they do to test Ford, Lincoln and Mercury cars for rust resistance. It's simple. Ford wants to be your car company.

Propositional Analysis

Number	Proposition
1.	Ford Motor Company hates rust.
2.	To fight rust,
3.	they do a lot of testing.
4.	Test cars get humidified for 22 hours.
5.	Sprayed
6.	and splashed
7.	with salt water.
8.	Splattered
9.	with salt
10.	and mud
11.	and humidified again.
12.	Then, (13) they do it all over again 60 times.
13.	except for the mud.
14.	That's what
15.	they do
16.	to test Ford, Lincoln and Mercury cars for rust resistance.
17.	It's simple.
18.	Ford wants
19.	to be your car company.

Note. The procedure used follows seven rules for separating constituent propositions, including the main rule that a proposition is defined as any clause/phrase containing a verb (from Gordon et al., Note 1).

viewers' free recalls of the commercial. Then the propositions recalled by the viewer can be compared to the propositions contained in the ad as an indication of how well the viewer recalled the verbal content as well as any inferences or conclusions that the ad elicited without making an explicit claim. A similar analysis can be applied to the visual content of the ad. Several expert judges can develop a verbal translation of the visual information in the ad. Assuming that there is a high degree of agreement among the judges, the resulting propositional analysis can be compared to the propositions recalled by viewers. An interesting question for research is whether viewers exposed to both the verbal and pictorial information in an ad tend to remember propositions contained only in the verbal portion of the ad or only in the video portion, or in both. Individual differences in viewers' modality preferences will surely affect what they remember. Learning researchers are aware that visualizers can respond to pictorial and verbal information differently than do verbalizers. Advertising researchers may learn the most about the impact of visual and verbal information in an ad when viewer characteristics are also considered.

The nature of the correspondence between the visual and verbal information in an ad is another issue that deserves careful study. Some studies from the learning literature would support the practice of providing pictorial equivalents for the verbal information. As mentioned earlier, theoretical models such as the dual-code model of memory (Paivio, 1971, 1974) predict that presenting visual information that repeats or duplicates the information presented verbally will facilitate learning and memory. However, a depth-of-processing or elaboration model such as that proposed by Craik and Lockhart (1972) would alternatively predict that supplementing verbal information with a relevant pictorial associate rather than an equivalent would facilitate memory because the viewer would have to expend more cognitive effort and process the information to a greater depth in order to see the relationship between the verbal and visual information. For example, an effective ad for Alaska Auto Wrecking Company should use an outline or picture of the state of Alaska (an equivalent), according to the dual-code model, whereas the depth-of-processing model would support the use of a penguin (an associate). Although several studies in the learning literature have not shown a facilitative effect for pictorial associates, those studies probably used associates that were too remote. For example, in a word-learning experiment, Willows (1978) used a picture of a dog as an associate of the word *cat*. Not surprisingly, children in the study made more word-naming errors in the associate picture condition than in a word-only condition. Research supports the use of visual strategies in advertising, but the most effective type of strategy to use—pictorial equivalent or pictorial associate—has not been determined and remains an issue for further research.

A final issue in advertising research relative to cognitive strategies is the type of outcome along the hierarchy of effects continuum that these strategies impact. As mentioned earlier, the bottom line in advertising effectiveness is whether the ad affects the purchase behavior of the consumer. Most advertising studies, however, assess only cognitive and attitudinal outcomes, with purchase behavior being estimated via self-reported behavioral intentions, a weak approximator at best. Although actual purchase behavior as a response to advertising manipulations is quite difficult to observe and record, Wright's (1979) study provides an exemplary model for advertising researchers who seek to investigate the effects of strategy use in advertising on actual behavior.

Reference Note

1. Gordon, L., Munro, A., Rigney, J. W., & Lutz, K. A. *Summaries and recalls for three types of texts* (Tech. Rep. 85). Los Angeles: University of Southern California, Behavioral Technology Laboratory, May 1978.

References

Alesandrini, K. L. Imagery-eliciting strategies and meaningful learning. *Journal of Mental Imagery,* 1982, *6,* 125–140.

Alesandrini, K. L. Strategies that influence memory for advertising communications. In R. J. Harris (Ed.), *Information processing research in advertising.* Hillsdale, NJ: Erlbaum, in press.

Alesandrini, K. L., & Sheikh, A. A. Research on imagery: Implications for advertising. In A. A. Sheikh (Ed.), *Imagery: Current theory, research and application.* New York: Wiley, in press.

Burke Marketing Research, Inc. *Burke color study.* Cleveland: AVCO Broadcasting Corp., 1960.

Craik, F. I. M., & Lockhart, R. S. Levels of processing: A framework for memory research. *Journal of Verbal Learning and Verbal Behavior,* 1972, *11,* 671–684.

Crock, S. FTC is seeking way to decide if pictures in advertising convey false impressions. *The Wall Street Journal,* August 1978, p. 6.

Federal Trade Commission. *Consumer information remedies.* Washington, DC: U.S. Government Printing Office, 1979.

Hendon, D. W. How mechanical factors affect ad perception. *Journal of Advertising Research,* 1973, *13,* 39–45.

Holbrook, M. B., & Lehmann, D. R. The role of message content versus mechanical features in predicting recognition of print advertisements. *Journal of Advertising Research,* 1980, *20,* 53–62.

Krugman, H. E. The impact of television advertising: Learning without involvement. *Public Opinion Quarterly,* 1965, *30,* 583–596.

Krugman, H. E. What makes advertising effective? *Harvard Business Review,* 1975, *53,* 96–103.

Lavidge, R. I., & Steiner, G. A. A model for predictive measurements of advertising messages. *Journal of Marketing,* 1961, *25,* 59–62.

Lutz, K. A., & Lutz, R. J. The effects of interactive imagery on learning: Application to advertising. *Journal of Applied Psychology,* 1977, *62,* 493–498.

Lutz, K. A., & Lutz, R. J. Imagery-eliciting strategies: Review and implications of research. In H. Keith Hunt (Ed.), *Advances in consumer research* (Vol. 5). Provo, UT: Association for Consumer Research, 1978.

Mitchell, A. A., & Olson, J. C. Are product attribute beliefs the only mediator of advertising effects on brand attitude? *Journal of Marketing Research,* 1981, *18,* 318–332.

Mowen, J. C. The availability heuristic: The effect of imaging the use of a product on product perceptions. In R. P. Bagozzi et al. (Eds.), *Marketing in the 80's: Changes and challenges* (Ser. 46). Chicago: American Marketing Association, 1980.

Paivio, A. *Imagery and verbal processes.* New York: Holt, Rinehart & Winston, 1971.

Paivio, A. Language and knowledge of the world. *Educational Researcher,* 1974, *3,* 5–12.

Paivio, A. Strategies in language learning. In M. Pressley & J. R. Levin (Eds.), *Cognitive strategy research: Educational applications.* New York: Springer-Verlag, 1983.

Percy, L. Psycholinguistic guidelines for advertising copy. In A. A. Mitchel (Ed.),

Advances in consumer research (Vol. 9). Ann Arbor, MI: Association for Consumer Research, 1982.

Pressley, M. Making meaningful materials easier to learn: Lessons from cognitive strategy research. In M. Pressley & J. R. Levin (Eds.), *Cognitive strategy research: Educational applications.* New York: Springer-Verlag, 1983.

Ray, M. L. When does consumer information processing research actually have anything to do with consumer information process? In W. D. Perreault, Jr. (Ed.), *Advances in consumer research* (Vol. 4). Ann Arbor, MI: Association for Consumer Research, 1977.

Rossiter, J. R. Visual and verbal memory in children's product information utilization. In B. B. Anderson (Ed.), *Advances in consumer research* (Vol. 3). Chicago: Association for Consumer Research, 1976.

Rossiter, J. R. Visual imagery: Applications to advertising. In A. A. Mitchell (Ed.), *Advances in consumer research* (Vol. 9.). Ann Arbor, MI: Association for Consumer Research, 1982.

Rossiter, J. R., & Percy, L. Visual imaging ability as a mediator of advertising response. In H. K. Hunt (Ed.), *Advances in consumer research* (Vol. 5). Ann Arbor, MI: Association for Consumer Research, 1978.

Rossiter, J. R., & Percy, L. Attitude change through visual imagery in advertising. *Journal of Advertising,* 1980, *9,* 10–16.

Rumelhart, D. E. Notes on a schema for stories. In D. G. Bobrow & A. Collins (Eds.), *Representation and understanding: Studies in cognitive science.* New York: Academic Press, 1975.

Schwartz, B. You can take cigarette ads out of television but you can't take television out of cigarette ads. *Media Industry Newsletter,* November 20, 1978. p. 7.

Sparkman, R., & Austin, L. M. The effect on sales of color in newspaper advertisements. *Journal of Advertising,* 1980, *9,* 39–42.

Stern, B. L., Krugman, D. M., & Resnik, A. Magazine advertising: An analysis of its information content. *Journal of Advertising Research,* 1981, *21,* 39–44.

Willows, D. M. A picture is not always worth a thousand words: Pictures as distractors in reading. *Journal of Educational Psychology,* 1978, *70,* 255–262.

Wright, P. Concrete action plans in TV messages to increase reading of drug warnings. *Journal of Consumer Research,* 1979, *6,* 256–269.

10. Cognitive Behavior Modification: The Clinical Application of Cognitive Strategies

William M. Reynolds and Kevin D. Stark

The past decade has witnessed the emergence of a cognitive-behavioral perspective in the field of clinical psychology. Basic to this perspective is a clearly delineated emphasis on cognitions as components of behavior change. The systematic use of cognitions to alter behavior, affect, and thoughts constitutes a class of strategies that have demonstrated their clinical utility. The application of cognitive strategies for therapeutic purposes is not new to the clinician. As Rosen and Orenstein (1976) note, the modification of cognitions for initiating behavior change can be traced back over a century to Lewis and the "art of controlling one's thoughts" (Lewis, 1875).

Cognitive behavior modification techniques have been applied to a myriad of educational and clinical concerns ranging from the treatment of academic deficits in children (see Lloyd, 1980; Meichenbaum & Asarnow, 1979; Ryan, 1981) to efficacy studies comparing cognitive-behavioral intervention with pharmacotherapy for the treatment of depression in adults (Kovacs, Rush, Beck, & Hollon, 1981; Rush, Beck, Kovacs, & Hollon, 1977). Between these points are numerous examples of treatment and research applications that utilize cognitive behavior modification as a training and/or intervention strategy.

In this chapter, we provide a brief account of the historical developments that have had an impact on cognitive behavior modification. Following this review of antecedents, an elucidation of what we refer to as the cognitive-behavioral perspective will be provided. The purpose of this section is to clarify the role of cognitive processes in the modification of behavior. The clinical perspective, as viewed by a number of applied cognitive-behavioral theorists, will also be presented. We will also illustrate the clinical application of cognitive behavior modification for the treatment of anxiety and depression. Lastly, methodological considerations as well as future directions in the clinical application of cognitive behavior modification are suggested. We consider our task an ambitious one. Given the parameters of theory and research that we propose to examine, our review will of necessity be selective. The entire field of cognitive behavior modification or even its clinical application cannot be reviewed in one chapter. Our goal is to blend breadth, as shown in the theory and scope of cognitive behavior modification, with depth, as illustrated by clinical applications to anxiety and depression.

A Cognitive-Behavioral Perspective

Cognitive behavior modification is a "purposeful attempt to preserve the demonstrated efficiencies of behavior modification within a less doctrinaire context, and to incorporate the cognitive activities of the client in the efforts to produce therapeutic change" (Kendall & Hollon, 1979, p. 1). It represents an attempt to integrate several varied perspectives (Mahoney, 1974) ranging from the formalized theories of Bandura (1971a, 1977a) and Bem (1972) to the clinical models of Ellis (1962), Kanfer (1971), Thoresen and Mahoney (1974), Beck (1976), and Bandura (1977b). Thus, while cognitive behavior therapists have incorporated cognitive-mediational phenomena into their treatment regimens, the commitment to the tenets and practices of contemporary behavioral research are clearly indicated (Mahoney & Kazdin, 1979). Although there is greater flexibility in terms of models, and the clinical strategies represent offshoots of social, cognitive, developmental, and other areas of psychology, the treatment approach stresses the experimental-clinical methodology that is basic to behavior therapy.

At present a monolithic theory representative of the cognitive-behavioral perspective does not exist. As Mahoney (1977a) has noted, if anything, the perspective appears to be "avoiding formalization," perhaps as a result of the empirical liberties afforded a developing theory. A number of attempts have been made to delineate a cognitive-behavioral theory of behavior change (e.g., Beck, 1976; Bolles, 1972; Mahoney, 1974; Meichenbaum, 1977a; Raimy, 1975; Seligman, 1975). These theories vary to a greater or lesser extent along two major dimensions: (a) the emphasis placed on the extent to which maladaptive cognitive processes and/or environmental determinants are responsible for maladaptive behavior; and (b) the emphasis placed on the use of cognitive and/or behavioral techniques to promote behavior change. This variability may be a result of the diverse schools of thought in which each theoretician was initially trained (e.g., psychoanalytic vs. behavioral), and—what is perhaps more important—of the types of clinical populations on which each theoretician focused (e.g., clinically depressed adults vs. hyperactive and impulsive children) at the time the theory evolved.

Behavioral Developments

Mahoney and Arnkoff (1978), in their review of the development of cognitive behavior modification, intimate that the cognitive-behavioral perspective is the result of two converging streams of influence, one from within behaviorism and the other from the cognitive movement. A brief examination of historical antecedents should provide a foundation for better understanding the current cognitive-behavioral perspective. This section describes a number of behavior therapies that were important to the development of this perspective.

Behaviorism. Behavior theories and therapies are much different today than they were a decade ago, which perhaps contributes to their continued existence (Mahoney & Arnkoff, 1978). Kazdin (1978) traces the evolution of behaviorism through three overlapping stages, each with a successive increase in the inclusion of mediational constructs.

The techniques employed by behavior therapists have generally been aligned with the dominant learning theory of the given era. Beginning with Watson's doctrine of metaphysical, or radical behaviorism, the existence of the mind was denied and all experiences were reduced to glandular secretions and muscle movements. Conscious processes, if they existed, were beyond the realm of scientific inquiry. Human behavior was considered to be almost exclusively determined by environmental influences. The stimulus-response theories have, however, demonstrated amazing resilience, as evidenced by their continued existence in the form of contemporary applied behavior analysis. As cognitive and social learning theorists developed models that included mediational constructs, the radical behaviorists countered with elaborate theoretical accounts with multiple levels of intervening variables (e.g., Wolpe, 1978).

Changing Perspectives. Within the past decade a number of behavior therapists have begun to express interest in the cognitive processes of their clients. Wilson (1978) states that a clearly discernible development within the field of behavior therapy is the emergence of what he refers to as the "cognitive connection." This cognitive connection, more commonly referred to as cognitive behavior modification, is considered to be the result of a "shotgun wedding" between behavior therapy and cognitive psychology (Mahoney, 1974). This merging of ideologies was delayed in its development as both perspectives appeared reluctant to accept the other. In recent years, however, both groups have for the most part recognized the limitations of their respective ideologies in isolation and welcomed the increased permeability between cognitive and behavioral perspectives (Mahoney & Arnkoff, 1978).

Behavioral Precursors. Early antecedents of cognitive behavior modification can be found in the clinical developments of behavior therapy. One critical milestone was the development of systematic desensitization by Joseph Wolpe (1958), and further refined in conjunction with colleagues Stanley Rachman and Arnold Lazarus. With its utilization of verbal instructions and heavy reliance on the client's self-reports and imagery, systematic desensitization was a first step in the liberalization of behavior therapy techniques. Goldfried (1971) reconceptualized systematic desensitization into a mediational framework in which the client is taught to cope actively with anxiety via relaxation. Goldfried proposed a number of procedural modifications that would enhance the efficacy of desensitization. This self-control paradigm for systematic desensitization has received empirical support (Goldfried & Trier, 1974; Spiegler, Cooley, Marshall, Prince, & Puckett, 1976), and appears to be more effective than standard desensitization (Goldfried, 1977).

Developments and advances in behavioral research on self-control (e.g., Bandura, 1971b; Kanfer, 1970; Mahoney, 1972) led to the general rejection of the behavioral assumption of environmental determinism. Another consequence was the development and subsequent acceptance of the model of reciprocal determinism (Bandura, 1974, 1978). Attention now centered on the human organism's capacity to influence his or her own behavioral acts as well as the environment. Clearly the organism was beginning to be viewed as a mediator for behavior change.

Covert conditioning procedures represent an additional behavioral technique that contributed to the trend toward modifying cognitions. Covert conditioning (i.e., the application of conditioning principles to covert events) is generally associated with the theory and procedures developed by Joseph Cautela and his colleagues. On the basis of experimental learning principles, Cautela developed a variety of covert therapy procedures, including covert sensitization (Cautela, 1966, 1967), covert reinforcement (Cautela, 1970a, 1970b), covert extinction (Cautela, 1971), and covert modeling. These therapies are important in that they represented procedures consistent with behavioral theory, yet emphasized the client's thoughts, feelings, and images as the central focus of change.

Summary. The foregoing developments represent but a few of the advances that occurred within the domain of behavior therapy that had an impact on the emergence of cognitive behavior modification. It should be noted that attempts at stemming the emergence of cognitive behavior modification as a viable treatment methodology were made (e.g., Eysenck, 1979; Ledwidge, 1978, 1979a, 1979b; Rachlin, 1977; Ullman, 1970), but these were quickly and soundly (to our perspective) met with argument supporting cognitive behavior modification (Ellis, 1977b; Locke, 1979; Mahoney, 1977b; Mahoney & Kazdin, 1979; Meichenbaum, 1979).

The Cognitive-Behavioral Perspective

The cognitive-behavioral theory of behavior change is based on the dual assertion that "(a) deficient or maladaptive cognitive processes are partly responsible for aberrant affect and behavior, and, (b) alteration of cognitive processes is a prerequisite for (or facilitator of) therapeutic improvement" (Mahoney, 1977b, p. 10). Although it appears that the processes that govern human adjustment are cognitive in nature, it may well be that behavioral procedures are among the most powerful methods for altering these cognitive processes (Bandura, 1977b; Mahoney & Kazdin, 1979; Meichenbaum, Note 1). Bandura (1969) was one of the first to emphasize this distinction between process (cognition) and procedure (behavioral performance). Consequently, the cognitive behaviorist is just as likely to employ behavioral procedures as is a behaviorist; however, the cognitive behaviorist views the consequences of behavioral acts as a source of information that guides and maintains behavior.

Similarities and Differences. One can find similarities between behavior therapy and cognitive behavior therapy. For instance, both approaches assume that a maladaptive reaction pattern can be unlearned without the absolute requirement that the individual obtain insight (in the psychodynamic sense) into the origin of the symptom. In addition, neither therapeutic approach draws substantially from recollections or reconstructions of childhood experiences or early family relationships (Beck, 1970). Thus the time reference is the here and now. Finally, both approaches adopt an experimental-clinical methodology. While commonalities between behavioral and cognitive-behavior approaches are evident, differences do exist between the two.

The major differences between behavior therapy and cognitive behavior therapy are theoretical ones (see Mahoney, 1974). The cognitive behaviorist, unlike the behaviorist, employs mediational constructs to explain the process of learning and behavior change. From the cognitive-behavioral perspective, the human organism is endowed with the capacity for self-control. The individual is an active participant in his or her environment rather than a passive receptor. Differences also extend to the actual procedures each therapist employs. The cognitive behavior modifier may utilize purely cognitive (semantic) means to promote change or any combination of cognitive and behavioral procedures aimed at any combination of cognitive or behavioral targets (Kendall & Hollon, 1979).

An Interactive Model of Individual and Environment. Central to the cognitive-behavioral perspective is a model in which the individual is an active participant in his or her existence. Unlike the unidirectional theory of environmental determinism, the model of reciprocal determinism (Bandura, 1977a) views behavior, internal personal factors, and environmental influences as interlocking determinants of each other. The environment influences behavior primarily through intermediary cognitive processes. Cognitive factors in part determine which external events will be attended to, as well as how they will be perceived and acted on. The individual's symbolic capacity allows for vicarious learning and the generation of novel thoughts and behavior. In addition, a self-regulatory capacity enables the individual to influence his or her behavior. Although behavior is influenced by the environment, the environment is also acted upon by the actions a person takes (Bandura, 1974).

Variability of Approaches. As previously indicated, there is a great deal of diversity in clinical procedures and theoretical perspectives that are considered or classified as cognitive behavior modification. Mahoney and Arnkoff (1978) list rational psychotherapies, coping skills therapies, self-instructional training, and problem-solving therapies all under the rubric of cognitive behavior modification. Meichenbaum and Genest (1980) note that each of these therapy procedures focuses on different aspects of the client's cognitive processes and each procedure intervenes at a different point in the chain of cognition-affect-behavior and environmental consequences. Proponents of a more cognitive orientation place greater emphasis on the role of cognition in aberrant behavior and in the behavior change process.

Within the scope of this chapter, we will briefly describe several cognitive (as well as cognitive-behavioral) approaches to behavior change. Included are the approaches formulated by Ellis (1962, 1980), Meichenbaum (1972; Meichenbaum & Genest, 1980), Goldfried (1971, 1977; Goldfried, Decenteceo, & Weinberg, 1974), and Beck (1967, 1976). The models of the latter two theorists will be described in the section on clinical applications, whereas the former are described below.

Ellis. Albert Ellis is commonly credited with being one of the pioneers in the fields of cognitive and cognitive behavior therapy. Ellis's (1962) rational-emotive therapy (RET) is based on the assumption that humans largely create their own emotional and behavioral disturbances by strongly believing in absolutistic irrational beliefs. This assumption is central to his *A-B-C-D-E* theory of change. Ellis (1977a) suggests that the average person assumes that an event in his or her life (*A*, activating event) automatically leads to an emotional or behavioral consequence (*C*). However, it is Ellis's contention that *C* does not automatically follow from *A*. Rather, the person causes his or her own emotional and behavioral consequences by strongly believing in things at *B* (the person's innately predisposed and acquired belief system). What the person is saying to himself or herself at *B* about *A* (the activating event) determines *C* (the emotional or behavioral consequence). Ellis further assumes that if the person is experiencing some sort of emotional or behavioral disturbance at *C*, it is the result of holding irrational beliefs at *B*.

In RET, the first task for the therapist is to help the client identify (or, in RET jargon, *detect*) his or her irrational and self-defeating beliefs. Ellis (1970) has identified 12 irrational beliefs that he views as the basis for emotional disturbance. The second major task of the therapist is to teach the client to replace his or her irrational beliefs with more adaptive ones (cognitive restructuring). The rational-emotive therapist does this through the use of the "logico-empirical method of scientific questioning, challenging, and debating" (Ellis, 1977a, p. 20). This process is called *disputing* (*D*) and consists of training the client to use four kinds of cognitive restructuring: *detecting, debating, discriminating,* and semantic *defining* (for further discussion see Ellis, 1977a). Although cognitive restructuring (disputing) is the primary therapeutic procedure in RET, the rational-emotive therapist employs emotional-evocative methods (i.e., rational-emotive imagery, shame-attacking exercises) and behavioral homework assignments. The goal, and the purported end result, of RET is a deep philosophical change or a new *effect* (*E*). Early foundations of RET emphasized the almost exclusive use of cognitive processes. More recently, however, there appears to be an emerging divergence within the RET camp, since Ellis (1980) has drawn the distinction between "preferred" (greater emphasis on cognitive processes in both process and procedure) and "general or nonpreferential" RET, which he states is synonymous with cognitive behavior therapy. The strengths and weaknesses of RET will not be discussed in this chapter. Instead, the reader is referred to descriptions and critical reviews by Lazarus (1979), Mahoney (1977c), and Meichenbaum (1977b).

Meichenbaum. Another major contributor to the advancement of cognitive behavior modification has been Donald H. Meichenbaum (1974, 1977a). While Meichenbaum's contribution to behavior change is generally associated with self-instructional therapies, this association is incomplete and too simplistic. Over the years Meichenbaum's model of behavior change has evolved, placing greater emphasis on the role of the cleint's cognitive structures or belief system (Meichenbaum & Butler, 1980). There is also increased attention to the role of the individual's behavioral acts and the outcomes of these actions. Internal dialogue (self-statements and images) remains a key factor in the process of change, although it seems to be on a level equal to that of the belief system, behavioral acts, and behavioral outcomes (see Meichenbaum & Butler, 1980).

Operationally, Meichenbaum and Genest (1980) have divided their version of cognitive behavior modification into three phases through which the client progresses at his or her own pace. The initial phase, "conceptualization of the problem," is designed to allow the therapist and the client to secure information about the problem, lay the groundwork for a common conceptualization, and decide on a means for therapeutic intervention. Since clients usually come into therapy with an idea of what their problem is, one of the primary goals of the initial phase is for the client and therapist to reformulate a common conceptualization of the problem. In this phase the client comes to recognize that his or her self-statements and/or images as well as his or her faulty thinking style or belief system may be causing the presenting problem. The initial phase of this procedure also capitalizes on what has been characterized as the "nonspecific factors" of therapy (i.e., the general therapeutic effect of client-therapist interaction). The basic goal of the initial and, as we will see, second phase is the modification of the client's internal dialogue (and thus his or her perceptions, expectations, and attributions) in regard to the presenting problem.

The second phase, "trying on the conceptualization," is designed to help the client explore, "try on," and consolidate the conceptualization of the presenting problem. Through self-monitoring and therapist-guided exercises the client discovers how his or her own thoughts help elicit and maintain the presenting problem. The therapy rationale and plan are discussed during this phase. Thus, the first two phases are directed toward enabling the therapist to understand the client's problems and concerns, having the client and therapist derive a common conceptualization, and preparing the client to accept the intervention procedures.

The third phase focuses on helping the client modify his or her cognitions and produce new adaptive behaviors. The therapist may choose to intervene at the point of cognitive structures (beliefs, meaning systems), cognitive processes, behavioral acts, and/or environmental consequences (Meichenbaum & Genest, 1980). In addition, the therapist may choose to intervene by influencing the client's thoughts and thinking style. The point of intervention and the types of procedures used vary according to the presenting problem and the orientation of the therapist. It is this third phase of therapy that is designed to alter the ongoing reciprocal interactions among cognition, affect, behavior, and environmental consequences.

Conclusions

It is evident from our perspective that cognitive behavior modification is a term used to describe a host of theories and techniques. It appears that at present we are no closer to a unified theory of cognitive behavior modification than we were 10 years ago. This, however, is not necessarily bad. In fact, it may be this very lack of direction toward formalizing a theory that allows the field to experiment with new procedures or reformulate old models. This continued evolution and resynthesis is evident in the work of Meichenbaum (Meichenbaum & Butler, 1980), Beck (1976, Beck, Rush, Shaw, & Emery, 1979), Bandura (1977a, 1977b), and others.

An increasing similarity can be seen in the emerging cognitive and behavioral approaches for behavior change. This resemblance appears to be largely the result of the adoption by both schools of thought of components from the other. Where this will lead we are uncertain. We have shown, however briefly, that the foundation of cognitive behavior modification rests on the premise that man interacts with the environment. What will be built on this foundation also remains to be seen.

Of the cognitive theorists we have described, Meichenbaum has produced work with a greater empirical basis for acceptance. This may be due in part to its continual reformulation (cf. Meichenbaum & Genest, 1980; Meichenbaum & Butler, 1980). While Ellis has not provided substantive modification to his approach, others have. Goldfried et al. (1974) utilize Ellis's model as a basis for what they refer to as "Systematic Rational Restructuring," which is described later in the subsection on the treatment of anxiety.

Cognitive behavior modification represents a diverse set of procedures and theoretical orientations that share a number of common characteristics. The actual expression of these theoretical formulations has resulted in numerous applications for a variety of clinical problems. The utility of the cognitive-behavioral perspective is best evaluated by examining its efficacy in applied situations.

Clinical Applications

The application of cognitive behavior modification in research and interventions has included therapies for chronic anger (Novaco, 1976, 1977, 1978), medical crises (Kendall, Williams, Pechacek, Graham, Shisslak, & Herzoff, 1979), control of pain (Beers & Karoly, 1979; Turk, 1978; Turk & Genest, 1979), test anxiety (Bruch, 1978; Goldfried, Linehan, & Smith, 1978; Holroyd, 1976; Meichenbaum, 1972), social anxiety (Mandel & Shrauger, 1980; Rathjen, Rathjen, & Hiniker, 1978), depression (Beck, 1967, 1976; Beck et al., 1979; Becker & Schuckit, 1978; Blaney, 1981; Comas-Diaz, 1981; Kovacs, 1980; Shaw, 1977; Shaw & Beck, 1977; Taylor & Marshall, 1977; Zeiss, Lewinsohn, & Munoz, 1979), assertiveness (Alden & Safran, 1978; Alden, Safran, & Weideman, 1978; Carmody, 1978; Derry & Stone, 1979; Hammen, Jacobs, Mayol, & Cochran, 1980; Jacobs & Cochran, 1982; Linehan, Goldfried, & Goldfried, 1979), and uncontrollable and/or impulsive behaviors (see Chapter 11 of this volume for reviews). Although this is not an exhaustive list of the behavioral and affective disorders for which cognitive-behavioral strategies have been applied, it does indicate that even a cursory review of all areas of application is beyond the scope of this chapter.

Our review of clinical applications will focus on cognitive-behavioral interventions for the reduction and/or amelioration of two clinical disorders: anxiety and depression. Anxiety and depression represent emotional disorders to which a number of cognitive strategy training procedures have been applied. While numerous cognitive intervention strategies have been developed for the treatment of these disorders, most base their foundations on the work of two pioneers of cognitive behavior therapy: Ellis (1962) and Beck (1967). Formulations of Ellis's rational-emotive approach most often have been applied to the management of anxiety, whereas Beck's cognitive therapy has had its greatest impact on therapies directed toward the amelioration of depression. The following subsections review the cognitive-behavioral strategies associated with the treatment of these disorders. Research pertaining to the clinical efficacy of these therapies will also be examined.

Treatment of Anxiety

The cognitive behavior therapist has a wide range of therapeutic procedures to choose from when approaching the problem of excessive anxiety. These procedures are specific to clients' individual needs. A multimethod approach to assessment (see Meichenbaum & Butler, 1981) is employed to determine what these needs are and, consequently, to arrive at the optimal procedure. The cognitive behavior therapist may, for example, choose to manipulate environmental consequences, teach the client coping skills, give the client training in problem solving, or employ cognitive restructuring. Conversely, the cognitive behavior therapist may decide that a combination of procedures (i.e., stress inoculation) will be most efficacious.

Cognitive Restructuring. Cognitive restructuring refers to a variety of therapeutic procedures in which the major agent of change is the modification of the client's self-statement as well as the premises, assumptions, and beliefs underlying these self-statements (Meichenbaum, 1977a). Mahoney and Arnkoff (1978) identified three major forms of cognitive restructuring: rational therapies (Ellis, 1962; Goldfried et al., 1974); self-instructional training (Meichenbaum et al., 1971); and cognitive therapy (Beck, 1970, 1976). The rational therapies and self-instructional training have received greater empirical attention in outcome research dealing with the treatment of anxiety, whereas research with Beck's cognitive therapy has centered around the treatment of depression.

Self-instructional training and the rational therapies accept Ellis's (1962) assumption that maladaptive feelings and behaviors are caused by maladaptive thought patterns. However, self-instructional training includes additional dimensions that stem from Soviet psychologists' theories concerning the development of covert speech in children (see Chapter 11 in this volume). The rational therapies and self-instructional training also differ in the relative emphasis placed on the logical analysis of irrational beliefs and the direct teaching of cognitive and behavioral coping strategies incompatible with anxiety. The rational therapist is more concerned with the content and incidence of irrational beliefs, whereas the self-instructional therapist places greater emphasis on teaching the client coping skills. Both therapists teach their clients a host of strategies that can be employed when confronted with an anxiety-provoking situation. The rational therapist teaches clients to monitor their internal dialogue and identify the irrational beliefs that give rise to maladaptive thought patterns. The client is further trained to reanalyze his or her irrational beliefs logically. The self-instructional therapist, on the other hand, teaches clients to use anxiety as a cue for generating a variety of cognitive and behavioral coping strategies. A basic strategy consists of the monitoring and identification of maladaptive self-statements. These anxiety-engendering self-statements are subsequently replaced with anxiety-incompatible coping statements. Thus, in both therapies the client is taught to monitor and identify maladaptive thoughts, and then to employ a variety of strategies to deal with these thoughts.

Early Studies. Contemporary research on the effectiveness of cognitive restructuring for the reduction of anxiety began in the late sixties and early seventies. The goal of the initial research was to establish cognitive restructuring as a viable treatment for reducing anxiety. The influence of Albert Ellis (1962) was evident in a study by Trexler and Karst (1972), who employed rational-emotive therapy to reduce speech anxiety. Similarly, Meichenbaum, Gilmore, and Fedoravicius (1971) employed an insight-oriented therapy that was "principally" derived from rational-emotive therapy to reduce speech anxiety. Meichenbaum et al. (1971) compared three forms of group therapy for their relative effectiveness in reducing the behavioral, self-report, and performance manifestations of speech anxiety. Treatments included group desensitization, self-instructional training, or a combination of systematic desensitization and self-instructional training. Two control conditions were included, an attention placebo group and a waiting-list control group.

Subjects in the self-instructional training group were given the rationale that speech anxiety is the result of self-verbalizations and automatic thoughts that are emitted while thinking about the speech situation. They were informed that the goals of therapy were to become aware of the maladaptive cognitions that are emitted in anxiety-provoking interpersonal situations, and to produce both self-statements and behaviors that are incompatible with anxiety. The combination group received the same treatment as the desensitization group for half of the sessions, while the time was split between the insight and systematic desensitization procedures (30 minutes each) during the final four sessions. The "speech discussion placebo" group was included to control for the improvement resulting from non-specific treatment factors and the therapeutic effects of simply discussing neutral topics in a group setting.

The results indicated that treatment emphasizing insight into maladaptive self-verbalizations was as effective as the systematic desensitization procedure in reducing speech anxiety. The insight-oriented therapy and desensitization therapy produced significantly greater reductions in anxiety than the combination group and the speech discussion group on behavioral and self-report measures. The waiting-list control group showed significantly less improvement than all other groups. Furthermore, on a cognitive measure of anxiety the three treatment groups showed significantly more improvement than the two control groups, but the three treatments did not differ significantly.

It should be noted that although the cognitive restructuring treatment emphasized insight into (awareness of) the maladaptive self-statements, it did not include the *direct* training of the production and employment of incompatible coping self-statements. Subjects were neither led through a hierarchy of anxiety-provoking situations in which they practiced the production of incompatible coping self-statements nor encouraged to employ the strategy of producing incompatible coping statements in vivo.

Based on the apparent clinical efficacy of the self-instructional procedure, Meichenbaum and his colleagues embarked on a research program designed to compare the efficacy of "standard" behavior therapy procedures (i.e., systematic desensitization) to behavior therapy procedures that included a self-instructional component (Meichenbaum & Cameron, 1974). One of the studies in this series has direct implications for the treatment of anxiety. Meichenbaum (1972) designed a two-phase "cognitive modification" treatment to deal with the worry (cognitive) and emotionality (physiological arousal) components (Liebert & Morris, 1967) of test anxiety. The treatment procedure combined an insight-oriented therapy that trained subjects to become aware of their anxiety-engendering thoughts and self-statements with a modified desensitization procedure in which subjects imaged coping with anxiety by employing relaxation and self-instructions to attend to the task. The study also included a standard systematic desensitization group (Paul & Shannon, 1966) and a waiting-list control group. At termination of treatment the cognitive modification group demonstrated the greatest decrement in test anxiety, with the high-anxious subjects in this group manifesting anxiety levels equivalent to the low-anxious control subjects on both subjective and performance measures of test anxiety. Subjects in the cognitive modification treatment also showed an increase in facilitative anxiety (Achievement Anxiety Scale; Alpert & Haber, 1960), suggesting that these subjects had relabeled their anxiety as facilitative, as a task-oriented cue to enhance their performance. All improvements were maintained at a 1-month follow-up.

The early cognitive restructuring procedures of Meichenbaum and his colleagues (Meichenbaum et al., 1971; Meichenbaum, 1972) and Trexler and Karst (1972) clearly suggested their clinical potential. Meichenbaum's self-instructional training (SIT) procedure also demonstrated clinical effectiveness in studies with impulsive children (Meichenbaum & Goodman, 1971) and hospitalized schizophrenics (Meichenbaum & Cameron, 1973). These early studies along with those conducted by Thorpe (1975) and Wein, Nelson, and Odom (1975) led to a component analysis of the SIT procedure by Thorpe, Amatu, Blakey, and Burns (1976). Thorpe et al. (1976) sought to isolate the relative contributions of (a) insight into maladaptive cognitions, and (b) rehearsal of anxiety-incompatible self-statements. The authors hypothesized that a combination procedure of insight plus rehearsal would be more effective in reducing speech anxiety than either component in isolation. The relative efficacy of the combination procedure was illustrated by comparing it to a general insight procedure, a specific insight procedure, and instructional rehearsal. Contrary to the original hypothesis, the specific insight procedure resulted in the greatest improvement on all self-report and behavioral measures of speech anxiety. The general insight treatment was the next most effective technique. Treatment gains were maintained at 3-month follow-up. Although the results suggest that emphasis should be placed on the insight component of the SIT procedure, generalizations should be tempered on the basis of several limiting factors. First, subjects did not manifest clinically relevant levels of anxiety; rather, they were seeking self-improvement. Second, and perhaps more critical, is that the failure to include a control group limited the analyses to within-group comparisons.

A more recent SIT component analysis was conducted by Glogower, Fremouw, and McCroskey (1978) with communication-anxious college students. The authors assessed the relative contributions of (a) extinction, (b) identification and monitoring of negative self-statements, (c) knowledge and rehearsal of coping statements, and (d) a combination of extinction, identification of negative self-statements, and rehearsal of coping statements. A waiting-list control condition allowed for between-group analyses. Contrary to the Thorpe et al. (1976) results, between-group and within-group analyses suggest that insight into negative self-statements and extinction contribute to the efficacy of SIT. Furthermore, rehearsal of coping statements was shown to be the primary component of the SIT procedure. The data suggest that the combination of the three components is more effective than any single component in alleviating communication anxiety.

In summary, the previously cited studies have demonstrated that cognitive restructuring in its various forms is (1) a viable treatment procedure for anxiety (Trexler & Karst, 1972); (2) as effective as systematic desensitization (Meichen-

Table 10-1 Selected Studies Utilizing Cognitive Restructuring for Anxiety

Study	Subjects	Target Behaviors	Therapy Format	Number of Sessions	Treatment Groups
Meichenbaum et al. (1971)	College volunteers	Speech anxiety	G	8; 60 min.	1. Desensitization (D) 2. Insight oriented (I) 3. Desensitization and Insight (D+I) 4. Speech discussion (S) 5. Waiting-list control (WL)
Meichenbaum (1972)	College volunteers	Test anxiety	G+I	8; 60 min.	1. Cognitive modification (CM) 2. Desensitization (D) 3. Waiting-list control (WL)

baum et al., 1971); and (3) more effective when combined with an imagery-based procedure that enables the individual to experience successful coping (Meichenbaum, 1972). Furthermore, component analyses of the self-instructional training procedure (Thorpe et al., 1976; Glogower et al., 1978) suggests that extinction, insight, and rehearsal of coping statements contribute to the efficacy of the procedure and that a combination of all components is more efficacious than any single component. Table 10-1 provides a selective review of studies utilizing cognitive restructuring for anxiety.

Further Developments. In the mid-seventies another variant of the cognitive restructuring procedure emerged. Goldfried et al. (1974) reconceptualized rational-emotive therapy within a behavioral framework, and delineated guidelines for a therapeutic intervention that they entitled systematic rational restructuring (SRR). The primary assumption underlying SRR is that an individual can learn to control his or her anxiety by modifying the cognitive set (the "internal sentences") with which (s)he approaches potentially anxiety-provoking situations. Thus, SRR is a self-control technique in which anxiety serves as a cue to reevaluate the reason(s) for the emotional reaction rationally.

The SRR procedure comprises four basic phases: (1) presentation of rationale; (2) overview of irrational assumptions; (3) analysis of the client's problems in rational-emotive terms; and (4) teaching the individual to modify his or her internal

Outcome Measures	Treatment Outcome[a]	
	Posttest	Follow-up
BCL	D=I>D+I=S>WL	
WdCt	D=I>D+I>S=WL	
DuSl	D=I=D+I>S=WL	
Ah	D=I=D+I>S=WL	
PRCS	D=I=D+I>S=WL	D=I=D+I>WL>S at 3 mo.
SADS	D=I=D+I>S=WL	D=I=D+I>S=WL at 3 mo.
FNE	D=I=D+I>S=WL	D=I=D+I>WL>S at 3 mo.
AACL	D=I>D+I=S>WL	
AD	D=I=D+I>S=WL	
AAT-D	CM=D>WL	CM=D>WL at 1 mo.
AAT-F	CM>D=WL	CM>D=WL at 1 mo.
AACL	CM>D=WL	
AD	CM>D>WL	
DST	CM=D>WL	
Raven	D>CM=WL	
GPA	CM>D>WL	

Table 10-1 (Continued)

Study	Subjects	Target Behaviors	Therapy Format	Number of Sessions	Treatment Groups
Glogower et al. (1978)	College volunteers	Communi-cation appre-hension	G	5; 60 min	1. Extinction (Ext) 2. Insight (I) 3. Coping statements (CS) 4. Combination (Comb) 5. Waiting-list control (WL)
Goldfried et al. (1978)[b]	Volunteers	Test anxiety	G	6; 60 min.	1. Systematic rational restructuring (SRR) 2. Prolonged exposure (PE) 3. Waiting-list control (WL)
Kanter & Goldfried (1979)[c]	Community volunteers	Inter-personal anxiety	G	7; 90 min.	1. Self-control desen-sitization (SCD) 2. Systematic rational restructuring (SRR) 3. Self-control desen-sitization TSRR (Comb) 4. Waiting-list control (WL)

Outcome Measures	Treatment Outcome[a]	
	Posttest	Follow-up
PRCA	Comb>I=Ext>WL CS>WL	Comb=CS=I=Ext>WL at 6 weeks
SAS	Comb=CS=I=Ext=WL	
SADS	Comb=CS=I=Ext=WL	Comb=CS=I=Ext=WL at 6 weeks
FNE	Comb=CS=I=Ext=WL	Comb=CS=I=Ext=WL at 6 weeks
No.V	Comb>I=Ext=WL CS>WL	
No.R$_3$	Comb>I=Ext=WL CS>WL	
IBM$_T$	Comb=CS=I=Ext=WL	
IBM$_R$	Comb=CS=I=Ext=WL	
IBM$_V$	Comb>I=Ext=WL CS>I	
S-RI$_{Ex}$	SRR>PE>WL	SRR=PE=WL at 6 weeks
S-RI$_Q$	SRR=PE>WL	SRR=PE=WL at 6 weeks
S-RI$_{Sp}$	SRR=PE=WL	SRR=PE=WL at 6 weeks
S-RI$_{Py}$	SRR>WL	SRR>PE at 6 weeks
S-RI$_J$	SRR>WL	SRR=PE=WL at 6 weeks
STABS	SRR>PE>WL	SRR>PE at 6 weeks
FNE	SRR>PE=WL	SRR=PE=WL at 6 weeks
SADS	SRR>PE=WL	SRR>PE at 6 weeks
TAS	SRR=PE=WL	SRR=PE=WL at 6 weeks
SAS	SRR=PE=WL	
AAT-D	SRR>PE>WL	SRR=PE=WL at 6 weeks
AAT-F	SRR=PE=WL	SRR=PE=WL at 6 weeks
TAQ-W	SRR=PE=WL	SRR=PE=WL at 6 weeks
TAQ-E	SRR=PE=WL	SRR=PE=WL at 6 weeks
ExpQ-W	SRR>WL	
ExpQ-E	SRR=PE=WL	
AD	SRR=PE=WL	
SADS	SRR=SCD=Comb>WL	SRR=Comb=SCD=WL at 9 weeks
FNE	SRR=Comb>WL	SRR>SCD at 9 weeks
S-RI$_{Py}$	SRR=Comb>WL	SRR=Comb=SCD=WL at 9 weeks
S-RI$_{Intro}$	SRR=Comb>WL	SRR=Comb=SCD=WL at 9 weeks
S-RI$_{Sp}$	SRR=SCD=Comb=WL	SRR=Comb=SCD=WL at 9 weeks
S-RI$_J$	SRR=Comb>Wl; Comb>SCD	SRR=Comb=SCD=WL at 9 weeks

Table 10-1 (Continued)

Study	Subjects	Target Behaviors	Therapy Format	Number of Sessions	Treatment Groups
Fremouw & Zitter (1978)	College volunteers	Speech anxiety	G	5; 60 min.	1. Skills training (ST) 2. Cognitive restructuring relaxation (CRR) 3. Discussion placebo (DP) 4. Waiting-list control (WL)

Note: G=group therapy; I=individual therapy; BCL=Behavioral Checklist (Paul, 1966); WdCt =word count; DuSl=duration of silences; Ah="ah" statements; PRCS=Personal Report of Confidence as a Speaker Scale (Paul, 1966); SADS=Social Avoidance and Distress Scale (Watson & Friend, 1969); FNE=Fear of Negative Evaluation (Watson & Friend, 1969); AACL=Affect Adjective Checklist (Zuckerman, 1960); AD=Anxiety Differential (Husek & Alexander, 1963); AAT=Achievement Anxiety Test (D=debilitating, F=facilitating); (Alpert & Haber, 1960); DST=Digit Symbol Test (Brown, Note 2); Raven=Raven's Progressive Matrices (Ravin, 1956); GPA=grade point average; PRCA=Personal Report of Communication Apprehension (McCroskey, 1970); TAS=Trait Anxiety Scale (Spielberger, Gorsuch, & Lushene, 1970); SAS= State Anxiety Scale (Spielberger et al., 1970); No.V=Number of verbalizations; No.R_3=Number of responses at least three words long with subject and predicate; IBM=Interaction Behavior

Outcome Measures	Treatment Outcome[a]	
	Posttest	Follow-up
S-RIT$_{ToSo}$	SRR=Comb>WL	SRR=Comb=SCD=WL at 9 weeks
TAS	SRR>SCD=WL	SRR>SCD at 9 weeks
IBT	SRR=Comb>WL; SRR>SCD	SRR>SCD at 9 weeks
S-RI$_{Ex}$	SRR=Comb=SCD=WL	SRR=Comb=SCD=WL at 9 weeks
S-RI$_{Wds}$	SRR=Comb=SCD=WL	SRR=Comb=SCD=WL at 9 weeks
S-RI$_D$	SRR=Comb=SCD=WL	SRR>Comb at 9 weeks
S-RI$_{Bt}$	SRR=Comb=SCD=WL	SRR=Comb=SCD=WL at 9 weeks
S-RI$_{TONS}$	SRR=Comb>WL	SRR=Comb=SCD=WL at 9 weeks
BCL	SRR=Comb=SCD=WL	
PR	SRR=Comb=SCD=WL	
SAS$_1$	SRR=Comb=SCD>WL	
SAS$_2$	SRR=Comb>WL; SRR=Comb>SCD	
AD	SRR=Comb=SCD>WL	
BC	CRR=ST>WL	
OR	CRR=ST>WL; CRR>DP	
DS	CRR=ST=DP=WL	
AD	CRR=ST=DP=WL	
PRCS	ST>CRR=WL; ST>CRR>DP	ST>WL; ST>DP; CRR>DP at 2 mo.
SADS	CRR=ST=DP=WL	CRR=ST=DP=WL at 2 mo.
PRCA	CRR=ST=DP=WL	CRR=ST=DP=WL at 2 mo.

Measure (T=tension, R=relevance, V=verbosity); (McCroskey, 1970); S-RI=S-R Inventory of Anxiousness (Ex=exam, Q=quiz, Sp=speech, Py=party, J=job interview, Intro=introduction, ToSo=total social, Wds=woods, D=dentist, Bt=boat, TONS=Total Nonsocial (Endler, Hunt, & Rosenstein, 1962); STABS=Suinn Test Anxiety Behavior Scale (Suinn, 1969); TAQ=Test Anxiety Questionnaire (W=worry, E=emotionality); (Liebert & Morris, 1967); ExpQ=Experience Questionnaire (W=worry, E=emotionality; Morris & Liebert, 1969); PR=Pulse Rate; BC= Behavior Checklist (Authors); OR=Overall rating of anxiety; DS=duration of silence.
[a] Explanation of outcome symbols: > denotes "more effective than"; = denotes "equal in overall efficiency." The expression presents logical representation of the outcome.
[b] For additional analyses see Goldfried et al. (1978).
[c] For additional analyses see Kanter and Goldfried (1979).

sentences. The goal of the first two phases of therapy is to impart the rationale that internal self-statements (however automatic) mediate emotional arousal, and that certain irrational beliefs give impetus to this covert self-talk. The third phase is designed to explore the nature of the client's problems, including specific situational parameters, and then through socratic dialogue to help the client reach the conclusion that his or her own feelings of anxiety are mediated by unrealistic expectations. The goal, therefore, of the first three phases is to have the client accept the rationale, agree that (s)he is causing his or her own emotional upset, and ideally, desire to learn how to change. In the fourth (active) phase the client is taught the cognitive strategy of rationally reevaluating his or her anxiety-engendering self-statements.

Goldfried et al. (1974) proposed a five-step procedure for training clients to modify the anxiety-producing set with which they may be approaching situations:

1. The client is exposed (in imagination or via role playing) to a hierarchy of anxiety-provoking situations with progression through the hierarchy being dependent on successful coping at each step.
2. The client is instructed to evaluate his or her anxiety level.
3. He or she is asked to use this anxiety as a signal for "ferreting" out any self-defeating anxiety-provoking attitudes or expectations regarding the situation.
4. These self-statements are rationally reevaluated.
5. Note is taken of the anxiety level after rational reevaluation.

For a more detailed description of the SRR treatment procedure see Goldfried and Davison (1976) and Goldfried and Goldfried (1975).

Inspection of the SRR procedure reveals multiple sources for the resulting therapeutic improvement. One salient source may be the exposure to progressively more anxiety-engendering situations in the hierarchy. Goldfried and Goldfried (1977) found that speech-anxious subjects who were given exposure to speech-giving situations without accompanying relaxation training showed significant anxiety decrements. Exposure alone, however, did not result in improvement across as many measures as was the case with a self-control desensitization group who used relaxation together with an imaginal exposure to the same hierarchy items. Several other studies have demonstrated that hierarchy exposure alone, particularly if it is prolonged or repeated, can be an effective therapeutic procedure for anxiety reduction (e.g., Aponte & Aponte, 1971; Barrett, 1969; D'Zurilla, Wilson, & Nelson, 1973; McGlynn, 1973; Raimy, 1975).

Goldfried et al. (1978) examined the effectiveness of the SRR version of cognitive restructuring in reducing test anxiety. College student volunteers were assigned to one of three conditions, systematic rational restructuring, prolonged exposure to hierarchy, or waiting-list control. The prolonged-exposure subjects received a plausible treatment rationale followed by exposure to the same hierarchy items as the SRR condition; they were further instructed to focus on their emotional reactions to the hierarchy items. The results revealed a consistent pattern in which the subjects in the SRR condition reported the greatest decrease in anxiety on self-report measures, followed by those who were exposed to the same hierarchy items, while the waiting-list control subjects did not change. Subjects in the SRR condition also reported greater generalization of anxiety reduction to social evaluative situations. The reduction in self-reported anxiety incurred by the exposure groups was consistent with earlier findings that hierarchy exposure alone is an effective treatment for anxiety and a contributing component to the therapeutic effect of SRR. However, this study illustrates that teaching anxious individuals to cope actively with their anxiety by means of cognitive reappraisal supplements any anxiety reduction associated with imaginary or role-play exposure to anxiety-provoking situations (extinction), and facilitates generalization to nontreated targets.

Kanter and Goldfried (1979) examined the clinical utility of SRR in a study comparing the effectiveness of systematic rational restructuring with self-control desensitization on a clinical sample of socially anxious individuals. The authors also investigated whether highly anxious individuals are too anxious to direct their own cognitions effectively. To meet the perceived special needs of the highly anxious individuals a third treatment was devised in which the subjects first received coping skills training emphasizing relaxation followed by rational restructuring (self-control desensitization and systematic rational restructuring).

Systematic rational restructuring was an effective intervention for clinically anxious individuals, and was equally effective with moderately and highly socially anxious individuals. It should be noted, however, that the measure used to differentiate between high- and moderate-anxious subjects (i.e., Social Avoidance and Distress Scale: Watson & Friend, 1969) assesses the pervasiveness rather than the intensity of anxiety. Although all three treatments effected significant change, the rational restructuring and combination procedures resulted in significant improvement on more self-report anxiety measures than the self-control desensitization procedure. Furthermore, the rational restructuring procedure was significantly more effective than desensitization in reducing state anxiety, trait anxiety, and irrational beliefs. There also was a tendency for the rational restructuring and combination treatments to result in greater generalization of treatment effects to nonsocial situations. The significant improvements in anxiety incurred by all groups were maintained or improved upon at a 9-week follow-up.

The previously cited studies have illustrated the relative effectiveness of the various cognitive restructuring procedures in reducing anxiety. Additional support for the efficacy of SIT-based interventions (Meichenbaum et al., 1971; Meichenbaum, 1972) are offered by D'Alelio and Murray (1981), Holroyd (1976), and Weissberg (1977), while further support for the SRR procedure (Goldfried et al., 1974) is provided by Malkiewich and Merluzzi (1980).

Combinatory Studies. A second line of research has been conducted that compares the relative efficacy of cognitive restructuring, skills training, and a combination of the two. Glass, Gottman, and Shmurak (1976) conducted an exemplary study in which they compared the effectiveness of a skills training intervention, a self-instructional training intervention, and a combination intervention with dating-anxious college men. The response-acquisition training consisted of coaching a model response, and recoaching for each of 11 problem dating situations. A competence-based model was followed in which subjects were taught the responses of "competent" daters. A self-instructional modification treatment based on Meichenbaum's self-instructional training procedure was employed. This training consisted of modeling effective self-statements, coping, and reinforcement following each problem situation. The combination procedure included major elements of each of these training procedures.

All three treatment groups improved to a significantly greater extent than a waiting-list control group in training situations. The skills training and the combination training resulted in significantly greater performance (more competent dating behavior) than did the self-instructional training. Although skills training resulted in the greatest improvement in training situations, subjects who received some form of self-instructional training showed greater transfer of training to nontraining situations. Only subjects who received self-instructional training significantly improved their in vivo performance on nontraining situations. Subjects in this group were more likely to make phone calls to females in real-life situations, and the impression they made on the women they called was superior to that of subjects in the other treatments. Furthermore, only for the self-instructional training group did scores on the role-play assessment for training, nontraining, and total situations increase from posttreatment to follow-up. The improvement in number of phone calls was also maintained upon follow-up. Once again the results for the combination group were surprising, since the group's performance never exceeded that of the component procedure groups.

Fremouw and Zitter (1978) compared public speaking skills training with a combination cognitive restructuring-relaxation procedure for the treatment of speech anxiety. The authors implemented a very complex skills training procedure that consisted of modeling, behavioral rehearsal, and videotape feedback on speaking tasks of increasing complexity. Training focused on seven components of public speaking skills: voice rate, voice volume, voice inflection, body stance, eye contact, gestures, and speech organization. Subjects were further instructed to practice specific skills at home between sessions. The self-instructional training format of cognitive restructuring was combined with coping skills training in relaxation. Subjects practiced overt rehearsal of coping statements while imaging a public speaking situation. They were further instructed to practice relaxation daily and monitor negative and coping self-statements on daily logs. A discussion placebo and waiting-list group were included as controls.

Both the skills training and cognitive restructuring-relaxation procedures significantly reduced the behavioral manifestations of speech anxiety relative to the waiting-list control group. The skills training procedure, relative to the other three procedures, significantly reduced anxiety on subjective measures. The cognitive restructuring-relaxation group showed significantly more improvement than the discussion placebo group and approached significance relative to the waiting-list control group. At the 8-week follow-up, both treatments showed additional improvement. However, the groups did not differ significantly on the generalization measures.

Summary. The foregoing subsections have illustrated a progression of research that has gone from simply demonstrating the utility of the cognitive restructuring procedure in reducing anxiety to comparing the relative effectiveness of cognitive restructuring, behavioral techniques (systematic desensitization and skills training), and combinations of cognitive restructuring and behavioral techniques. Components such as imaginal exposure to a hierarchy were added to the cognitive restructuring procedure and resulted in increased efficacy. Furthermore, an additional cognitive restructuring procedure was introduced (SRR) that has demonstrated clinical utility.

The aforementioned studies suggest that cognitive restructuring is an effective therapeutic procedure for reducing anxiety. However, there appear to be limitations to its effectiveness. Most of the research suggests that it is very effective at reducing subjective levels of anxiety. However, inconsistent results have been reported when using behavioral and performance measures of anxiety. These equivocal results may occur because cognitive restructuring is primarily designed to change the client's internal dialogue, the way he or she views the stressor.

The cognitive restructuring procedure has evolved over the years and now incorporates numerous components. The primary components are (1) insight into maladaptive thoughts; (2) training in replacing maladaptive thoughts; and (3) exposure to a hierarchy of anxiety-engendering situations. Lastly, it should be noted that the cognitive restructuring procedure is one of many cognitive-behavioral procedures that have been effective in reducing anxiety. Unfortunately, the length of this chapter precludes examination of these other worthwhile techniques.

Treatment of Depression

Depression is an emotional disorder of major consequence. It is one of the most prevalent affective disorders, and despite a long history of study, its etiology remains uncertain. A number of theories have evolved that attempt to conceptualize depression and provide mechanisms for its amelioration. The four principal theoretical avenues of thought are biological and biochemical (Maddison & Duncan, 1965; Morris & Beck, 1974; Schildkraut, 1965; Schuyler, 1974), psychoanalytic (Abraham, 1927; Bibring, 1953), behavioral (Ferster, 1965, 1973; Lazarus, 1968; Lewinsohn, 1974; Lewinsohn, Weinstein, & Shaw, 1969; Wolpe, 1971), and cognitive (Beck, 1963, 1967). Of these approaches, the cognitive model of depression provides a theoretical rationale for utilizing cognitive strategy training in the treatment of this disorder. This section briefly describes Beck's (1976) cognitive model of depression and its application. Research studies comparing cognitive behavior therapy with other psychotherapies (e.g., behavior therapy) and with pharmacotherapy will follow. Our purpose in reviewing these studies is to examine the relative efficacy of cognitive behavior modification for the treatment of depression. It should be noted that these studies focus on the treatment of what is generally viewed as unipolar depression, rather than bipolar (psychotic) depression.

Cognitive Therapy. The application of cognitive strategies as an intervention for depression is the basic foundation of the cognitive therapy formulated by Beck

(1970, 1976). Beck's cognitive-behavioral approach is the model on which most cognitive treatments are based, although research studies using Ellis's (1962) rational-emotive approach have recently appeared (Gardner & Oei, 1981; Oliver, 1977). The cognitive model of depression (Beck, 1976; Beck et al., 1979) suggests that psychological elements of depression can be delineated by three specific concepts: the cognitive triad, schemas, and cognitive errors in information processing. The cognitive triad consists of cognitive patterns in which the individual regards self, current experiences, and the future in a systematically and negatively distorted manner. Schemas are stable cognitive patterns that are the basis on which the individual interprets different experiences and situations. In depression, dysfunctional schemas are responsible for the individual's distorted conceptualization of specific situations and events. Beck et al. (1979) view this as the "structural organization of depressive thinking." Beck (1967) describes the third component as the sytematic errors in thinking that enable the individual to maintain a negative view despite conflicting data. These errors in information processing include: arbitrary interference, selective abstraction, overgeneralization, magnification and minimization, personalization, and absolutistic, dichotomous thinking (see Beck et al., 1979; Rush & Giles, 1982; and Young & Beck, 1982, for further descriptions of these concepts).

Cognitive therapy as a treatment operationalizes the cognitive model of depression by focusing on the specific cognitive elements described above. Implementation utilizes cognitive and behavioral techniques to "(1) define and detect cognitions or automatic thoughts; (2) examine and test these cognitions; (3) develop alternative constructions of day-to-day events; (4) record dysfunctional thoughts; (5) develop alternative, more flexible schemas; and (6) rehearse both cognitive and behavioral responses based on these new assumptions" (Rush & Giles, 1982, p. 164). The basic premise of cognitive therapy is the utilization of cognitive strategies to ameliorate distorted cognitions that are viewed as responsible for the individual's depressive affect.

Cognitive-Behavioral Interventions. While most of the studies utilizing cognitive therapy for depression follow the basic tenets of Beck's approach, there is variability among treatments. A major continuum on which these interventions vary is the degree to which behavioral procedures are used to supplement the cognitive therapy. For example, Beck's cognitive therapy has been utilized as a strictly cognitive treatment by some investigators (e.g., Shaw, 1977), while other investigators include such behavioral components as daily activity schedules and/or graded homework assignments. Current thinking by Beck and colleagues (Beck et al., 1979) stresses the inclusion of behavioral techniques in cognitive therapy, but qualifies its application: "For the behavior therapist, the modification of behavior is an end in itself; for the cognitive therapist it is a means to an end—namely, cognitive change" (p. 119). For the most part, recent applications of cognitive therapy as proposed by Beck and his colleagues (Beck, 1970, 1976; Beck et al., 1979; Burns & Beck, 1978; Rush, Khatami, & Beck, 1975) include a combined cognitive-behavioral approach that stresses the use of behavioral techniques, yet maintains the importance of modifying cognitions.

One potential problem in reviewing outcome studies in which cognitive strategy training has been used is the treatment nomenclature. The terminology used to identify the therapeutic intervention is often inconsistent, partly because clinical interventions (psychotherapies) fall on a continuum rather than into discrete categories. For purposes of this review we suggest an intervention continuum with therapies that are purely cognitive or strictly behavioral procedures as endpoints. An example of a purely cognitive therapy would be Ellis's RET, which is semantic in nature, whereas Lewinsohn's reinforcing events therapy (Lewinsohn, Youngren, & Grosscup, 1979) is consistent with a behavioral perspective. Between these two points lie a number of intervention strategies. Some, like Beck's, are primarily cognitive in nature but do utilize behavioral components. Likewise, some therapies that are considered behavioral, such as Rehm's self-control model (Rehm, 1977), also demonstrate flexibility by attending to cognitive factors. This leads to confusion with regard to what the primary intervention strategy is. For instance, Hollon (1981) classifies Rehm's self-control treatment of depression as a behavior therapy, while Kovacs (1979, 1980) categorizes self-control behavior therapies (Rehm's among them) as cognitive behavior therapies. However, since the primary target of the therapy is behavior, it may be more useful to consider such interventions as behavioral-cognitive therapies. Toward the middle of this continuum are interventions that use a combined cognitive *and* behavioral treatment (e.g., Coats & Reynolds, Note 3; Taylor & Marshall, 1977), although the combination of treatment components is idiosyncratic in each study.

In this review, we will generally adhere to the term provided by each investigator for describing the therapeutic intervention. What follows is a selective review of intervention studies that have utilized cognitive or cognitive-behavioral treatments for the alleviation or reduction of depressive symptomatology.

Comparative Efficacy. Within the past 10 years, a number of studies have appeared that allow for comparison between cognitive treatments and other forms of therapy for depression. Although research designs, subjects, duration of treatment, outcome measures, and other relevant variables for contrasting studies have varied, an examination of these studies provides a basis for judging the efficacy of cognitive therapy.

This selective review focuses on studies that utilized a cognitive-behavioral treatment for depression. While we recognize that several treatment approaches, such as the behavioral self-control model (Fuchs & Rehm, 1977; Rehm, 1977; Rehm, Fuchs, Roth, Kornblith, & Romano, 1979) and the reformulated learned helplessness theory of depression (Abramson, Seligman, & Teasdale, 1978; Seligman, 1981), have decidedly cognitive components (e.g., maladaptive self-evaluations, selective attention to negative events), space limitations preclude a detailed review of these intervention strategies in this chapter. We will, however, include a study by McLean and Hakstian (1979) where a behavior therapy that emphasized cognitive self-control was used, and a study by Roth, Bielski, Jones, Parker, and Osborn (1982) in which self-control therapy was implemented to help subjects "identify and modify dysfunctional, self-defeating styles of thinking and behaving" (p. 137).

Although a number of case studies (e.g., Rush et al., 1975) have reported substantial decreases in depressive symptomology as a function of cognitive behavior therapy, design constraints limit outcome generalizability. Because of the episodic nature of most depressive disorders, the lack of no-treatment (i.e., waiting-list) or placebo control groups seriously attenuates judgment regarding treatment efficacy. Our literature review will focus on research utilizing comparison group designs. Of these, two major categories can be delineated: studies comparing cognitive therapy to other forms of psychotherapy and studies comparing cognitive therapy with pharmacotherapy.

Table 10-2 Selected Studies Utilizing Cognitive Therapy for Depression

Study	Subjects	Therapy Format	Treatment Groups	N at Posttest Completers
Rush et al. (1977)	Clinic outpatients	I	1. Cognitive therapy (C) 2. Pharmacotherapy (Ph)	18 14
Shaw (1977)	College outpatients	G	1. Cognitive therapy (C) 2. Behavior therapy (B) 3. Nondirective (ND) 4. Waiting-list control (WL)	8 8 8 8
Taylor & Marshall (1977)	College volunteers	I	1. Cognitive therapy (C) 2. Behavior therapy (B) 3. Cognitive & Behavior (CB) 4. Waiting-list control (WL)	7 7 7
Zeiss et al. (1979)	Community volunteers	I	1. Cognitive therapy (C) 2. Social skills (SS) 3. Behavior therapy (B) 4. Delayed-treatment control (DT)	— — — 44 total
McLean & Hakstian	Clinic outpatients	I	1. Insight therapy (IT) 2. Behavioral-cognitive (BC) 3. Relaxation (R) 4. Pharmacotherapy (Ph)	37 40 38 39
Beck et al. (1979)	Clinic outpatient	I	1. Cognitive therapy (C) 2. Cognitive & pharmacotherapy (CPh)	14 12
Fleming & Thornton (1980)	Community volunteers	G	1. Cognitive therapy (C) 2. Behavior therapy (B) 3. Nondirective (ND)	13 13 9

Comparisons with Other Psychotherapies. The efficacy of cognitive behavior therapies for the treatment of depression can best be demonstrated when a control group
methodology is utilized. As the studies below indicate, the flexibility to incorporate
a waiting-list control group is often a function of subject characteristics. Ethical
considerations discourage the use of no-treatment control groups with clinic (in-
and outpatient) populations. It is generally the case that studies using volunteer
subjects not actively soliciting treatment do include control groups. However,
although waiting-list groups control for the potentially confounding episodic nature
of some depressions, a significant reduction of depression in a treatment-group-
only design indicates that some treatment is better than no treatment. Table 10-2
provides a summary of published studies that have included a cognitive-behavioral
treatment group for depression.

N at Posttest Dropouts	Outcome Measures	Treatment Outcome[a]	
		Posttest	Follow-up
1	BDI	C>Ph	C>Ph at 3 mo., C=Ph at 6 mo.
8	HRSD	C>Ph	
	Raskin	C=Ph	
0	BDI	C>B=ND>WL	C=B at 1 mo.
0	HRSD	C>B=ND=WL	C=B at 1 mo.
0	VAS	C=B=ND=WL	C=B at 1 mo.
0			
0	BDI	CB>C=B>WL	CB>C=B at 5 weeks
0	D-30	CB=C=B>WL	CB>C=B at 5 weeks
0	VAS	CB=C=B>WL	CB=C=B at 5 weeks
6	MMPI-D	C=SS=B>DT	C=SS=B>DT at 2 mo.
6			
3			
7	BDI	BC>IT, all other	BC=IT=R=Ph at 3 mo.
2		comparisons	
		nonsignificant	
5			
10			
4	BDI	C=CPh	C=CPh at 6 mo.
3	HRSD	C=CPh	C=CPh at 6 mo.
—	BDI	C=B=ND	C=B=ND at 6 weeks
—	D-30	C=B=ND	C=B=ND at 6 weeks
—	DAS	C=B=ND	C=B=ND at 6 weeks
	IBT	C=B=ND	C=B=ND at 6 weeks

Table 10-2 (Continued)

Study	Subjects	Therapy Format	Treatment Groups	N at Posttest Completers
Comas-Diaz (1981)	Community volunteers	G	1. Cognitive therapy (C)	8
			2. Behavior therapy (B)	8
			3. Waiting-list control (WL)	10
Rush & Watkins (1981)	Clinic outpatients	G/I	1. Group cognitive therapy (Cg)	23
			2. Individual cognitive therapy (C$_i$)	8
			3. Individual cognitive & Pharmacotherapy (C$_i$Ph)	7
Gardner & Oei (1981)	Community volunteers	G	1. Cognitive therapy (C)	8
			2. Behavior therapy (B)	8
Roth et al. (1982)	Community volunteers	G	1. Self-control (SC)	13
			2. Self-control & pharmacotherapy (SCPh)	13
Coats & Reynolds (Note 3)	High school student volunteers	G	1. Cognitive & behavior therapy (CB)	6
			2. Relaxation (R)	8
			3. Waiting-list control (WL)	9

Note. Cognitive therapy as a treatment group includes treatments that vary from purely cognitive to cognitive-behavioral. I=individual therapy; G=group therapy; BDI=Beck Depression Inventory; HRSD=Hamilton Rating Scale for Depression; VAS=Visual Analogue Scale; MMPI-D =Minnesota Multiphasic Personality Inventory-Depression scale; DAS=Dysfunctional Attitude Survey; D-30=Dempsey 30-Item MMPI-D; IBT=Irrational Beliefs Test; Zung=Zung Depression

In a study with 32 mildly to moderately depressed students referred from a university health service, Shaw (1977), using a group treatment format, compared Beck's cognitive therapy to the behavioral social skills training approach of Lewinsohn (1974) as well as to a nondirective therapy and waiting-list control group. Beck Depression Inventory (BDI; Beck, Ward, Mendelson, Mock, & Erbaugh, 1961) scores at termination of treatment indicated that all three therapy groups were significantly less depressed than the waiting-list control, and the cognitive therapy treatment was more effective than the behavioral and nondirective groups. The latter two groups did not differ significantly in their effectiveness. Examining group outcome means on the modified form of the Hamilton Rating Scale for Depression (HRSD; Hamilton, 1960) showed that the cognitive therapy group was superior to the behavioral, nondirective, and waiting-list groups. All other group comparisons were not significant. None of the groups differed on the Visual Analogue Scale (VAS; Aitken, 1969; Aitken & Zealley, 1970), a subjective rating scale of depressed

N at Posttest	Outcome Measures	Treatment Outcome[a]	
Dropouts		Posttest	Follow-up
0	BDI	$C=B>WL$	$C=B$ at 5 weeks
0	HRSD	$C=B>WL$	$B>C$ at 5 weeks
0			
5	BDI	$CPh=C_i, C_iPh>Cg$	
1			
0			
0	BDI	$C=B$	$C=B$ at 5 weeks
0	Zung	$C=B$	$C=B$ at 5 weeks
0	BDI	$SC=SCPh$	
0	HRSD		
3	BDI	$CB=R>WL$	$CB=R>WL$ at 5 weeks
3	RADS	$CB=R>WL$	$CB=R=WL$ at 5 weeks
1	BID	$CB=R>WL$	$CB=R>WL$ at 5 weeks

Rating Scale; RADS=Reynolds Adolescent Depression Scale; BID=Bellevue Index of Depression; Raskin=Raskin Three Area Rating Scale.

[a]Explanation of outcome symbols: $>$ denotes "more effective than"; $=$ denotes "equal in overall efficiency." The expression presents logical representation of the outcome.

mood. At 1-month follow-up the cognitive and behavioral groups did not differ significantly on any of the outcome measures.

There are several components of the Shaw (1977) study that are noteworthy. The design included an attention control (nondirective therapy) and no-treatment (waiting-list) control group, thus allowing for the assessment of general therapeutic effects common to any treatment. Assessment was based on two extensively used depression measures that maximized assessment method variance. Although both instruments measure depressive symptomatology, the BDI is a self-report scale while the HRSD is a clinician rating scale. Differential efficacy was indicated as a function of assessment measure. Lastly, this study incorporated a posttreatment follow-up. Given the episodic nature of depression, maintenance of treatment gains is an important outcome consideration.

Taylor and Marshall (1977) reported a study comparing the relative efficacy of cognitive, behavioral, and a combined cognitive *and* behavioral treatment to a waiting-list control group. Subjects were 28 mildly to moderately depressed college student volunteers. Results based on BDI, VAS, and D-30 (Dempsey, 1964) scores at termination of treatment indicated significant improvement by all three treatment groups compared to the waiting-list control group. Between-group comparisons of BDI scores showed the combined cognitive and behavioral treatment to be more effective than either of these treatments alone. Comparisons between treatment groups using the VAS and D-30 measures were nonsignificant. At a 5-week follow-up, the combined treatment was superior to the cognitive and behavioral therapies on the BDI and VAS. Differences between the individual therapies remained nonsignificant on all measures. These results suggest an additive effect of cognitive and behavior therapies.

Zeiss, Lewinsohn, and Munoz (1979) investigated the efficacy of cognitive, behavioral (increasing the rate of pleasant activities), and social skills (interpersonal) treatments, and a waiting-list control group with 44 depressed community volunteers. Treatments were individually administered and focused on teaching specific skills. Outcome measures included the depression scale of the Minnesota Multiphasic Personality Inventory (MMPI-D) and a number of treatment-specific behavioral, interpersonal, and cognitive assessment measures. At posttest, all treatments were more effective than the waiting-list control, although there were no discernible differences among treatment groups on the MMPI-D. All groups also demonstrated comparable effectiveness across the treatment-specific measures, a result that was contrary to the authors' expectation. Zeiss et al. (1979) suggest that Bandura's (1977b) self-efficacy model provides a rationale for the failure to find differential effects on the treatment modality-specific measures.

In a related study focusing on training coping skills within cognitive and behavioral treatment modalities, Fleming and Thornton (1980) compared these two treatments with a nondirective group that did not receive self-help skills training. Subjects were 35 moderately depressed community volunteers. The cognitive therapy followed specifications of Shaw (1977), while the behavioral treatment utilized Fuchs and Rehm's (1977) self-control therapy. The nondirective group was unstructured but conducted as an active treatment condition rather than an attention control. As Table 10-2 indicates, numerous depression measures were administered, including the Dysfunctional Attitude Survey (DAS, Weissman, 1979). Significant decreases in depression were found across all three treatment conditions at posttest and were maintained at the end of a 6-week follow-up. There were no significant between-group differences at posttest or follow-up, as measured by self-report depression measures. An interesting outcome of this study was the efficacy of the nondirective therapy, which did not teach specific coping skills, for reducing depression. Although a number of methodological questions exist regarding the treatments and design of this study, the results appear to expand upon the findings of Zeiss et al. (1979). While Zeiss et al. (1979) concluded that the specific content of skill training may not be as critical to treatment as previously thought, Fleming and Thornton (1980) found that a treatment without specific skills training components may also be effective in reducing depressive symptomatology. If generalized treatment gains are attributed to a self-efficacy model (as in the Zeiss et al., 1979, study), then the basis for an individual's expectations of personal efficacy, if not a function of skills training, needs further investigation.

The relative efficacy of cognitive and behavioral group therapy was also investigated by Comas-Diaz (1981) in her study of 26 moderately depressed Puerto Rican women. Scores on the BDI and HRSD showed the cognitive and behavioral treatment groups to be significantly less depressed at posttest than a waiting-list control group. The treatment group maintained lower depression scores at a 5-week follow-up. While differences between treatment groups were nonsignificant on the BDI and HRSD at posttest, at follow-up the behavior therapy group manifested lower HRSD scores than the cognitive treatment group, results contrary to the findings of Shaw (1977). Comas-Diaz (1981) speculated that subject characteristics (e.g., minority, low education level) may explain the differential effectiveness in favor of the behavioral treatment found at follow-up. It should also be noted that at follow-up, the cognitive group showed a significant *increase* in depression scores from the posttest assessment.

One additional study comparing cognitive and behavioral treatments for depression, in which a cognitive therapy consistent with Ellis's rational-emotive therapeutic approach (RET, Ellis & Harper, 1976) was used, will be considered here. Gardner an Oei (1981) contrasted an RET cognitive treatment with a pleasant activities behavioral treatment for 16 depressed community volunteers. Results obtained using the BDI and Zung Depression Rating Scale (Zung, 1965) showed significant decreases in depression by both groups without differential between-group effectiveness at posttest and 5-week follow-up.

Coats and Reynolds (Note 3) examined the efficacy of cognitive-behavioral and relaxation therapies for the treatment of depression with a sample of 28 moderately depressed adolescents. Outcome measures included a slightly modified form of the BDI, the Bellevue Index of Depression (BID, Petti, 1978) and the Reynolds Adolescent Depression Scale (RADS, Reynolds, Note 4; Reynolds & Coats, Note 5). The cognitive-behavioral intervention followed Beck's cognitive therapy and incorporated pleasant-event activity components of Lewinsohn's behavior therapy as well as self-control components of Rehm. Treatment format was group and consisted of 10 sessions over a 5-week period. At termination, both treatments showed significant reductions in depression on all measures and were significantly different than a waiting-list control group. There were, however, no between-treatment-group differences. Treatment gains were maintained at a 1-month follow-up on the BDI and BID. The lack of differential treatment effects found by Coats and Reynolds is similar to the findings of Zeiss et al. (1979) and McLean and Hakstian (1979), and lends further credence to Bandura's (1977b) self-efficacy formulation.

Comparisons with Pharmacotherapy. Several investigations have focused on the efficacy of cognitive-behavioral interventions in comparison with pharmacotherapy. Studies of this nature are important since, as perusal of the psychiatric literature indicates, pharmacotherapy is a major treatment modality for a psychiatrist treating depression. Further impetus for such comparison studies is provided by Morris and

Beck (1974), who in their review of the efficacy of antidepressant drugs found that drugs were superior to a placebo in approximately two thirds of the studies.

In a study with 41 unipolar depressed outpatients, Rush et al. (1977) compared cognitive therapy to pharmacotherapy (imipramine). Significant decreases in depressive symptomatology were found in both groups as assessed by the BDI, HRSD, and Raskin Three Area Rating Scale (Raskin, Schulterbrandt, Reatig, & McKeon, 1969). On the BDI and HRSD the cognitive therapy group showed significantly more improvement than the pharmacotherapy group. These results were based on subjects who completed treatment. A follow-up at 3 months with the BDI showed the cognitive group maintaining significantly lower scores than the pharmacotherapy group. This trend continued at 6 months, although the difference between groups was not significant. Further support for the cognitive-behavioral treatment was also suggested by the significantly greater number of dropouts from the pharmacotherapy group (eight vs. one). The authors indicate that overall, 78.9% of the original subjects in the cognitive therapy group showed marked clinical improvement or complete remission, whereas only 22.7% of the subjects in the pharmacotherapy treatment did.

Becker and Schuckit (1978) questioned the generalizability of the Rush et al. (1977) results on a number of points. In response to Becker and Schuckit's concerns, Rush, Hollon, Beck, and Kovacs (1978) provided further data and analyses specific to the outcome of the Rush et al. (1977) study. After adding three subjects whose data were incomplete at the time of the original report, Rush et al. (1978) differentiated subjects as either "acute" or "chronic" depressives within each treatment modality. Contrary to Becker and Schuckit's suggestion that comparing cognitive therapy to pharmacotherapy may be inappropriate with chronic depressed outpatients when using tricyclic antidepressant drugs (such as imipramine), Rush et al. (1978) found that according to the BDI and HRSD, chronic subjects showed significant improvement with either treatment, whereas acute subjects were significantly more improved in the cognitive therapy group than in the pharmacotherapy group at posttreatment assessment.

Kovacs et al. (1981) conducted a 12-month follow-up assessment of 35 of the 44 subjects who had participated in the Rush et al. (1977, 1978) study. Based on their scores on the BDI, both groups maintained posttreatment levels of self-reported depression 12 months later. At follow-up, subjects in the cognitive therapy group reported significantly lower scores on the BDI than the pharmacotherapy group (adjusted for pretreatment scores). Furthermore, at follow-up, 67% of the subjects in the cognitive therapy and 35% of the subjects in the pharmacotherapy group reported nondepressed levels of clinical symptomatology.

McLean and Hakstian (1979) in an outpatient treatment study with 154 moderately depressed subjects examined short-term insight psychotherapy, relaxation therapy, behavioral-cognitive therapy, and pharmacotherapy (amitriptyline) for the treatment of depression. Multiple outcome measures (including the BDI) were obtained for each subject. At termination, all treatments showed significant improvement on the BDI, with the behavioral-cognitive group significantly less depressed than the psychotherapy group. Fifty percent of the behavioral-cognitive therapy group had BDI scores in the normal (nondepressed) range at posttest compared to

25–28% for the other three groups. Only 7% of the subjects in the behavioral-cognitive treatment were still moderately to severely depressed, compared to 19–30% for the other treatments. At a 3-month follow-up the differential gains by the behavioral-cognitive group at posttest were no longer evident. This study is noteworthy for the rigorous screening procedure used to select subjects, the substantial sample size, and the methodological procedures implemented by the investigators, including replacement subjects for dropouts and attention to treatment conformity, such as blood serum checks for self-medication compliance by the pharmacotherapy group.

An interesting study was conducted by Rush and Watkins (1981) that investigated the differential efficacy of group versus individual cognitive therapy and individual cognitive therapy plus medication. The cognitive therapy followed the methodology suggested by Beck et al. (1979), while the pharmacotherapy was varied and included tricyclic antidepressants ($N = 5$), a monoamine oxidase inhibitor ($N = 1$), and lithium carbonate ($N = 1$). Subjects were 38 moderately depressed outpatients. Contrary to the authors' expectation, individual cognitive therapy and individual cognitive therapy plus medication treatments were more effective than group cognitive therapy in alleviating depression, although all groups showed significant pretest-posttest differences. Follow-up data 2 months later on fewer than half the subjects in the group therapy condition revealed a maintenance of gains. Unfortunately, follow-up information on the individual therapy groups was not obtained, precluding discussion of generalization effects.

Finally, Roth et al. (1982) investigated self-control and combined self-control with antidepressant medication treatments for depression. The self-control therapy utilized cognitive strategy components and was "oriented toward helping patients identify and modify dysfunctional, self-defeating styles of thinking and behaving" (p. 137). Subjects were 26 community volunteers who received 12 weeks of group therapy. The combined condition medication was desipramine (a tricyclic). A repeated measures design indicated that both treatments were significant in their effect upon reducing depressive symptomatology at posttesting. While the difference between groups at posttest was nonsignificant (on the BDI), the authors found a significant time by condition interaction, indicating that improvement was more rapid for the self-control plus antidepressant medication treatment group. At a 3-month follow-up, treatment gains were maintained by both groups.

It should be noted that none of the foregoing studies that compared cognitive behavior therapy with pharmacotherapy incorporated a control group in their design. While ethical considerations often mitigate the use of a waiting-list or placebo control group in studies utilizing clinic samples, the lack thereof leaves some questions unanswered. This is not to say that control groups cannot be used with clinic samples. In a study comparing the efficacy of interpersonal psychotherapy (although not cognitive therapy) Weissman and her colleagues (Weissman, Prusoff, DiMascio, Neu, Goklaney, & Klerman, 1979; Weissman, Klerman, Prusoff, Sholomskas, & Padian, 1981) found a combined psychotherapy plus pharmacotherapy (tricyclic) group treatment to show greater effectiveness than either treatment individually, while all three treatments were more effective than a nonscheduled treatment control group. Furthermore, the inclusion of a placebo plus psychotherapy group when comparing the efficacy of combinatory psychotherapy and pharmacotherapy treatments (cf. Bellack, Hersen, & Himmelhock, 1981) adds further rigor to such outcome studies.

Summary. The studies reviewed in this section examined the efficacy of cognitive therapies for the treatment of depression. Although there was variability with regard to the concomitant behavioral procedures utilized with the cognitive therapy, all studies included a treatment condition that emphasized the training of a cognitive strategy. Two general classes of efficacy studies were described, those comparing cognitive therapy with other forms of psychotherapy (e.g., behavior therapy) and studies comparing cognitive therapy to pharmacotherapy. Results of these investigations suggest that at termination of therapy, the cognitive therapy is as effective as, and in some studies more effective than, other psychotherapies and pharmacotherapies. Treatment gains are often maintained, although differential effectiveness of cognitive therapy is usually not found at follow-up assessments. Overall, in the studies reviewed, cognitive therapy was comparable in its effectiveness with other forms of therapy. An examination of the cognitive therapy variations suggests that cognitive therapy when combined with another psychotherapy or pharmacotherapy may be more effective than cognitive therapy alone. Also, cognitive treatments utilizing an individual therapy format appear to be more effective than group therapy, although further research is needed before this trend can be firmly established.

Cognitive behavior modification has gained acceptance as an intervention strategy for the treatment of depression. One question raised by a number of these studies is whether the specific type of psychotherapy makes a difference to the outcome. Several studies have found nonspecific treatment effects (e.g., Coats & Reynolds, Note 3; Fleming & Thornton, 1980; Zeiss et al., 1979) that were contrary to expectations. It would seem from this review that comparative efficacy studies may no longer provide as much new information as studies that examine commonalities among treatment components and *their* relative effectiveness.

Lastly, from this review, we would like to suggest the examination of subject dropout rate as one additional criterion for evaluating the efficacy of a treatment. This appears particularly relevant when examining differential effectiveness of cognitive therapy with pharmacotherapy. As the results of these studies indicate, pharmacotherapies appear less effective in maintaining subjects in treatment. These results are also consistent with the findings of Bellack et al. (1981) in which psychosocial therapies with either antidepressant or placebo realized a significantly greater proportion of completers than did the pharmacotherapy group. Given an equal effectiveness for reducing or alleviating depressive symptomatology, a therapy of choice would be one that maintains clients. In this respect, cognitive therapies have a small edge.

Overview

We have presented a number of clinical approaches for the treatment of anxiety and depression that follow the general tenets of cognitive behavior modification.

All of these approaches have as a common base a focus on cognitions, and vary with regard to the strategies used to implement change. Anxiety and depression represent disorders whose etiologies and/or maintenance have been in part explained by cognitive theories. If one ascribes a cognitive basis to these disorders, then a logical choice of treatment might be a cognitive-behavioral one. It should be recognized that many competing theories (e.g., behavioral, biochemical) do exist, thus providing the rationale for other forms of therapeutic intervention.

Our purpose in this section was the presentation of empirical investigations that have utilized cognitive-behavioral interventions. Recognizing the numerous methodological problems inherent in generalizing from such diverse studies, we can only claim that cognitive-behavioral therapies appear to be as effective as most contemporary therapeutic interventions.

Methodological Issues

In our review of studies comparing cognitive-based treatments with other therapies, we attempted to synthesize outcomes in order to provide a general overview of treatment efficacy. It should be recognized that a generalization of this type is limited by the variability of the outcome studies examined. Differences among studies occur on such variables as subjects, treatment, therapist, assessment, analysis, and design.

Subjects

Subject variability can be found on a number of salient characteristics. These include subject background and motivation for participation. Subjects may be community volunteers, student volunteers (who may participate for class credit and/or requirements), and/or various outpatients who are actively seeking therapeutic assistance. Sex, age, marital status, race, socioeconomic status, and prior histories of emotional disorders and previous participation in therapy also vary between and within studies. One of the most important subject characteristics is the very nature of the clinical problem. For instance, in both anxiety and depression, subjects vary in regard to the depth of their malady (e.g., mild, moderate, severe) as well as its duration. Added to these subject differences is the problem of sample size. Many of the studies reported have treatment groups with 10 or fewer subjects. With such low numbers a differential response to treatment by one or two subjects can distort outcome results. Furthermore, at follow-up assessments one generally finds even fewer subjects, which creates additional problems with regard to the power of the analysis.

Treatments

Differences among treatments also lead to ambiguity in comparing therapeutic effectiveness. Clearly there are idiosyncratic components in treatments labeled cognitive, cognitive-behavioral, and cognitive restructuring, as well as in the many combinations of treatments. In the depression literature, a treatment that Zeiss et al. (1979) refer to as a cognitive therapy differs from that used by Shaw (1977). Likewise, the combination cognitive *and* behavioral treatment by Coats and Reynolds (Note 3) is not the same as that employed by Taylor and Marshall (1977). It needs to be recognized that treatments are often study specific. Another structural variation is the treatment format employed (i.e., group or individual). As the intervention research on depression illustrates, therapy formats are varied, without any obvious modality preference. Except for the study by Rush and Watkins (1981), differences in treatment formats have not been examined in a controlled manner. The problem of comparing treatment efficacy from one investigation to the next is also exacerbated by what are often very brief reports of actual treatment components by the author of the study. Uniformity in the reporting of procedures and therapeutic components would lend greater generalizability to future studies.

Therapist

When applying therapeutic interventions to clinical or subclinical populations, the training and experience of the therapist is a critical variable (Sundberg, Tyler, & Taplin, 1973). In the intervention studies described, the therapists involved in the direct administration of therapy have varied from highly experienced psychiatrists to first-year graduate students in psychology. Often, the former are found in studies using clinic outpatients, whereas the latter are generally responsible for dissertation studies. Whatever the impetus for the study, there is clearly a very wide gulf in training and experience among individuals responsible for implementation of the therapeutic regimen. Another concern lies in the specific psychological orientation of the therapist and the degree of congruence between this orientation and the philosophical underpinnings of the treatment approach. When the experimenter acts as a therapist for multiple treatments, the potentially confounding effect of his or her orientation may cloud judgments regarding differential treatment efficacy. In addition to these issues, it is not known whether individual differences in age, sex, race, and other characteristics between therapist and subject may impinge on treatment effectiveness.

Assessment

Assessment procedures and techniques are important components of treatment outcome research. As Sundberg, Snowden, and Reynolds (1978) note, the aim of assessment is to discern individual characteristics that are important for decision making. In therapy research, assessment forms the basis for making decisions regarding subject selection, individual subject characteristics (e.g., level of depression), efficacy of treatment, and generalizability of outcome. Assessment when applied to cognitive behavior modification raises many critical questions. For instance, do we demonstrate treatment efficacy by showing a reduction in depressive symptomatology (as might be measured by the Beck Depression Inventory), a change or reduction in maladaptive cognitions (as measured by a thought-sampling procedure or measure of irrational beliefs), or in peer or professional ratings of cognitive style? Clearly, assessment needs to be related to what we wish to modify. Furthermore, the tendency for researchers to develop study-specific behavioral assessment measures for which validity and reliability are doubtful only serves to reduce generalizability. The issue of bandwidth and fidelity is also worthy of note. For instance, the Beck Depression Inventory was used in the majority of the depression studies cited, thus allowing for generalization, at least on the assessment measure level. However, this scale is probably best considered a broad bandwidth measure and therefore may not be sensitive to subtle or specific changes in depression. As shown in several of the studies reviewed, differential results were found within a study as a function of different outcome measures. This raises questions regarding the efficacy of the assessment procedures and techniques.

Analysis and Design

As with any body of research, one finds variability in the design and analysis of studies. However, there are a number of analyses that do not allow for direct comparison of results. For example, repeated measures designs and analyses of covariance, which in most instances use pretest scores as covariates, create differences in interpretation, especially when examining gains made on a subsequent follow-up assessment. The design of intervention studies also is a factor that shows substantial variability. In general, the studies reviewed demonstrate efficacy by comparing the treatment of interest to (a) one or more different, yet recognized, therapies; (b) a waiting-list or delayed-treatment control group; *and/or* (c) a placebo, attention, or nondirective treatment control group (we recognize that these groups are not equivalent, yet their purpose is similar). Furthermore, a number of studies did not include control groups of any type, a distinct weakness. While studies with control group designs generally show treatment groups to be superior to controls, without a control group this outcome *cannot* be inferred.

Summary

Consideration of methodological issues serves a number of purposes. It allows us to see limitations in the studies reviewed and the degree to which we can feel secure making global statements of treatment efficacy. It also illustrates a number of components that can be incorporated in future investigations in order to provide or enhance efficacy and study generalizability. We are not stating that the studies reviewed are flawed and do not provide useful information. On the contrary, a number of these studies are, from our perspective, exemplary. Our purpose in this section is simply to note a number of variables on which studies differ, and how differences between studies on these variables limits direct comparisons.

Summary

In this chapter we have shown that cognitive strategy training, as elaborated by cognitive behavior modification, is an effective technique for the treatment of clinical problems. As demonstrated by current research on the treatment of depression and anxiety, there is a great deal of interest in cognitive behavior modification. Given the rapidly increasing research, theory, and application literature, cognitive behavior modification can be viewed as the zeitgeist of behavior change procedures.

As procedures for effecting changes in behavior go, cognitive behavior modification is still in its adolescence. As such, there is room for growth and development, as well as searching of new avenues for experimentation. As our brief historical overview of the cognitive-behavioral perspective suggests, cognitive behavior modification is still evolving. This can be seen in the variety of cognitive-behavioral approaches that are continually undergoing modification or combination with other techniques.

This chapter has illustrated the clinical approaches to cognitive behavior modification through a selective review of research on the treatment and amelioration of anxiety and depression. Yet, these domains represent only the tip of the iceberg in relation to the myriad applications of cognitive behavior modification. Furthermore, although our review highlighted the use of cognitive behavior modification with adults, the application to academic, behavioral, and emotional problems of children is also a burgeoning area of research (Craighead, 1982; Craighead, Meyers, Craighead, & McHale, 1982; Kendall & Braswell, 1982; Kirschenbaum & Ordman, in press; Meyers & Craighead, in press).

The continuing evolution of theory and procedures reflects the turmoil of cognitive behavior modification. When research shows that components within an approach are effective, they are retained or added; if they prove ineffective, they are dropped or earmarked for further study. Our methodology section indicated a number of areas to which future studies should attend in order to maximize outcome generalizability. Cognitive behavior modification is clearly a major force within the field of clinical psychology. Its application shows promise for the amelioration of many clinical problems. We expect future developments and formulations of cognitive behavior modification to further its widespread use and application.

Acknowledgments. The authors wish to express their appreciation to Maribeth Gettinger and Gloria E. Miller for their constructive comments on an earlier version of this chapter, and to Karen Kraemer for the typing of this chapter.

Reference Notes

1. Meichenbaum, D. H. Personal communication. December, 1981.
2. Brown, M. *A set of eight parallel forms of the digit symbol test.* Unpublished set of tests, University of Waterloo, Ontario, Canada, 1969.
3. Coats, K. I., & Reynolds, W. M. *A comparison of cognitive-behavioral and relaxation therapies for depression with adolescents.* Unpublished manuscript, University of Wisconsin, 1982.
4. Reynolds, W. M. *Development and validation of a scale to measure depression in adolescents.* Unpublished manuscript, 1981.
5. Reynolds, W. M., & Coats, K. *Depression in adolescents: Incidence, depth and correlates.* Paper presented at the 10th International Congress of the Interna-

tional Association for Child and Adolescent Psychiatry, Dublin, Ireland, July 1982.

References

Abraham, K. *Selected papers of Karl Abraham.* London: Hogarth Press, 1927.

Abramson, L. Y., Seligman, M. E. P., & Teasdale, J. D. Learned helplessness in humans: Critique and reformulation. *Journal of Abnormal Psychology,* 1978, *87,* 49–74.

Alden, L., & Safran, J. Irrational beliefs and non-assertive behavior. *Cognitive Therapy and Research,* 1978, *2,* 357–364.

Alden, L., Safran, J., & Weideman, R. A comparison of cognitive and skills training strategies in the treatment of unassertive clients. *Behavior Therapy,* 1978, *9,* 843–846.

Alpert, R., & Haber, R. Anxiety in academic achievement situations. *Journal of Abnormal and Social Psychology,* 1960, *61,* 207–215.

Aitken, R. C. B. Measures of feeling using analogue scales. *Proceedings of the Royal Society of Medicine,* 1969, *62,* 989–993.

Aitken, R. C. B., & Zealley, A. K. Measurement of mood. *British Journal of Hospital Medicine,* 1970, *4,* 214–224.

Aponte, J. F., & Aponte, C. F. Group preprogrammed systematic desensitization without the simultaneous presentation of aversive scenes with relaxation training. *Behavior Research and Therapy,* 1971, *9,* 337–346.

Bandura, A. *Principles of behavior modification.* New York: Holt, Rinehart & Winston, 1969.

Bandura, A. *Social learning theory.* Morristown, NJ: General Learning Press, 1971. (a)

Bandura, A. Vicarious self-reinforcement processes. In R. Glaser (Ed.), *The nature of reinforcement.* New York: Academic Press, 1971. (b)

Bandura, A. Behavior theory and the models of man. *American Psychologist,* 1974, *29,* 859–869.

Bandura, A. *Social learning theory.* Englewood Cliffs, NJ: Prentice-Hall, 1977. (a)

Bandura, A. Self-efficacy: Toward a unifying theory of behavioral change. *Psychological Review,* 1977, *84,* 191–215. (b)

Bandura, A. The self-system in reciprocal determinism. *American Psychologist,* 1978, *33,* 344–358.

Barrett, C. L. Systematic desensitization versus implosive therapy. *Journal of Abnormal Psychology,* 1969, *74,* 587–592.

Beck, A. T. Thinking and depression. *Archives of General Psychiatry,* 1963, *9,* 324–333.

Beck, A. T. *Depression: Causes and treatment.* Philadelphia: University of Pennsylvania Press, 1967.

Beck, A. T. Cognitive therapy: Nature and relation to behavior therapy. *Behavior Therapy,* 1970, *1,* 184–200.

Beck, A. T. *Cognitive therapy and the emotional disorders.* New York: International Universities Press, 1976.

Beck, A. T., Rush, A. J., Shaw, B. F., & Emery, G. *Cognitive therapy of depression.* New York: Guilford Press, 1979.

Beck, A. T., Ward, C. H., Mendelson, M., Mock, J., & Erbaugh, J. An inventory for measuring depression. *Archives of General Psychiatry,* 1961, *4,* 561–571.

Becker, J., & Schuckit, M. The comparative efficacy of cognitive therapy and pharmacotherapy in the treatment of depression. *Cognitive Therapy and Research,* 1978, *2,* 193–197.

Beers, T. M., Jr., & Karoly, P. Cognitive strategies, expectancy, and coping style in the control of pain. *Journal of Consulting and Clinical Psychology,* 1979, *47,* 179–180.

Bellack, A. S., Hersen, M., & Himmelhoch, J. Social skills training compared with pharmacotherapy and psychotherapy in the treatment of unipolar depression. *American Journal of Psychiatry,* 1981, *138,* 1562–1567.

Bem, D. J. Self-perception theory. In L. Berkowitz (Ed.), *Advances in experimental social psychology* (Vol. 6). New York: Academic Press, 1972.

Bibring, E. The mechanism of depression. In P. Greenacre (Ed.), *Affective disorders.* New York: International Universities Press, 1953.

Blaney, P. H. The effectiveness of cognitive and behavioral therapies. In L. P. Rehm (Ed.), *Behavior therapy for depression: Present status and future directions.* New York: Academic Press, 1981.

Bolles, R. C. Reinforcement, expectancy, and learning. *Psychological Review,* 1972, *79,* 394–409.

Bruch, M. A. Type of cognitive modeling, imitation of modeled tactics, and modification of test anxiety. *Cognitive Therapy and Research,* 1978, *2,* 147–164.

Burns, D., & Beck, A. Cognitive behavior modification of mood disorders. In J. Foreyt and D. Rathjen (Eds.), *Cognitive behavior therapy: Research and application.* New York: Plenum, 1978.

Carmody, T. Rational-emotive, self-instructional, and behavioral assertion training: Facilitating maintenance. *Cognitive Therapy and Research,* 1978, *2,* 241–253.

Cautela, J. R. Treatment of compulsive behavior by covert sensitization. *Psychological Record,* 1966, *16,* 33–41.

Cautela, J. R. Covert sensitization. *Psychological Reports,* 1967, *20,* 459–468.

Cautela, J. R. Covert negative reinforcement. *Journal of Behavior Therapy and Experimental Psychiatry,* 1970, *1,* 273–278. (a)

Cautela, J. R. Covert reinforcement. *Behavior Therapy,* 1970, *1,* 33–50. (b)

Cautela, J. R. Covert conditioning. In A. Jacobs and L. B. Sachs (Eds.), *The psychology of private events: Perspectives on covert response systems.* New York: Academic Press, 1971.

Comas-Diaz, L. Effects of cognitive and behavioral group treatment on the depressive symptomatology of Puerto Rican women. *Journal of Consulting and Clinical Psychology,* 1981, *49,* 627–632.

Craighead, W. E. A brief clinical history of cognitive-behavior therapy with children. *School Psychology Review,* 1982, *11*(1), 5–13.

Craighead, W. E., Meyers, A. W., Craighead, L. W., & McHale, S. M. Issues in cognitive behavior therapy with children. In M. Rosenbaum, C. M. Franks, & Y. Jaffe (Eds.), *Perspectives on behavior therapy in the eighties.* New York: Springer-Verlag, 1982.

D'Alelio, W. A., & Murray, E. J. Cognitive therapy of test anxiety. *Cognitive Therapy and Research,* 1981, *5,* 299–308.

Dempsey, P. A. A unidimensional depression scale for the MMPI. *Journal of Consulting Psychology,* 1964, *28,* 364–370.

Derry, P., & Stone, G. Effects of cognitive-adjunct treatments on assertiveness. *Cognitive Therapy and Research*, 1979, *3*, 213–221.

D'Zurilla, T. J., Wilson, G. T., & Nelson, R. A preliminary study of the effectiveness of graduated prolonged exposure in the treatment of irrational fear. *Behavior Therapy*, 1973, *4*, 672–685.

Ellis, A. *Reason and emotion in psychotherapy*. New York: Lyle Stuart, 1962.

Ellis, A. *The essence of rational psychotherapy: A comprehensive approach to treatment*. New York: Institute for Rational Living, 1970.

Ellis, A. The basic clinical theory of rational-emotive therapy. In A. Ellis and R. Grieger (Eds.), *Handbook of rational-emotive therapy*. New York: Springer-Verlag, 1977. (a)

Ellis, A. Can we change thoughts by reinforcement: A reply to Howard Rachlin. *Behavior Therapy*, 1977, *8*, 666–672. (b)

Ellis, A. Rational-emotive therapy and cognitive behavior therapy: Similarities and differences. *Cognitive Therapy and Research*, 1980, *4*, 325–340.

Ellis, A., & Harper, R. *A new guide to rational living*. Englewood Cliffs, NJ: Prentice-Hall, 1976.

Endler, N., Hunt, J., & Rosenstein, A. An S-R Inventory of anxiousness. *Psychological Monographs*, 1962, *76*(Whole No. 536).

Eysenck, H. J. Behavior therapies and the philosophies. *Behaviour Research and Therapy*, 1979, *17*, 511–514.

Ferster, C. B. Classification of behavioral pathology. In L. Krasner and L. Ullmann (Eds.), *Research in behavior modification*. New York: Holt, Rinehart & Winston, 1965.

Ferster, C. B. A functional analysis of depression. *American Psychologist*, 1973, *28*, 857–870.

Fleming, B. M., & Thornton, D. W. Coping skills training as a component in the short-term treatment of depression. *Journal of Consulting and Clinical Psychology*, 1980, *48*, 652–654.

Fremouw, W. J., & Zitter, R. E. A comparison of skills training and cognitive re-structuring-relaxation for the treatment of speech anxiety. *Behavior Therapy*, 1978, *9*, 248–259.

Fuchs, C. Z. & Rehm, L. P. A self-control therapy program for depression. *Journal of Consulting and Clinical Psychology*, 1977, *45*, 206–215.

Gardner, P., & Oei, T. P. S. Depression and self-esteem: An investigation that used behavioral and cognitive approaches to the treatment of clinically depressed clients. *Journal of Clinical Psychology*, 1981, *37*, 128–135.

Glass, C. R., Gottman, J. M., & Shmurak, S. H. Response-acquisition and cognitive self-statement modification approaches to dating skills training. *Journal of Counseling Psychology*, 1976, *23*, 520–526.

Glogower, F. D., Fremouw, W. J., & McCroskey, J. C. A component analysis of cognitive restructuring. *Cognitive Therapy and Research*, 1978, *2*, 209–223.

Goldfried, M. R. Systematic desensitization as training in self-control. *Journal of Consulting and Clinical Psychology*, 1971, *37*, 228–234.

Goldfried, M. R. The use of relaxation and cognitive relabeling as coping skills. In R. B. Stuart (Ed.), *Behavioral self-management: Strategies, techniques and outcomes*. New York: Brunner/Mazel, 1977.

Goldfried, M. R., & Davison, G. L. *Clinical behavior therapy*. New York: Holt, Rinehart & Winston, 1976.

Goldfried, M. R., Decenteceo, E. T., & Weinberg, L. Systematic rational restructuring as a self-control technique. *Behavior Therapy,* 1974, *5,* 247–254.

Goldfried, M., & Goldfried, A. Cognitive change methods. In F. H. Kanfer and A. P. Goldstein (Eds.), *Helping people change: A textbook of methods.* New York: Pergamon, 1975.

Goldfried, M. R., & Goldfried, A. P. Importance of hierarchy content in the self-control of anxiety. *Journal of Consulting and Clinical Psychology,* 1977, *45,* 124–134.

Goldfried, M., Linehan, M. M., & Smith, J. C. Reduction of test anxiety through cognitive restructuring. *Journal of Consulting and Clinical Psychology,* 1978, *46,* 32–39.

Goldfried, M. R., & Trier, C. Effectiveness of relaxation as an active coping skill. *Journal of Abnormal Psychology,* 1974, *83,* 348–355.

Hamilton, M. A rating scale for depression. *Journal of Neurology, Neurosurgery, and Psychiatry,* 1960, *23,* 56–62.

Hammen, C. L., Jacobs, M., Mayol, A., & Cochran, S. Dysfunctional cognitions and effectiveness of skills and cognitive-behavioral assertion training. *Journal of Consulting and Clinical Psychology,* 1980, *48,* 685–695.

Hollon, S. D. Comparisons and combinations with alternative approaches. In L. P. Rehm (Ed.), *Behavior therapy for depression: Present status and future directions.* New York: Academic Press, 1981.

Holroyd, K. A. Cognition and desensitization in the group treatment of test anxiety. *Journal of Consulting and Clinical Psychology,* 1976, *44,* 991–1001.

Husek, T., & Alexander, S. The effectiveness of the anxiety differential in examination stress situations. *Educational and Psychological Measurement,* 1963, *23,* 309–318.

Jacobs, M. K., & Cochran, S. D. The effects of cognitive restructuring on assertive behavior. *Cognitive Therapy and Research,* 1982, *6,* 63–76.

Jones, R. G. *A factored measure of Ellis' irrational belief system, with personality and maladjustment correlates.* Unpublished doctoral dissertation, Texas Technological College, 1968.

Kanfer, F. H. Self-regulation: Research, issues, and speculations. In C. Neuringer & J. L. Michael (Eds.), *Behavior modification in clinical psychology.* New York: Appleton-Century-Crofts, 1970.

Kanfer, F. The maintenance of behavior by self-generated stimuli and reinforcement. In A. Jacobs & L. B. Sachs (Eds.), *The psychology of private events: Perspectives on covert response systems.* New York: Academic Press, 1971.

Kanter, N. J., & Goldfried, M. R. Relative effectiveness of rational restructuring and self-control desensitization in the reduction of interpersonal anxiety. *Behavior Therapy,* 1979, *10,* 472–490.

Kazdin, A. E. *History of behavior modification: Experimental foundations of contemporary research.* Baltimore: University Park Press, 1978.

Kendall, P. C., & Braswell, L. Cognitive-behavioral self-control therapy for children: A components analysis. *Journal of Consulting and Clinical Psychology,* 1982, *50,* 672–689.

Kendall, P. C., & Hollon, S. D. Cognitive-behavioral interventions: Overview and current status. In P. C. Kendall & S. D. Hollon (Eds.), *Cognitive-behavioral interventions: Theory, research, and procedures.* New York: Academic Press, 1979.

Kendall, P. C., Williams, L., Pechacek, T. F., Graham, L. E., Shisslak, C., & Herzoff, N. Cognitive-behavioral and patient education intervention in cardiac catheterization procedures: The Palo Alto Medical Psychology Project. *Journal of Consulting and Clinical Psychology,* 1979, *47,* 49-58.

Kirschenbaum, D. S., & Ordman, A. M. Preventive interventions for children: Cognitive-behavioral perspectives. In A. W. Meyers & W. E. Craighead (Eds.), *Cognitive behavior therapy for children.* New York: Plenum, in press.

Kovacs, M. Treating depressive disorders: The efficacy of behavior and cognitive therapies. *Behavior Modification,* 1979, *3,* 496-517.

Kovacs, M. The efficacy of cognitive and behavior therapies for depression. *American Journal of Psychiatry,* 1980, *137,* 1495-1501.

Kovacs, M., Rush, A., Beck, A. T., & Hollon, S. D. Depressive outpatients treated with cognitive therapy or pharmacotherapy: A one year follow-up. *Archives of General Psychiatry,* 1981, *38,* 33-39.

Lazarus, A. A. Learning theory and the treatment of depression. *Behavior Research and Therapy,* 1968, *6,* 83-89.

Lazarus, A. A. A critique of rational-emotive therapy. In A. Ellis & J. M. Whiteley (Eds.), *Theoretical and empirical foundations of rational-emotive therapy.* Monterey, CA: Brooks/Cole, 1979.

Ledwidge, B. Cognitive behavior modification: A step in the wrong direction? *Psychological Bulletin,* 1978, *85,* 353-375.

Ledwidge, B., Cognitive behavior modification: A rejoinder to Locke and to Meichenbaum. *Cognitive Therapy and Research,* 1979, *3,* 133-139. (a)

Ledwidge, B. Cognitive behavior modification or new ways to change minds: Reply to Mahoney and Kazdin. *Psychological Bulletin,* 1979, *86,* 1050-1053. (b)

Lewinsohn, P. M. A behavioral approach to depression. In R. J. Friedman & M. M. Katz (Eds.), *The psychology of depression: Contemporary theory and research.* New York: Wiley, 1974.

Lewinsohn, P. M., Weinstein, M. S., & Shaw, D. A. Depression: A clinical-research approach. In R. D. Rubin & C. M. Franks (Eds.), *Advances in behavior therapy: 1968.* New York: Academic Press, 1969.

Lewinsohn, P. M., Youngren, M. A., & Grosscup, S. J. Reinforcement and depression. In R. A. Depue (Ed.), *The psychobiology of the depressive disorders: Implications for the effects of stress.* New York: Academic Press, 1979.

Lewis, D. *Chastity; or our secret sins.* Philadelphia: Maclean, 1875.

Liebert, R., & Morris, L. Cognitive and emotional components of test anxiety: A distinction and some initial data. *Psychological Reports,* 1967, *20,* 975-978.

Linehan, M., Goldfried, M., & Goldfried, A. Assertion therapy: Skill training or cognitive restructuring. *Behavior Therapy,* 1979, *10,* 372-388.

Lloyd, J. Academic instruction and cognitive behavior modification: The need for attack strategy training. *Exceptional Education Quarterly,* 1980, *1,* 53-64.

Locke, E. A. Behavior modification is not cognitive—and other myths: A reply to Ledwidge. *Cognitive Therapy and Research,* 1979, *3,* 119-126.

Maddison, D., & Duncan, G. (Eds.) *Aspects of depressive illness.* Edinburgh: Livingston, 1965.

Mahoney, M. J. Research issues in self-management. *Behavior Therapy,* 1972, *3,* 45-63.

Mahoney, M. J. *Cognition and behavior modification.* Cambridge, MA: Ballinger, 1974.

Mahoney, M. J. Reflections on the cognitive-learning trend in psychology. *American Psychologist*, 1977, *32*, 5–13. (a)

Mahoney, M. J. On the continuing resistance to thoughtful therapy. *Behavior Therapy*, 1977, *8*, 673–677. (b)

Mahoney, M. J. A critical analysis of rational-emotive theory and therapy. *The Counseling Psychologist*, 1977, *7*, 44–46. (c)

Mahoney, M. J., & Arnkoff, D. Cognitive and self-control therapies. In S. L. Garfield & A. E. Bergin (Eds.), *Handbook of psychotherapy and behavior change* (2nd ed.). New York: Wiley, 1978.

Mahoney, M. J., & Kazdin, A. E. Cognitive behavior modification: Misconceptions and premature evacuation. *Psychological Bulletin*, 1979, *86*, 1044–1049.

Malkiewich, L., & Merluzzi, T. Rational restructuring versus desensitization with clients of diverse conceptual levels: A test of a client-treatment matching model. *Journal of Counseling Psychology*, 1980, *27*, 453–461.

Mandel, N. M., & Shrauger, J. S. The effects of self-evaluative statements on heterosocial approach in shy and nonshy males. *Cognitive Therapy and Research*, 1980, *4*, 369–381.

McCroskey, J. Measures of communication-bound anxiety. *Speech Monographs*, 1970, *37*, 269–277.

McGlynn, F. D. Graded imagination and relaxation as components of experimental desensitization. *Journal of Nervous and Mental Disease*, 1973, *156*, 377–385.

McLean, P. D., & Hakstian, A. R. Clinical depression: Comparative efficacy of outpatient treatments. *Journal of Consulting and Clinical Psychology*, 1979, *49*, 818–836.

Meichenbaum, D. Cognitive modification of test anxious college students. *Journal of Consulting and Clinical Psychology*, 1972, *39*, 370–380.

Meichenbaum, D. *Cognitive behavior modification*. Morristown, NJ: General Learning Press, 1974.

Meichenbaum, D. Dr. Ellis, please stand up. *The Counseling Psychologist*, 1977, *7*, 43–44.

Meichenbaum, D. H. *Cognitive-behavior modification*. New York: Plenum, 1977.

Meichenbaum, D. Cognitive behavior modification: The need for a fairer assessment. *Cognitive Therapy and Research*, 1979, *3*, 127–132. (b)

Meichenbaum, D., & Asarnow, J. Cognitive-behavioral modification and metacognitive development; Implications for the classroom. In P. Kendall & S. Hollon (Eds.), *Cognitive-behavioral interventions: Theory, research, and procedures*. New York: Academic Press, 1979.

Meichenbaum, D., & Butler, L. Toward a conceptual model for the treatment of test anxiety: Implications for research and treatment. In I. Sarason (Ed.), *Test anxiety: Theory, research, and applications*. Hillsdale, NJ: Erlbaum, 1980.

Meichenbaum, D., & Butler, L. Cognitive ethology: Assessing the streams of cognition and emotion. In K. Blankstein, P. Pliner, & J. Polivy (Eds.), *Advances in the study of communication and affect: Assessment and modification of emotional behavior* (Vol. 6). New York: Plenum, 1981.

Meichenbaum, D. H., & Cameron, R. Training schizophrenics to talk to themselves: A means of developing attentional controls. *Behavior Therapy*, 1973, *4*, 515–534.

Meichenbaum, D. H., & Cameron, R. The clinical potential of modifying what clients say to themselves. *Psychotherapy: Theory, Research and Practice*, 1974, *11*, 103–117.

Meichenbaum, D., & Genest, M. Cognitive behavioral modification: An integration of cognitive and behavioral methods. In F. Kanfer & A. Goldstein (Eds.), *Helping people change* (2nd ed.). New York: Pergamon, 1980.

Meichenbaum, D., Gilmore, J., & Fedoravicius, A. Group insight vs. group desensitization in treating speech anxiety. *Journal of Consulting and Clinical Psychology*, 1971, *36*, 410–421.

Meichenbaum, D. H., & Goodman, J. Training impulsive children to talk to themselves: A means of developing self-control. *Journal of Abnormal Psychology*, 1971, *77*, 115–126.

Meyers, A. W., & Craighead, W. E. (Eds.). *Cognitive behavior therapy for children.* New York: Plenum, in press.

Morris, J. B., & Beck, A. T. The efficacy of antidepressant drugs: A review of research (1958–1972). *Archives of General Psychiatry,* 1974, *30*, 667–674.

Morris, L., & Liebert, R. Effects of anxiety on timed and untimed intelligence tests. *Journal of Consulting and Clinical Psychology*, 1969, *33*, 240–244.

Novaco, R. W. Treatment of chronic anger through cognitive and relaxation controls. *Journal of Consulting and Clinical Psychology*, 1976, *44*, 681.

Novaco, R. W. Stress inoculation: A cognitive therapy for anger and its application to a case of depression. *Journal of Consulting and Clinical Psychology*, 1977, *45*, 600–608.

Novaco, R. W. Anger and coping with stress: Cognitive behavioral interventions. In J. Foreyt & D. Rathjen (Eds.), *Cognitive behavior therapy: Research and application.* New York: Plenum, 1978.

Oliver, R. The "empty nest syndrome" as a focus of depression: A cognitive treatment model based on rational emotive therapy. *Psychotherapy: Theory, Research and Practice,* 1977, *14*, 87–94.

Paul, G., & Shannon, D. Treatment of anxiety through systematic desensitization in therapy groups. *Journal of Abnormal Psychology,* 1966, *71*, 124–135.

Paul, G. L. *Insight vs. desensitization in psychotherapy: An experiment in anxiety reduction.* Stanford, CA: Stanford University Press, 1966.

Petti, T. A. Depression in hospitalized child psychiatry patients: Approaches to measuring depression. *Journal of the American Academy of Child Psychiatry,* 1978, *17*, 49–59.

Rachlin, H. Reinforcing and punishing thoughts. *Behavior Therapy,* 1977, *8*, 659–665.

Raimy, V. *Misunderstandings of the self.* San Francisco: Jossey-Bass, 1975.

Raskin, A., Schulterbrandt, J. G., Reatig, N., & McKeon, J. J. Replication of factors of psychopathology in interview, ward behavior, and self-ratings of hospitalized depressives. *Journal of Nervous and Mental Disease,* 1969, *148*, 87–98.

Rathjen, D., Rathjen, E., & Hiniker, A. A cognitive analysis of social performance: Implications for assessment and treatment. In J. Foreyt & D. Rathjen (Eds.), *Cognitive behavior therapy: Research and application.* New York: Plenum, 1978.

Raven, J. *Guide to using progressive matrices.* London: H. E. Lewis Press, 1956.

Rehm, L. P. A self-control model of depression. *Behavior Therapy,* 1977, *8*, 787–804.

Rehm, L. P., Fuchs, C. Z., Roth, D. M., Kornblith, S. J., & Romano, J. M. A comparison of self-control and assertion skills treatments of depression. *Behavior Therapy,* 1979, *10*, 429–442.

Rosen, G. M., & Orenstein, H. A historical note on thought stopping. *Journal of Consulting and Clinical Psychology,* 1976, *44*, 1016–1017.

Roth, D., Bielski, R., Jones, M., Parker, W., & Osborn, G. A comparison of self-control therapy and combined self-control therapy and antidepressant medication in the treatment of depression. *Behavior Therapy,* 1982, *13,* 133–144.

Rush, A. J., Beck, A. T., Kovacs, M., & Hollon, S. Comparative efficacy of cognitive therapy and pharmacotherapy in the treatment of depressed outpatients. *Cognitive Therapy and Research,* 1977, *1,* 17–37.

Rush, A. J., & Giles, D. E. Cognitive therapy: Theory and research. In A. J. Rush (Ed.), *Short-term psychotherapies for depression: Behavioral, interpersonal, cognitive, and psychodynamic approaches.* New York: Guilford Press, 1982.

Rush, A. J., Hollon, S. D., Beck, A. T., & Kovacs, M. Depression: Must pharmacotherapy fail for cognitive therapy to succeed? *Cognitive Therapy and Research,* 1978, *2,* 199–206.

Rush, A. J., Khatami, M., & Beck, A. T. Cognitive and behavior therapy in chronic depression. *Behavior Therapy,* 1975, *6,* 398–404.

Rush, A. J., & Watkins, J. T. Group versus individual cognitive therapy: A pilot study. *Cognitive Therapy and Research,* 1981, *5,* 95–103.

Ryan, E. B. Identifying and remediating failures in reading comprehension: Toward an instructional approach for poor comprehension. In T. G. Waller & G. E. MacKinnon (Eds.), *Advances in reading research* (Vol. 2). New York: Academic Press, 1981.

Schildkraut, J. J. The catecholamine hypothesis of affective disorders. *American Journal of Psychiatry,* 1965, *122,* 509–522.

Schuyler, D. *The depressive spectrum.* New York: Aronson, 1974.

Seligman, M. E. P. *Helplessness.* San Francisco: W. H. Freeman, 1975.

Seligman, M. E. P. A learned helplessness point of view. In L. P. Rehm (Ed.), *Behavior therapy for depression: Present status and future directions.* New York: Academic Press, 1981.

Shaw, B. F. Comparison of cognitive therapy and behavior therapy in the treatment of depression. *Journal of Consulting and Clinical Psychology,* 1977, *45,* 543–551.

Shaw, B. F., & Beck, A. T. The treatment of depression with cognitive therapy. In A. Ellis & R. Grieger (Eds.), *Handbook of rational-emotive therapy.* New York: Springer-Verlag, 1977.

Spiegler, M. D., Cooley, E. J., Marshall, G. J., Prince, H. T., & Puckett, S. P. A self-control versus a counter-conditioning paradigm for systematic desensitization: An experimental comparison. *Journal of Counseling Psychology,* 1976, *23,* 83–86.

Spielberger, C., Gorsuch, R., & Lushene, R. *Manual for the State-Trait Anxiety Inventory.* Palo Alto, CA: Consulting Psychologist Press, 1970.

Suinn, R. The STABS, a measure of test anxiety for behavior therapy: Normative data. *Behaviour Research and Therapy,* 1969, *7,* 335–339.

Sundberg, N. D., Snowden, L. R., & Reynolds, W. M. Toward assessment of personal competence and incompetence in life situations. In M. R. Rosenzweig & L. W. Porter (Eds.), *Annual review of psychology* (Vol. 29). Palo Alto, Calif.: Annual Reviews Inc., 1978.

Sundberg, N. D., Tyler, L. E., & Taplin, J. R. *Clinical psychology; Expanding horizons* (2nd ed.). Englewood Cliffs, NJ: Prentice-Hall, 1973.

Taylor, F. G., & Marshall, W. L. Experimental analysis of a cognitive-behavioral therapy for depression. *Cognitive Therapy and Research,* 1977, *1,* 59–72.

Thoresen, C. E., & Mahoney, M. J. *Behavioral self-control.* New York: Holt, Rinehart & Winston, 1974.

Thorpe, G. L. Desensitization, behavioral rehearsal, self-instructional training and placebo effects on assertive-refusal behavior. *European Journal of Behavioral Analysis and Modification,* 1975, *1,* 30–44.

Thorpe, G. L., Amatu, H. I., Blakey, R. S., & Burns, L. E. Contributions of overt instructional rehearsal and "specific insight" to the effectiveness of self-instructional training: A preliminary study. *Behavior Therapy,* 1976, *7,* 504–511.

Trexler, L. D., & Karst, T. O. Rational-emotive therapy, placebo, and no-treatment effects on public-speaking anxiety. *Journal of Abnormal Psychology,* 1972, *79,* 60–67.

Turk, D. C. Cognitive behavioral techniques in the management of pain. In J. P. Foreyt & D. P. Rathjen (Eds.), *Cognitive behavior therapy: Research and application.* New York: Plenum, 1978.

Turk, D. C., & Genest, M. Regulation of pain: The application of cognitive and behavioral techniques for prevention and remediation. In P. C. Kendall & S. D. Hollon (Eds.), *Cognitive-behavioral interventions: Theory, research, and procedures.* New York: Academic Press, 1979.

Ullman, L. P. On cognitions and behavior therapy. *Behavior Therapy,* 1970, *1,* 201–204.

Watson, D., & Friend, R. Measurement of social evaluative anxiety. *Journal of Consulting and Clinical Psychology,* 1969, *33,* 448–457.

Wein, K. S., Nelson, R. O., & Odom, J. V. The relative contributions of reattribution and verbal extinction to the effectiveness of cognitive restructuring. *Behavior Therapy,* 1975, *6,* 459–474.

Weissberg, M. A comparison of direct and vicarious treatments of speech anxiety: Desensitization, desensitization with coping imagery, and cognitive modification. *Behavior Therapy,* 1977, *8,* 606–620.

Weissman, A. N. The Dysfunctional Attitude Scale: A validation study (Doctoral dissertation, University of Pennsylvania, 1979). *Dissertation Abstracts International,* 1979, *40,* 1389B–1390B. (University Microfilms No. 79-19533)

Weissman, M. M., Klerman, G. L., Prusoff, B. A., Sholomskas, D., & Padian, N. Depressed outpatients: Results one year after treatment with drugs and/or interpersonal psychotherapy. *Archives of General Psychiatry,* 1981, *38,* 51–55.

Weissman, M. M., Prusoff, B. A., DiMascio, A., Neu, C., Goklaney, M., & Klerman, G. L. The efficacy of drugs and psychotherapy in the treatment of acute depressive episodes. *American Journal of Psychiatry,* 1979, *136,* 555–558.

Wilson, G. T. Cognitive behavior therapy: Paradigm shift or passing phase? In J. P. Foreyt & D. P. Rathjen (Eds.), *Cognitive behavior therapy: Research and application.* New York: Plenum, 1978.

Wolpe, J. *Psychotherapy by reciprocal inhibition.* Stanford: Stanford University Press, 1958.

Wolpe, J. Neurotic depression: Experimental analog, clinical syndromes and treatment. *American Journal of Psychotherapy,* 1971, *25,* 362–368.

Wolpe, J. Cognition and causation in human behavior and its therapy. *American Psychologist,* 1978, *33,* 437–446.

Young, J. E., & Beck, A. T. Cognitive therapy: Clinical applications. In A. J. Rush (Ed.), *Short-term psychotherapies for depression: Behavioral interpersonal, cognitive, and psychodynamic approaches.* New York: Guilford Press, 1982.

Zeiss, A. M., Lewinsohn, P. M., & Munoz, R. F. Nonspecific improvement effects in depression using interpersonal skills training, pleasant activity schedules, or cognitive training. *Journal of Consulting and Clinical Psychology*, 1979, *47*, 427–439.

Zuckerman, M. The development of an affect adjective check list for the measurement of anxiety. *Journal of Consulting Psychology*, 1960, *24*, 457–462.

Zung, W. W. K. A self-rating depression scale. *Archives of General Psychiatry*, 1965, *12*, 63–70.

11. Cognitive Strategy Training and Children's Self-Control

Michael Pressley, William M. Reynolds, Kevin D. Stark, and Maribeth Gettinger

The training of self-control behavior in children is an area of research that for many years, at least in the United States, was the almost exclusive domain of the strict behaviorists. In the past 15 years a growing body of literature has emerged suggesting the utility of cognitive and verbally mediated approaches for self-control interventions. This chapter will overview recent experimental work on cognitive interventions affecting children's self-control. We will focus on ways in which children manipulate their own cognitions to increase self-control and, to a lesser extent, on ways in which tasks and materials can be manipulated to influence children's cognitions and self-control. Thus, both subject strategies and environmental strategies will be explored. As will become evident during the survey of the literature, self-control strategy research has contributed greatly to both theoretical and practical issues of child study.

Much of the experimental work on induced cognitive self-control in children has been conducted in three areas. These are (1) verbal control of motor behavior; (2) strategy use in resistance-to-temptation situations, and (3) cognitive modification of children's "impulsive" behaviors. In each situation, there is a high probability of children's executing inappropriate responses. Within each research area, the subjects were taught strategies, or the environment was manipulated, so as to increase the likelihood of a priori less probable, but more desirable, behaviors. These three research areas will be reviewed in the above-cited order. For each, definitions of the problems and relevant strategies will be presented, a brief summary of research findings will be offered, and suggestions for future research directions will be considered.

Readers interested in more detailed comments on general issues of strategy research and self-control relating to each of the three areas covered are referred to an earlier article by Pressley (1979) on increasing children's self-control through cognitive interventions. An effort has been made in this chapter to highlight the advances in the field since the publication of the 1979 article. Most notably, a more detailed version of Luria's position has appeared in English (Luria, 1982); there have been advances in understanding the mechanisms underlying children's failures in delay-of-gratification situations (e.g., Yates & Mischel, 1979); and studies of cognitive control of impulsivity have appeared that are more ambitious as well as more systematic in their scope than previous efforts (e.g., Kendall & Braswell, 1982). These advances and others will be considered in light of the previous conceptualizations and research.

Development and Verbal Control of Motor Behavior

No discussion of cognitive control in children would be complete without commentary on the work of Alexander R. Luria. Much of contemporary thinking about children's verbal control of behavior has as its basis the thoughts and ideas of Luria, even though Luria's conception of verbal-behavioral linkages has frequently been misunderstood (Wilder, 1976; Wozniak, 1972). However, recent translations of Luria's writing (e.g., Luria, 1982) provide better summaries of Soviet work, and consequently there should be less confusion in the future about Soviet viewpoints concerning verbal influences on behavior.

The Paradigms

Luria researched the development of two types of verbal-behavioral relations, the development of external verbalizations as regulators of motor behavior and the ontogeny of self-speech as a controlling influence on motor behavior. Both of these lines of inquiry inspired follow-up investigations in the West (e.g.,Wozniak, 1972). The developmental progressions described by Luria (1961, 1982) are considered here in some detail because of the frequent confusion in the literature regarding Luria's claims about verbal control of motor behavior.

External Verbalizations and Children's Motor Behaviors. The development of external verbal control extends over the first 3½ to 4 years of life and is far from a simple progression (Luria, 1982). Even during the first year of life, adult verbalizations exert some influence on children's behaviors, primarily in the form of orienting responses that disrupt ongoing behavior sequences of the infant. By the end of the first year of life, the meaning of adult speech influences the child's orientations. Thus, a 1-year-old who is asked, "Where is the cup?" is likely to turn toward the cup and perhaps even reach for it. At this age, whether children respond appropriately to verbalizations is dependent on the environment in which the speech is encountered. For instance, if a child were instructed to "pick up the fish," success would depend on whether there were other toys in the environment, how physically proximate the fish was relative to other toys, and how perceptually salient the fish was compared to other objects near it. Thus, if the fish were farther away than the chicken, the child might pick up the chicken. If a cup near the fish were more colorful, the child might go for the cup. Although the adult commands somewhat control the behavior of the child at this stage, compliance with these commands is easily disrupted by objects in the environment that "evoke a direct orienting response" (Luria, 1982, p. 92) inconsistent with the adult's command.

Luria (1982) argued that "it is possible to strengthen the regulative function of speech at this stage [by] highlighting the appropriate object" (p. 92). This can be done by shaking the object, tapping it, or pointing to it. Presumably these maneuvers result in orienting responses to the appropriate object that are more powerful than distractions provided by other objects.

Children up to 1½ to 2½ years of age are also susceptible to a phenomenon described by Luria (1982) as "inertia," which can result in failure to follow a command. Inertia is illustrated by the following two examples:

> Consider the case of a small child of 14 to 16 months who is given the task of placing rings on a rod to build a toy pyramid. The child is told, "Put on the ring!", "Put it on!", "Put it on!" every time a ring is placed on the rod. Then, in the same tone of voice, the child is told, "Take it off!" "Take it off!" . . . [However,] the child will continue putting the rings on and will do this even more energetically than before. Even if the command "Take it off!" is given in a loud voice, the child may continue more energetically than before to put on rings. The inertia of his/her own action prevents him/her from carrying out the command. (p. 92)

As a second example:

> A goblet and a cup were placed before the child. A coin was dropped into the goblet while the child was watching, and the experimenter said, "Now, come on, find the coin!" . . . If this command was repeated five or six times, the child always responded appropriately by reaching toward the goblet. However, if the coin was then dropped into the cup (again, while the child is observing) and the child was told, "Now the coin is in the cup, find it!", the child often continued reaching for the goblet. Even if the child understood the instructions, the inertia of the previous action was so powerful that the child was unable to overcome it. (pp. 92–93)

Even when children develop to the point of not showing inertia in the goblet-cup situation as just described, it is possible to produce such inertia by increasing the task demands slightly. One way is to delay the child's reactions by physically restraining the child's hands, and a second way is to eliminate visual cues from the situation. Thus, when children did not see the coin actually drop into the goblet because the dropping action was shielded, they showed much more inertia. Only by the third or fourth year of life do children consistently carry out verbal commands when delay is imposed or visual input is restricted.

Even after 3 years of age there are deficiencies in preschoolers' motor responses to verbal commands in some circumstances. For instance, if a child simultaneously observes a behavior inconsistent with the one he or she is asked to perform, errors occur. Thus, children may have difficulty following a conditional command such as,

"When I raise my fist you are to raise your finger." Similarly, if presented with a toy fish and rooster similar to toys in the experimenter's possession, 3-year-olds also have difficulty following commands such as, "When I pick up the fish, you pick up the rooster, and when I pick up the rooster you pick up the fish." Luria (1982) contends that it is not until 3½ years of age that children can overcome such direct visual interference when responding to a spoken command.

Finally, it is not until the very late preschool years (4–4½ years) that children can carry out a complex sequence of motor behaviors under verbal command, such as following: "Put down the pieces in the following way—one red checker, then two white ones, one red one, two white ones," when arranging red and white checkers; or can conform to the instruction, "Draw a vertical line, draw a horizontal line across the vertical line."

Self-Verbalizations and the Regulation of Motor Behavior. By far the most frequently cited task in Soviet studies of children's verbal control of their motor behavior is bulb squeezing. In the relevant experiments, a child was given a balloon-like rubber bulb that fits in the palm of the hand and could be easily squeezed (Luria, 1959, 1961, 1969). In the bulb-squeezing task, children between the ages of 1½ and 3 years will squeeze the bulb when instructed to do so by an adult, but tend to perseverate in their responding (e.g., Wozniak, 1972). When instructed to "stop pressing" or any variant on this command, the young child does not obey the command, but in fact continues to press and may press even harder. Moreover, children 1½–3 years of age do not benefit from an instruction to instruct themselves verbally to "squeeze" only when squeezing was appropriate (Luria, 1961; Yakovleva, 1976). In summary, in the studies described above neither the speech of others nor self-speech produces controlled motor responding. In general, speech can initiate squeezing but cannot inhibit it.

Between the ages of 3 and 4½–5½ years, children continue to respond perseveratively when instructed to squeeze the bulb (Luria, 1959, 1961, 1969, 1982; Tikhomerov, 1976; Yakovleva, 1976). When instructed to squeeze a bulb without instructions to verbalize while squeezing, they squeeze both when they are supposed to squeeze and when they are not supposed to. If instructed to verbalize, however, children can execute some control over their motor behaviors. For instance, if a child is instructed to squeeze and simultaneously say "Go," the child can give a discrete squeeze without perseverating. If two squeezes are required and the child says, "Go, go," the child can give two discrete squeezes (e.g., Luria, 1961; Tikhomerov, 1976). However, if the subject says, "Squeeze two times," the result is three squeezes (Luria, 1961, 1969, 1982; Tikhomerov, 1976; Wozniak, 1972).

Why do we obtain this pattern of results? According to the Soviets, because the feedback mechanisms between the hand and the cortex are not mature in preschoolers, the children perseverate in bulb squeezing because they fail to realize when they have completed a response (Luria, 1969; Tikhomerov, 1976; Yakovleva, 1976). In order to inhibit a motor response that the immature nervous system fails to sense completely (such as bulb squeezing), the child must supplement the motor response with a signal that the response has been executed. One way to do this is to have the child make a discrete vocalization simultaneous with a bulb squeeze. The meaning of the vocalization does not matter, for it is the impulsive aspect of the speech that regulates the motor responding. Thus, if required to make two motor responses, the child can say, "One, two," "Go, go," or "Dog, dog" and two responses should occur. However, the semantically correct verbalization "I shall squeeze twice" should result in more than two responses, since there are four discrete vocalizations (syllables in this case; Luria, 1961, 1969, 1982; Tikhomerov, 1976; Wozniak, 1972). The motor response is determined by the number of speech impulses and not the semantic meaning of the command.

Eventually (by 4½–5½ years of age) the semantic aspect of the verbal self-instruction assumes dominance over the impulsive aspect of the speech. Thus, at this point, when the child self-instructs to "press once," he or she presses once, following the meaning of the verbalization, rather than pressing twice, consistent with the impulse of the verbalization.

The Data

External Verbalizations and Children's Motor Behavior. No exact replications of Luria's tasks have been successfully implemented in the West. A number of studies using other tasks have confirmed that during the preschool years there are improvements in children's motor responses to verbal commands. For instance, Birch (1966) reported that between 2 and 7 years of age, children's compliance with instructions to push a bar down and hold it down increased. Strommen (1973) reported that between 4 and 8 years of age children's accuracy in a Simon Says-type game increased. Masters and Binger (1978) permitted children to play with an attractive toy and then ordered them to stop playing with it. The amount of compliance to such an instruction increased between 2 and 4 years of age.

Two studies used situations very similar to Luria's "delay, then respond" setup in the goblet-cup task. These studies included children in the 2- to 3-year-old range, roughly corresponding to the ages of the children Luria (1982) commented on in his "delay, then respond" task. Golden, Montare, and Bridger (1977) presented 2- and 2½-year-olds with two tasks. In one of the tasks, a cookie was placed under one of three small boxes in full view of the subject. The subject was instructed to "find the cookie" but to wait for a whistle before looking for it (i.e., delay, then act). In another game the child was put in front of a toy train with a switch. In this task the subject was instructed to "start the train," but only when signaled to do so. Even 2-year-olds were able to execute the "delay, then respond" response sequences over 50% of the time. By 2½ years the children executed the sequences correctly 90% of the time. Bain (1976) used a task very similar to the cookie task in Golden et al. (1977), and found that 2-year-olds were able to execute "delay, then respond" sequences correctly 60% of the time. In summary, all of the results considered in this section are in accord with Luria's (1982) position that young preschoolers experience difficulties in reacting to external verbal commands and that responses to such commands become more accurate during the later preschool years. In closing, however, it must be noted that some data have been produced by

Western researchers suggesting that the completion of the development of motor compliance to external verbalizations extends well into the grade school years. See, for example, Strommen (1973), and especially LaVoie, Anderson, Fraze, and Johnson's (1981) work on mismatching of verbal and visual input in motor response situations.

Self-Verbalizations and the Regulation of Motor Behavior. For the most part Western researchers have not been able to replicate the developmental progression proposed by Luria. This type of research has usually been conducted within a bulb-squeezing paradigm (Joynt & Cambourne, 1968; Miller, Shelton, & Flavell, 1970; Wilder, 1969), although other motor tasks have occasionally been employed (e.g., Beiswenger, 1968; Jarvis, 1968; Meacham, 1973, 1978). In all of the above-cited studies, children improved on the experimental task as they became older during the preschool years. In general, however, vocalization did not improve performance, and crucial age X vocalization condition interactions were not obtained.

Wozniak (1972) has leveled devastating criticisms at Western attempts at replication of Soviet research. Difficulties noted include instructions to the child to vocalize and then respond (in contrast to the simultaneous procedures used by the Soviets), overly complex instructions, inappropriate use of warm-up procedures, and low statistical power. In general, we find Wozniak's criticisms reasonable, especially the criticism of vocal-motor order of responding in the Western studies. Only if the vocalization occurs concurrently with or very shortly after the motor response can the verbal response supplement the motor response in the manner discussed by Luria (1961, 1969, 1982), Tikhomerov (1976), and Yakovleva (1976).

A series of studies by Rondal (1976) attempted to correct some of the problems associated with previous Western research. It is not possible to review completely this extensive series of studies. Suffice to summarize here that on the positive side, Rondal (1976) found that motor responding in preschoolers could be affected by the impulsive aspect of vocalization, with the effects most pronounced in the 3½- to 4½-year range. Thus, preschoolers were more likely to respond two times if they said, "Press, press." On the negative side, with older children (5½-7 years of age), Rondal (1976) did not find that semantically appropriate verbalizations increased the probability of correct motor responding. Thus, Rondal's (1976) findings supported only part of the Lurian position.

Discussion and Future Research

In the past, the greatest difficulty for Western researchers interested in Lurian ideas was finding out exactly what occurred in the Lurian investigations. Very little of Luria's writing was translated from Russian, and that which was translated included unfamiliar terminology and allusions to non-Western theory and data not available to Western workers. The situation has been improved by recent translations (e.g., Luria, 1982; Tikhomerov, 1976; Wertsch, 1981) and enlightening commentaries on Soviet psychology (e.g., Wozniak, 1972). It is hoped that the availability of these resources will permit future Western researchers to avoid some of the fundamental errors made by previous investigators.

It is unfortunate that Western researchers have spent so much effort on the bulb-squeezing task. That task is an artificial laboratory procedure that does not correspond to demands that children typically encounter in the real world. There is little reason to be interested in motor movements so slight that preschoolers' sensory systems can hardly detect and monitor them! Fortunately, in recent years, Western psychologists have been examining verbal control of motor behavior in more relevant situations.

When one examines studies such as those of Golden et al. (1977), Bain (1976), and Masters and Binger (1978), it is apparent that Western hypotheses about the effects of external verbalization on motor behaviors are not as articulated as Luria's position on the topic. Thus, the general framework provided by Luria (1982) could be heuristic for researchers interested in verbalization and motor responding. Luria (1982) raised many fundamental questions about possible situational effects on external verbal control of behavior, suggesting a developmental progression from only very limited external verbal control to verbal control of complex motor behaviors carried out in diverse environments. In addition, many of Luria's (1982) specific ideas are relevant to contemporary work on child development outside the area of motor control. Luria's (1982) hypotheses about the primacy of visually salient events over verbal events in very young preschoolers interfaces with other theoretical traditions making similar claims (e.g., Bruner, 1973). Also, Luria (1982) suggests work on mismatching of visual and verbal input that would complement mismatching research in the area of reading (e.g., Willows, 1978). In summary, Luria seems to have offered a rich set of hypotheses that await systematic investigation.

It is hoped that researchers will do follow-up work on Luria's ideas with a careful eye toward the actual information processing of the child. For example, some of the failures of external verbal control of behavior reported by Luria are as likely due to failures in memory of the verbalizations as to the mechanisms suggested by Luria (e.g., orienting responses to irrelevant stimuli). Also, it is known that directions in many Soviet studies were overly complex (e.g., Yakovleva's commentary, 1976), and thus some failures observed by Luria may have been nothing more than failures to comprehend the directions. Finally, use of terms like *inertia* by Luria do not explain behaviors, but merely label them. It is essential to identify the processes actually causing behaviors like inertia. Solid information processing analyses of the behaviors Luria describes could reveal much about the control of children's behaviors, and such work should be encouraged.

Cognitive Intervention Effects on Children's Delay of Gratification and Resistance to Temptations

The Paradigms

A great deal of research has been conducted in recent years on cognitive effects on delay of gratification and resistance to temptation. In resistance-to-temptation tasks children have typically been left in a situation with tempting stimuli (e.g., toys) and have been instructed to resist the temptation. Delay of gratification involves foregoing a smaller reward presently available (e.g., one piece of candy) in order to obtain a larger reward later (e.g., two pieces of candy). Of course, delay of gratification is a specific case of resistance to temptation, since the subjects resist the smaller reward that is presumably very tempting. These two paradigmatic situations can be illustrated by considering two specific operationalizations.

Hartig and Kanfer's (1973) study employed a resistance-to-temptation task in which children were taken to a room and attractive toys were placed in back of them. The preschool participants were left alone with the toys and instructed not to turn around and look at the toys. The main dependent variable was the amount of time that passed before the child turned around and looked at the toys.

Mischel and Patterson (1976, 1978; Patterson & Mischel, 1975, 1976) conducted a series of studies on children's delay of gratification. A typical scenario in these experiments was the following: A child was brought to an experimental room and was shown a box of "fun toys" and a box of "broken toys." The child was then introduced to a boring, repetitive task (such as copying or putting pegs in a pegboard) and was told that this was his or her work for the session. The subject was then introduced to a talking clownlike toy that was also in the room, Mr. Clown Box. The subject was warned that the clown box would try to distract her or him from the task by trying to get the child to play with the toys that the clown box would display. The child was instructed to ignore the clown box's distractions. Before the experimenter left the room, it was explained to the child that if he or she worked on the task for the entire period while the experimenter was absent, then he or she would be allowed to play with the fun toys. The subject was also told that if he or she did not work for the entire period, then only the broken toys would be available later.

The Data

A variety of cognitive manipulations have been shown to increase children's resistance to temptation and delay of gratification, and thus their self-control.

Self-Verbalization Effects. Mischel and his colleagues have documented that preschoolers can be taught self-verbalizations that will increase their willingness to resist temptations. However, the effectiveness of a verbalization depends on the content of the verbalization. For instance, Mischel and Patterson (1976; Patterson & Mischel, 1976) reported that in the clown box situation, a temptation-inhibiting verbalization, such as, "No, I'm not going to look at Mr. Clown Box," increased resistance over no verbalization, as did a reward-relevant verbalization, such as, "I want to play with the fun toys and Mr. Clown Box later." In contrast, verbalizations emphasizing the monotonous task failed to increase self-control.

Research conducted outside of Mischel's laboratory confirms the efficacy of instructions to preschoolers to engage in self-verbalization, with numerous investigations in the area confirming that only certain types of self-verbalizations increase preschoolers' self-control (e.g., Hartig & Kanfer, 1973; Toner, Lewis, & Gribble, 1979; Toner & Smith, 1977). Research on elementary school age children's use of self-verbalizations has not been as systematic as the research conducted with preschoolers. However, when elementary school children have been instructed to use verbalizations that Mischel and his colleagues found to be effective with preschoolers, resistance to temptation has increased (e.g., Hartig & Kanfer, 1973; Sawin & Parke, 1979). See Pressley (1979) for a thorough analysis of studies of school-aged children's self-verbalizations and the effects on self-control.

External Verbalization: The Effects of Rationales. The main types of external verbalizations investigated by self-control researchers are rationales that can be provided to children about why they should engage in resistance to deviation. The effectiveness of these rationales has been explicitly compared with the effectiveness of alternative procedures, such as punishment for deviation.

A study by Parke (1969) illustrates the type of data obtained in experiments on rationale effects. In that study, first- and second-grade boys were instructed not to play with some attractive toys. Using a 2^4 factorial design, half of the subjects were punished for deviation by hearing a loud buzzer, and half were punished with a soft buzzer. Half were punished early in the deviation sequence, and half were punished late in the deviation sequences. Half interacted with a highly nurturant person, and half interacted with a not so nurturant person. Half were given no rationale for the prohibition on play with the toys, and half were told that they should not play with the toys because the experimenter feared the toys would be broken, and thus would no longer be of use to the experimenter.

When no rationale was provided, intense punishment, early punishment, and nurturant interaction produced more self-control than low-intensity punishment, late punishment, or non-nurturant interaction. When a rationale was provided, self-control was evident regardless of intensity of punishment, timing of punishment, or nurturance of the experimenter. Thus, the rationales had a potent and pervasive effect. In general, provision of rationales to children and adolescents increases the effectiveness of punitive feedback (e.g., Blackwood, 1970; Cheyne & Walters, 1969; LaVoie, 1973, 1974a; MacPherson, Candee, & Hohman, 1974).

Just as the type of self-instruction a child uses is crucial in determining self-control, the type of rationale provided to subjects has been shown to be a determinant of rationale effectiveness. Furthermore, the effectiveness of some types of rationales changes with age (Parke, 1970, 1974, 1977). Rationales that emphasize physical consequences of acting in an uncontrolled manner increase the self-control of preschoolers, elementary school age children, and adolescents (e.g., LaVoie, 1974a, 1974b; Parke, 1974; Verna, 1977). Rationales that emphasize property rights, feelings and intentions of others, and the points of view of others become effective with increasing age (e.g., Cheyne, 1972; Jensen & Buhanan, 1974; LaVoie, 1974b). This finding is consistent with theories of social cognitive development that contend that understanding of property rights and perspectives different from one's own increases with age (e.g., Kohlberg, 1969). The interested reader is referred to Parke (1970, 1974, 1977) for extensive and interesting discussions of rationale effects with children.

Affect Manipulations. If children are instructed to think about "fun" things during delay of gratification or resistance to temptation, they are more likely to wait or resist temptation compared to no-instruction control subjects (e.g., Fry, 1977; Masters & Santrock, 1976; Mischel, Ebbesen, & Zeiss, 1972; Moore, Clyburn, & Underwood, 1976; Santrock, 1976; Yates, Lippett, & Yates, 1981). Conversely, if children produce sad thoughts while waiting, they do not wait as long as non-instructed control subjects (e.g., Fry, 1977; Masters & Santrock, 1976; Moore et al., 1976; Santrock, 1976). Thus self-produced affect is a powerful determinant of children's self-control.

Cognitive Ideations and Transformations of Temptations. Readers familiar with contemporary theory in cognitive behavior modification (e.g., Mahoney, 1974) know that ideations are presumed to affect behavior. Although there is relatively little work on cognitive transformations and ideations in children, there is some evidence to suggest that ideations affect children's self-control. The two studies that best document this relation are considered here in detail.

In Mischel and Baker (1975), preschool subjects were left alone in a room with a preferred food, under an instruction that they would receive twice as much of the food if they waited for the experimenter to return than if they called the experimenter back. Subjects in four experimental conditions were instructed to execute one of four strategies during the delay period. In one experimental condition, subjects were to think about the consummatory aspects of the reward (the taste, how much fun it would be to eat the reward). In a second experimental group, the subjects were instructed to think about the consummatory qualities of a food different from the one for which they were waiting. In a third group subjects were instructed to think about nonconsummatory aspects of the contingent reward. They were instructed to think about the reward and transform the food. Thus, subjects who waited for marshmallows were instructed to do the following:

> Think about how white and puffy they are. Clouds of white and puffy, too.— When you look at marshmallows think of clouds. Or you can think how round and white a marshmallow is. The moon is round and white. When you look at marshmallows, think about the moon. Or you can think about how round a marshmallow is on top. A ball is round. When you look at marshmallows think about playing ball. (p. 257)

In a fourth condition, the preschoolers mentally transformed in a nonconsummatory fashion a food for which they were not waiting. Subjects who mentally transformed the food for which they were waiting and those who concentrated on the consummatory aspects of another food waited longer than subjects in the two control conditions.

Mischel and Moore (1980) also provided data documenting the powerful role of ideations in determining self-control. Subjects in that study delayed gratification in order to obtain an additional quantity of a preferred food. During the period of waiting, one third of the subjects saw a slide depicting foods between which they had chosen in expressing their preference. Thus, they saw both the preferred and the rejected food. One third saw a slide of two other foods not relevant to the contingency (i.e., these foods were not otherwise involved in the experiment as far as the subjects knew). One third of the subjects saw no slide. Within each slide condition, consummatory relevant subjects thought about consummatory aspects of the two food choices (e.g., if they chose between marshmallows and pretzels, they thought about how yummy marshmallows and pretzels are). Consummatory-irrelevant subjects thought about the yumminess of foods other than the ones on which they made a decision. No-ideation control subjects did not ideate.

In previous work, Mischel and Moore (1973) had shown that exposure to slides of relevant rewards led to longer delays than exposure to slides of irrelevant rewards, presumably because the relevant pictures reminded the subjects of the contingency between their waiting and receiving the reward. However, in Mischel and Moore (1980), the positive effect of viewing the relevant slide was wiped out by the instruction to ideate about the consummatory aspects of the relevant foods. In general, ideation instructions were a much more powerful determinant of behavior than the content of the slides. Consummatory-relevant ideations decreased delay and consummatory-irrelevant ideations increased self-control, regardless of the slide presented. See Moore, Mischel, and Zeiss (1976) for additional data substantiating the importance of ideations over setting variables in children's delay of gratification.

Attentional Manipulations. One way to interpret the data on ideations discussed in the last subsection is to argue that delay-increasing ideations direct the *attention* of subjects away from the consummatory and arousing aspects of temptations, whereas delay-decreasing ideations orient the attention of subjects to the rewards. Indeed, the evidence is overwhelming that manipulations that increase attention to arousing properties of rewards decrease control, whereas factors decreasing attention to arousing properties increase control (e.g., Anderson, 1978; Hartig & Kanfer, 1973; Miller, Weinstein, & Karniol, 1978; Mischel et al., 1972; Mischel & Patterson, 1976; Mischel & Underwood, 1974; Moore, 1977; Patterson & Carter, 1979; Perry, Bussey, & Perry, 1975; Perry & Parke, 1975; Sawin & Parke, 1979; Toner et al., 1979; Toner & Smith, 1977). See Pressley (1979) for a complete discussion.

Discussion and Future Research

The data are convincing that even very young children can execute cognitive strategies to increase their resistance to temptation. The evidence is also compelling that the cognitive content of the strategy is a critical determinant of strategy effectiveness. For instance, the type of verbalization a child utters determines whether self-verbalizations increase self-control or not. Also, positive affect induction increases self-control, but negative affect induction decreases it. Attentional manipulations emphasizing nonconsummatory aspects of rewards increase self-control, but drawing attention to consummatory features decreases control.

There are a number of research tactics with respect to cognitive self-control that should be used. Work is needed in comparing the effectiveness of the various cognitive interventions with each other. Only a few studies (e.g., Anderson, 1978; Patterson & Mischel, 1975) have taken this comparative strategy approach.

Further work is also needed documenting children's spontaneous cognitions when confronted with temptation. In particular, more needs to be known about how young children's cognitive activities result in "uncontrolled" behavior. Work such as that of Yates and Mischel (1979) is a good start in this direction. During delay intervals in that study, preschoolers consistently preferred to view stimuli that would produce uncontrolled responding, such as the actual reward rather than a picture of the reward. In addition, preschoolers evidenced little knowledge of strategies to increase self-control, such as knowing stimulus dimensions that increase or decrease self-control. In contrast, older children (e.g., third graders) spontaneously chose less arousing stimuli (e.g., pictures instead of the actual object) to view during the delay interval. They also seemed more aware that choosing these stimuli would increase self-control.

One striking aspect of the literature on cognitive effects in resistance to temptation is that very few of the studies were conducted developmentally (i.e., most included children at a single age level, usually preschoolers). One probable reason for this is that as children get older, their self-control improves dramatically. Nonetheless, even older children (e.g., sixth graders) exhibit some deficiencies in self-control. Thus, it is important to do self-control research spanning a wider age range than has typically been included in previous studies. It is encouraging to note that in recent years there has been a tendency to conduct multiple-age studies in investigations of cognitive control (e.g., Miller et al., 1978; Yates et al., 1981; Yates & Mischel, 1979).

There are undoubtedly many other cognitive strategies and processes that can positively affect self-control in children. It is hoped that investigators will creatively examine extant cognitive theory and data with an eye toward designing such interventions. Exemplary recent contributions in this vein include work in attribution theory showing that by changing subjects' representations of themselves it is possible to affect self-control (e.g., Perry, Perry, Bussey, English, & Arnold, 1980; Toner, Moore, & Emmons, 1980). Also, Kanfer, Stifter, and Morris (1981) demonstrated that how one feels about the beneficiary of one's delay behaviors is a determinant of self-control.

Effects of Cognitive Strategies in Modifying Impulsive Behaviors

The cognitive dimension of reflection-impulsivity (Kagan, Rosman, Day, Albert, & Phillips, 1964) refers to the manner in which people respond to problems under conditions of high response uncertainty. People who respond very rapidly and fail to consider all of the possible alternatives, and consequently make many errors, are labeled impulsive. Conversely, people who weigh all of the possible alternatives and take longer to respond and make fewer errors are labeled reflective. The most frequently employed instrument to measure the dimension of reflection-impulsivity is the Matching Familiar Figures (MFF) test (Kagan et al., 1964; Kagan, 1966). The MFF consists of 12 items that require the subject to select, from an array of perceptually similar drawings, the one drawing that exactly matches the standard. Amount of time taken to respond initially (latency) and the number of errors are recorded. Researchers commonly employ a median split to classify subjects as reflective or impulsive. Individuals who respond above the median in response time and below the median in errors are labeled reflective. Individuals who respond below the median in response time and above the median in errors are labeled impulsive. Messer (1976) noted the limitations of using a median split procedure for classification, and consequently established preliminary norms for the MFF.

The impulsive child, in contrast to the reflective child, has been characterized as less attentive, less able to inhibit motor responding, more aggressive, more pessimistic about overcoming obstacles, and less mature in moral judgment (Messer, 1976). Furthermore, Messer (1976) discusses the relationship between impulsivity and educational problems. He noted that impulsive children perform less well in school, are less adept at problem solving, and are more likely to have reading problems. Moreover, impulsivity is found in greater proportion among children from special populations, such as the learning disabled, mentally retarded, hyperactive, brain damaged, and epileptic (Messer, 1976).

Researchers have attempted to teach impulsive children cognitive strategies for self-control to help them process information more completely and efficiently. The two most widely researched interventions, attention training and self-instructional training, will be discussed below.

Self-Instructional Training

Soviet research and theorizing concerning the developmental relationships between language and behavior (e.g., Luria, 1961; Vygotsky, 1962) have contributed to the development of intervention programs designed to modify impulsivity. One of the primary components of these interventions is teaching impulsive children to use directive self-instructions to slow down and think carefully. Palkes, Stewart, and Kahana (1968) conducted one of the earliest studies of this genre. Palkes et al. (1968) trained hyperactive boys to use a verbal self-direction strategy in solving perceptual-motor tasks. Experimental subjects received 1 hour of training in which they were taught to verbalize overtly the commands to "stop, listen, look, and think" before responding to a task. A control group of hyperactive boys were exposed to the same training tasks but they did not receive directive self-verbalization training. Although the two groups did not differ in their performance on Porteus (1955) maze problems at pretesting, the experimental subjects significantly outperformed the control subjects at posttesting. Specifically, the experimental subjects "cut fewer corners, crossed over fewer lines, lifted their pencils less, and threaded the maze with fewer irregular lines than did the control group" (p. 823). These results were later replicated by Palkes, Stewart, and Freedman (1972).

Meichenbaum and Goodman (1971) developed a more comprehensive intervention program for modifying impulsive behavior. Their self-instructional training procedure was designed to teach impulsive children to replace their maladaptive sequence of behaviors with directive self-instructions and adaptive problem-solving strategies. A multicomponent procedure including modeling, overt and covert rehearsal of self-statements, prompts, feedback, and social reinforcement were employed to facilitate the acquisition of verbal self-instructions and concomitant less impulsive behavior. The self-instructional training procedure served as the vehicle for training impulsive children to use new and more efficient cognitive strategies when confronted with a problem. The training procedures followed a specific sequence of steps that parallels the Soviet position that external behavior precedes speech in a developmental progression. In the sequence:

1. The child observes the therapist as the therapist guides his or her performance via overt self-instructions.
2. The child performs the task while the therapist guides the child's performance.
3. The child performs the task while guiding his or her own performance via overt self-instructions.
4. Overt self-instructions are faded as the child guides his or her performance via whispering self-instructions.
5. The child performs the task while guiding his or her own performance via covert self-instructions.

Through this sequence, the child is taught several problem-solving strategies: (1) defining the problem; (2) focusing attention and response guidance; (3) self-reinforcement; and (4) coping statements.

Meichenbaum and Goodman (1971) reported two studies in which they utilized their self-instructional training procedure to reduce the impulsive behavior of hyperactive school children. In the first study they compared the relative efficacy of four half-hour sessions of self-instructional training to attention-control and assessment-control conditions. Subjects in the attention-control group were exposed to the same training materials and had the same opportunity as the experimental group to perform the training tasks, but without training in directive self-instructions. The subjects' performance was assessed at pretest, posttest, and follow-up on the Porteus Maze Test, MFF latencies and errors, and three performance subtests of the WISC. In addition, the children's classroom behavior was rated by observers and classroom teachers. The results across all of the paper-and-pencil measures indicated at least a trend toward superior performance by the self-instructional treatment subjects. However, the improvements did not generalize to the classroom ratings. Analyses of posttest performance relative to pretest performance further demonstrated the superiority of the self-instructional procedure. The self-instructional group also maintained their improved performance at a 1-month follow-up.

In the second study, Meichenbaum and Goodman (1971) examined the relative efficacy of cognitive modeling and cognitive modeling plus self-instructional training in modifying cognitive impulsivity. Fifteen cognitively impulsive kindergarten and first-grade children were assigned to either a cognitive modeling condition, cognitive modeling plus self-instruction condition, or an attention-control condition. Subjects in the cognitive modeling condition observed the therapist as he or she verbalized self-instructions and demonstrated the strategies that reflective children use to solve visual discrimination matching tasks like the MFF. After observing the model, children were given the opportunity to perform a similar task and received encouragement and social reinforcement for using the modeled strategy. Subjects in the cognitive modeling plus self-instruction condition were exposed to the same behavior by the therapist, but in addition, they were trained to use directive self-instructions. Subjects in the attention-control condition observed the therapist perform a task and were given an opportunity to perform the same tasks. At posttesting (after one 20-minute training session) both treatment groups significantly increased their decision time (latency) relative to their pretest performance on the matching tasks. The cognitive modeling plus self-instruction group slowed down the most and was significantly different from the cognitive modeling alone group with respect to decision time. Furthermore, only subjects who received self-instructional training (in addition to cognitive modeling) significantly reduced their errors relative to the other two groups and to their pretest performance.

Bender (1976) extended the work of Meichenbaum and Goodman (1971) and further investigated the contribution made by the various components of the self-instructional training procedure. Bender compared five conditions: (1) verbal self-instruction training in which children were taught to verbalize specific problem-solving strategies; (2) therapist modeling of specific problem-solving strategies; (3) general verbal self-instruction training in which children were trained to verbalize the self-instructions to "go slowly and find the match" (p. 348) but not any specific strategies; (4) attention control; and (5) assessment control. The inclusion of the five conditions enabled Bender to compare the differential contributions of self-verbalization versus therapist verbalization, and direct strategy training versus no direct strategy training. Subjects were 70 impulsive first-grade students. The four experimental conditions received 10–25 minutes of training on each of 4 consecutive days. Each child had the same number of trials on the same materials. Subjects were tested immediately after each training session on a visual discrimination matching test like the MFF, and on the MFF following completion of the training sessions.

Analyses of the immediate posttest data indicated that the self-verbalization condition was significantly more effective than the therapist verbalization condition in increasing response latencies and reducing errors. Additional analyses revealed that explicit strategy training was significantly more effective than no explicit strategy training for increasing response latencies but not for decreasing total errors. Post hoc analyses revealed that the verbal self-instruction strategy-training condition was significantly more effective than the other conditions in increasing response latencies. Response latencies in the other conditions did not differ significantly from each other. A similar nonsignificant trend was found for total errors. Analyses of the MFF posttest data did not reveal significant differences among the various conditions. Thus, the treatment effects either did not generalize to the MFF test, or were highly transient and were not maintained at posttesting (1 day after completion of the four training sessions). Bender (1976) suggested that the training period was too short to allow for a transfer of the training effect.

Nelson and Birkimer (1978) evaluated the relative efficacy of the various components of Meichenbaum and Goodman's self-instructional training procedure. Their study was designed to determine whether both the self-instruction and the self-reinforcement components were necessary to produce change in an impulsive response style. Forty-eight impulsive second and third graders (as measured by the MFF) were divided into four groups: (1) self-instruction training without self-reinforcing statements; (2) self-instruction training with self-reinforcing statements; (3) attention control; and (4) assessment control. The training techniques for the experimental groups were similar to those of Meichenbaum and Goodman (1971). The attention-control group received the same training as the experimental groups, but without the self-verbalization training. Subjects' performance was assessed at pretreatment and posttreatment with the MFF. Analyses of the MFF data indicated that children in the self-instruction condition with self-reinforcing statements made significantly fewer errors and had significantly longer response latencies from pretest to posttest. No significant changes were found for subjects in any of the other conditions. These results suggest that it is necessary to include the self-reinforcement component (statements) of the self-instructional training procedure in order to modify impulsive behavior.

A number of researchers have expanded on Meichenbaum and Goodman's (1971) self-instructional training procedure and have successfully employed it to modify the impulsive cognitive style of schoolchildren in the regular classroom (latency scores only on the MFF; Genshaft & Hirt, 1979), children diagnosed as hyperactive (both latency and error scores on the MFF; Douglas, Parry, Marton, & Garson, 1976), children diagnosed as emotionally disturbed (both error and latency scores of the MFF; Finch, Wilkinson, Nelson, & Montgomery, 1975), and children in a Head Start program (Arnold & Forehand, 1978). Further support for the efficacy of this procedure is offered by Bornstein and Quevillon (1976), who dramatically increased the on-task behavior of three "overactive" preschoolers following self-instructional training; and by Snyder and White (1979), who reported a significant decrease in the impulsive behaviors (i.e., drug taking, physical aggression, stealing, and destruction of property) of institutionalized adolescents following self-instructional training.

Attention Training and the Modification of Impulsivity

Although there has not been a great deal of research on the effects of self-verbalizations on impulsive children's attention, the available evidence indicates that self-verbalization by impulsive children influences their attention. Goodman's (1974) dissertation at the University of Waterloo continues to be one of the most analytical studies of the problem. Goodman (1974) first showed that while doing the MFF, impulsive children's attentional deployment differs from that of normal children. Specifically, the eye movements of normal children were much more systematic than those of impulsive children, with more thorough visual analyses of the stimulus array by the normal children, accompanied by a progressive narrowing of attention to the most relevant stimuli in the array. In a follow-up study, impulsive children were taught a self-verbalization strategy for the modification of impulsivity. This training increased the systematicity of scanning in the impulsives. Thus, it may be that positive self-verbalization effects are actually due to the changes in attention they produce. Given that attention modification is a possible explanation of why self-verbalization increases performance, it is noteworthy that investigators have attempted to modify attention directly without training self-verbalization as a mediator. It is to that research that attention now turns.

There have been two general approaches to modifying children's attention. One tactic has been to instruct children explicitly to change their information processing of visually presented materials. When impulsive children have been explicitly instructed about how to deploy their attention in visual discrimination tasks, their impulsive behaviors in those tasks have been greatly reduced. That is, they take more time in making decisions and make fewer errors (e.g., Albert, 1970; Cole & Hartley, 1978; Egeland, 1974; Heider, 1971; Nelson, 1968).

Egeland's (1974) study is a good example of this type of work. In that study impulsive children in the experimental condition were taught to do matching-to-sample visual discrimination tasks by scanning all of the alternatives. The subjects were instructed to:

1. Look at the standard and *all* the alternatives.
2. Break the alternatives down into component parts.
3. Select one component part and compare it across all alternatives. Look for similarities and differences across alternatives on the particular component part being studied.
4. Check the standard to determine the correct form of the component part.
5. Successively eliminate alternatives that deviate from the standard on the particular component being studied. Continue to eliminate alternatives based on an analysis of component parts until only the correct alternative remains. (p. 167)

After training, the children in the experimental group completed the MFF in a less impulsive fashion than untrained control subjects. Interestingly, Egeland (1974) observed general academic improvement in his trained subjects, with better reading comprehension for trained versus untrained children. However, it should be noted that this observation of generalization is an isolated one; other researchers have failed to observe generalization to academics after attention strategy training (e.g., Albert, 1970; Nelson, 1968).

A second approach to attention modification has not involved direct instruction, but evaluates the facilitative effects of various training tasks designed to direct subjects' attention to relevant processing dimensions. Most of this work has been conducted by Tamar Zelnicker and her colleagues. Zelnicker, Jeffrey, Ault, and Parsons (1972) presented three tasks to groups of reflective and impulsive 9-year-olds. Control subjects were presented with three MFF tasks in succession. Experimental subjects were presented with an MFF task, then a discriminating familiar figures (DFF) task, and finally a second MFF task. Whereas in the MFF task subjects must pick a match for a standard from an array of perceptually similar items, in the DFF task the subject must find an object that is different from the standard in an array of figures. In doing this second task, experimental subjects' attention was drawn to the possible dimensions of differences between figures. Thus, when subjects picked an item identical to the standard from the array (i.e., the subject made an error), the subject was asked to show the difference between the standard and the choice.

The critical dependent variable in Zelnicker et al. (1972) was performance on the third MFF task. Among impulsive subjects, there were dramatic processing differences on this task between subjects given three MFFs and those give the MFF-DFF-MFF sequence. The experimental impulsive subjects examined the standards and choices more completely and made many more visual comparisons between the standards and choices. In a series of follow-up experiments (Zelnicker & Oppenheimer, 1973, 1976), Zelnicker and her colleagues offered additional evidence indicating that visual discrimination exercises emphasizing differences between objects can modify visual analysis skills of impulsive children.

Unfortunately, Zelnicker's original work has not inspired follow-up research, and this is somewhat disappointing. It should be noted, however, that in recent years psychologists have become increasingly interested in materials- and/or task-induced modifications in cognitive processing, and there is increasing speculation that such task-induced modifications may lead to permanent changes in processing approaches (see Pressley, 1983, for a discussion). Thus, we do not think that the Zelnicker work is merely of historical significance. Instead, we feel that if interest in the impulsivity treatment area turns to creating materials to assist in the rehabilitation of impulsives, then the studies of Zelnicker and her associates may prove to be invaluable.

When one contrasts attention strategy directions (e.g., Egeland, 1974) with self-verbalization instructions (e.g., Meichenbaum, 1977), they seem to differ only in that attention instructions do not include the self-verbalization component. Is there really a difference between the verbal self-instruction and attention-training procedures? Perhaps both boil down to attention training, as suggested by Goodman's (1974) dissertation results. Alternatively, perhaps they do produce differential effects, and additional profit might be gained by a combined approach. Only recently has a direct test of the two procedures been reported that suggests preliminary resolutions of these issues.

Parrish and Erickson (1981) included (1) an attention-training condition with directions similar to the ones used by Egeland (1974), (2) a verbal self-instruction condition using procedures similar to those employed by Meichenbaum (e.g., 1977; Meichenbaum & Goodman, 1971), (3) a combined attention-training and verbal self-instruction condition, and (4) a no-strategy control condition. Impulsive children in all three of the training conditions improved MFF performance and improved performance on academic materials similar to the ones used during training. Subjects in all three training conditions outperformed no-strategy control subjects on the posttests. However, the performance differences among the three treatment conditions were minimal.

Thus, the Parrish and Erickson (1981) data support the hypothesis that verbal self-instruction and attention training may be training the same underlying processes. However, caution must be exercised in interpreting these results, and the conclusions should be accepted as only tentative. First, it is always difficult to draw conclusions from results showing no differences among conditions, but the problem is compounded when the conditions include too few subjects in order to have reasonable statistical power for detecting differences between conditions. This was the case in the study of Parrish and Erickson (1981), which included only six subjects per condition. Second, the measures taken by Parrish and Erickson (1981) were not nearly as process oriented as they could have been. Visual scanning measures such as those obtained by Goodman (1974) and measures of verbalization as in Kendall and Finch (1979b) should be collected in such strategy comparison studies in order to obtain better clues to the processing consequences of different types of instruction. It is hoped that the general insensitivity of researchers in this area to more direct process measures will decline in the near future.

From the foregoing review, and the programmatic line of research to be described below, it is clear that training cognitive strategies (i.e., attention training and self-instructional training) is a viable treatment for impulsive behavior. However, as we will indicate at the end of this section, these studies are not totally free from criticism.

Cognitive-Behavioral Intervention: A Programmatic Example

A systematic program of research that has focused on the efficacy of a cognitive-behavioral treatment of impulsivity has been conducted by Philip Kendall (1981a, 1982) and colleagues (Kendall & Braswell, 1982; Kendall & Finch, 1976, 1978, 1979b; Kendall & Wilcox, 1979, 1980; Kendall & Zupan, 1981; Kendall, Zupan, & Braswell, 1981). In our opinion, the sum of this research is a noteworthy contribution to the literature on the treatment of self-control problems in children. As such, we will describe this research in some detail.

In their initial investigation, Kendall and Finch (1976) reported a case study in which treatment consisted of self-instructional training combined with a response-cost contingency. The subject was a 9-year-old impulsive boy seen at a children's outpatient psychiatric clinic. Multiple outcome measures were used, including the MFF and observations of target behaviors ("switches" in behavior with respect to conversation topics, games played with, and rules of play).

Generalization of treatment effects was examined by (1) varying the treatment setting (different room with new walls, rugs, view, etc.); (2) changing the array of games (which had previously been held constant); and (3) changing the therapist. Results showed an increase in mean latency on the MFF from 4.59 seconds to 18.73 seconds with errors reduced from nine to five. The frequency of switches in the three behaviors decreased dramatically and was maintained during the generalization phase. A follow-up 6 months later showed a mean latency of 24.7 seconds and four errors on the MFF. Furthermore, the authors indicated that unsolicited reports from the subject's classroom teacher suggested improvement in his study skills and effort in the classroom.

Following this study, Kendall and Finch (1978) conducted a control group investigation to examine the efficacy of the cognitive-behavioral treatment. Subjects were 20 new admissions to a treatment clinic who met the criteria of a mean MFF latency score of 8.5 seconds or less and an error rate of 7 or more. Subjects were quite heterogeneous with regard to specific diagnosis (e.g., adjustment reactions of childhood or adolescence, overanxious, neurotic, aggressive, as well as psychotic organic brain damage). Conditions included an experimental group that received verbal self-instruction training coupled with a response-cost contingency for errors made during training, and a control group. Both groups also received exposure to training materials. All subjects received six 20-minute sessions. Assessment measures at pre- and posttest and at a 2-month follow-up included the MFF, Impulse Control Categorization Instrument (ICCI, Matsushima, 1964), Impulsivity Scale (IS, Hirschfield, 1965), Impulsive Classroom Behavior Scale (ICBS, Weinriech, 1975) and the Locus of Conflict Scale (LOC, Armentrout, 1971).

Results on the MFF showed a significant increase in latency and a significant reduction in errors for the experimental group but not for the control group. The experimental treatment gains were maintained at the 2-month follow-up. Differences between groups on MFF latency and error scores were significant at both posttesting and follow-up. Analysis of scores on the IS and ICCI, on the other hand, indicated nonsignificant main effects for groups and assessment periods. Results on the ICBS were somewhat confounded as a result of a significant difference between groups at pretesting, with controls manifesting significantly lower impulsivity scores. Furthermore, the control group showed a significant increase in ICBS impulsivity scores from pre- to posttest, while the experimental group showed a significant decrease. Trends for both groups continued at follow-up.

Abikoff and Ramsey (1979) reanalyzed Kendall and Finch's (1978) data using an analysis of covariance to adjust for initial group differences. As one might expect, when adjusted means were examined, differences between groups on posttest and follow-up ICBS scores were nonsignificant. Abikoff and Ramsey (1979) concluded that there was no evidence to support the efficacy of the cognitive-behavioral treatment, a conclusion subsequently rebutted by Kendall and Finch (1979a). Both sets of investigators, however, failed to point out that the MFF, which is more widely used than the nine-item ICBS as a measure of impulsivity, did differentiate between groups at posttest and follow-up, but revealed no differences between groups at pretest. Thus, a question arises regarding the utility of the ICBS as a measure of impulsivity.

In an attempt to measure change in self-verbalizations resulting from a cognitive-behavioral intervention for impulsivity, Kendall and Finch (1979b) examined six categories of verbal behavior among groups of impulsive subjects who received treatment, impulsive subjects who did not receive treatment (controls), and subjects who were reflective (MFF latency $\geq$ 16 seconds, fewer than 5 errors). Verbal behavior was recorded during each child's performance on the MFF at each of the three assessment points. Results were inconclusive. Nonsignificant effects were obtained for the five specific verbal codes. Impulsive subjects who received treatment showed a significant increase in total on-task verbal behaviors from pretest to posttest. This gain, however, was negated at follow-up, where verbal behaviors were assessed at a level similar to that found on the pretest. As the authors note, difficulty exists in inferring "internalization" of verbal behavior from children's self-statements.

This last point alludes to a critical issue underlying all of the studies cited above—assessment methodology. Clearly, assessment is a complex issue of great importance if treatment efficacy, maintenance, and generalization are to be demonstrated. Reviews and commentaries on this topic have recently appeared in the literature and will not be discussed in detail in this chapter. The interested reader is directed to articles and/or chapters by Cole and Kazdin (1980), Kendall (1981b), Kendall and Hollon (1981), Kendall and Korgeski (1979), and Kendall, Pellegrini, and Urbain (1981).

In an effort to improve upon assessment methodology, Kendall and Wilcox (1979) developed the Self-Control Rating Scale (SCRS), a 33-item teacher or parent scale for rating children's cognitive-behavioral self-control. In subsequent investigations by Kendall and his colleagues to be cited, the SCRS was used as a consistent outcome measure for evaluating the effectiveness of various treatment interventions on children's self-control. Thus, a brief description of this measure and its psychometric qualities precedes discussion of those investigations.

Self-Control Rating Scale items were written to conform to a cognitive-behavioral description of self-control and clinical and research descriptions of impulsivity. Ten items pertain to self-control (e.g., "Does the child stick to what he or she is doing until he or she is finished with it?"), 13 items pertain to impulsivity (e.g., "Does the child grab for the belongings of others?"), and 10 items have both possibilities (e.g., "Does the child interrupt inappropriately in conversations with peers, or wait his or her turn to speak?"). Items are rated from 1 (maximum self-control) to 7 (maximum impulsivity) with a score of 4 (the scale's physical mean) indicating where the average child would be rated on the item.

Kendall and Wilcox (1979) report internal consistency reliability (coefficient alpha) of .98 with a sample of 110 children from Grades 3–6, and test-retest reliability (with a 3- to 4-week interval) of .84 with a subsample of 24 children. Correlations between the SCRS and MFF errors and latency, Porteus maze Q scores, and total behavioral observation scores were statistically significant, but of weak (Marascuilo, 1971) magnitude, ranging from −.19 (MFF latencies) to .35 (Porteus Q). A significant difference in SCRS scores was obtained between 32 children referred because of self-control problems and a matched group of 32 nonreferred children, suggesting contrasted-group validity. In a subsequent report, Kendall et al. (1981) provided further evidence as to the validity of the SCRS. While the data are not overwhelmingly positive, they do lend some support for the utility of the SCRS.

Kendall and Wilcox (1980) examined the differential effectiveness of concrete versus conceptual self-instructional training as components of a cognitive-behavioral treatment for impulsivity. The concrete approach was designed so that self-instructional training was worded in a task-specific manner. The conceptual approach utilized more globally worded directions that would apply to a variety of problem situations. The authors hypothesized that the conceptual training procedures would show greater behavior change and facilitate greater generalization of treatment effects. An attention-control group was also included. Subjects were 33 8- to 12-year-olds who received six 30- to 40-minute treatment sessions spread over a 3-week period.

In the concrete training condition, children were instructed to self-verbalize with reference only to the task at hand. For instance, the following self-verbalizations were taught for an oddity discrimination task:

> Problem definition: I'm going to find the picture that doesn't match.
> Problem approach: This one's a clock, this one's a clock, this is a cup and saucer, and this one is a clock.
> Focusing of attention: Look at the pictures.
> Self-reinforcement: The cup and saucer are different (check answer sheet). I got it right. Good job!
> Coping statement: Oh, it's not the clock that's different, it's the teacup. I can pick out the correct one next time. (p. 83)

Kendall and Wilcox (1980) reasoned that generalization of treatment effects would be more likely to occur if subjects were taught self-verbalizations that were not so tightly tied to the actual tasks used in training. Thus, for the same oddity discrimination problem, subjects in the conceptual training condition were taught to self-verbalize in the following fashion:

> Problem definition: My first step is to make sure I know what I'm supposed to do.
> Problem approach: Well, I should look at all the possibilities.
> Focusing of attention: I should think about only what I'm doing right now.
> Self-reinforcement: (Checking the answer sheet) Hey, good job. I'm doing very well.
> Coping statement: Well, if I make a mistake I can remember to think more carefully next time, and then I'll do better. (p. 83)

Throughout training in both of the self-instruction conditions, the therapist first modeled the use of the self-verbalization strategy overtly. Then subjects self-verbalized overtly. Then the trainer self-verbalized in a whisper and the subject was subsequently required to do likewise. Gradually, the initially overt strategy was made covert. A cue card telling the child to "stop, listen, look, and think" was continually available. Also, whenever a child made a mistake, a token was taken away; thus, the procedures of the study were not entirely cognitive. In the last two training sessions, the children were explicitly encouraged to extend the self-instructional tactics they had learned to their classrooms and everyday life. Subjects in the attention-control condition also had six "therapy" sessions involving the same practice materials, but were not taught any strategies to use with the materials.

Multiple treatment-outcome measures were obtained at pretreatment, posttreatment, and 1-month follow-up. Scores on the Porteus mazes (Q score, pencil lifts, test age), MFF (latency and errors), ICCI, and SCRS failed to show significant between-group differences. Analysis of SCRS ratings across assessment times, however, did reveal the following: Ratings of the conceptual group improved significantly from pretreatment to posttreatment and to 1-month follow-up. The

concrete group also made significant pre- to posttreatment gains, but these were not maintained at follow-up. Finally, the control group did not show significant improvement in ratings at either posttreatment or follow-up assessments. These results suggest that more general instructions may be more likely to lead to increased self-control. Interested readers are referred to Schleser, Meyers, and Cohen (1981) for additional data documenting that more general instructions produce more general self-control effects, as well as to Kendall and Finch's (1979c) discussion of the Kendall and Wilcox (1980) data.

Kendall (1981a) reported a 1-year follow-up (1 year after the 1-month follow-up) of the cognitive-behavioral treatment conducted by Kendall and Wilcox (1980). Unfortunately, only 17 of the 33 children were located (7 from the concrete, 4 from the conceptual, and 6 from the attention-control group). Conceptually trained children, when interviewed, showed significantly better recall of the training material than either the concrete or control group children. Documentation of long-term treatment effectiveness as assessed by the treatment-outcome measures was impeded by the small sample size.

Kendall and Zupan (1981) conducted a study in which individual and group treatments utilizing cognitive-behavioral self-control training, as well as a nonspecific treatment-control group, were compared. Subjects were 30 children from Grades 3–5 who were referred by their teachers because of lack of self-control. All subjects received 12 45- to 55-minute treatment sessions conducted over a 6-week period. All subjects received similar tasks, instructions, and performance feedback. In addition to this, the experimental groups recieved cognitive-behavioral self-control training in either an individual or group therapy format. The cognitive-behavioral treatment conditions received verbal self-instruction training via modeling, along with rewards for correct performance and behavior and response-cost contingencies for errors during training. The major components of the self-instruction were similar to those used by Kendall and Wilcox (1980). In the last four sessions, cognitive-behavioral strategies aimed at enhancing subjects' cognitive awareness of emotions and interpersonal skills were implemented.

Outcome measures included the MFF (Egeland & Weinberg, 1976, alternate forms), the Means-Ends Problem-Solving (MEPS) test (Spivack & Shure, 1974), SCRS, Chandler's (1973) social role-taking test, and Conners's (1969) hyperactivity rating scale. At posttreatment, both experimental groups showed significant improvement in SCRS scores from pretreatment, and were also significantly lower than the nonspecific treatment group, although not different from each other. All three groups manifested improved performance on the MFF, hyperactivity scale, and role-taking test, and significant decreases in MEPS scores. Between-group differences were not evident at posttreatment on any of these four measures.

At a 2-month follow-up, individual and group cognitive-behavioral treatment groups maintained significant improvement on the SCRS, but did not differ significantly from the control group. Similar results were found on the hyperactivity ratings and on the MFF errors (but not on latency scores). MEPS scores similarly maintained performance decrements. Both experimental groups maintained improvement at follow-up, while the control group did not.

Subsequently, Kendall (1982) presented data from a 1-year follow-up on 23 of the 30 children, and added another comparison group of nonproblem children from Grades 2–5. At 1-year follow-up, all treatment groups maintained significant differences from pretreatment on the SCRS, hyperactivity ratings, MEPS, MFF latencies and errors, and the role-taking test. In comparison to nonproblem children, children receiving group treatment did not differ significantly on the SCRS; children receiving individual treatment did not differ significantly on the hyperactivity ratings. Interviews with the children indicated that subjects in the individual therapy group were significantly better at recalling what they had learned and provided more examples of how they used this information than either the group treatment or control group.

The most recent study by Kendall and his colleagues examining cognitive-behavioral therapy for self-control is an impressive component analysis investigation conducted by Kendall and Braswell (1982). Subjects were 27 teacher-referred children from Grades 3–6 who exhibited non-self-controlled behavior. Experimental groups were a cognitive behavior therapy group and a behavior therapy group. Treatment consisted of 12 45- to 55-minute sessions spread over 6 weeks. An attention-control group, in which subjects also received 12 sessions involving similar therapy (training) materials but no cognitive or behavioral treatment components, was also included.

The cognitive behavior therapy was similar to that used in the investigation by Kendall and Zupan (1981), with self-instructions consistent with the conceptual-style approach by Kendall and Wilcox (1980). The behavioral treatment group was exposed to the same training materials as the cognitive-behavioral and attention-control groups, but unlike the cognitive-behavioral group it received neither self-instructional training nor cognitive modeling in problem solving. The behavioral group differed from the attention-control group by the inclusion of reward and response-cost contingencies.

Outcome measures included the SCRS, Conners's hyperactivity scale, the MFF, Wide Range Achievement Scale (WRAT); Jastak, Bijou, & Jastak, 1965), Piers-Harris Children's Self-Control Scale (PH; Piers & Harris, 1969), and behavioral observations of six classroom behaviors. Hyperactivity ratings and SCRS were completed by both teachers and parents.

Results of the MFF latency scores showed significant improvement by the cognitive-behavioral and behavioral groups from pretreatment to posttreatment. Only the behavioral group maintained significant changes between pretreatment and 10-week follow-up assessment. All three groups showed significant reduction in MFF errors between pretreatment and posttreatment and 10-week follow-up. On the WRAT, only the cognitive-behavioral group showed significant change between pretreatment and posttreatment scores on the reading subtest, although all three groups manifested significant reading score gains between pretreatment and 10-week follow-up. Both the cognitive-behavioral and behavior therapy groups showed significant changes from pretreatment to posttreatment and to 10-week follow-up on WRAT spelling and math scores. Differences between groups for MFF latency and error scores and for all achievement scores were nonsignificant.

Teacher ratings of self-control on the SCRS showed that the cognitive-behavioral group was significantly more improved at posttreatment and 10-week follow-up than either the behavioral or attention-control group. Furthermore, only the cognitive-behavioral group showed significant improvement from pretreatment at posttreatment and 10-week follow-up. On the self-concept measure, only the cognitive-behavioral group manifested significantly improved self-concept scores from pretreatment to posttreatment and to follow-up. Between-group differences, however, were nonsignificant.

Space limitations preclude extensive descriptions of results on all outcome measures utilized by Kendall and Braswell (1982). The interested reader is directed to the original research report for further edification. Overall, the results at post-treatment and 10-week follow-up tend to favor the cognitive-behavioral treatment. The authors (Kendall & Braswell, 1982) note (and rightly so) that because of inconsistent effects found on outcome measures, caution must be used in inter-preting the data. Kendall and Braswell (1982) also conducted a 1-year follow-up of 20 subjects. All three groups showed significant improvement on MFF latency and errors, and WRAT reading, math, and spelling. At the 1-year follow-up, signifi-cant group differences previously found were no longer evident on any of the outcome measures.

Summary. The results of the investigations by Kendall and colleagues on the efficacy of cognitive-behavioral treatments for self-control in children are mixed, but provide some support for cognitive-behavioral therapy. That results are incon-sistent depending on different outcome measures suggests two things. First, non-self-controlled behavior is difficult to assess in children. Second, significant gains in self-controlled behavior or its analog can be realized in children, although the exact mechanism responsible for these gains remains unclear.

A number of methodological concerns come to our attention in some of the studies (e.g., sample size, therapist characteristics, subjects' level of pathology, failure to set experimentwise error rate, and other concerns). (See Chapter 10 in this book for a detailed discussion of some of these issues.) These concerns are, in our opinion, offset by the noteworthy programmatic path that Kendall and his colleagues have taken in their research on cognitive-behavioral interventions for self-control in children.

Discussion

It is regrettable that impulsivity researchers have devoted so much of their effort to simple visual analysis tasks administered in laboratory settings. When one reads these studies, it is easy to get the impression that investigators in the area are interested only in modifying MFF performance! It is hoped that the development of reliable instruments for assessing impulsivity more globally (e.g., Kendall & Wilcox, 1979) will lead to research concerned with the whole child, not just the child's perceptual-motor discriminations on standard psychometric devices.

The urgency of thinking about the whole child is made obvious by the fact that when impulsivity interventionists have looked for generalization of treatment effects, they usually have found little or inconsistent transfer of training, especially to academic performance. Recently, there has been some rethinking that has resulted in a set of suggestions for redesigning training so that generalization will be more likely.

Some suggestions are very concrete and consistent with behavioral principles of generalization (e.g., Stokes & Baer, 1977), such as varying the settings in which training takes place, varying the training materials, and gradually fading the training out rather than looking for generalization after an abrupt cessation of instructions (Kendall & Finch, 1979b). Others are more concerned with modifying children's cognitions so that they know when to use a strategy and do so. These investigators argue that failure to generalize may be remedied by metacognitive interventions. These interventions include making the child aware of the need for a strategy, making the child knowledgeable about situations in which strategies can be helpful, teaching the child to monitor strategy effects, and getting the child to use knowledge gained through monitoring and feedback to direct future strategy deployment (e.g., Borkowski & Cavanaugh, 1979; Meichenbaum & Asarnow, 1979). Given the widespread attention that metacognitive theory has generated and specifically the growing awareness of its relevance to issues of transfer (e.g., Borkowski, in press; Pressley, Heisel, McCormick, & Nakamura, 1982), it is likely that a great deal of research on metacognition and transfer of self-control strategies will follow in the near future.

General Discussion

If one reads the research literature discussed here from the perspective of a rigorous experimental psychologist, one can point with pride to the large volume of carefully controlled and reasonably analytical research on teaching self-control strategies to children. The research reported here scores high when one assesses internal validity (e.g., Campbell & Stanley, 1966). Nonetheless, internal validity is not the sole criterion used to evaluate the success of a research enterprise.

Most of the studies reviewed here were conducted in laboratory settings using laboratory tasks. In contrast, most self-control problems experienced by children occur in real-world settings. For clinicians who treat self-control problems, the analyses offered of motor control based on bulb squeezing and of impulsivity based largely on perceptual-motor performance must seem wholly inadequate. Thus, it is fair to conclude that research on strategy intervention and self-control scores low on ecological validity (e.g., Bracht & Glass, 1968). Despite suggestions to the contrary (e.g., Meichenbaum, 1977), a set of real-world cognitive interventions for increasing self-control is not yet a reality. At the same time, it is possible to point with enthusiasm to recent experimental studies of interventions that have been implemented successfully in classrooms and clinical settings (e.g., Kendall & Finch, 1978; Kendall & Wilcox, 1980; Sagotsky, Patterson, & Lepper, 1978). The only way that an effective self-control technology can be developed is for researchers to carry out more of their experiments in naturalistic settings.

The most obvious accomplishment of the studies reported here is that they document that even very young children have the competence to execute a variety of self-control strategies. However, little evidence was provided that children would or could apply the techniques in a setting other than the training setting. When self-control tactics are needed in the real world, the subject must recognize that he or she is in a situation where self-control might be a problem, and must recognize environmental variables that might induce noncontrolled responding. The child must then formulate and execute a strategy for dealing with the problem. In contrast, in most of the studies reviewed here, such a high degree of subject analysis and initiative was not required. Generally, subjects were simply instructed to execute a strategy, with the occasions for strategy execution clearly specified. Much work is needed on training children when to deploy strategies. Metacognitive training procedures may have much to offer for this particular problem (e.g., Meichenbaum & Asarnow, 1979).

In closing, we would argue that the body of research covered here provides reason to believe that it will be possible to develop techniques to aid children in having greater control over themselves. The results of these studies suggest many new avenues that self-control researchers might pursue profitably in order to reach this goal. When one considers the enormous problems associated with poor self-control during childhood, from reading disability (e.g., Margolis & Brannigan, 1978; Roberts, 1979) to conduct disorders (e.g., Paulsen & O'Donnell, 1979), the motivations are great for pursuing the promising directions suggested.

Acknowledgments. The authors wish to thank Karen Kraemer for the typing of this chapter.

References

Abikoff, H., & Ramsey, P. P. A critical comment on Kendall and Finch's cognitive-behavioral group comparison study. *Journal of Consulting and Clinical Psychology*, 1979, *47*, 1104–1106.

Albert, J. A. Modification of the impulsive conceptual style (Doctoral dissertation, University of Illinois, 1969). *Dissertation Abstracts International*, 1970, *30*, 3377B. (University Microfilms No. 70-778)

Anderson, W. H., Jr. A comparison of self-distraction with self-verbalization under moralistic versus instrumental rationales in a delay-of-gratification paradigm. *Cognitive Therapy and Research*, 1978, *2*, 299–303.

Armentrout, J. A. Parental child rearing attitudes and preadolescents' behavior problems. *Journal of Consulting and Clinical Psychology*, 1971, *37*, 278–285.

Arnold, S., & Forehand, R. A comparison of cognitive training and response cost procedures in modifying cognitive styles of impulsive children. *Cognitive Therapy and Research*, 1978, *2*, 183–187.

Bain, B. Verbal regulation of cognitive processes: A replication of Luria's procedures with bilingual and unilingual infants. *Child Development*, 1976, *47*, 543–546.

Beiswenger, H. Luria's model of the verbal control of behavior. *Merrill-Palmer Quarterly*, 1968, *14*, 267–284.

Bender, N. Self-verbalization versus tutor verbalization in modifying impulsivity. *Journal of Educational Psychology*, 1976, *68*, 347–354.

Birch, D. Verbal control of nonverbal behavior. *Journal of Experimental Child Psychology*, 1966, *4*, 266–275.

Blackwood, R. The operant conditioning of verbally mediated self-control in the classroom. *Journal of School Psychology*, 1970, *8*, 257–258.

Borkowski, J. G. Signs of intelligence: Strategy generalization and metacognition. In S. R. Yussen (Ed.), *The development of reflection*. New York: Academic Press, in press.

Borkowski, J. G., & Cavanaugh, J. C. Maintenance and generalization of skills and strategies by the retarded. In N. R. Ellis (Ed.), *Handbook of mental deficiency, psychological theory and research* (2nd ed). Hillsdale, NJ: Erlbaum, 1979.

Bornstein, P., & Quevillon, R. The effects of a self-instructional package on overactive preschool boys. *Journal of Applied Behavior Analysis*, 1976, *9*, 179–188.

Bracht, G. H., & Glass, G. V. The external validity of experiments. *American Educational Research Journal*, 1968, *5*, 437–474.

Bruner, J. S. *Beyond the information given*. New York: W. W. Norton & Co., 1973.

Campbell, D., & Stanley, J. *Experimental and quasi-experimental designs for research*. Chicago: Rand McNally, 1966.

Chandler, M. J. Egocentrism and antisocial behavior: The assessment and training of social perspective-taking skills. *Developmental Psychology*, 1973, *9*, 326–332.

Cheyne, J. A. Punishment and reasoning in the development of self-control. In R. D. Parke (Ed.), *Recent trends in social learning theory*. New York: Academic Press, 1972.

Cheyne, J. A., & Walters, R. H. Intensity of punishment, timing of punishment, and cognitive structure as determinants of response inhibition. *Journal of Experimental Child Psychology*, 1969, *7*, 231–244.

Cole, P. M., & Hartley, D. G. The effects of reinforcement and strategy training on impulsive responding. *Child Development*, 1978, *49*, 381–384.

Cole, P. M., & Kazdin, A. E. Critical issues in self-instruction training with children. *Child Behavior Therapy*, 1980, *2*(2), 1–21.

Connors, C. K. A teacher rating scale for use in drug studies with children. *American Journal of Psychiatry*, 1969, *126*, 884–888.

Douglas, V. I., Parry, P., Marton, P., & Garson, C. Assessment of a cognitive training program for hyperactive children. *Journal of Abnormal Child Psychology*, 1976, *4*, 389–410.

Egeland, B. Training impulsive children in the use of more efficient scanning strategies. *Child Development*, 1974, *45*, 165–171.

Egeland, B., & Weinberg, R. A. The Matching Familiar Figures Test: A look at its psychometric creditability. *Child Development*, 1976, *47*, 483–491.

Finch, A., Wilkinson, M., Nelson, W., & Montgomery, L. Modification of an impulsive cognitive tempo in emotionally disturbed boys. *Journal of Abnormal Child Psychology*, 1975, *3*, 49–52.

Fry, P. S. Success, failure and resistance to temptation. *Developmental Psychology*, 1977, *13*, 519–520.

Genshaft, J., & Hirt, M. Race effects in modifying cognitive impulsivity through self-instruction and modeling. *Journal of Experimental Child Psychology*, 1979, *27*, 185–194.

Golden, M., Montare, A., & Bridger, W. Verbal control of delay behavior in two-year-old boys as a function of social class. *Child Development*, 1977, *48*, 1107–1111.

Goodman, J. B. Impulsive and reflective behavior: A developmental analysis of attentional and cognitive strategies (Doctoral dissertation, University of Waterloo, 1973). *Dissertation Abstracts International*, 1974, *34*, 5190-B.

Hartig, M., & Kanfer, F. The role of verbal self-instructions in children's resistance to temptation. *Journal of Personality and Social Psychology*, 1973, *25*, 259–267.

Heider, E. R. Information processing and the modification of an "impulsive conceptual tempo." *Child Development*, 1971, *42*, 1276–1281.

Hirschfield, P. P. Response set in impulsive children. *Journal of Genetic Psychology*, 1965, *107*, 117–126.

Jarvis, P. E. Verbal control of sensory-motor performance. A test of Luria's hypothesis. *Human Development*, 1968, *11*, 172–183.

Jastak, J. F., Bijou, S. W., & Jastak, S. R. *Wide Range Achievement Test.* Wilmington, DE: Guidance Associates, 1965.

Jensen, L., & Buhanan, K. Resistance to temptation following three types of motivational instructions among four-, six-, and eight-year-old female children. *Journal of Genetic Psychology*, 1974, *125*, 51–59.

Joynt, D., & Cambourne, B. Psycholinguistic development and the control of behavior. *British Journal of Educational Psychology*, 1968, *38*, 249–260.

Kagan, J. Reflection-impulsivity: The generality and dynamics of conceptual tempo. *Journal of Abnormal Psychology*, 1966, *71*, 17–24.

Kagan, J., Rosman, B. L., Day, D., Albert, J., & Phillips, W. Information processing in the child: Significance of analytic and reflective attitudes. *Psychological Monographs*, 1964, *78*(1, Whole No. 578).

Kanfer, F. H., Stifter, E., & Morris, S. J. Self-control and altruism: Delay of gratification for another. *Child Development*, 1981, *52*, 674–682.

Kendall, P. C. One-year follow-up of concrete versus conceptual cognitive-behavioral self-control training. *Journal of Consulting and Clinical Psychology*, 1981, *49*, 748–749. (a)

Kendall, P. C. Assessment and cognitive-behavioral interactions: Purposes, proposals, and problems. In P. C. Kendall & S. D. Hollon (Eds.), *Assessment strategies for cognitive-behavioral interventions.* New York: Academic Press, 1981. (b)

Kendall, P. C. Individual versus group cognitive-behavioral self-control training: 1-year follow-up. *Behavior Therapy*, 1982, *13*, 241–247.

Kendall, P. C., & Braswell, L. Cognitive-behavioral self-control therapy for children: A component analysis. *Journal of Consulting and Clinical Psychology*, 1982, *50*, 672–689.

Kendall, P. C., & Finch, A. J., Jr. A cognitive-behavioral treatment for impulse control: A case study. *Journal of Consulting and Clinical Psychology*, 1976, *44*, 852–857.

Kendall, P. C., & Finch, A. J., Jr. A cognitive-behavioral treatment for impulsivity: A group comparison study. *Journal of Consulting and Clinical Psychology*, 1978, *46*, 110–118.

Kendall, P. C., & Finch, A. J., Jr. Reanalysis: A reply. *Journal of Consulting and Clinical Psychology*, 1979, *47*, 1107–1108. (a)

Kendall, P. C., & Finch, A. J., Jr. Analyses of changes in verbal behavior following a cognitive-behavioral treatment for impulsivity. *Journal of Abnormal Child Psychology*, 1979, *7*, 455–463. (b)

Kendall, P. C., & Finch, A. J., Jr. Developing nonimpulsive behavior in children: Cognitive-behavioral strategies for self-control. In P. C. Kendall & S. D. Hollon (Eds.), *Cognitive-behavioral interventions: Theory, research, and procedures.* New York: Academic Press, 1979. (c)

Kendall, P. C., & Hollon, S. D. Assessing self-referent speech: Methods in the measurement of self-statements. In P. C. Kendall & S. D. Hollon (Eds.), *Assessment strategies for cognitive-behavioral interventions.* New York: Academic Press, 1981.

Kendall, P. C., & Korgeski, G. P. Assessment and cognitive-behavioral interventions. *Cognitive Therapy and Research*, 1979, *3*, 1–21.

Kendall, P. C., Pellegrini, D. S., & Urbain, E. S. Approaches to assessment for cognitive-behavioral interventions with children. In P. C. Kendall & S. D. Hollon (Eds.), *Assessment strategies for cognitive behavioral interventions.* New York: Academic Press, 1981.

Kendall, P. C., & Wilcox, L. E. Self-control in children: Development of a rating scale. *Journal of Consulting and Clinical Psychology*, 1979, *47*, 1020–1029.

Kendall, P. C., & Wilcox, L. E. Cognitive-behavioral treatment for impulsivity: Concrete versus conceptual training in non-self-controlled problem children. *Journal of Consulting and Clinical Psychology*, 1980, *48*, 80–91.

Kendall, P. C., & Zupan, B. A. Individual versus group application of cognitive-behavioral self-control procedures with children. *Behavior Therapy*, 1981, *12*, 344–359.

Kendall, P. C., Zupan, B. A., & Braswell, L. Self-control in children: Further analyses of the Self-Control Rating Scale. *Behavior Therapy*, 1981, *12*, 667–681.

Kohlberg, L. Stage and sequence: The cognitive developmental approach to socialization. In D. A. Goslin (Ed.), *Handbook of socialization theory and research.* Chicago: Rand McNally, 1969.

LaVoie, J. C. Punishment and adolescent self-control. *Developmental Psychology*, 1973, *8*, 16–24.

LaVoie, J. C. Aversive, cognitive, and parental determinant of punishment generalization in adolescent males. *Journal of Genetic Psychology*, 1974, *124*, 29–39. (a)

LaVoie, J. C. Cognitive determinants of resistance to deviation in seven-, nine-, and eleven-year-old children of low and high maturity of moral judgment. *Developmental Psychology*, 1974, *10*, 393–403. (b)

LaVoie, J. C., Anderson, K., Fraze, B., & Johnson, K. Modeling, tuition, and sanction effects on self-control at different ages. *Journal of Experimental Child Psychology*, 1981, *31*, 446–455.

Luria, A. R. The directive function of speech in development and dissolution. *Word*, 1959, *15*, 341–352.

Luria, A. R. *The role of speech in the regulation of normal and abnormal behavior.* New York: Pergamon, 1961.

Luria, A. R. Speech development and the formation of mental processes. In M. Cole & I. Maltzman (Eds.), *Handbook of contemporary Soviet psychology.* New York: Basic Books, 1969.

Luria, A. R. *Language and cognition.* New York: Wiley, 1982.

MacPherson, E. M., Candee, B. L., & Hohman, R. J. A comparison of three methods of eliminating disruptive classroom behavior. *Journal of Applied Behavior Analysis*, 1974, *7*, 287–297.

Mahoney, M. J. *Cognition and behavior modification.* Cambridge, MA: Ballinger, 1974.

Marascuilo, L. A. *Statistical methods for behavioral science research.* New York: McGraw-Hill, 1971.

Margolis, H., & Brannigan, G. G. Conceptual tempo as a parameter for predicting reading achievement. *Journal of Educational Research*, 1978, *71*, 342–345.

Masters, J. C., & Binger, J. C. Interrupting the flow of behavior: The stability and development of children's initiation and maintenance of complaint response inhibition. *Merrill-Palmer Quarterly*, 1978, *24*, 229–242.

Masters, J. C., & Santrock, J. W. Studies in the self-regulation of behavior: Effects of contingent cognitive and affective events. *Developmental Psychology*, 1976, *12*, 334–348.

Matsushima, J. An instrument for classifying impulse control among boys. *Journal of Consulting Psychology*, 1964, *28*, 87–90.

Meacham, J. A. Verbal-motor interactions during sequences of motor activity (Doctoral dissertation, University of Michigan, 1972). *Dissertation Abstracts International*, 1973, *33*, 5545B. (University Microfilm No. 73-11, 205)

Meacham, J. A. Verbal guidance through remembering the goals of actions. *Child Development*, 1978, *49*, 188–193.

Meichenbaum, D. *Cognitive behavior modification.* New York: Plenum, 1977.

Meichenbaum, D., & Asarnow, J. Cognitive-behavioral modification and metacognitive development: Implications for the classroom. In P. C. Kendall & S. D. Hollon (Eds.), *Cognitive-behavioral interventions: Theory, research, and procedures.* New York: Academic Press, 1979.

Meichenbaum, D., & Goodman, J. Training impulsive children to talk to themselves. A means of developing self-control. *Journal of Abnormal Psychology*, 1971, *77*, 115–126.

Messer, S. B. Reflection-impulsivity: A review. *Psychological Bulletin*, 1976, *83*, 1026–1052.

Miller, D. T., Weinstein, S. M., & Karniol, R. Effects of age and self-verbalization on children's ability to delay gratification. *Developmental Psychology*, 1978, *14*, 569–570.

Miller, S. A., Shelton, J., & Flavell, J. H. A test of Luria's hypothesis concerning the development of verbal self-regulation. *Child Development*, 1970, *41*, 651–665.

Mischel, W., & Baker, N. Cognitive appraisals and transformations in delay behavior. *Journal of Personality and Social Psychology*, 1975, *31*, 254–261.

Mischel, W., Ebbesen, E. B., & Zeiss, A. Cognitive and attentional mechanisms in delay of gratification. *Journal of Personality and Social Psychology*, 1972, *21*, 204–218.

Mischel, W., & Moore, B. S. Effects of attention to symbolically presented rewards upon self-control. *Journal of Personality and Social Psychology*, 1973, *28*, 172–179.

Mischel, W., & Moore, B. The role of ideation in voluntary delay for symbolically presented rewards. *Cognitive Therapy and Research*, 1980, *4*, 211–221.

Mischel, W., & Patterson, C. J. Substantive and structural elements of effective plans for self-control. *Journal of Personality and Social Psychology*, 1976, *34*, 942–950.

Mischel, W., & Patterson, C. J. Effective plans for self-control in children. In W. A. Collins (Ed.), *Minnesota symposium on child psychology* (Vol. 11). Hillsdale, NJ: Erlbaum, 1978.

Mischel, W., & Underwood, B. Instrumental ideation in delay of gratification. *Child Development,* 1974, *45,* 1083–1088.

Moore, B. S. Cognitive representation of rewards in delay of gratification. *Cognitive Therapy and Research,* 1977, *1,* 73–83.

Moore, B., Clyburn, A., & Underwood, B. The role of affect in delay of gratification. *Child Development,* 1976, *47,* 273–276.

Moore, B., Mischel, W., & Zeiss, A. Comparative effects of the reward stimulus and its cognitive representation in voluntary delay. *Journal of Personality and Social Psychology,* 1976, *34,* 419–424.

Nelson, T. F. The effects of training in attention deployment on observing behavior in reflective and impulsive children (Doctoral dissertation, University of Minnesota, 1968). *Dissertation Abstracts International,* 1968, *29,* 2659-B. (University Microfilm No. 68-17, 703)

Nelson, W., & Birkimer, J. Role of self-instruction and self-reinforcement in the modification of impulsivity. *Journal of Consulting and Clinical Psychology,* 1978, *46,* 183.

Palkes, H., Stewart, M., & Freedman, J. Improvement in maze performance of hyperactive boys as a function of verbal training procedures. *Journal of Special Education,* 1972, *5,* 337–342.

Palkes, H., Stewart, M., & Kahana, B. Porteus maze performance after training in self-directed verbal commands. *Child Development,* 1968, *39,* 817–826.

Parke, R. D. Effectiveness of punishment as an interaction of intensity, timing, agent nurturance and cognitive structuring. *Child Development,* 1969, *40,* 213–236.

Parke, R. D. The role of punishment in the socialization process. In R. A. Hoppe, G. A. Milton, & E. C. Simmel (Eds.), *Early experiences and the process of socialization.* New York: Academic Press, 1970.

Parke, R. D. Rules, roles, and resistance to deviation in children: Explorations in punishment, discipline, and self-control. In A. Pick (Ed.), *Minnesota symposium on child psychology* (Vol. 8). Minneapolis: University of Minnesota Press, 1974.

Parke, R. D. Punishment in children: Effects, side effects and alternative strategies. In H. L. Hom, Jr., & P. A. Robinson (Eds.), *Psychological processes in early education.* New York: Academic Press, 1977.

Parrish, J. M., & Erickson, M. T. A comparison of cognitive strategies in modifying the cognitive style of impulsive third-grade children. *Cognitive Therapy and Research,* 1981, *5,* 71–84.

Patterson, C. J., & Carter, D. B. Attentional determinants of children's self-control in waiting and working situations. *Child Development,* 1979, *50,* 272–275.

Patterson, C. J., & Mischel, W. Plans to resist distraction. *Developmental Psychology,* 1975, *11,* 369–378.

Patterson, C. J., & Mischel, W. Effects of temptation-inhibiting and task-facilitating plans on self-control. *Journal of Personality and Social Psychology,* 1976, *33,* 209–217.

Paulsen, K., & O'Donnell, J. P. Construct validation of children's behavior problem dimensions: Relationship to activity level, impulsivity, and soft neurological signs. *Journal of Psychology,* 1979, *101,* 273–278.

Perry, D. G., Bussey, K., & Perry, L. Factors influencing the imitation of resistance to deviation. *Developmental Psychology*, 1975, *11*, 724–731.

Perry, D. G., & Parke, R. D. Punishment and alternate response training as determinants of response inhibition in children. *Genetic Psychology Monographs*, 1975, *91*, 257–279.

Perry, D. G., Perry, L. C., Bussey, K., English, D., & Arnold, G. Processes of attribution and children's self-punishment following misbehavior. *Child Development*, 1980, *51*, 545–551.

Piers, E. V., & Harris, D. B. *The Piers-Harris Children's Self-Concept Scale.* Nashville: Counselor Recordings and Tests, 1969.

Porteus, S. D. *The maze test: Recent advances.* Palo Alto, CA: Pacific Books, 1955.

Pressley, M. Increasing children's self-control through cognitive interventions. *Review of Educational Research*, 1979, *49*, 319–370.

Pressley, M. Making meaningful materials easier to learn: Lessons from cognitive strategy research. In M. Pressley & J. R. Levin (Eds.), *Cognitive strategy research: Educational applications.* New York: Springer-Verlag, 1983.

Pressley, M., Heisel, B. E., McCormick, C. G., & Nakamura, G. V. Memory strategy instruction with children. In C. J. Brainerd & M. Pressley (Eds.), *Verbal processes in children.* New York: Springer-Verlag, 1982.

Roberts, T. Reflection-impulsivity and reading ability in seven-year-old children. *British Journal of Educational Psychology*, 1979, *49*, 311–315.

Rondal, J. A. Investigation of the regulatory power of the impulsive and meaningful aspects of speech. *Genetic Psychology Monographs*, 1976, *94*, 3–33.

Sagotsky, G., Patterson, C. J., & Lepper, M. R. Training children's self-control. A field experiment in self-monitoring and goal-setting in the classroom. *Journal of Experimental Child Psychology*, 1978, *25*, 242–253.

Santrock, J. W. Affect and facilitative self-control: Influence of ecological setting, cognition, and social agents. *Journal of Educational Psychology*, 1976, *68*, 529–535.

Sawin, D. B., & Parke, R. D. Development of self-verbalized control of resistance to deviation. *Developmental Psychology*, 1979, *15*, 120–127.

Schleser, R., Meyers, A. W., & Cohen, R. Generalization of self-instructions: Effects of general versus specific content, active rehearsal, and cognitive level. *Child Development*, 1981, *52*, 335–340.

Snyder, J., & White, M. The use of cognitive self-instuction in the treatment of behaviorally disturbed adolescents. *Behavior Therapy*, 1979, *10*, 227–235.

Spivack, G., & Shure, M. B. *Social adjustment of young children: A cognitive approach to solving real-life problems.* San Francisco: Jossey-Bass, 1974.

Stokes, T., & Baer, D. An implicit technology of generalization. *Journal of Applied Behavior Analysis*, 1977, *10*, 349–367.

Strommen, E. A. Verbal self-regulation in a children's game: Impulsive errors on "Simon Says." *Child Development*, 1973, *44*, 849–853.

Tikhomerov, O. K. The formation of voluntary movements in children of preschool age. *Soviet Psychology*, 1976, *14*, 48–125.

Toner, S. J., Lewis, B. C., & Gribble, C. M. Evaluative verbalization and delay maintenance behavior in children. *Journal of Experimental Child Psychology*, 1979, *28*, 205–210.

Toner, S. T., Moore, L. P., & Emmons, B. A. The effect of being labeled on subsequent self-control in children. *Child Development*, 1980, *51*, 618–621.

Toner, I. J., & Smith, R. A. Age and overt verbalization in delay-maintenance behavior in children. *Journal of Experimental Child Psychology*, 1977, *24*, 123-128.

Verna, G. B. The effects of four-hour delay of punishment under two conditions of verbal instruction. *Child Development*, 1977, *48*, 621-624.

Vygotsky, L. S. *Thought and language*. New York: Wiley, 1962.

Weinriech, R. J. *Inducing reflective thinking in impulsive, emotionally disturbed children*. Unpublished master's thesis, Virginia Commonwealth University, 1975.

Wertsch, J. V. *The concept of activity in Soviet psychology*. Armonk, NY: M. E. Sharpe, 1981.

Wilder, L. The role of speech and other extra-signal feedback in the regulation of the child's sensorimotor behavior. *Speech Monographs*, 1969, *36*, 425-434.

Wilder, L. Recent developments in Soviet research on the verbal control of voluntary motor behavior. In K. F. Riegal & J. A. Meacham (Eds.), *The developing individual in a changing world*. Chicago: Aldine, 1976.

Willows, D. M. A picture is not always worth a thousand words: Pictures as distractors in reading. *Journal of Educational Psychology*, 1978, *70*, 255-262.

Wozniak, R. H. Verbal regulation of motor behavior: Soviet research and non-Soviet replications. *Human Development*, 1972, *15*, 13-57.

Yakovleva, S. V. Conditions for the formation of the simplest voluntary actions in very young children. *Soviet Psychology*, 1976, *14*, 13-47.

Yates, B. T., & Mischel, W. Young children's preferred attentional strategies for delaying gratification. *Journal of Personality and Social Psychology*, 1979, *37*, 286-300.

Yates, G. C., Lippett, R. M., & Yates, S. M. The effects of age, positive affect induction, and instructions on children's delay of gratification. *Journal of Experimental Child Psychology*, 1981, *32*, 169-180.

Zelnicker, T., Jeffrey, W. E., Ault, R., & Parsons, J. Analysis and modification of search strategies of impulsive and reflective children in the Matching Familiar Figures test. *Child Development*, 1972, *43*, 321-335.

Zelnicker, T., & Oppenheimer, L. Modification of information processing of impulsive children. *Child Development*, 1973, *44*, 445-450.

Zelnicker, T., & Oppenheimer, L. Effect of different training methods on perceptual learning in impulsive children. *Child Development*, 1976, *47*, 492-497.

Author Index

Page numbers set in italic type refer to pages on which complete reference information appears.

Aagard, J.A., 57, *68*
Abelson, R., 61, 62, *73, 195*
Abikoff, H., 286, *293*
Abraham, K., 241, *257*
Abrams, J.C., 129, 131, *153*
Abramson, L.Y., 243, *257*
Acerman, P., 132, *149*
Actkinson, T.R., 58-60, *68, 70*
Adams, N., 62, *73*
Adams, P.A., 130, *151*
Ainsworth, J.S., 57, *68*
Aitken, R.C.B., 247, *257*
Aivano, S., 6, 17, *23*
Albert, J.A., 278, 283, *293, 295*
Alden, L., 228, *257*
Alesandrini, K.L., 211, 212, *219*
Alexander, S., 236, *260*
Algozzine, R., 130, *149*
Allen, V., 155, *171*
Alpert, R., 231, 236, *257*
Alwitt, L., *184*
Amatu, H.I., 231-233, *265*
Anderson, D., *184*
Anderson, J., 190, *191*
Anderson, J.R., 60, 64, *68*
Anderson, M.C., 61, *69*
Anderson, R.C., 61, 62, *69*
Anderson, W.H., 277, *293, 296*
Andreasson, C.S., 25, *27*

Aponte, C.F., 237, *257*
Aponte, J.F., 237, *257*
Appel, L.F., 17, *21*
Arbitman-Smith, R., 119, *127,* 155, 164, *173*
Arenberg, D.L., 35, *47,* 75-77, 83, *96, 98, 99*
Armentrout, J.A., 286, *293*
Arnkoff, D., 222, 223, 225, 229, *262*
Arnold, G., 278, *293*
Arnold, S., 282, *299*
Aron, J., 155, *173*
Asarnow, J., 113, *125,* 221, *262,* 292, *293, 297*
Ashcraft, M.H., 41, *46*
Atkinson, R.C., 29, *44,* 54, 57, *69,* 103, 119, *125*
Ault, R., 283, 284, *300*
Ausubel, D.P., 66, *69*

Babad, E., 162, *171*
Bachen, C., *179*
Baddeley, A.D., 51, *69*
Baer, D., 292, *299*
Bahrick, H.D., 78, *96*
Bahrick, P.O., 78, *96*
Bailey, S., 82-84, 95, *96*
Bain, B., 271, 273, *294*
Baker, N., 276, *297*

Bakker, D.J.,   151, *152, 153*
Ball, D.W.,   133, 141, 142, *150, 151*
Ball, S.,   *179, 192*
Balla, D.,   123, *125*
Baltes, P.B.,   75, 77, 79, *96, 99*
Bandura, A.,   189, 222, 224, 225, 228,
    248, 249, *257*
Barclay, C.,   162, 163, *171*
Barclay, C.R.,   27, 28, *44*, 54, *70*, 109,
    112, *126*
Barrett, C.L.,   237, *257*
Bauer, R.H.,   134, 136, 137, 139, 148,
    149
Baver, R.,   156, *171*
Beach, D.R.,   35, *45*
Bean, J.P.,   29, 38, *48*
Beck, A.T.,   221, 222, 225, 226, 228,
    229, 241, 242, 244, 246, 250, 251,
    257, 258, 261, 264, 266
Beck, P.,   88, *98*
Becker, J.,   228, 250, *258*
Beers, T.M. Jr.,   228, *258*
Begg, I.,   38, *47*
Beiswenger, H.,   272, *294*
Bell, J.A.,   41, *47*
Bellack, A.S.,   252, *258*
Bellezza, F.S.,   25, 52, 54, 55-67, *69, 73*
Belmont, J.,   27, 41, *44, 45*, 162, 163,
    171, 172
Belmont, J.M.,   103, 105, 107, 108, 113,
    115, 116, 119, 121, *125, 126*
Belson, W.,   *179*
Bem, D.J.,   222, *258*
Bender, B.G.,   37, *44*
Bender, N.,   281, *294*
Benton, A.L.,   131, 133, *149*
Bereiter, C.,   159, *171*
Berkman, P.L.,   76, *98*
Berkowitz, L.,   *179, 189*
Berndt, T.J.,   *189*
Berry, J.K.,   39, 41, *46*, 64, 65, *68*
Beuhring, T.,   30, 41, *43*
Bibring, E.,   241, *258*
Bielski, R.,   244, 246, 251, *264*
Bijov, S.W.,   290
Bilsky, L.H.,   41, *44*, 107, 108, *125*
Binger, J.C.,   271, 273, *297*
Binks, M.G.,   55, *71*
Birch, D.,   271, *294*

Birkimer, J.,   282, 283, *298*
Bisanz, G.L.,   27, *44*
Bispo, J.G.,   35, *48*
Blackwood, R.,   275, *294*
Blakey, R.S.,   231, 232, 233, *265*
Blaney, P.H.,   228, *258*
Blick, K.A.,   53, 58, *69, 72*
Bobrow, S.A.,   61, *69*
Bogatz, G.,   *179, 192*
Bogdonoff, M.D.,   78, *99*
Bolles, R.C.,   222, *258*
Boltwood, C.E.,   53, *69*
Borkovec, T.D.,   105, *128*
Borkowski, J.B.,   104-113, 115, 116,
    119-122, *124-126, 127*, 163, 166,
    168, 171
Borkowski, J.C.,   18, *21*
Borkowski, J.G.,   40, 41, 42, *44-46, 49*,
    292, *294*
Bornstein, P.,   282, *294*
Borys, S.V.,   104, 110, *126*
Botwinick, J.,   77, 78, 90, *96*
Bower, G.H.,   54, 56, 61, 64, *68, 69*
Braby, R.,   57, *68*
Bracht, G.H.,   37, *44, 292, 294*
Branigan, G.G.,   *293, 297*
Bransford, J.D.,   65, 66, *69*, 140, *152*
Braswell, L.,   256, *260*, 268, 285, 290,
    291, 295, *296*
Bray, N.W.,   18, *21*, 27, *44*
Bridger, W.,   271, 273, *295*
Broadbent, D.E.,   133, *149*
Brooks, P.,   104, *126*
Brown, A.L.,   17, 18, *21, 23*, 26, 27,
    31-34, 36, 37, 41, *44, 45*, 54, 63, *70*,
    104, 109, 110, 112, *126*, 136, 138,
    140, 146, *149, 152*
Brown, H.,   155, 159, 160, 162-164,
    167, 168, *171, 172*
Brown-Graves, S.,   *192*
Bruce, D.R.,   7, *21*
Bruch, M.A.,   228, *258*
Bruner, J.S.,   273, *294*
Bryant, S.L.,   38, 40, *48*
Buchel, F.P.,   120, 121, *126*
Budoff, M.,   159, 161, 162, *171, 172,
    173*
Budwig, N.,   155, 157, *170, 174*
Buehler, J.A.,   76, *98*

Bugelski, B.R., 55, *70*
Buhanen, K., 275, *295*
Buium, N., 108, *128*
Buonassissi, J.V., 53, *69*
Burger, A.L., 106, 109, 111, 112, *126*
Burke, D., 4, *22*, 143, *151*
Burns, D., 242, *258*
Burns, L.E., 231, 232, *265*
Bussey, K., 277, 278, *299*
Butler, L., 227-229, *262*
Butterfield, E.C., 27, 41, *45*, 103, 105, 107, 108, 113, 116, 119, 121, *125, 126*, 162, 163, 168, *171, 172*

Calvert, S., *184, 185*
Cambourne, B., 272, *295*
Cameron, R., 231, *262*
Camino, L., *179*
Campbell, D., 165, 168, *172*, 292, *294*
Campione, J.C., 18, *21*, 26, 27, 41, *44*, 63, *70*, 104, 109, 110, 112, *126*, 136, 138, *152*, 155, 159, 162, 163, 167, 169, *171, 172*
Canestrari, R.E., 77, 82, 83, *96*
Candee, B.L., 275, *296*
Cannizzo, S., 5, 17, *22*, 162, *173*
Carlomusto, M., 80, *98*
Carmody, T., 228, *258*
Carpenter, P., *152*
Carroll, J.B., 121, 122, *126*
Carroll, K., 87, 88, *97*
Carter, D.B., 277, *298*
Case, R., 134, *149*
Catchpole, M.J., 37, 41, *49*
Cautela, J.R., 224, *258*
Cavanaugh, J.C., 41, *44, 45*, 104-107, 109, 110, 113, 115, 116, 119, 120-122, *125-127*, 163, 166, *171*, 292, *294*
Ceci, S.J., 137, 143, 148, *149*
Cermak, L.S., 35, *47*, 75, 77, 85, *97, 98*, 135, *150*
Cermak, S., 135, *150*
Chaffee, S., 179, *189*
Chandler, M.J., 289, *294*
Chase, W.C., 59, *70*
Chatelanat, G., 164, *173*
Cheesman, F.L., 66, *69*
Cheyne, J.A., 275, *294*

Chi, M., *186*
Chi, M.T.H., 4, *21*, 134, *150*
Chinsky, J.M., 35, *45*
Clark, H.T., 106, 112, *126*
Clark, P.A., 104, 110, *127*
Clark, W.C., 94, *97*
Clarke, A.D., 159, *172*
Clarke, A.M., 159, *172*
Clarke-Stewart, K., 168, *172*
Clyburn, A., 276, *298*
Coats, K.I., 243, 246, 249, 252, 254, *258*
Cochrane, S., 228, *260*
Cody, W.J., 108,*128*
Cofer, C.N., 7, *21*
Cohen, G., 93, 94, *97*
Cohen, R., 120, *128, 289, 299*
Cohen, R.L., 134, 135, 148, *150*
Coie, J.D., *189*
Cole, K.D., 86-88, *100*
Cole, M., 8, 17, *22, 24*, 155, 170, *172, 173*
Cole, P.M., 283, 287, *294*
Collins, A., 155, *172*
Collins, K.W., 39, *45*, 64, *70, 71*
Collins, W.A., 179, 181, *183*, 184, *185, 187*, 188, *189, 193-196*
Comez-Diaz, L., 228, 246, 249, *258*
Comstock, G., 179, *189*
Conger, J.J., 25, *45*
Connors, C.K., 289, *294*
Cook, L.K., 25, 32, 38, 40, *45*, 53, 61, 63, 66, *70*, 180, 183, 195
Cooley, E.J., 224, *264*
Cooper, R.G., 17, *21*
Corder-Bolz, C., 191, *193*
Cordoni, B.K., 132, *150*
Corman, L., 159, *171*
Cort, R., 144, *149*
Costanzo, P.R., *189*
Cox, D., 10, 11, 15, *21*
Craighead, W.E., 256, *258, 263*
Craik, F.I.M., 6, 7, *22*, 77, 78, *97*, 209, 218, *219*
Cravioto, J., 132, *150*
Crock, S., 216, *219*
Cronbach, L.J., 59, *70*, 119, *127*
Cruickshank, W.M., *150*
Cubberly, W.E., 39, *49*, 58, *73*

Cuvo, A.J., 6, 27, *22, 45*

D'Alelio, W.A., 239, *258*
Dallago, M.L.P., 136, 137, 139, 143, *150*
Damburg, P.R., 104, *126*
Daniels, P.R., 129, 131, *152*
Danner, F.W., 37, *45*
Dansereau, D.F., 39, *45,* 64, 70, *71*
Davidson, E., *189*
Davies, D., 120, *127*
Davison, G.L., 237, *260*
Dawson, M.M., 141, 142, *150*
Day, D., 278, *295*
Day, J., 165, 167, 168, *170*
Day, J.D., 26, 27, *44*
Dean, R.S., 63, *70*
Decenteceo, E.T., 226, 228, 229, 233, 237, 239, *260*
Delaney, H.D., 29, 35, 38, *48,* 51, *72*
DeLeon, J.M., 84, *96*
DeLicardie, E.R., 132, *150*
DeLuca, D., 135, *150*
Dempsey, P.A., 248, *258*
Dennis-Rounds, J., 29, 31, 37, 38, 41, *47, 57, 72,* 84, *99,* 166, *174*
Denny, N.W., 80, *97*
DeRose, T.M., 92, *98*
Derry, P., 228, *259*
Desrochers, A., 35, *47,* 51, 56, *72*
Detterman, D.K., 103, 104, 110, 122, *127*
Devillis, R.F., 110, *128*
Diekhoff, G., 39, *45,* 64, *70*
Dimascio, A., 251, *265*
DiVesta, F.J., 59, 62, *70, 73*
Divine-Hawkins, P., 63, 66, *71*
Divoky, D., 132, *152*
Dixon, T.R., 38, *45*
Donaldson, W., 7, *24,* 38, *49*
Dorans, B.A., 104, 110, *126*
Dorr, A., *192*
Douglas, V.I., 134, 141, *150, 282, 294*
Douglass, L.C., 139, *148*
Drake, C., 135, *150*
Dretzke, B.J., 29, 30, *43, 46*
Drucker, J.F., 133, *150*
Dugas, J., 110, *128*

Duncan, G., 241, *261*
Duty, D.C., 58, *73*
Dykman, R.A., 132, *149*
D'Zurilla, T.J., 237, *259*

Easter, A., *194*
Ebbesen, E.B., 276, 277, *297*
Egeland, B., 283, 284, 289, *294*
Eisdorfer, C., 78, *97, 99*
Eisenberg, L., 130, *150*
Ellis, A., 222, 224, 226, 229, 230, 242, 249, *259*
Ellis, N.R., 103, 104, *127*
Ellsworth, P., *188*
Emery, G., 228, 242, 244, 251, *257*
Emmons, B.A., 278, *299*
Endler, N., 236, *259*
Engle, R.W., 119, 120, *127*
English, D., 278, *299*
Eoff, J., 35, 38, *48*
Erbaugh, J., 246, *258*
Erber, J.T., 80, *97*
Erickson, M.T., 284, *298*
Ericsson, K.A., 59, *70,* 121, *125*
Eron, L., *179*
Evans, R.A., 41, *44, 45*
Evans, S.H., 39, 64, *70*
Eysenck, H.J., 224, *259*

Faris, R.E.L., 156, *172*
Farnill, D., *189*
Fedoravicius, A., 229-232, 239, *263*
Feiss, K., 155, *173*
Feldman, R., 155, *171*
Ferguson, G., 165, *172*
Ferrara, R., 155, 167, *171*
Ferretti, R.P., 108, 115, 116, *125*
Ferster, C.B., 241, *259*
Feshbach, S., *189*
Feuerstein, R., 118, 119, *127,* 155, 159, 163, 164, *172, 173*
Filler, J., 164, *173*
Finch, A.J., 282, 285, 286, 289, 292, *294-296*
Fisher, S., 130, *151*
Fiske, D., 165, 168, *172*
Flavell, J., 5-8, 14, 16, 17, 19, *21-24,* 35, 36, *45,* 54, *70,* 105, 106, 111, 115, *127,* 139, *151,* 162, 164, *173,*

1

272, *297*
Fleischner, J., 144, *149*
Fleming, B.M., 244, 248, 252, *259*
Fletcher, J.M., 133, *152*
Flueloep, S., 114, 119, *128*
Fokkema, S.D., *150*
Foley, M., 18, *21*
Ford, C.E., 142, *149*
Forehand, R.A., 282, *293*
Forrest, T., 130, *151*
Forrest-Pressley, D.L., 66, *70,* 139-141, *150*
Foth, D., 61, *72,* 136, 137, 143, *153*
Fozard, J.L., 35, *47,* 75, 77, 78, 82, 84, 88, 90, *97-99*
Frank, B., 144, *149*
Frankel, F., 8, *22*
Frase, B., 272, *296*
Frederiksen, J.R., 135, *150*
Freedman, J., 279, *298*
Freeman, R.D., 131, *150*
Fremouw, W.J., 233-234, 236, 240, *259, 260*
French, L., 155, 159, 160, *171*
Friedlander, B., *184*
Friedman, A., 65, *70*
Friedrich, L., *179,* 189, *193*
Friel, J., 132, *152*
Friend, R., 236, 239, *265*
Fry, P.S., 276, *294*
Fuchs, C.Z., 243, 248, *259, 264*
Fuentes, E.J., 40, *45*
Furth, H.G., 9, *22*

Gabourie, P., 136, 138, 139, 145, 146, *153*
Gabriesheski, A.S., 92, *98*
Gagne, E., 17, *24*
Gagne, R.M., 67, *70*
Gallistel, C.R., 38, *45*
Galanter, E., 55, 56, *72*
Galton, F., 59, *70*
Gardner, B., 135, *148*
Gardner, P., 242, 246, 249, *259*
Gardner, W., 155, 170, *173*
Garguilo, R., 17, *24*
Garland, J., 39, *45,* 64, *70, 71*
Garson, C., 282, *294*
Geen, R., *189*

Gelman, R., 38, *45*
Genest, M., 225-228, *262, 265*
Genshaft, J., 282, *295*
Ghatala, E.S., 41, *47*
Gibson, E.J., 14, *22*
Gibson, J.J., 14, *22*
Giles, D.E., 242, *264*
Gillies, L.A., 66, *70,* 139-141, *150*
Gilmore, J., 229-232, 239, *263*
Giordani, B., 133, *151*
Gladis, M., 80, *97*
Glaser, R., *150*
Glass, C.R., 239, *259*
Glass, G.V., 37, *44,* 292, *294*
Glenn, C., *186*
Glidden, L.M., 106, *128*
Glowgower, F.D., 232-234, *260*
Goetz, E.T., 61, 62, *69*
Goklaney, M., 251, *265*
Goldberg, S., 8, *22*
Goldberg, W.J., 135, *150*
Golden, M., 271, 273, *295*
Goldfried, A., 228, 237, *260, 261*
Goldfried, M.R., 223, 224, 226, 228, 229, 233, 234, 236, 237, 239, *259-261*
Goldman, T., 139, 141, *153*
Gombrich, E.H., 65, 66, *70*
Gonda, J.N., 79, *97*
Goodman, J.B., 231, *263,* 279-282, 284, *295, 299*
Gordon, L., 216, 217, *218*
Gordon, N., *189*
Gordon, S.K., 94, *97*
Gorsuch, R., 236, *264*
Gottlieb, J., 162, *172*
Gottman, J.M., 239, *259*
Graham, L.E., 228, *261*
Grandon, G.M., 104, *128*
Graves, S., *189*
Gray, K., 87, 88, *97*
Greer, R.N.E., 30, 35, *43, 45*
Gribble, C.M., 274, 277, *299*
Griffith, D., 57-60, *68, 70*
Grosscup, S.G., 243, *261*
Grossman, J.L., 82, 83, *97*
Grover, S.C., 118, 119, *125*
Gruenenfelder, T.M., 30, 41, *44,* 113, *125,* 163, *171*

Grumet, J.F., *189*
Gruneberg, M.M., 52, 53, *70*
Guider, R.L., 86-88, *100*

Haber, R., 231, 236, *257*
Hagen, J.W., 4, 6, *22*, 35, *45*, 133, *150*
Haines, D.J., 139, 141, 142, *150*
Hakstian, A.R., 243, 244, 249, 250, *262*
Hale, G., *150, 153, 185*
Halff, H.M., 66, *70*
Hall, J.P., 58, *71*
Hall, J.W., 29, *46*
Hall, L., 165, 167, 168, *170*
Hallahan, D.P., 133, 141, 142, 148,
    150, 151, 153
Hamilton, J., 159, 161, *172, 173*
Hamilton, M., 246, *260*
Hammen, C.L., 228, *260*
Hammill, D.D., 131, *153*
Hance, J., 82-84, 95, *96*
Hans, T., 82-84, 95, *96*
Hansen, C.L., 138, *151*
Harding, C.J., 133, *153*
Harper, R., 249, *259*
Harris, A.J., 131, 132, *151*
Harris, D.B., 290, *299*
Harris, J.E., 53, *71*
Harrison, R., 159, 162, *172*
Hartig, M., 274, 275, 277, *295*
Hartley, D.G., 283, *294*
Hastie, R., *188*
Hastorf, A., *188*
Hatano, G., 55, *71*
Haugen, D.M., 41, *47*
Hausman, C.P., 83, *99*
Hawkins, R.P., *185*
Hawles, T.G., 7, 17, *23*
Hayes-Roth, B., 51, 52, *71*
Haywood, C., 119, 124, *127*, 155, 164,
    173
Heider, E.R., 283, *295*
Heisel, B.E., 35, *47, 292, 299*
Hendon, D.W., *219*, 221
Hersen, M., 252, *258*
Herzoff, N., 228, *261*
Hess, V.L., *189*
Hicks, D.J., *191*
Higbee, K.L., 51, 52, 55, 57, *71*
Hilbert, N.M., 76, *97*

Himmelhoch, J., 252, *258*
Hiniker, A., 228, *263*
Hirschfield, P.P., 286, *295*
Hirt, M., 282, *295*
Hofland, B., 79, *95*
Hogaboam, T., 135, *152*
Hohman, R.J.A., 275, *296*
Holbrook, M.B., 205, *219*
Holley, C.D., 39, *45*, 64, *70, 71*
Hollon, S.D., 221, 222, 225, 243, 244,
    250, *260, 261, 264, 287, 296*
Holmes, M., 109, 111, *126*
Holroyd, K.A., 228, 239, *260*
Hood, L., 155, 170, *173*
Hope, D.J., 35, *48*
Hornik, R., *197*
Horton, D.L., 38, *45*
Horton, R., *191*
Houck, D.G., 134, 135, 141, 142, 147,
    148, *153*
Huesmann, L.R., *179*
Hughes, J.R., 131, *151*
Hughes, S.E.D., 7, *22*
Hultsch, D.F., 77, 80, 81, *97*
Hunt, J., 236, *259*
Hunter, I.M.L., 55, 58, *71*
Huntsman, N.J., 133, *150*
Husek, T., 236, *260*
Huston, A., *183, 184*
Huston-Stein, A., 179, *185, 192, 193*
Huttenlocher, J., 4, *22*, 143, *151*
Hyde, T.S., 7, *22*

Jackson, M., 134, *151*
Jackson, P., 20, *23*
Jacobs, M., 228, *260*
Jacobs, M.K., 228, *260*
Jarvis, P.E., 272, *295*
Jastak, J.F., 290, *295*
Jastak, S.R., 290, *295*
Jeffrey, W.E., 283, 284, *300*
Jenkins, J.J., 7, *22*
Jensen, L., 275, *295*
Johnson, D.D., 40, *45*
Johnson, K., 272, *296*
Johnson, M., 116, 117, 119, *127*
Johnson, M.B., 116, 117, 119, *127*
Johnson, M.K., 65, 66, *69*
Johnson, N., *186*

Johnson, N.S., 41, *46,* 65, *71,* 138, 145, *151*
Johnson, P.J., 15, *22*
Jones, B.F., 29, *46*
Jones, M., 244, 246, 251, *264*
Jones, R.G., 236, *260*
Jones, W., 146, *149*
Jorm, A.J., 133, *151*
Joynt, D., 272, *295*
Jusczyk, P.W., 30, *46*
Just, M., *152*
Justice, E.M., 18, *21*

Kagen, J., 278, *295*
Kahana, B., 279, *298*
Kahn, J.V., 118, 119, *125*
Kahn, R.L., 76, *97*
Kail, R.V., Jr., 4, *22*
Kanfer, F., 222, 224, *260,* 274, 275, 277, 278, *295*
Kanter, N.J., 234, 236, 239, *260*
Karasov, R., *193*
Karniol, R., 277, 278, *297*
Karoly, P., 228, *258*
Karst, T.O., 230-232, *265*
Katzman, N., 179, *189*
Kauffman, J.M., 133, 141, 142, *150, 151, 153*
Kaufman, A.S., 131, *151*
Kavale, K., 133, *151*
Kazdin, A.E., 222-224, *260, 262,* 287, *294*
Kee, D.W., 135, *148*
Keeney, T., 5, 17, 22, *162, 173*
Kellas, G., 6, *22,* 27, 41, *46,* 110, *128*
Kemler, D.G., 30, *46*
Kendall, C.R., 109, 111, 112, 115, 119, 120, 122, *124,* 127
Kendall, P.C., 222, 225, 228, 256, *260, 261,* 268, 285, 286-292, *295, 296*
Kendler, H.D., 15, *22*
Kendler, T.S., 15, *22*
Keniston, A., 181, 185, *194*
Kennedy, B., 163, *173*
Kennedy, B.A., 17, *23,* 113, 119, *127*
Kennedy, S.P., 35, *46*
Keogh, B.K., *151*
Kestner, J., 30, 41, *46*
Khatami, M., 242, 244, *264*

Kincaid, J.P., 57, *68*
Kingsley, P.R., 35, *45*
Kinsbourne, M., 130, *153*
Kintsch, W., 61, *71*
Kirschenbaum, D.S., 256, *261*
Klerman, G.L., 251, *265*
Knights, R.M., *151-153*
Kobasigawa, A., 9, *23*
Kohlberg, L., 275, *296*
Konnor, M., 156, *174*
Koppitz, E.M., 130, 137, *151*
Korgeski, G.P., 287, *296*
Kornblith, S.J., 243, *264*
Kovacs, M., 221, 228, 243, 244, 250, *261, 264*
Kramer, J.J., 119, *127*
Krebs, E.W., 63, 66, *71, 73*
Kreutzer, M.A., 115, *127,* 139, *151*
Krugman, D.M., 212, *220*
Krugman, H.E., 204, *219*
Kuiper, N.A., 40, *48*
Kulhavy, R.W., 63, *70, 73*
Kunen, S., 17, *24*
Kurtz, B., 106, 108, 115, *125, 126,* 168, *171*
Kurtz, J., 132, *150*
Kussmann, T., 156, 157, *173*

Labouvie, V., 75, 77, *96*
Labouvie-Vief, G., 75, 79, 91, 93, 94, 96, *97*
Lachman, J.L., 78, 90, *97, 98*
Lachman, R., 78, 90, *97, 98*
Lange, G., 17, 20, *23, 25, 46*
Langer, E.J., 88, *98*
Laurence, M.W., 9, 16, 20, *23,* 80, *98*
Laver, A.B., 51, *71*
LaVoie, J.C., 272, 275, *296*
Lawrence, K.A., 56, *72*
Lawson, M.J., 114, 119, *128*
Lawton, S.Q.C., 33, *45,* 146, *149*
Lazarus, A.A., 226, 241, *261*
Lea, S.E.G., 137, 143, 148, *149*
Ledwidge, B., 224, *261*
Lefkowitz, M.M., *179*
Lehmann, D.R., 205, *219*
Leifer, A., *189*
Leonard, C., 115, *127,* 139, *151*

Leont'ev, A.N.,   157, *173*
Lepper, M.R.,   292, *299*
Lesgold, A.M.,   38, *46,* 64, *71,* 134,
    135, 142, *150, 151, 152*
Levers, S.R.,   30, 41, *44,* 113, *125,* 163,
    171
Levin, B.B.,   29, *46*
Levin, J.R.,   7, 17, *23, 24,* 29, 30, 33,
    35-41, *43, 44, 46-49,* 51, 52, 57, 62-
    66, *68, 71, 72,* 92, *98, 150, 152*
Levin, S.,   *184*
Lewinsohn, P.M.,   228, 241, 243, 244,
    246, 248, 249, 252, 254, *261, 266*
Lewis, B.C.,   274, 277, *299*
Lewis, D.,   221, *261*
Lewis, M.,   *150, 153*
Leyens, J.,   *179*
Liberty, C.,   6, 15, 20, *23*
Liebert, R.,   *189,* 231, 236, *261, 263*
Lindauer, B.K.,   35, *47*
Lindsay, P.H.,   64, *73*
Linehan, M.M.,   228, 234, 236, 238,
    260, 261
Lippett, R.M.,   276, 278, *300*
List, J.,
Lloyd, J.,   221, *261*   -
Lockhart, L.,   63, 66, *73*
Lockhart, R.S.,   6, *22,* 209, 218, *219*
Lodico, M.G.,   41, *47*
Lomenick, T.,   20, *24*
Lomov, B.,   156, *173*
Long, M.K.,   80, *99*
Lorayne, H.,   55, *71*
Lorch, E.,   *184*
Lowenthal, M.F.,   76, *98*
Lucas, J.,   55, *71*
Luria, A.,   155, 156, 159, 160, 162, *173,*
    268-273, 275, 279, *296*
Lushene, R.,   236, *264*
Lutz, K.A.,   206, 209, 210, 216-218, *219*
Lutz, R.J.,   206, 209, 210, 216, *219*

Maccoby, E.,   189
MacPherson, E.M.,   275, *296*
Maddison, D.,   241, *261*
Mahoney, M.J.,   222-226, 229, *261, 262,*
    265, 276, *297*
Malkiewich, L.,   239, *262*
Malmgren, I.,   136, 138, 145, 146, *153*

Mandel, N.M.,   228, *264*
Mandler, J.,   *186*
Mandler, J.M.,   65, *71,* 138, 145, *151*
Manis, F.R.,   135, *151*
Mar, H.H.,   106, *128*
Marascuilo, L.A.,   287, *297*
Margolis, H.,   293, *297*
Marshall, G.J.,   224, *264*
Marshall, W.L.,   228, 243, 244, 248,
    254, *265*
Marton, P.,   282, *294*
Mason, S.E.,   83, *98*
Masters, J.C.,   271, 273, 276, *297*
Matsushima, J.,   286, *297*
Mayer, R.E.,   25, 32, 38, 40, *45,* 53, 61,
    63, 66, *70, 71,* 180, 183, *195*
Mayol, A.,   228, *260*
McCarrell, N.,   17, *21*
McCarty, D.L.,   57, *72*
McCauley, C.,   8, *22, 27, 46,* 104, 110,
    126-128
McClelland, J.,   134, *151*
McCombs, M.,   179, *189*
McCormick, C.B.,   29, 30, 35, 39, 41,
    43, 44, 36-48, 292, *299*
McCroskey, J.C.,   232-234, 236, *260,*
    262
McDermott, R.,   170, *173*
McDonald, B.A.,   39, *45,* 64, *70, 71*
McFarland, C.E.,   6, *22, 27, 46*
McGivern, J.,   30, *43*
McGlynn, F.D.,   237, *262*
McHale, S.M.,   256, *258*
McKeon, J.J.,   250, *263*
McLane, J.,   155, 157, 170, *174*
McLean, P.D.,   243, 244, 249, 250, *262*
McLeish, J.,   156, *173*
McLuhan, M.,   *197*
McMannis, D.L.,   41, *47*
McNamee, G.,   155, 157, 170, *174*
McVey, K.A.,   104, 105, 124, *128*
Meacham, J.,   155, *173, 174,* 272, *297*
Meichenbaum, D.,   112, 113, 120, *125,*
    128, 221, 222, 224-233, *262,* 279-
    282, 284, 292, 293, *297*
Mendelson, M.,   246, *258*
Merluzzi, T.,   239, *262*
Mervis, C.B.,   39, *47*
Meskin, J.,   159, 162, *172*

Messer, S.B., 279, *297*
Meyer, B.F.J., 38, *47,* 94, *98*
Meyers, A.W., 120, *128, 256, 258, 263,*
    289, *299*
Meyers, C.E., 124, *127*
Miceli, L., 93, *98*
Michener, S., 40, *48*
Middleton, D.B., 9, *23*
Milgram, N.A., 9, *22*
Miller, D., 113, 119, *127,* 163, *173*
Miller, D.J., 17, *23*
Miller, D.T., 277, 278, *297*
Miller, G.A., 55, 56, *72*
Miller, G.E., 29, 39-41, *46, 48,* 52, 57,
    72
Miller, L., *185*
Miller, S.A., 272, *297*
Minsky, M.A., 61, *72*
Mischel, W., 268, 274, 276-278, *297,*
    298, 300
Mitchell, A.A., 209, *219*
Mitchell, D.W., 108, 115, 116, *125*
Miyake, Y., 55, *71*
Mock, J., 246, *258*
Moely, B.E., 7-9, 17, *23, 24,* 136, 137,
    139, 143, *150*
Money, J., 130, *150, 151*
Monge, R.H., 80, *98*
Montare, A., 271, 273, *295*
Montgomery, L., 282, *294*
Moore, B.S., 276, 277, *297, 298*
Moore, L.P., 278, *299*
Moore, R.F., 117, *128*
Morris, C.D., 140, *152*
Morris, J.B., 241, 250, *263*
Morris, L., 231, 236, *261, 263*
Morris, P.E., 52, *70*
Morris, S.J., 278, *295*
Morrison, F.J., 133, 135, *151*
Mowen, J.C., 213, *219*
Moyer, S.C., 133, 153
Moynahan, E.D., 19, *23,* 30, 41, *47*
Mueller, H., 80, *98*
Munoz, R.F., 228, 244, 248, 249, 252,
    254, *266*
Munro, A., 216, 217, *218*
Murphy, M., 162, 163
Murphy, M.D., 17, *23,* 41, *44,* 80-82,
    92, *98, 99*

Murray, E.J., 239, *258*
Myers, N., 8, *22*

Nagle, R.J., 119, 120, *127*
Nagy, J., 133, *151*
Nakamura, G.V., 35, *47, 48,* 138, 139,
    145, 146, *153,* 292, *299*
Naus, M.J., 6, 15, 17, 20, *23,* 25, 27,
    47
Neale, J., *189*
Neimark, E., 8, *23*
Nelson, K.J., 16, *23*
Nelson, R., 237, *259*
Nelson, R.O., 231, *265*
Nelson, W., 282, 283, *294, 298*
Netley, C., 134, 135, 148, *150*
Neugarten, B.L., 92, *98*
New, C., 251, *265*
Newcomb, A.F., 181, *183*
Newman, R.S., 104, 105, 124, *128*
Nicholas, D.W., 35, *49*
Niederche, G., 76, *97*
Niles, J.A., 133, *153*
Nisbett, R., *188*
Norman, D.A., 52, 64, *72, 73*
Novaco, R.W., 228, *263*
Nowlin, J., 78, *97*
Nye, W.C., 41, *47*

Oakley, D.D., 136, 138, *152*
Odom, J.V., 231, *265*
O'Donnell, J.P., 132, *150,* 293, *298*
Oei, T.P.S., 242, 246, 249, *259*
O'Hanlon, A., 82-84, 95, *96*
O'Leary, K.D., 105, *128*
O'Leary, S., 155, *174*
Oliver, R., 242, *263*
Olson, F., 7, 17, *23*
Olson, J.C., 209, *219*
Ong, W.J., 56, *72*
Oppenheimer, L., 284, *300*
Ordman, A.M., 256, *261*
Orenstein, H., 221, *264*
Ornstein, P.A., 4, 6, 15, 17, 20, *23,* 25,
    27, *47*
Orton, S.T., 133, *151*
Ortony, A., 61, *72, 73*
Osborne, G., 244, 246, 251, *264*
O'Sullivan, J., 30, 41, *43*

Owen, F.W.,   130, *151*
Owings, R.,   139, *152*

Padian, N.,   251, *265*
Page, E.B.,   104, *128*
Paivio, A.,   29, 35, 38, 41, *47*, 51-57,
  59-61, *72*, 82, *98*, 147, *152, 184*,
  209, 210, 218
Palkes, H.,   273, *298, 299*
Paris, S.G.,   35, *47*, 104, 105, 124, *128*
Parke, R.,   155, *174*
Parke, R.D.,   *179*, 275, 277, *298, 299*
Parker, W.,   244, 246, 251, *264*
Parrish, J.M.,   284, *298*
Parry, P.,   282, *294*
Parsons, J.,   283, 284, *300*
Pascarella, E.T.,   119, *128*, 132, *153*
Pash, J.R.,   58, *72*
Patterson, C.J.,   274, 277, 292, *297-299*
Patterson, R.J.,   58, *71*
Paul, G.,   231, *263*
Paul, G.L.,   236, *263*
Paulshock, D.,   90, *98*
Paulson, K.,   293, *298*
Pearson, P.D.,   40, *45*
Pechacek, T.F.,   228, *261*
Peck, V.A.,   104, *126*
Pedersen, F.,   168, *175*
Peleg, Z.R.,   117, *128*
Pelham, W.E.,   134, 142, *149, 152*
Pelligrini, D.S.,   287, *296*
Pelligrino, J.W.,   18, *23, 150*
Percy, L.,   212, 213, 219, *220*
Perfetti, C.A.,   134, 142, *151, 152*
Perlmutter, M.,   8, *22*, 90, *98*
Perry, D.G.,   277, 278, *299*
Perry, L.C.,   277, 278, *299*
Persensky, J.J.,   58, *72*
Peters, J.E.,   132, *149*
Peters, K.G.,   134, 141, *150*
Petersen, G.,   140, *152*
Peterson, P.L.,   19, *24*, 26, 35, 40, *47*,
  54, 59, *72*, 106, *128*, 136, *152*, 186,
  187
Petti, T.A.,   249, *263*
Pezdek, K.,   93, *98*
Pflaum, S.W.,   119, *128*, 132, *153*
Phelps, E.,   *192*
Phillips, W.,   278, *295*

Piaget, J.,   36, *47*, 155, *174*
Pichert, J.W.,   61, *69*
Pierce, R.C.,   76, *98*
Piers, E.V.,   290, *299*
Pigott, S.,   38, *48*
Plemons, J.K.,   79, *98*
Poon, L.W.,   35, *47*, 75, 77, 82, 84, 88,
  90, 91, *96, 98, 99*
Popkin, S.J.,   88, *99*
Portevs, S.D.,   279, *299*
Posnansky, C.,   18, *23*
Powell, A.H. Jr.,   78, *99*
Pressley, M.,   7, 17, *23, 24*, 29-31, 33,
  35-41, *43, 46-48*, 51, 52, 57, 65, *72*,
  82-84, 92, *95, 96, 98, 99*, 138, 148,
  150, 152, 157, 166, *174*, 182, 184,
  188, *194*, 213, 220, 268, 284, 292,
  299
Pribram, K.H.,   55, 56, *72*
Prince, H.T.,   224, *264*
Prusoff, B.A.,   251, *265*
Puckett, S.P.,   224, *264*
Purdie, S.,   181, 184, 189, *195*

Quevillion, R.,   282, *294*

Rachlin, H.,   224, *263*
Rahmani, L.,   156, *174*
Raimy, V.,   222, 237, *263*
Raines, J.M.,   35, 38, *48*
Ramanaiah, N.,   35, *48*
Ramaniah, N.B.,   132, *150*
Ramsey, P.P.,   286, *293*
Rapuczynski, W.,   *192*
Raskin, A.,   250, *263*
Rathjen, D.,   228, *263*
Rathjen, E.,   228, *263*
Raugh, M.R.,   57, *69*
Raven, J.,   236, *263*
Rawlings, E.,   *189*
Ray, M.L.,   204, *220*
Reatig, N.,   250, *263*
Reddy, B.G.,   66, *69*
Reece, H.W.,   82, 83, *99*
Reeve, R.E.,   134, 141, 142, *150, 151*
Rehm, L.P.,   243, 248, *259, 264*
Reichart, G.J.,   108, *128*
Reid, M.K.,   106, *126*
Reis, E.,   106, 112, *126*

Reitman, J.S., 56, *69*
Resnick, L., 159, *174*
Resnik, A., 212, *220*
Reynolds, R.E., 62, *69*
Reynolds, W.M., 243, 246, 249, 252, 254, *258, 264*
Ribich, F., 35, *48*
Rice, G.E., 94, *98*
Rice, M., *183*
Rie, H., *152*
Riegel, K., 155, 159, *174*
Rigney, J.W., 216, 217, *218*
Ringstrom, M.D., 137, 143, 148, *149*
Roberts, D., *179, 189*
Roberts, K.H., 51, *72*
Roberts, P., 56, 82-84, *95, 96*
Roberts, T., 293, *299*
Robertson-Tchabo, E.A., 83, *99*
Robinson, B.C., 76, *98*
Rodin, J., 88, *98*
Rogoff, B., 155, 170, *173*
Rohwer, W.D. Jr., 29, 30, 35-38, 41, 42, *48*, 65, *72*
Romano, J.M., 243, *264*
Rondal, J.A., 272, *299*
Roney, L.K., 58, *73*
Rose, T.L., 84, *96*
Rosen, G.M., 221, *264*
Rosenshein, K., 132, *150*
Rosenstein, A., 236, *259*
Rosman, B.L., 278, *295*
Rosner, S.L., 129, 131, *153*
Ross, A.O., 142, *149*
Ross, J., 56, *72, 152*
Ross, L., *188*
Rossiter, J.R., 204, 212, 213, *220*
Roth, D., 244, 246, 251, *264*
Roth, D.M., 243, *264*
Rothkopf, E.Z., 60, *73*
Rourke, B.P., 132, *152*
Royer, J.M., 42, *48*
Ruben, H., 84, *96*
Rubenstein, J., 168, *175*
Rumelhart, D.E., 38, *48*, 61, 64, *73*, 216, *220*
Rush, A., 221, 250, *261*
Rush, A.J., 221, 228, 242, 244, 246, 250, 251, *254, 257, 264*
Rushton, J.P., *179*

Ryan, E.B., 124, *125,* 221, *264*

Sabo, R., 133, *150*
Safran, J., 228, *257*
Sagotsky, G., 292, *299*
Salomon, G., *183*
Sameroff, A., 155, *174*
Sanders, H., 90, *100*
Sanders, R.E., 76, 80, 81, 82, 92, *98, 99*
Santogrossi, D., *191*
Satz, P., 131-133, *152*
Sautrock, J.W., 276, 297, *299*
Sawin, D.B., 275, 277, *299*
Schaie, K.W., 75, 90, *96, 99*
Schallert, D.L., 38, *48*, 61, 62, 64, *73*
Schank, R., 61, 62, *73, 195*
Schell, D.A., 91, 93, 94, *96*
Schiffman, G.B., 129, 131, *153*
Schildkraut, J.J., 241, *264*
Schleser, R., 120, *128*, 289, *299*
Schmeck, R.R., 35, *48*
Schmitt, F.A., 80, 81, 82, 92, *98, 99*
Schneider, D., *188*
Schonfield, D., 89, *99*
Schorr, D., 62, *73*
Schrag, P., 132, *152*
Schuckit, M., 228, 250, *258*
Schulman, A.I., 57, 63, *68*
Schulterbrandt, J.G., 250, *263*
Schultz, C.B., 62, *73*
Schuman, H., 159, 163, 167, *174*
Schuyler, D., 241, *264*
Schwartz, B., 205, *220*
Schwartz, N.H., 63, *73*
Scott, J., *184*
Scribmer, S., 155, *172*
Scruggs, T.E., 30, *43*
Seligman, M.E.P., 222, 243, *257, 264*
Senter, R.J., 58, *72*
Shannon, D., 231, *263*
Shaw, B.F., 228, 242, 244, 246-249, 251, 254, *257, 264*
Shaw, D.A., 241, *261*
Sheikh, A.A., 211, 212, *219*
Shelton, J., 272, *297*
Shepherd, M.J., 144, 148, *149*
Shiffrin, R.M., 54, *69*, 103, 119, *125*
Shifman, M., 164, *173*

Shimmerlik, S.M.,   63, *73*
Shisslak, C.,   228, *261*
Shmurak, S.H.,   239, *259*
Sholomskas, D.,   251, *265*
Short, E.J.,   124, *125*
Shrarger, J.S.,   228, *262*
Shriberg, L.K.,   29, 39, *46, 48,* 64, 65,
    68
Shure, M.B.,   289, *299*
Siegel, A.,   *189*
Siegler, R.,   166, *174*
Silberstein,   90, *100*
Silver, L.B.,   132, *152*
Simon, E.W.,   86, *100*
Simon, H.A.,   60, *73,* 121, *125*
Singer, D.,   *192*
Singer, J.,   *192*
Singer, R.,   *189*
Smiley, S.S.,   32, 33, 36, 37, *44, 45,*
    136, 138, 140, 146, *149, 152*
Smith, A.D.,   80, 83, *98, 99*
Smith, E.E.,   62, *73*
Smith, J.C.,   228, 234, 236, 238, *260*
Smith, R.A.,   274, 277, *300*
Smith, S.H.,   63, 66, *71*
Snow, R.E.,   59, *70,* 119, *127*
Snowden, L.R.,   254, *264*
Snowman, J.,   63, 66, *71, 73*
Snyder, J.,   282, *299*
Sobol, B.,   *194*
Sperber, R.,   104, 120, *126, 127*
Spiegler, C.,   236, *264*
Spiegler, M.D.,   224, *264*
Spielberger, C.,   236, *264*
Spiro, R.J.,   38, *49,* 61, *69*
Spitz, H.H.,   104, 110, *126*
Spitzer, L.,   89, *96*
Spivack, G.,   289, *299*
Squire, L.R.,   90, *99*
Stainback, S.,   133, *151*
Stanley, J.,   292, *294*
Steger, B.M.,   133, *153*
Stein, A.H.,   *179, 186, 189, 193*
Stein, B.S.,   140, *152*
Steiner, G.A.,   204
Stern, B.,   212
Sternberg, R.J.,   104, 121, *128*
Sterns, H.L.,   76, *99*
Stevens, A.,   155, *172*

Stevens, K.V.,   61, *69*
Stevenson, H.,   *185*
Stewart, M.,   279, *298*
Stifter, E.,   278, *295*
Stokes, T.,   292, *299*
Stolz, L.M.,   130, *151*
Stone, G.,   228, *259*
Storandt, M.,   78, 90, *99*
Strommen, E.A.,   271, 272, *299*
Suinn, R.,   236, *264*
Sundberg, N.D.,   254, *264, 265*
Sunshine, P.M.,   59, *70*
Sutherland, J.,   130, *149*
Sutton, A.,   159, *174*
Suzuki, N.S.,   30, 35, *43, 46*
Swanson, J.M.,   130, *153*
Sweeney, C.A.,   57, 61, *73*
Swing, S.R.,   26, 35, 40, *47,* 54, 59, *72,*
    106, *128,* 136, *152,* 186, *187*
Switsky, H.N.,   124, *127*
Sykes, R.N.,   52, *70*

Taplin, J.R.,   254, *265*
Tarver, S.G.,   133, 134, 136, 141, 148,
    153
Taub, H.A.,   80, *99*
Taylor, A.M.,   37, *45*
Taylor, F.G.,   228, 243, 244, 248, 254,
    265
Teasdale, J.D.,   243, *257*
Thomas, J.C.,   84, 90, *96, 98*
Thompson, L.W.,   35, *47,* 75, 77, *98, 99*
Thoresen, C.E.,   222, *265*
Thorndyke, P.W.,   62, *73*
Thornton, D.W.,   244, 248, 252, *259*
Thorpe, G.L.,   231-233, *265*
Thurlow, M.L.,   108, *128*
Tikhomerov, O.K.,   270-272, *299*
Toner, S.J.,   274, 277, 278, *299, 300*
Torgesen, J.K.,   134-136, 139, 141-145,
    147, 148, *150, 153*
Toye, A.R.,   35, *48*
Trabasso, T.,   35, *49*
Treat, N.J.,   82-84, 88, *98, 99*
Trexler, L.D.,   230-232, *265*
Trier, C.,   224, *260*
Trier, M.L.,   76, *98*
Trollip, S.R.,   61, *69*
Tulkin, S.,   156, *174*

Tulving, E., 38, *49*
Turk, D.C., 228, *265*
Turnure, J.E., 108, *128*
Turnbull, A.P., 41, *49*
Tyler, L.E., 254, *265*

Ullman, L.P., 224, *265*
Underwood, B., 276, 277, *298*
Underwood, V.L., 39, *49, 58, 73*
Urbain, E.S., 287, *296*

Van Nostrand, G.K., 131, *152*
Venable, V., 156, *174*
Verna, G.B., 275, *300*
Vesonder, G.T., 27, *44*
Vlietstra, A.G., 185
Voss, J.F., 27, *44*
Vygotsky, L.S., 155, 156, 159, 167, *174, 175,* 279, *300*

Wachs, T., 164, *173*
Wackman, D.B., *193*
Wagner, M., 35, 38, *48*
Wambold, C., 103, 107, 108, 119, *126*
Walder, L.O., 179
Walker, C., 51, 52, *71*
Walsh, D.A., 80-82, *99*
Walsh-Sweeney, L., 82, 84, *99*
Walters, R.H., 275, *294*
Wanschura, P.B., 107, 108, *128*
Wanshura, P.B., 41, *49*
Ward, C.H., 246, *258*
Ward, S., *193*
Wark, D., 112, *128*
Warrington, E.K., 90, *100*
Wartella, E., *193*
Waters, H.S., 25, 27
Watkins, B., 179, *184, 185,* 192, *193*
Watkins, J.T., 246, 251, 254, *264*
Watson, D., 236, 239, *265*
Weaverdyck, S.E., 91, 93, 94, *96*
Weidman, R., 228, *257*
Wein, K.S., 231, *265*
Weinberg, L., 226, 228, 229, 233, 237, 239, *260*
Weinberg, R.A., 289, *294*
Weiner, B., 123, *128*
Weinman, C., 89, *98*
Weinriech, R.J., 286, *300*

Weinstein, C.E., 39, *49, 58,* 63, *73*
Weinstein, M.S., 241, *261*
Weinstein, S.M., 277, 278, *297*
Weisberg, M.A., 239, *266*
Weisberg, R., 51, *72*
Weissman, A.N., 248, *265*
Wellman, H., 181, 183, 185, 187, *194*
Wellman, H.M., 35, *45*
Wender, P.H., 132, *153*
Wertsch, J., 155, 157, 169, 170, *174*
Wertsch, J.V., 272, *300*
Westby, S., 181, 184, 185, 187, 189, *194, 195*
Wetstone, H., *189*
White, C.V., 132, *153*
White, M., 282, *299*
White, R.T., 67, *70*
Whitman, T.L., 116, 117, 119, *127*
Whittemore, C.L., 107, 108, *125*
Wicker, F.W., 39, *49, 58,* 73
Wight-Felske, A., 118, 119, *125*
Wilcox, B.L., 27, *44*
Wilcox, L.E., 285, 287-292, *296*
Wilder, L., 268, 272, *300*
Wilkie, F., 78, *97*
Wilkinson, M., 282, *294*
Williams, L., 228, *261*
Willis, S.L., 79, *98*
Willows, D.M., 218, 273, *300*
Wilson, G.T., 223, 237, *259, 265*
Wilson, K.P., 58, *71*
Wilson, M., 140, *149*
Winograd, E., 86, *100*
Wittlinger, R.P., 78, *96*
Wittrock, M.C., 63, *73*
Wolff, P., 37, *49*
Wolpe, J., 223, 241, *265*
Wong, B.Y.L., 136, 137, 140, 143, 146, 148, *149, 153*
Wong, R., 136, 137, 143, *153*
Worden, P.E., 54
Worden, P.W., 135, 136, 138, 139, 145, 146, *148, 153*
Worthen, D., 136, 138, *152*
Wozniak, R., 155, 156, 159, 167, *174, 175*
Wozniak, R.H., 268, 270-272, *300*
Wright, J., 179, *183-185,* 192, *193*
Wright, P., 211, 213, 218

Wright, R.E.,   80, *100*

Yakovleva, S.V.,   270, 272, 273, *300*
Yarrow, L.,   168, *175*
Yates, B.T.,   268, 278, *300*
Yates, F.A.,   51, 56, 62, *73*
Yates, G.C.,   276, 278, *300*
Yates, S.M.,   276, 278, *300*
Yesavage, J.A.,   84, *96*
Young, J.E.,   242, *266*
Youngran, M.A.,   243, *261*
Yuille, J.C.,   37, 41, *49*
Yussen, S.R.,   92, *98*

Zarit, S.H.,   76, 86, 87, 88, *97, 100*
Zealley, A.K.,   247, *257*
Zeiss, A.,   276, 277, *297, 298*
Zeiss, A.M.,   228, 244, 248, 249, 252, 254, *266*
Zelnicker, T.,   283, 284, *300*
Zetlin, A.,   109, 111, *126*
Zigler, A.,   109, 111, *126*
Zitter, R.E.,   236, 240, *259*
Zuckerman, D.,   192
Zuckerman, M.,   236, *266*
Zung, W.W.K.,   249, *266*
Zupan, B.A.,   289, 290, *296*

Subject Index

Page numbers set in roman type refer to *Cognitive Strategy Research: Psychological Foundations*. Page numbers set in italic type refer to *Cognitive Strategy Research: Educational Applications*.

Adolescence, memory, 25-36
Adult memory, 51-73, 75-99
Advanced organizers, 66, 117-118, 215
Advertising, 203-218
Affect and self-control, 275-276
Ambiguity and prose learning, *245-248*
Analogies, 215
Anxiety, 229
Applied versus basic research, in reading, *161-181*
Aptitude X treatment interactions (ATIs), 119-120, *18, 124-126, 173, 180*
Arithmetic and mnemonics, *231*
Assessment of reading skills, *179-180*
Attentional strategies, 277, 282-285, *9-13, 104-116, 124-126*
Attitudinal effects
  of advertisements, 204
  of television, 188-191
Automaticity, 120-121

Basic versus applied research, in reading, *161-181*
Behavioral effects
  of advertisements, 204
  of television, 188-191
Behaviorism, 223

Behavior modification, cognitive, 221-256

Classroom applications, 39-40, 42
Classroom implementation of strategies, *267-287*
Cognitive approach to reading, *93-126*
Cognitive behavior modification, 221-256, *285-291*
Cognitive deficiencies and learning materials, *239-266*
Cognitive re-structuring, 229-241
Communication, *29-42*
  and moral education, *53-83*
Comparison strategies in communication, *34-36*
Comprehension, 117-118
  of television content, 179-188
  versus production of language, *190*
Concreteness and comprehension, 184, 212-213
Conservation, *4-27*
Content knowledge of prose, *93-98*
Contexts of language learning, *191-207*

Delay of gratification, 273-278
Deliberate Psychological Education, *59-67, 76*

Depression,   241-253
Developmental lag hypothesis,   131-132
Developmental strategy hypothesis,   36-
   37, 42
Dialectics,   155-158
Didactic instruction and moral educa-
   tion,   *67-70*
DRTA,   *121-123*

Elaborating text,   *89*
Elaboration,   29-31, 37-38, 82-86, 206-
   211
Elderly,   75-95
Encoding, during reading,   90-91
Executive functioning,   115-116

Familiarity effects on strategy use,   14-17,
   79-80
Feedback,   111-114, *19-21*
Formal language learning,   *189-190, 193-
   207*

Generalization,   3-5, 12-19, 28-29, 31,
   41-42, 43, 84-85, 105-124, 160-169,
   285-291, *6, 8, 35-37, 277-279*
Goals and learning,   105

Hardware of reading,   *173-182*
Hook mnemonic for language learning,
   201-203

Ideations and self-control,   276-277
Illogical prose,   245-248
Imagery,   29-31, 37-42, 51-68, 82-87,
   253-258
   abstract materials,   55
   advertising,   206-214, 218
   language learning,   *198-203*
   therapy,   229-237
Impulsivity,   278-292
Individual differences
   in strategy use,   26-36, 108, 119-120,
      39, 269-275
   in imagery,   59-60
   and picture effects,   *216, 231-233*
   and susceptibility to moral educa-
      tion,   *55-56*
   in TV comprehension,   183-184
Inefficiency in strategy execution,   253-

258
Inferences
   moral judgment of,   *251-253*
   prose structure of,   *248-251*
   of television viewing,   181-188, 193-
      197, 251
Information processing strategy for moral
   growth,   70-73, 76
Instrumental enrichment,   118-119, 163-
   165
Integration,   *110*
Intelligence assessment,   158-170
Internalization,   169-170

Journal of Educational Psychology, impact
   on reading research,   *166-181*
Just Community,   *73-74*

Keyword mnemonic,   29, 31, 37-42, 57-
   58, 84-85, *198-210, 222-226, 256-
   258, 269, 279-281*

Language acquisition,   118
Language learning,   *189-210*
Learning and development
   Piagetian theories of,   *3-27*
   Soviet theories of,   157-158
Learning disabled,   129-148, 130-132,
   159, 165-169
Levels of processing,   *103*
Limits of training, Piagetian concepts,   *7-
   10*
Listening,   *31, 36-37*
Loci, method of,   56-57, 63
Long-term memory,   54, 77-78, 136-139

Maintenance,   41, 160, *277-278*
Maps as recall aids,   63
Materials
   effects on strategy use,   11-14, 90-94
   effects on TV comprehension,   184
Mathematics learning from self-instruc-
   tion,   116-117
Memory,   1-99
Memory decline during adulthood,   76-78
Mentally retarded,   103-129, 159, 165-
   169
Metacognition,   163-169, *37-39, 273-275*
   and reading,   *133-156*

Metamemory, 111, 114-115, 124, 139-140, *178-179*

Methodological issues in cognitive behavior modification, 253-255

Microcomputers in referential communications research, *39*

Minimal brain dysfunction, 131-132

Mnemonics, *41*

Modeling, *16-18, 31-36, 45-59*

Monitoring, *142-145, 190*

Moral education, *43-83*

Moral judgment, stages and assessment, *43-44*

Motivation and strategy use
in elderly, 88-90
in retarded, 123-124

Motor behavior, 268-273

Notetaking, *89, 104-112*

Organizational strategies, 7-21, 80-82, 106-116, 134-139, 142-147, *108-110*
in advertising, 214

Peers and moral education, *47-54*

Pegword, *83*

Perceptual deficits and learning disabilities, 132-133

Perceptual learning, 14-15

Perceptual strategies, *10-13*

Piagetian concepts, *1-2, 3-27, 43-83*

Piagetian tasks, 165, *29-42*

Pictures and memory, 38, 64-66, *253-259*
in advertising, 206-213, 218
language learning, *195-198, 216-232*
school learning, *213-237*

Plans, *135*

Plus-one exchange strategy, in moral education, *45-59, 75*

Practice and intellectual improvement, 79-80

Prior knowledge, 61-62, 66-67, *94-102*, 183-184, 194-196, *272-273*

Processing knowledge of prose, *94, 102-104*

Production of language, *190, 196-207*

Prose learning, 31-34, 38, 61-67, 91-93, 138-140, 145-147, *87-131, 226-233, 253-259*

advertising prose, 216-217
stages in, 62-63

Prose structure and learning, 241-245

Questioning strategies, 146, *18-21, 31-33, 89, 112-119, 123-124, 146-149*

Rational-emotive therapy, 226

Reading, *87-132, 133-156, 157-187*
history of reading research, *158-161*
pictures in reading, *216-221*

Reading Research Quarterly, impact on reading research, *166-181*

Real-world memory, 37-38, 42, 148

REAP, *117-119*

Referential communication, *27-42*

Rehearsal, 5-21, 27-29, 103-104, 106-116, 134-139, 141-145

Reinforcement of verbal behavior, *193-194*

Resistance to temptation, 273-278

Retention of TV plots, 181-188

Retrieval, 33-34, 60, *21-22*

Role-taking, *31, 55-77, 203-204*

Rule learning and Piagetian concepts, *13-16*

Schemata, 61-62, 66-67, *258-260*
in learning TV content, 183-184, 194-196

Selective attention and learning disabilities, 133-134, 185-186

Self-control, 267-293

Self-esteem and strategy use, 88-90

Self-instructional strategies, 112-113, 116-117, 120, 226-241, 270-275, 279-291, 280

Self-reports, 30, 76

Semantic processing, 7-21, 40-41, 106-116, 142-145, 214-218

Sensory memory, 77

Sex differences, 10-11

Short-term memory, 54, 77, *21-22*
learning disabilities, 134-136, 141-142

Silent method of language learning, *204-206*

Skill differences in reading, *174-183*

Social input and learning, 157-158, 169-170

Social learning and Piagetian con-
  cepts, *16-18*
Social strategies, *16-18*
Social studies content, *230-231*
Software of reading, *173-182*
Soviet theories, 155-170, 229, 268-273
Speaking, *33, 36-37*
SQ3R, *116-117, 147-149*
S-R approach in reading, *92-93*
Story grammar, *99-100, 241-245*
Structural knowledge of prose, *94, 98-
  102*
Structured overview of text, *119-121*
Study skills training, *116-124, 145-149*
Style, cognitive, and strategy use, 92-94
Summarizing, *89, 104-112*

Teacher-lead discussions and moral
  growth, *54-55*
Television, 179-197

Temporal integration of televised information, 181-188
Total Physical Response strategy of language learning, *203-204*
Transfer appropriate processing, *103*

Underlining, 31-33, 66, *89, 104-112*

Verbal contexts and language learning, *194-195*
Verbal instruction, 17-19
Verbalizations and motor control, 268-
  273
  and delay-of-gratification, 274-275
Vocational training, 118

World knowledge and TV viewing, 183-
  184

Zone of proximal development, 155-170

Cognitive Strategy Research
Educational Applications
(Companion volume to Cognitive Strategy Research: Psychological Foundations)

Contents

Part I   Strategy Training of Piagetian Concepts

Chapter 1   Varieties of Strategy Training in Piagetian Concept Learning
Charles J. Brainerd, Department of Psychology, University of
Western Ontario

Chapter 2   Training Cognitive Strategies for Oral Communication
W. Patrick Dickson, Department of Child and Family Studies,
University of Wisconsin, Madison

Chapter 3   Moral Education Strategies
Robert D. Enright, Department of Educational Psychology,
University of Wisconsin, Madison

Part II   Cognitive Strategies in Reading and Language

**Chapter 4   Reading Strategies Training for Meaningful Learning
from Prose**
Linda K. Cook, Department of Psychology, University of
California, Davis and Richard E. Mayer, Department of
Psychology, University of California, Santa Barbara

Chapter 5   Children's Flexible Use of Strategies During Reading
D. L. Forrest-Pressley, Psychology Department, Children's
Psychiatric Research Institute, London, Ontario, Canada and
Laurie A. Gillies, Department of Psychology, Dalhousie
University

**Chapter 6   From Theory to Practice in Reading Research: Toward the
Development of Better Software**
Dale M. Willows, Department of Curriculum, Ontario Institute for
Studies in Education, Diane M. Borwick, Department of
Psychology, University of Waterloo, and Irwin S. Butkowsky,
Family Court Clinic, Clarke Institute of Psychiatry, Toronto,
Ontario, Canada

Chapter 7   **Strategies in Language Learning**
             Allan Paivio, Department of Psychology, University of Western
             Ontario

Part III   **Educational Applications of Cognitive Strategy Research**

Chapter 8   **Pictorial Strategies for School Learning:**
             Practical Illustrations
             Joel R. Levin, Department of Educational Psychology and
             Wisconsin Center for Education Research, University of
             Wisconsin, Madison

Chapter 9   **Making Meaningful Materials Easier to Learn: Lessons from**
             Cognitive Strategy Research
             Michael Pressley, Department of Psychology, University of
             Western Ontario

Chapter 10   **Problems in Classroom Implementation of Cognitive**
             Strategy Instruction
             Penelope L. Peterson, Department of Educational Psychology and
             Wisconsin Center for Education Research, University of
             Wisconsin, Madison and *Susan R. Swing, Department of*
             Educational Psychology and Wisconsin Center for Education
             Research, University of Wisconsin, Madison